1857

War of Independence

or

Clash of Civilizations?

British Public Reactions

First appearence of the Mutiny

A Fakir of Bengal   The Lotus Flower

The Chapatties

An Englishman's View of the Indian Mutiny. (See appendix 1 for detailed comments)

1857
War of Independence
or
Clash of Civilizations?
British Public Reactions

SALAHUDDIN MALIK

OXFORD
UNIVERSITY PRESS

OXFORD
UNIVERSITY PRESS

Great Clarendon Street, Oxford OX2 6DP

Oxford University Press is a department of the University of Oxford.
It furthers the University's objective of excellence in research, scholarship,
and education by publishing worldwide in

Oxford New York

Auckland Cape Town Dar es Salaam Hong Kong Karachi
Kuala Lumpur Madrid Melbourne Mexico City Nairobi
New Delhi Shanghai Taipei Toronto

with offices in

Argentina Austria Brazil Chile Czech Republic France Greece
Guatemala Hungary Italy Japan Poland Portugal
South Korea Singapore Switzerland Turkey Ukraine Vietnam

Oxford is a registered trade mark of Oxford University Press
in the UK and in certain other countries

ISBN 978-0-19-547422-0

Typeset in Minion Pro
Printed in Pakistan by
Namaa Lica Printers, Karachi.
Published by
Ameena Saiyid, Oxford University Press
No. 38, Sector 15, Korangi Industrial Area, PO Box 8214
Karachi-74900, Pakistan.

With love, affection, and prayers
for our beloved daughter
Nadia S. Malik

Contents

List of Illustrations

Frontispiece: An Englishman's View of the Indian Mutiny.

1. Bahadur Shah Zafar, 24 October 1774–7 November 1862, the octogenarian King of Delhi in his royal regalia.
2. Zeenat Mahal, wife of Bahadur Shah Zafar, d. 1886.
3. The King's Palace at Delhi.
4. View of Delhi from the Palace Gate.
5. Repulse of a Sortie from Delhi.
6. Penetrating Delhi's defences—Blowing up the Cashmere (sic) Gate.
7. British re-entry into Delhi: Assault on Delhi—Capture of Cashmere (sic) Gate.
8. Contingent Force of Sikh Irregular Cavalry (See appendix 2 for detailed comments).
9. Blowing Mutinous Sepoys from the Guns.
10. Capture of the King of Delhi by Captain Hodson.
11. Bahadur Shah Zafar's permanent abode, Rangoon, Myanmar (Burma).
12. The Palace at Agra.
13. Siege of Delhi.
14. The Siege of Lucknow.

Acknowledgements:

- Frontispiece: *Narrative of the Indian Revolt from its Outbreak to the Capture of Lucknow* by Sir Colin Campbell (London: George Vickers, 1858).

- Bahadur Shah Zafar's permanent abode, Rangoon, Myanmar (Burma)–Author.

- All other photographs and maps from *History of the Indian Mutiny* by Charles Ball with the permission of Sang-e-Meel Publications.

Foreword

There is nothing more important after the events of 11 September 2001 than promoting the understanding between the US and the world of Islam. That tragic event has led to wars with two Muslim nations, Afghanistan and Iraq, and has also involved many other Muslim societies. The ignorance and prejudice against Muslims has grown, and it has become imperative that the scholars of Islam assume the role of interpreters of their faith both on and off campus. There are far too few Muslim scholars studying and writing about the history of Muslim peoples. There is, therefore, an unfortunate lack of knowledge about Muslim history among both Muslims and non-Muslims alike.

Why should the world try to understand Islam? The events of 11 September have created one of the greatest paradoxes of the twenty-first century: Islam, which sees itself as a religion of peace, is now associated with murder and mayhem. The ever-growing Muslim population is now estimated at 1.5 billion living in fifty Muslim states, with at least one state holding nuclear capabilities. Perhaps in the next few years we may well see several more nuclear nations. Many of these Muslim states play a pivotal role either as close ally or adversary in the United States' 'War on Terror'. The Muslim community is not isolated to one part of the world; roughly 7 million Muslims live in the United States and many millions more in Europe. Some of the most wanted names on the terrorist list of the US are Muslim; but so are the closest allies of the US—the presidents of Egypt, Jordan, Afghanistan and Pakistan to give a few examples. Therefore, if both implacable opponents and close allies are Muslims, it is imperative to begin to understand Islam.

We need to be grateful therefore to Professor Salahuddin Malik for providing an intellectual lead in creating bridges between the US and Muslim society and helping to explain Muslim history through his work. His new book is of particular relevance, as it underlines the need to both understand Islam and its history.

Current tensions and conflict between Muslims and non-Muslims or even within the Muslim community itself revolve around the concept of identity. The question of identity has defined much of world affairs since the nineteenth century. Globalization in the form of media, commerce and governance is challenging our ideas of cultural tradition, religious custom and national identity. This crisis in society began in the nineteenth century when British Imperialism and South Asian nationalist forces clashed in the uprising of 1857–8. That seminal event was a defining time for both Western colonialism and Muslim society. Contemporary analysis of the South Asian crisis of 1857 allows us a glimpse into the development of local identity and also the international community as a whole. The question of what embodies the South Asian identity or nation is one that has affected both British Imperial India and post-partition Pakistan and India. Whether it is the idea of a united front opposing the British or the notion of what comprises the Indian nation itself, the question of identity has played a decisive role in South Asian affairs since the crisis of 1857. Scholars have not been able to agree even on a definition of the uprisings. To the British, it was the 'Great Mutiny' and to South Asians it was the 'First War of Independence'. The disagreement over a proper name for the events of 1857 demonstrates to us such a divide between perspectives. Therefore, a work on such subject matter by a Muslim scholar who can relate those events to developments today in the post 9/11 world is not only enlightening but also ever important.

Many books have been written on the crisis of 1857, but we have yet to see an account as exhaustive as this. Professor Malik is able to highlight through a new set of eyes the way the British mind saw inhabitants of the Indian subcontinent. Placing the events of 1857 in a contemporary context, allows us a glimpse into how the West sees the Muslim world both historically and currently. We know that in part, the rebellion stemmed from oppressed peoples defending what is most important to them. Religious customs were outlawed and mocked. Muslims and Hindus felt that their religion was under attack by British strong-arm rule. This lack of respect for the Muslim and Hindu cultures and religion became a flashpoint for the uprising. We can observe even now how a lack of cultural and religious concern can exacerbate or even create a contentious environment.

Analysing the messy rebellion of 1857, Professor Malik draws a historical parallel between nineteenth century South Asia and contemporary events, where we may draw lessons from the British imperial past to the trying events of today. Great historians utilize the experience of events past to present us with lessons to deal with the challenges of today. In a world where careless rhetoric and confrontation is pervasive, the lessons of 1857 can provide us with the wisdom to embrace dialogue and cooperation. Professor Malik does not restrict himself to the nineteenth century or to South Asia; he even refers to Muslim Spain a thousand years ago. Drawing from the Andalusian experience, where communities of the three Abrahamic religions and other faiths created a: 'New Ornament of the World', Professor Malik illustrates this is possible today.

The British view of the 1857 crisis as a clash of civilizations between Christianity and Islam causes us to reflect on current tensions. With so many Muslims now living in non-Muslim nations, major world civilizations are experiencing problems in accommodating or even understanding Islam, both within their borders and outside them. An absence of mutual respect and recognition of culture and custom has created and worsened this relationship. It is obvious that any situation where all parties feel as if they are under siege will result in conflict. Only through cooperative understanding and respect can these communities co-exist in peace. Within our ever-shrinking world this lesson must be learned. Respect for cultural and religious customs has become a need. This is no longer simply a policy lesson for an imperial power or occupying force but a means of interaction between global and real neighbours. It is, therefore, essential that we create by any and all means a process of mutual understanding and dialogue. If we do not, then we may be entering a phase of history dominated by the nightmare scenario of a perpetual clash of civilizations between the West and the Muslim world.

Professor Malik has contributed a significant work with considerable relevance to the contemporary world. He suggests that we understand the past so that we can look into the future and together find solutions to bridge the gap between cultures and religions. A sentiment such as this deserves a scholar on the level of Professor Malik. His work speaks for itself. He has written extensively on Muslim history, especially on British imperial rule in the subcontinent. His voice warrants contemplation and his writings demand application by anyone attempting to understand the conflict between the West and the Muslim world. In this post-9/11 world, authors such as Salahuddin Malik are conduits of change. They fulfill the need for research that explores the gap between cultures and provide us with enlightened analysis.

Professor Akbar S. Ahmed
Ibn Khaldun Chair of Islamic Studies
American University
Washington, D.C., USA

Preface

The year 1957, a year in which I obtained my Master's degree at the University of the Punjab, Lahore, Pakistan, was the centenary of the Indian uprising of 1857. In this year the peoples of India and Pakistan elaborately celebrated the 100th anniversary of what they considered to be the first war of Indo-Pakistan independence. Numerous articles were written, books published, public meetings held, processions arranged, and public monuments erected to mark the historic occasion. Almost every history examination paper, at all levels, contained one question in common and it was on the rebellion or the mutiny of 1857. This highly stimulating politico-intellectual atmosphere of the year was a significant factor in my decision to investigate at some future date the so far neglected subject of British public attitudes towards the Indian mutiny—an inspiration which today has taken the shape of reality.

From the beginning up until the end of this research I had to change its title no less than three times. Starting off with 'British Public Opinions towards the Indian Mutiny', a year later I changed the word 'Opinions' to 'Attitudes'. Still later I discovered that British opinions were neither opinions nor attitudes but reactions, and at that, very sharp reactions; now the word 'Reactions' took the place of 'Attitudes'. Finally, when I started to write I was overwhelmed by the immensity of material which I had gathered together over a period of more than two years. I was then compelled to trim down the scope of this dissertation to its present form.

Although a large variety of books and research papers have been written on this most interesting chapter of British Indian history, virtually none of them touched the present theme in detail. The nearest approach to the present work was Professor George D. Bearce's scholarly book, *British Attitudes towards India, 1784-1858*. This book touches on the year 1858, but because of the wide scope of Professor Bearce's inquiry, 'the intellectual basis and ideological atmosphere which underlay British rule in India', the book naturally could not give more than ten pages to the inexhaustible subject of the Indian mutiny. This study is, therefore, designed to fill the gap left by researchers in comprehending the Great Indian Rebellion or Mutiny.

An investigation of British reactions towards the Indian uprising of 1857 offers an interesting field of research and provides a fascinating study of the British nation, mind and thinking in the mid-nineteenth century. It offers a study of that nation's political, social, religious, moral, commercial and imperial mode of thought. At the same time it also furnishes an illuminating picture of the inhabitants of the Indo-Pakistan subcontinent, both Hindu and Muslim, through the eyes of their British contemporaries. It is an inquiry into

a multiform body of thought and attitudes towards India as caused by the
Indian mutiny—an inquiry that probes into various intellectual, political and
religious tendencies, i.e., Conservatism, Liberalism, Imperialism, Evangelism,
Chartism, mercantilism, and what we might call 'moralism'. The variety of
attitudes shown by the adherents to each of these 'isms' (towards the Indian
mutiny) reveals the conflict and tension which existed in Britain's intellectual
environment in the middle of the nineteenth century. In addition to this, the
study also throws light, though indirectly, on the amazing amount of liberty
of speech and expression enjoyed by the British. The freedom of expression
and the intellectual conflict invariably provided an opportunity for an open
debate on all important subjects. Such occasions enabled the British to pool
their thought processes for nation building activity. As in other cases, the
great response of the British to the uprising had a beneficial effect on future
British policies towards India. The detailed analysis of the whole situation
made it possible for the government to diagnose the disease and apply
relevant remedies.

Generally, researchers have considered the insurrection to have been either
a mutiny or a war of Indian independence. Surprisingly, one aspect of it never
seems to have been touched by any recent research, namely that it could
conceivably be called a Muslim revolt as well. A booklet appearing even as
late as 1963, *1857 in India, Mutiny or War of Independence,* edited by Professor
Ainslee T. Embree, while it takes into account all different interpretations put
upon the outbreak (including the mutiny as a 'Brahmanical Protest'), fails to
discuss this important possible interpretation. In contemporary Britain and
for a long time after, however, if there was one point on which there was
almost unanimous agreement, it was in calling the outbreak a Muslim
rebellion; moreover, some sections even viewed it as a struggle between the
Cross and the Crescent. This study, though it presents the picture as seen only
by the British, attempts to throw some light on this so far neglected aspect of
the rebellion and opens up an interesting field of research for those interested
in the Muslim history of India such as: Anglo-Muslim relations in South Asia
before and after the mutiny; widening of the already existing cleavage between
Hindus and Muslims following the failure of the revolt and the role of these
events in the establishment of Pakistan.

This work also lays open some other aspects of historical research into the
Britain of the mid-nineteenth century, e.g., the exclusion of British
missionaries and settlers from the Company's Indian empire until 1813, in
particular, and 1833 in general, by the governments of Britain and India as
two factors which precipitated the outbreak; Ireland and India as seen through
the Irish views towards the revolt of 1857; comparison of Irish and Scottish
reactions towards the insurrection; the relationship between the Indian
mutiny and the British Evangelical movement in India, the opinion the British
had as to the degree to which they could control the events in India and the
extent to which these events were in the hands of God; lack of tolerance
exhibited by Christian Europe, in general, Christian Britain, in particular,

toward other religions, especially by the clerical community; imperial phobias, from the Spartans to the British and Americans; well-documented history of comparative imperialisms, especially European versus Arab and Ottoman imperialisms with focus on social, economic, political, cultural, and religious costs, and, most significantly, historical analysis of the cause and effect of Christian-Muslim hostility and who is responsible for this oldest on-going clash of civilizations: the cause or the effect.

Apart from all this, the competitive atrocities committed by the three peoples, Hindus, Indian Muslims, and the British, the motives behind their uncivilized behaviour and the mixed reactions shown by all three towards these acts of oppression and repression, usually verging on barbarism, also offer a highly interesting subject for sociological and historical study.

This research has also made a definite contribution to the source material on the Indian mutiny by an accidental discovery of a large number of hitherto unknown pamphlets in the National Library of Scotland, and some in other libraries. In addition to these an abundant supply of sermons on the Indian mutiny discovered in various libraries, especially church and missionary (of which a real wealth must still be lying hidden), has brought to light, virtually for the first time, a new kind of material on this most controversial subject.

The chief purpose of this research is to describe certain aspects of British public reactions towards the Indian revolt as they took place. Thus the attempt is made to present public opinion in Britain faithfully. My own opinions I have tried to let obtrude as little as possible, and where they seemed necessary, I have indicated that they are mine.

Since I am dealing with public opinion only, I have used published accounts and have not consulted private papers, or other unpublished matter on the subject.

The terms mutiny, revolution, social revolt, uprising, insurrection and the like, have been used interchangeably. As the controversy on the character of the outbreak is still unresolved and since these were the terms used by contemporary Britons, I have retained them as such. My use of them, therefore, does not in any way reflect my opinion on the subject.

Acknowledgements

My debt to archivists and librarians is very profound. Without their help and active assistance this manuscript would not have been able to achieve the breadth and the depth it now has. I am especially grateful to the inter-library loans departments which enabled me to secure books, pamphlets, and other research materials virtually from across the globe. It is impossible to mention individuals by name. With a couple of exceptions, here I acknowledge the staffs of various libraries and archives: Baptist Missionary Society, London, Church Missionary Society, London, Society for the Propagation of the Gospel, London, London Missionary Society, Scottish Missionary Society, Edinburgh, British Museum Library, the National Library of Scotland, Edinburgh, Dr. William's Library, London, the Church of England Library, London, Public Library of Edinburgh, the Westminster Cathedral Library, London, the War Office Library, London, the India Office Library, London, and the Newspaper Library of the British Museum in Colindale, the Redpath Library of McGill University, Montreal and the Loyola College Library, Montreal.

Locally, I am very grateful to Robert Gilliam of the Inter-Library Loans-Department at Drake Memorial Library, State University College at Brockport. In the Photographic Division of the College I am indebted to Jim Dusen for duplicating important images and drawings for reproduction in this book. In our department I am beholden to our secretary, Teri Rombaut, for coming to my assistance whenever I needed it. I am also grateful to James Swiatek, our graduate student helper, for his patient guidance in helping me due to my lack of familiarity in navigating the internet.

I am particularly grateful to the late Dr Robert I. Crane, Ford-Maxwell Professor of South Asian History, Syracuse University, to have read the manuscript at my request. Dr Crane, whom I never had the pleasure to meet, liked the manuscript and strongly commended it for publication. He described the work as 'a good study, judicious, and very carefully researched…(with) scholarly objectivity…the most exhaustive examination of British opinion taken from the widest range of sources, I have yet seen.' The die was cast and the decision to publish the manuscript was made. However, a wide variety of commitments and other pursuits did not permit me to get to it for several years.

Recently, the push came from my daughter, Nadia S. Malik, who read the manuscript, liked it and started to nag me on a daily basis to submit it for publication. Nadia's dogged persistence forced me to take the time out, further upgrade the manuscript, and actually submit it for publication. But for Nadia's daily reminders, this research might still have been sitting on a shelf in my office. I am therefore dedicating this book to Nadia.

I am also grateful to my other daughter, Sumaiya S. Malik, for her encouragement and regular inquiries regarding the 'welfare' of this manuscript. Above all, I am ever beholden to my wife, Sarwat Malik for her patience and willing support in my research. I am grateful to her for taking over a lot of my functions in the house and allowing me unfettered time to pursue this research to publication.

I owe a special debt of gratitude to my scholarly peers, Dr Akbar S. Ahmad, Ibn Khaldun Chair of Islamic Studies, American University, Washington, D.C., Dr John L. Esposito, al-Walid Chair of Center for Christian-Muslim Understanding, Georgetown University, Washington, D.C., and Dr Anand A. Yang, Guleb Professor of International Studies, Washington University, Seattle, and current President of the Association of Asian Studies, for taking the time out of their very busy schedules and writing a foreword and introductions. Their different backgrounds provide different perspectives to the book.

Additionally, I am beholden to Professor Emil Homerin, Chairman, Department of Religion, University of Rochester, Dr Ainslee T. Embree, Professor Emeritus, Columbia University and a past President of the Association of Asian Studies, and Professor Sharif al Mujahid, Sitara-i-Imtiaz, and a Distinguished Professor, Karachi University, for their insightful and provocative blurbs.

I also owe a special debt of gratitude to the editors of Oxford University Press for their patience with my tardy responses and their ability to work with me. My gratitude to Aquila Ismail who edited the manuscript and suggested changes wherever needed is also great.

In my department I am greatly indebted to Drs Kathleen and John Kutloowski for proof reading the edited copy of this manuscript.

Before closing, I would like to express my eternal gratitude to my grandparents, Ghulam Farid Malik and Abida Khanum Malik, and my parents, Abdul Rehman Malik, Tamgha-i-Shujaat, and Saeeda Khanum Malik, for the attention, love, care, inspiration, and resources they provided to me. Their constant emphasis on my education and their pride and confidence in my talent gave me my personality.

Introduction

If those who ignore history are bound to repeat it, then Salahuddin Malik's 1859, War of Independence becomes a must read.

As a graduate student in the late 1960s and early 1970s studying Islam in South Asia, 1857 was invariably described as the Sepoy Mutiny. The use of the term 'mutiny' by historians of course already prejudged the good guys and the bad guys, the legality and authority of British colonial rule and authority vs. their 'rebellious subjects.'

The Sepoy Mutiny, what many South Asian historians, in contrast to British historians of the time, would call the first war for independence, was a defining moment in South Asian history and politics. However, understanding the root causes of this defining moment, the diverse actors, the subsequent fallout and consequences, long and short term, has been a major challenge for historians as it was for Britain and British society in the nineteenth century. Was it simply a military mutiny, a Muslim-led religious uprising or a 'jihad,' an incipient nationalist struggle against colonial rule, or a sign and yet another historical example of the clash of civilizations between East and West, Islam and Christianity?

This book is a timely reminder that South Asian Islam offers an important perspective for understanding Muslim responses to European colonialism as well as lessons that remain relevant in a post 9/11 world. For decades there has been a tendency to read Islamic history through the lens of Arab history. This, of course, has meant that Turkish, Persian and especially South Asian Islam are often seen as peripheral, when in fact their contributions (intellectual, scientific, religious, cultural, architectural) not only complemented but also rivalled and at times outstripped that of the Arab world. This is certainly the case when it comes to political and religious responses to British colonial rule, from rejection to accommodation.

Muslim Responses to European Colonialism: Conflict, Co-Existence or Clash of Civilizations?

By the nineteenth century, a clear shift of power occurred as the decline of Muslim fortunes reversed the relationship of Islam to the West. Increasingly, Muslims from North Africa to South-East Asia found themselves on the defensive in the face of European expansion, which constituted a singular challenge to Islam: politically, economically, morally, and culturally. European imperialism threatened both Muslim political and religio-cultural identity and history. The impact of Western rule and modernization raised new questions and challenged time-honored beliefs and practices. With the dawn of European domination of the Muslim world, the image, if not always the reality, of Islam as an expansive worldwide force had now been shattered.

Muslim views of the West and their responses to its power and ideas varied from rejection and confrontation to admiration and imitation. For many, colonialism conjured up images of the Crusades; the European challenge/ aggression was but another phase of militant Christianity's war with Islam; Europe was the enemy that threatened both the faith of Islam and the political life of the Muslim community.

Muslim images of a Crusader West, of colonialism as a religio-cultural as well as political and military battle between European Christendom and the Muslim world, were reinforced by the reality and policies of colonial powers. Colonialism was experienced as a threat to Muslim identity and faith. Implicit in its policies and explicit in the statements of many government officials and missionaries was the belief that Europe's expansion and domination was due to its inherent Christian cultural superiority. Thus, educating the 'natives' in the language, history, and sciences of the West and Christian virtues was part of an 'enlightened' policy to civilize.

However different regional experiences may have been, four diverse Muslim responses to the West took shape: rejection, withdrawal and non-cooperation, secularism and Westernization, and Islamic modernism. For some Muslims, the example of the Prophet's response to his Meccan detractors was the answer—emigration (*hijra*) or sacred struggle (*jihad*) to leave a territory no longer under Muslim rule or fight to defend the faith and land of Islam. Emigration proved impractical for large numbers of people, and given the superior military strength of Europe, holy war was doomed to defeat.

For many religious leaders, the alternative was simply to refuse to deal with their colonial masters, shun their company, schools, and institutions. Any form of cooperation or involvement was regarded as a form of capitulation to the enemy, or treason. Modern (European) education was regarded as alien, superfluous, and a threat to religious belief.

If some preached rejection and resistance, others were eager to learn from and emulate the strength of Europe, to modernize. For many, the realities of European ascendancy had to be acknowledged and dealt with, its lessons discerned in order to survive. A new intellectual elite was born; modern, educated, and Western oriented. Though Islamic rationales were employed by some to legitimize the transformation, implicit in this process was the gradual acceptance of a secular outlook that restricted religion to personal life while turning to the West for development models in public life. The traditional Islamic basis and legitimacy of Muslim societies were slowly altered as the ideology, law, and institutions of the state, indebted to imported models from the West, were increasingly secularized.

A fourth response to the challenge of the West, the Islamic modernist movement, sought to bridge the gap between Islamic traditionalists and secular oriented reformers. Islamic modernists incorporated the internal community concerns of eighteenth century revivalism with the need to respond to the power and external threat of European colonialism and the demands of modernity.

Like secular reformers, Islamic reformers responded to European colonialism and were influenced by their perception of the 'Success of the West.' The West was strong and successful, Muslims were weak and subject to domination and dependence. Thus, they believed that the sources of the West's strength must be accommodated and assimilated. This posture would stand in sharp contrast to Islamic activism (fundamentalism) in the latter half of the twentieth century, with its denunciation of the 'neocolonialism of the superpowers' and its emphasis on the 'Failure of the West' and in its place the autonomy and self-sufficiency of Islam.

Islamic modernism, like much of the modern Muslim response to the West in the twentieth century, had an ambivalent attitude towards the West, a simultaneous experience of attraction and repulsion. Europe was admired for its strength, technology and political ideals of freedom, justice, and equality, but often rejected for its imperialist goals and policies. Reformers like Jamal al-Din al-Afghani and Muhammad Abduh in Egypt and Sayyid Ahmad Khan and Muhammad Iqbal in the Indian subcontinent argued the compatibility of Islam with modern science and the best of Western thought. They preached the need and acceptability of a selective synthesis of Islam and modern (Western) thought, condemned the unquestioned veneration and imitation of the past, reasserted their right to reinterpret (*ijtihad*) Islam in light of modern conditions, and sought to provide an Islamically-based rationale for educational, legal, and social reform (modernization) to revitalize a dormant and impotent Muslim community. Islamic modernism did not simply seek to restore a pristine past but instead wished to reformulate its Islamic heritage. It provided an Islamic rationale for the acceptability of modern ideas and institutions, whether they be scientific, technological, or political (constitutionalism and representative government).

Islamic modernism was often associated with nationalist movements that emerged in the late nineteenth and early twentieth century from Egypt and North Africa to South Asia and beyond. For most movements and reformers, the renaissance of the Muslim community was the first step to national independence or liberation from the hated yoke of colonialism—the restoration of Muslim power. Muslims, they believed, must look to Islam, their source of strength and unity, but learn the secrets of Western power in order to cast off foreign rule and regain their identity and autonomy. However, Islamic modernism in South Asia offered an example of a more nuanced approach.

In contrast to Islamic modernist reformers like the prominent and influential Jamal al-Din al-Afghani, who roamed the Muslim world preaching a message of Islamic intellectual reform and political liberation, Sayyid Ahmad Khan's Islamic modernist message in South Asia argued for religious reform but also that Indian Muslims could balance being loyal British citizens as well as Muslim nationalists at one and the same time. He worked tirelessly, writing to convince the British, many of whom believed that Islam was not only a backward faith incompatible with modernity but also an inherently violent and dangerous religion, that Muslims and Islam were not a threat. At the same time, he reinterpreted Islam, seeking to produce a new theology that responded to the demands of modernity and also strove to build modern educational and scientific organizations that would implement his reformist vision. His message to both Christians and Muslims was an ecumenical one that emphasized what their faiths shared in common, and that co-existence rather than a clash of civilizations was both possible and desirable.

1857/2001: A Clash of Civilizations?

Salahuddin Malik's analysis of the British public's reaction to the crisis of 1857 is a sober reminder that historical causes for the conflict were easily overshadowed at times by the tendency of many to see the uprising in India as a 'Jihad waged by world-wide Islam against world-wide Christianity—a modern day name change would make it a clash of civilizations'. As he notes in Chapter IX, ironically, there is a significant connection between 1857 and post 11 September 2001. However different the world of the twenty-first century is from that of the nineteenth century, some pitfalls are enduring. The dangers of Islamophobia, of the demonization of the other in relations between the Muslim world and the West, belief in a clash of civilizations, fallout from the impact of colonial power and policies, and the need for significant inter-religious dialogue and reform—remain critical global issues.

This book is a reminder that conflicts, and indeed the Sepoy Mutiny and the 9/11 attacks, have to be viewed within their specific historical context. Their root causes are primarily political and economic (occupation, marginalization, repression, exploitation) but that religion can also be an important factor, a source of identity, legitimacy and mobilization as well as triumphalism, arrogance, dehumanization, expansionism and colonization. As Salahuddin Malik notes: 'Events surrounding 1857 in South Asia and the events which have betaken the world today have striking similarities: the same disregard for cause and effect in history, the same irresponsible and hateful rhetoric, the same exploitations and dehumanizations and the same display of ruthless and relentless power against the powerless and the have-nots'.

The challenge today as in post-1857 British India is, where do we go from here? How do we build a global consensus to address the causes of global terrorism and the widening gap between the West and much of the Muslim world? How do we contain and counter the dangerous increase in both

Islamophobia and anti-Americanism? While there is no simple answer, Salahuddin points us in the right direction: 'Enough is enough. The past has to become consigned to history books. Now the world has become more like a global village, "dangerously educated and dangerously equipped". Continued human welfare depends on mutual recognition, respect, justice, equity and fair play at the global level. With a broader understanding and cooperation between Christianity and Islam, the two religions certainly have the potential to solve half the problems of the world between them. Should not this be the case? This, indeed, is our survival kit.'

John L. Esposito
Founding Director, Prince Alwaleed bin Talal Center for Muslim-Christian Understanding at the Walsh School of Foreign Service, Georgetown University, Washington, D.C., USA.

Introduction

There is no time like the present to look back at the past, specifically the dramatic events of 1857 in South Asia. Indeed, the year 2008 is another critical vantage point from which to consider that past, as Salahuddin Malik does in this excellent new book on an episode that has been much studied and debated ever since its occurrence a century and a half ago. Now, as on all the other occasions when that uprising excited considerable attention—for instance, 1907 and 1957—its analyses have understandably been partly viewed through the lenses of those times.

This book clearly signals the current global moment and preoccupation. That now familiar phrase was first utilized at the beginning of the 1990s and then made [in]famous by Samuel Huntington's 1996 book entitled *The Clash of Civilizations and the Remaking of World Order*. It addresses three interpretations of the uprising that have had currency from the very outset (especially the third one) in order to understand the past but also to suggest its connections to and implications for our present conditions and concerns. This study also touches on other explanations that have been advanced, for instance, the notion that 1857 resulted from 'a revolutionary conspiracy... aimed at the restoration of native authority' or 'Russian intrigue' or even a 'Brahman' plot.

 For most contemporaries, the uprising was predominantly a 'Sepoy Mutiny,' a characterization that the British Raj and its administrators and supporters favoured because it downplayed the scope and scale of the uprising. From the very start, however, a few writers recognized its wider context, although the mutiny thesis continued to dominate most accounts, and understandably so, because they were overwhelmingly written in English by British men and some women residing in Britain or in India. Indian voices rarely ever appeared in print in 1857 and its immediate aftermath; their speaking parts took the form of actions and reactions enacted on the battlefield and in everyday forms of resistance. One notable exception was Syed Ahmad Khan whose *Causes of the Indian Revolt* was first issued in 1858 and whose account is deserving of attention, not only because it is the first published work on 1857 written by an Indian but also because it attempts to depict Muslims as loyal subjects.

Fifty years later, in 1907, with South Asia still under British rule, the military mutiny thesis continued to dominate the discourse on the uprising. But other views were beginning to question the validity of this argument. One intellectual salvo that fired up the existing historiography in the early twentieth century was V.D. Savarkar's 1909 book on *The Indian War of*

Independence, whose title boldly announces this author's different interpretation of 1857, namely, that it was much more than a mutiny; that it was a nationalist war of independence.

By 1957 the shift away from the military mutiny paradigm was abundantly evident. Scholars in both India and Pakistan began to dig into the archives in the 1950s and '60s to generate better identifications of the mutineers and rebels and more compelling interpretation of why they instigated and participated in the uprising. While some of the writing of this era celebrated the centenary by reviving the Savarkar thesis, the new versions differed from the original thesis, especially in Pakistan, where the accent was on recognizing it as the 'first war of Indo-Pakistan independence.'

Most scholarly work in the post-independence era, however, assumed a different line of reasoning in highlighting the popular nature and character of the uprising. Surendranath Sen's *Eighteen Fifty-Seven*, published in 1957 under the auspices of the Government of India, is a case in point. According to Sen, the uprising 'had its origin in sepoy discontent' but 'derived its strength from the widespread disaffection among the civil population.' Many other studies, too, underscore the 'civil' and 'popular' dynamics of the uprising, often by detailing its dynamics in specific localities and regions.

The historian C. A. Bayly has recently attempted to synthesize the old and new arguments by emphasizing the complex and multiple origins of the uprising. In his words, 'army mutinies and rebellions against the British in 1857-9' occurred 'at the political level' and 'combined with a wide range of local tensions arising from the emergence of new-style landlordism, conflicts over forested and nomadic land, and inequalities in the suffering from the competition of British imported manufactures, played a role. Here the rebellion sometimes took on a popular Islamic form.' (p. 154)

Professor Malik addresses this 'popular Islamic form' by examining 'British Public Reactions' or 'Public Opinions' or 'Attitudes' that treated the uprising as a 'Muslim Rebellion'. He reconstructs these reactions and attitudes through a close reading of published works, some of which are familiar to historians but many that are not particularly well known. His careful tracking of public opinion leads him through the pages of major newspapers published in London and Manchester as well as in Dublin and Edinburgh, and through the periodical literature, which, as he rightly observes, has not been mined in depth. His skillful survey of 'church, missionary and lay' periodicals enables him to uncover 'a wealth of material in the shape of articles, sermons, diaries, journals, editorials, dialogues, poems, letters, extracts of letters and on the spot reports ' and to point out the considerable influence that 'missionaries and clergymen' wielded in shaping the British imagination about 1857.

As a result of such exhaustive research, he is able to state with confidence that British representations treated the uprising as a 'Mahomedan Rebellion'. Indeed, as his sources reveal, a large segment of British public opinion regarded 1857 as 'a Jihad waged by world-wide Islam against world-wide Christianity...[and a] clash of civilizations'. In fact, he argues that the 'only aspect of public opinion in which there was virtual unanimity among all schools of thought on the Indian uprising was that it was a Muslim rebellion. The Muslims were considered the main culprits, the spirit and the body of the whole movement.' In this respect, Professor Malik's historical study accords well with cultural and literary studies of British discourse in Britain and India that consider the 'mutinies and rebellions in 1857-9' as critical in generating a profound change in the British imagination, which, thereafter fixated on Muslims in South Asia as a corporate body unified in its implacable opposition to British colonial rule. A thoughtful epilogue seeks to connect past events and discourses to present-day conditions and realities.

Anand A. Yang
Director
Jackson School of International Studies
University of Washington, Seattle, USA

Abbreviations

BC	*British Controversialist*
BM	*Baptist Magazine*
BMCPB	British Museum Catalogue of Printed Books
BQR	*British Quarterly Review*
c	Column
cc	Columns
CEM	*Church of England Magazine*
CEQR	*Church of England Quarterly Review*
CMI	*Church Missionary Intelligence*
CS	*Christian Spectator* (Monthly)
DNB	*Dictionary of National Biography*
DUM	*Dublin University Magazine*
Ext	Extract
ER	*Eclectic Review*
Edin. Rev.	*Edinburgh Review*
HW	Household Words
LG	*Literary Gazette*
LH	Leisure Hour
LQR	*London Quarterly Review*
MH	*Missionary Herald*
MMC	*Missionary Magazine and Chronicle*
NR	*National Review*
pt	Part
QR	*Quarterly Review*
SR	*Saturday Review*
TEM	*Tait's Edinburgh Magazine*
UPM	*United—Presbyterian Magazine*
WMM	*Wesleyan—Methodist Magazine*
WR	*Westminster Review*

Changed Spellings of Place Names

New	Old
Agarpara	Agarparah
Ambala	Umbala
Azamgarh	Azimgurh
Bakarganj	Backergunj
Ballabgarh	Ballubgurh
Banaras	Benares
Bangalore	Banglore
Belgaum	Belgaun
Bhagalpur	Bhagulpur
Bharatpur	Bhurtpore
Bijnor	Bijnor
Bithur	Bithoor
Budaun	Badaun
Bulandshahr	Boolundsher
Bushire	Bushaire
Chhota Nagpur	Chotta Nagpore
Comilla	Comillah
Dinapore	Dinapur
Etawah	Etwah
Faizabad	Fyzabad
Farrukhabad	Faruckabad, Furruckabad
Fatehgarh	Futtehghur
Fatehpur	Futtehpur
Gonda	Ghond
Gorakhpur	Gorruckpore
Govindgarh	Gobindgurh
Haryana	Hurrianah
Hissar	Hisar
Hooghly	Hoogly
Hoshangabad	Hashungabad
Jaunpur	Jaunpore
Kanpur	Cawnpore
Kasauli	Kassoulie

Khurramshahr	Muhammorah, Mohammerah, Mohammareh, Mohamra
Kolapur	Kolapoor
Kulu	Kooloo
Ludhiana	Ludhianah
Mainpuri	Mynpoorie
Mathura	Muttra
Murshidabad	Moorshidabad
Muzaffarnagar	Moozuffernugger
Mymensingh	Mymensing
Nagina	Nugeenah
Najibabad	Nujeebabad
Nani Tal	Nynetal
Nargund	Noorgund
Nimach	Neemuch
Punjab	Panjab
Patiala	Puttiala, Pattiala, Putteela
Rampur	Rampore
Ratnagiri	Rectnagherry
Rohilkhand	Rochilchund, Rochilkhund
Sanaur	Sunawur
Satara	Sattara
Sawantwadi	Sawuntwaree
Sind	Sindh, Scinde, Scindh
Sitapur	Seetapur
Udaipur	Oudeypore
Vellore	Velore

Elizabeth C Moss
13 Collaway Road
Waterloe
Liverpool
L22 4QX

CHAPTER 1

Background of British Reaction to the Crisis of 1857

Commercial relations between Britain and India had already existed for some 250 years at the time of the outbreak of hostilities by the people of India against the British, in 1857. These relations had by degrees become political as well and in the first half of the nineteenth century religious issues also arose between them. In addition to these three links, the civilian and military services of the East India Company combined with the Queen's regiments stationed in India, the arrival of a limited number of British settlers in the country,[1] and the development of an Anglo-Indian press provided further interface between Britain and South Asia. In the main, these links tended to create conflict and tension. Apart from the traditional hostility between the civilian and military services of the Company, clashes also arose from imperial, commercial, religious and private interests which were difficult, and in some cases, impossible, to reconcile. Moreover, the serious proportions which the outbreak of the revolt in India assumed led to a search for the causes of the aggression in an effort to attach responsibility. The very existence of the empire had been endangered; the lives and occupations of hundreds of thousands of Britons were jeopardized at home and in India. It is no wonder that corresponding echoes were heard in strife-torn India as well as in crisis-ridden Britain.

There were several reactions to the revolt. To many it appeared a mere mutiny of the pampered sepoys; to a still larger number a revolutionary conspiracy which aimed at the restoration of native authority; to others, another highly important episode in a losing battle between the Crescent and the Cross; a few advanced the theory of a Russian intrigue designed to expand Russian influence in central and southern Asia; and there were even those who insisted that it was inspired by Brahman attempts to restore the influence they had lost as a result of the modernization of India. These explanations for the uprising were offered either by vested interests seeking to direct responsibility away from themselves, or by secular and religious schools of thought endeavouring to justify their convictions. In the case of vested interests, however, responsibility for the uprising became a subject of mutual accusations.

Apart from the above mentioned reactions which dealt with the character of the outbreak, it was also seen by the Evangelicals as an inevitable result of the policy of debarring Christians and Christianity from India and as such a divine chastisement. The Irish, however, looked at it from their own point of view, through their own past history and experience; hurriedly drew parallels between the British rule in India and in their own country;[2] called the uprising a revolution[3] and at once compared it with the French Revolution and the American War of Independence.[4]

Even after excluding these highly interested elements, which tried to influence public opinion in the light of their own views, the fact remains that this diversity of reactions shown by the British public was also a natural phenomenon, and was to be expected. As in nature, the same object has a different appearance to those who behold it from different angles and from different positions, so was it true in regard to India as well as the events which took place in that country during the fateful years of the outbreak. Even those individuals who tried to view the India of 1857 honestly, could not help doing so through their own personality, circumstances and environments, or through what they had themselves experienced, seen or heard. The result was that even the uninvolved sections of British society were likely to be influenced by their own preconceptions and surroundings. Placed as they were in different positions, from such perfectly different countries, among such perfectly different populations throughout the immense and vast subcontinent of India, they were sure to present a different account of the same object—the Indian mutiny.

The immediate impression in Britain, however, was that the outbreak was an army mutiny. The first official news which arrived in London on 26 June 1857, reported a military uprising. Lord Canning either did not want to be an alarmist, or he really could not comprehend the gravity of the situation or perhaps he failed to calculate the importance of Delhi in the hands of rebels. The people, quite naturally, reacted mildly as they were already used to receiving news of mutinies, disbandments and disarming. They knew about the mutiny at Vellore in 1805; the disbandment of the 47th Regiment in 1824 for refusing to serve in Burma; the refusal of four Bengal regiments in 1844 to serve in Sindh till extra allowances were made to them; the mutiny of the 66th Native Infantry at Govindgarh in 1849, and the refusal of the 38th

Bengal Native Infantry to go to Burma in 1852. In fact, the year 1857 had started with mutinies. Apparently there was nothing new in the news. This time the extent appeared to be a little wider, and for that the government, the press and the people strongly chided the Indian sepoys for their wrong-headedness and advocated immediate and stern action.

As the government in Britain decided not to become alarmed, the people and most of the press either followed its cue or adopted the wise policy of wait and see. The government denied that the empire was in danger and hoped that the outbreak would soon be effectually suppressed by the military forces already present in India. V.A. Smith, President of the Board of Control for India, speaking in the Commons on 29 June 1857, ardently pinned his hopes on the gallantry and quick action of his friend General George Anson, the Commander-in-Chief of India. He deplored the fact that since the mail left India on the 18th of May, he could not, therefore, inform the House that the insurgent headquarters at Delhi was already 'razed to the ground'. He however felt convinced that the next mail would bring the news of its reduction.[5] If *The Scotsman*,[6] the *Manchester Guardian*,[7] the *Illustrated London News*[8] and others entertained no doubts regarding the prompt and easy suppression of the Mutiny, *The Times* took it still more lightly.[9] Expressing its delight that the mutiny was confined to only a few regiments at Meerut and Delhi and that all other stations were reported to be quiet, the paper resolutely but cheerily advocated, as a safeguard for the future, the obliteration of everything that was Indian. In its editorial of 29 June 1857, the paper observed:

> Now that we have conquered India from the Indus to the frontiers of Siam it is our own interest to establish in it a homogeneity which it has never before possessed.... Why, for instance, should there be a Mogul at Delhi, whose very existence, as we see in the present case, preserves the memory of what we should endeavour to obliterate? We would even hope that the death of the Nizam may be the occasion of the Deccan being brought more completely under British sovereignty. We cannot now refuse our part or change our destiny. To retain power in India, we must sweep away every political establishment and every social usage which may prevent our influence from being universal and complete.[10]

Before long news brought by the Indian mail spread throughout the length and breadth of Great Britain. The first delivery alone brought 20,000 letters.[11] Though the letters elaborated details of the sanguinary happenings at Meerut and Delhi; though the participation of the people was reported; though it looked more than a mere military mutiny; though the views and thoughts of quite a few had started to change, still the majority was quite composed and unaffected. After all, the rising was confined to Delhi only for the mutineers had already been driven out of Meerut. European troops would very soon march against Delhi and the city would fall prostrate at their feet. Many must have known that in 1803 General Lake had reduced the same city with only 3000 troops. The next mail, many thought, would bring cheerful news. Thus it was that the British public tried to soothe its fears.

But the fears were not to be calmed so easily. The next mail, and the mail for quite some time after, brought news only of killings and massacres. As a result, the stream of public opinion began to take a different turn. Many analysts were no longer prepared to dismiss the uprising as a simple mutiny. It looked like a serious affair—in fact more like the most formidable danger that had ever threatened the British empire in India. The seriousness of the situation naturally caused criticism of the British Indian administration, both civil and military; of the missionary 'crusade'[12] which had been launched by the British Evangelicals at the start of the eighteenth century and of blind territorial expansion. It was this criticism of the various bonds linking Britain with India that brought all the interested parties into the field in an attempt to safeguard their own names and put the blame upon others before public opinion could reach boiling point. The public was soon deluged with pamphlets and articles, statements and letters, speeches and sermons, works of poetry and fiction, and tracts— military, religious and political—largely written anonymously, by officers and officers' wives, civilians, and missionaries, enthusiasts in theology and aspirants in politics. Public meetings began to be held on an unprecedented scale; lectures were delivered and speeches made in an attempt to bring public opinion in tune with their interests.

The anxiety of the Britons was so great that even the Commons, which earlier could hardly produce a quorum for debates on India, not only attracted virtually the entire House but also began crisis sittings. Prolonged and late night debates on this issue became a common feature in the British Parliament.[13] In fact whatever the topic for discussion, references to India became frequent. Parliamentary sessions on the war with Persia[14] and later on the country's monetary crisis, when the Commons had to be reconvened on 3 December 1857, around a fortnight ahead of the schedule,[15] virtually became Indian debates. The *Manchester Guardian*, a paper which on 29 September 1857, was highly critical of the large mass of matter published on India and had described it as 'rubbish', soon itself felt so anxious about the empire that it did not hesitate to contradict its three day old stand:

It is not strange to find at the present juncture that the minds of the politicians, of every class and party, are filled with one topic–the state of our Indian Empire. Every eye is turned towards India, every ear is intent to catch the last fragment of information from thence, or to anticipate the least whispers of the approaching news. The newspapers are filled with every detail which can be obtained throughout the length and breadth of Hindostan. There is no room for any speech or thought of other or less urgent matters. The empire, the prestige, the honour of England are felt to be at stake.[16]

It appears as if everybody tried to say or write something irrespective of his knowledge of India and all seemed to be nervous. The government of the time did not lag behind in this respect. Outwardly trying to belittle the outbreak, it played a major role in contributing to this national nervousness by throwing an additional 'Sunday' into the middle of the week when it appointed Wednesday, 7 October 1857, as the Day of National Humiliation, Fasting and Prayers. The special services, often three in the day, were held in the churches all over Britain and attracted large congregations. The press publicity of the day and the publication of hundreds of sermons on the mutiny acquainted even the most ignorant of Britons, if not with the people of India, their history and, complex problems, then at least with the outbreak in that country, and the serious threats it posed to Britain's economy, and her world-wide political and military image.

Before dealing with the rising streams of thought in Britain, it will be necessary to say a few words on the sources of British information on India—sources which eventually helped in shaping the public reactions. The first important thing to be noted here is the distance between Britain and India. The physical distance between the two countries was from 6,000 to 11,160 miles via the Red Sea and Cape routes respectively and the time distance was from six to thirteen weeks.[17] The time required and the high cost of transportation must have made a trip to India beyond the capacity of an average Englishman to undertake. Thus with few exceptions only government servants, settlers, missionaries or a few businessmen could go to India—all backed by certain collective or individual interests.

Written inquiries to some of those newspapers and periodicals which continue to publish to the present time have given me the impression that none had a professional reporter stationed in India at the time of the outbreak. The fact that several of the newspapers, at times, reported the news as originating from what they called 'our own correspondent', reveals that these correspondents actually belonged to one of the interests discussed on page one of the introduction.

Naturally, their reports were coloured by their own interests and opinion. As a result of this the people of Britain received a distorted and misleading picture of contemporary Indian society. This situation improved somewhat when *The Times* sent W.H. Russell, its one-time Crimean War correspondent, to India to cover the outbreak. But he arrived at the scene of insurrection only in 1858.

In addition to these difficulties, it should be borne in mind that generally the East India Company discouraged free movement of people to India. The obvious argument for such a policy was the fear of inciting the religious and social prejudices of the people of India. Yet also the Company's own fear of engendering criticism of its Indian policies at home led it to follow this restrictive policy. The Court of Directors, so sensitive to any public criticism, barred representatives of the press from their meetings. As late as 3 February 1858, the *Manchester Guardian* complained:

> India as we have before observed was a sealed book. The Directors by excluding the reporters of the press from their councils, had kept the public in the dark as to what was going on. It was only when something was wrong that we got the information.

The result of this failure of the East India Company to keep their countrymen informed on the affairs of India was a general indifference towards India caused by lack of interest and ignorance. A large number of Britons, actually conscious of this weakness, did not hesitate to point it out.[18] A writer in the *British Controversialist* went to the extent of saying that there were 'not even ten men in the country who had such a knowledge of India so as to entitle them to speak even in the tone of ordinary confidence.'[19] This apathy, however, was rudely broken by the outbreak of insurrection in India. As already pointed out, there was a sudden and intensely felt concern about Indian affairs among the people, but their knowlede of the matter was perhaps no better than that of a man who is suddenly awakened from deep, prolonged slumber.

The time distance combined with past indifference, vast dissimilarity between the people of Britain and India in almost all fields—social, political, religious, educational and economic, and absence of unbiased news media from India, proved a major handicap in both receiving and evaluating accurate information from India. It easily took more than three months to exchange information or else to verify a certain report. The Britons, therefore, had to depend upon their own critical faculty to sift out the truth by comparing different pieces of information, by making some allowance for reporters' own affiliations, or else entirely to depend upon what they were told. It cannot, however, be doubted that almost the entire countryside as well as a sizeable section of Britons living in the cities must have behaved as docile and credulous beings, unfamiliar as they were with the history and the people of India.

That there was enough room for fabrication and concoction is proven by some of the widely circulated but unfounded rumours and stories. One such very important and frequently accepted report concerned a serious rift between Lord Canning, the Governor-General of India, and Lord Clyde (then Sir Colin Campbell), the newly appointed Commander-in-Chief of India. *The Scotsman* repeatedly tried in October 1857, albeit in vain, to discredit all such rumours.[20] Next month the *Saturday Review* similarly censured the wide currency this story had gained.[21] Finally, in an attempt to root out the falsehood, Lord Panmure, Secretary for War, had to quote on 12 December an extract of a letter from Lord Clyde himself to the Duke of Cambridge, the Commander-in-Chief of Britain, dated 26 October 1857. In it Lord Clyde recorded his deep sense of obligation to Lord Canning for his confidence, support and kindness shown to him.[22]

The Nation, likewise, took the wind out of an atrocity story which had no foundation at all. Under the title 'The Atrocity Press', this paper drew attention to the two versions of a fabricated tale of the killing of a certain Mrs Farquharson. According to one version published by *The Freeman*, the lady in question was burnt alive by the rebels after they had committed most frightful and revolting atrocities on her. The other version, said to be the 'truer' one, describing the fate of the 'hapless lady' was published by the *Dublin Evening Post*. Reporting its source as a private letter, this paper informed its readers that 'after suffering a series of indescribable brutalities, she [Mrs Farquharson] was placed alive between two boards and cut through with a saw.' *The Nation* reported that this story was at once taken up by those whom the English papers called 'our own correspondent' and reproduced in England. The reality in this case, however, was that Mrs Farquharson was still alive and was then residing in Europe.[23]

The *Illustrated London News* successfully passed the picture of Joti Prasad, a native Indian banker, for that of Nana Sahib, the 'hero' of the Kanpur massacre. William Forbes-Mitchell, late sergeant of the 93rd Highlanders, in his reminiscences of the 'Great Mutiny', published in 1894, was just as successful in exposing the proxy nature of the portrait. Joti Prasad, who was earlier involved in a case with the

Government of India, had in 1851 hired the services of John Lang, a London barrister, to go out to India and defend his client before a special court at Meerut. After Joti's honourable acquittal through the successful pleading of Lang, the former was so grateful to his defendant that he presented him with an honorarium of £30,000 in addition to the fees on his brief. Lang happened to ask for a portrait of his generous client, and presented with one, took it with him to London. After the news of Kanpur massacre had arrived in England, the artists of the *Illustrated London News* started to call on Britons of Indian experience residing in London in order to get a portrait of The Nana. Failing in that, they finally secured the portrait of Joti Prasad. Despite Lang's protestations that 'the picture no more resembled the Nana of Bithoor than it did her Gracious Majesty the Queen of England; that neither the dress nor the position of the person represented in the picture could pass in India for a Mahratta chief,' the artist contended that 'he did not care for people in India; he required the picture for the people of England.' In this way the picture of poor Joti was passed 'as that of the arch-assassin of the Indian Mutiny.' Although the picture in question was at once recognized in India as being not that of the Nana but that of Joti, the mystery behind it could come to light only after thirty-seven years.[24]

The spirit of sensationalism was not confined to the British press or less important individuals. Highly responsible persons like Lord Shaftesbury were also carried away by sympathy for their fellow countrymen in India and their excessive zeal for evangelical activity. In his speech at Wimborne, delivered on 30 October 1857, he reported to his audience in these words:

> Hundreds, thousands have been massacred in the onslaughts of towns, provinces have been ravaged, thousands have been put to death...but where have you heard of such cruelties perpetrated in cold blood when I tell you that I myself saw a letter from the highest lady now in India stating that day by day ladies were coming to Calcutta with their ears and noses cut off and their eyes put out–When I tell you that children of the tenderest years have been reserved to be put to death under circumstances of the most exquisite torture, not in moments of excitement as you read of in history when the town of Magdeburg was sacked by the imperialists....[25]

In the subtitle of the published version of the 'Great Speech', it was described as a 'most fearful but faithful exposure' of the scene in India. The speech, published as a 'penny-dreadful', must have attracted readers country-wide. However, when challenged on his statement, the noble lord changed his stand from 'he had seen' to 'he had heard of' with a further addition that his informant was perhaps in error.[26] Ninety-nine days after the speech was delivered, the *Manchester Guardian*, a paper that had earlier endorsed Shaftesbury's speech *in toto* on 3 November 1857, and had then done it without journalistic evidence or investigation, decided to censure Shaftesbury for the mischief—a mischief that had already done its job. The paper regretfully observed:

> Whether all people who had made similar statements have also been in error, or have wilfully endeavoured to mislead the public mind in regard to the moral complexion of the Indian mutiny we will not pretend to determine.[27]

Censuring this particular instance and other similar fabrications and reporting that the amount of deliberate lying in England, both by the press and the people had touched frightful heights, *The Nation* itself was carried away by its sentiments, when it went on to observe:

> There is an atmosphere of untruth all over England. Lords lie and commoners lie, merchants lie and forge, banks and companies of all kinds are founded on lies (unlimited), the leading journal is the greatest liar in the world and the little journals try to lie as such as the great one. The war with India has given a powerful stimulus to the lie manufacture and at the same time increased the popular demand for the article.[28]

These were not the only instances of fabrications. In fact, a large number of such concoctions seemed current at that time.[29] In fact the majority of the European residents in India, especially those living in Calcutta, as well as the European press had turned hostile to Canning because of his Press and Arms Acts. They bitterly resented the equal treatment which Lord Canning afforded to the two communities, the rulers and the ruled, in these two matters.[30] It was reported that only one out of ten residents in Bengal liked the governor-general.[31] Many European residents of Calcutta even petitioned the Commons for recalling Canning.[32] These people presented Indians in the worst colours and showed the Governor-General as too mild a person for the situation. All this, naturally, resulted in misrepresentations, which contributed to the formation of public opinion in Britain. Thus in this atmosphere of nervousness, tension, gossip, fabrication, absence of any familiarity with the people of India and, above all, claimed racial superiority over the natives that the British formed their attitudes towards the Indian mutiny.

Before discussing the actual British reactions to the uprising, it is advisable to investigate the motivations which impelled certain sections to throw themselves so ardently into instructing the public. These included all those who might conceivably be held responsible for the catastrophe in India as well as those East Indian groups with something at stake in the rebel country, and who feared that an adverse public opinion would materially endanger their vested interest. The desire to defend their Indian policies in England, and the natural instinct of self-preservation in India dictated these reactions.

The most important element which made a substantial contribution in moulding public opinion was the Government of India. The outbreak, call it a 'mutiny', a 'revolution', 'first war of Indian independence', or a 'Muslim rebellion' was essentially a revolt against government policies—civil and military, social and administrative and political and religious—justified or unjustified. Naturally the government had to be cautious against coming under heavy criticism in Britain. The fear was justified and later on fully supported by a vigorous demand for the recall of Lord Canning. In addition it was not in the interest of the Indian administration to appear alarmed. In India there was not only the need to maintain the confidence of European inhabitants for their own safety, but also to suppress bad news in order to retain the wavering confidence and support of loyal Indians. The result was a carefully planned effort to suppress the news or belittle the outbreak. There is no lack of evidence in this regard. The government led by Canning tried to hold back news of the uprising from the people of Calcutta until the following Thursday. When the rumour of the uprising reached Calcutta on the 14th and *The Harkaru* published it in its issue of the 15th, *The Englishman* was instructed, complained Henry Mead, to publish a contradiction to it.[33]

Canning was so cautious that he declined even the offer of Lord Elphinstone, Governor of Bombay, to convey the news to London by special steamer, then luckily available at Bombay.[34] H. Baillie later on criticized Canning and others in Calcutta for suppressing the news of the uprising and minimizing its extent for around two months.[35] In fact, this cautious attitude led the governor-general to turn down the offer of voluntary service made by a deputation of loyal European residents of Calcutta. The offer first made on the 21st of May was repeated four days later. This discourtesy later proved to be a serious handicap for Lord Canning. He had also turned down the offer of help made by the Prime Minister of Nepal.[36] Interestingly, however, later on Canning willy-nilly accepted all these offers. To top it all, still later he made a vigorous attempt to control the news by gagging the press in India, both native and Anglo-Indian. This, however, misfired. Instead of suppressing the news, Canning's action magnified it. A tide of rumours issued forth, and the wrath of the European community for the percieved lack of confidence in them fell heavily upon the governor-general. Thus while the government kept underestimating the situation, the European residents of Calcutta decided to sift the government policies and expose its acts of omission and commission.

Another element responsible in helping to shape public opinion in Britain was the government of Viscount Palmerston. Unlike the Tories, the Whigs had all along advocated a forward policy in India. They wanted to usher into India an era of reform in social, religious, educational and administrative fields. As they wanted to carry the blessings of British rule to every corner of India, extension of territories and modernization of India were also included in their programme. Consequently, Pitt's India Act of 1784 established a Board of Control for India to be presided by a responsible cabinet minister. This clearly led to a closer scrutiny of the affairs of the East India Company by the British government. Henceforth, all correspondence with India, commercial, political, financial and military, was closely examined by the Board. Many times the contents of the outgoing letters were changed. The British government was thus always heavily involved in the policies pursued in India, especially in territorial expansion.

These policies reached their nadir during the tenure of Governor-General Lord Dalhousie—a Whig nominee. Naturally, Palmerston's government carried a major share in the matter of responsibility for the outbreak. The Tory party and its press virulently criticized Whig policies. *The Press* called for ministerial responsibility.[37] V.A. Smith, President of the Board of Control for India, found it difficult to defend the Whig policies, except by feebly maintaining that the outbreak in India was not caused by either territorial expansion or disturbance of landed property in the country.[38] To avoid causing public alarm the government belittled both the nature and the scope of the outbreak. To back-up its low-level concern in the public eye, it chose to send reinforcements to India via the much longer route around Africa rather than the shorter route of Mediterranean-overland-Red Sea to the west coast of India. Palmerston's logic was that the British government did not want to be indebted to any foreign government or entity in its suppression of the revolt. However, government's attempt to marginalize the revolt failed. For this additional error of judgment the government was taken to task by the media, the House of Commons as well as the House of Lords. Naturally, the Whigs and their cohorts in the press started a vigorous campaign to justify their policies by insisting that the uprising in India was a mere military mutiny and that there was nothing to be worried.

A majority of the shareholders of the East India Company, their courts of Proprietors and Directors and other allied shipping, mercantile and financial interests were another group who had their interests to safeguard. The allied interests of the Company enjoyed a privileged position with regard to India, and were in the same position vis-a-vis the Company as an Awadh sepoy was to his state. Just as the Awadh sepoy did not wish the Company to annex Awadh, similarly these allied interests did not want the abolition of the Company. In both cases their extinction meant the abolition of privileges. As to the shareholders of the Company, it was certainly far from their interest to speak of popular disaffection in India and thereby renounce their right to rule. They, therefore, tried their utmost to convince the people of Britain of the military nature of the revolt. *The Nation* editorially pointed out that the Company was trying to corrupt the press and even intimidate it.[39]

In spite of the fact that public opinion in England had overwhelmingly turned against the anomaly of the dual government in India, and stood for a quick transfer of power from the Company to the Crown, the former did not lose heart. As late as 11 February 1858, in an attempt to prove its innocence the Company petitioned the Crown and vigorously endeavoured to transfer the responsibility for the uprising to it. Disavowing all responsibility for internal as well as external wars, for all territorial extensions in India, the petitioners argued that the army was that part of the Indian administration most directly under the administration of the Crown. It contended that since the governor-general was virtually appointed by the British government, the Company had no say whatever in the appointment of the commander-in-chief. Since the outbreak was a military uprising, the Government of Britain rather than the Company was to be held accountable.[40]

The next group to expound their views of the Indian mutiny were the missionaries and clergymen of various denominations. Like the Company, they represented special interests. The difficulties faced by William Carey, Josiah Marshman and William Ward, all pioneer British missionaries in India, were still fresh in their minds. They had not forgotten the strong opposition of the East India Company to the introduction of missionary activity in India. Even after the passage of the Charter Act of 1813, the Company in the eyes of the missionaries was lamentably tardy in recognizing India's great need for reforms.[41] Above all they were not prepared to forgive the Company for dismissing a sepoy from service for his conversion to Christianity, simply because it feared that this might cause some misgivings among Hindu soldiers.[42] Although policies of the Company had considerably changed since its taking over, it took several steps to eradicate the social evils of *sati*, infanticide, ban on Hindu widows' remarriage, and although the Religious Disabilities Act abolished the disability of a Hindu convert to Christianity to inherit ancestral property, the irrefutable fact remained that the army cantonments were still 'off limit' places for the missionaries. Their activities were still confined to settled areas, and the Bible had still not been introduced in government schools. The Evangelicals and the clergy of Britain held the Company responsible for all this, and were not prepared to give it any consideration.

To make matters worse many Britons regarded the excessive missionary activity to be largely responsible for the uprising in India. It was believed that the Indians had begun to identify the missionaries with the government and thus feared that it was in fact the government that intended to impose Christianity on them by force, with the employment of missionaries as a means to that end. The government of India felt so convinced of the missionary element in causing the uprising by exciting religious prejudices of the Indians, that they imposed censorship to the press and even considered suppressing the chief missionary paper, *Friend of India*.[43]

When called upon to share the responsibility for the insurrection, the missionaries washed their hands of the blame. Together with the clergymen of Britain, especially the Anglicans, they declared with one voice that Christian preaching was not at all responsible for the outbreak of mutiny in India. Indeed they contended that the lack of sufficient missionary activity had led to it. The sepoy army was never allowed to be tamed by Christian love; on the contrary its caste and religious prejudices were pampered beyond limits. No wonder that, untaught, untamed and unenlightened as the sepoys were, they revolted. Moreover, the greater loyalty of the Madras and Bombay presidencies, where Christian missionary activity was of much longer standing and much more widespread, proved that conversion and Christianity were a deterrent rather than a cause of the revolt. Instances of loyalty of native converts to Christianity were profusely reported from all over India and emphasized. At places like Delhi and Lucknow, the missionaries argued, their programme was introduced only recently, thus the agitation. To prove the sincerity of their point of view all the missionary societies launched a vigorous campaign for stepping up evangelistic activity in India. Meetings of various missionary societies were held, lectures quoted figures on insufficient missionary work and huge amounts of funds were raised.

To extricate themselves completely from all blame for the outbreak, the Evangelical party successfully pointed to Muslim hostility towards the followers of Christ. This enmity, they stressed, was not born of the missionary programme but had existed in spite of it. The followers of Islam, they maintained, had always remained deadly enemies of Christianity and would continue to be so in the future. This hatred was alleged to be universal and was not confined to India. Muslims were thought to be constantly obsessed with fear of the Christian truth. Whenever opportunity presented itself to them to express this hatred and animosity towards Christianity, they readily availed of it. In India the situation was presented as still worse for political enemity was believed to have been added to the existing religious hatred. The Muslims of India always felt ill at ease under the British rule. They were anxious to re-establish their past glory in India, and reportedly indulged in ceaseless conspiracies for the overthrow of the British rule. The revolt of 1857, the missionaries emphasized, was simply another, albeit more vigorous outburst of Muslim bigotry towards Christianity and Christian. Muslims were held responsible for every move in the uprising. In short, by presenting all these arguments, both against the Company and the Muslims, the Evangelists tried to absolve themselves of all responsibility for the outbreak.

In like manner, the civilian and military servants of the East India Company, with of course a few renegades on both sides, were at loggerheads over the nature of the revolt. Just as it was not in the interest of the military servants to accept the mutiny view, the civilian service equally disliked the revolution theory. Since acceptance of either notion involved shouldering responsibility, an implied admission of incompetence, and loss of prestige for the service, both tried to hide any fact damaging to them and bring to light only those which transferred all blame to the other party. To this end, news and information were tailored to the general interest of the service.

Among all the contending factions, the Conservatives enjoyed a happier position. They all along advocated a policy of caution and gradual advancement in India; quick changes were as noxious to them as the thought of a revolution itself. To them maintenance of native rule in the princely states of India was a source of strength to the British, because it presented a favourable contrast between the oppressive native despotism and enlightened British rule. Rapid social and educational changes did not much appeal to them. They believed that Indian culture and civilization had much to offer to them and that its weaknesses should be overcome gradually. The Conservatives thus enjoyed a higher moral plane in putting forward their opinions on the subject of the outbreak and an air of confidence pervaded their utterances. As they had always opposed liberal Whig policies, virtually stood in opposition to the missionary 'crusade' and had warned them of the serious consequences liable to follow in the wake of their laudable motives, they viewed the uprising through these convictions.

The Conservatives patiently waited for a month listening to the government pronouncements, and finally refused to put any faith in the Whig version that the outbreak was not a people's protest against recent government policies but a military mutiny caused chiefly by the introduction of greased cartridges. Describing the uprising as a national war, they predicted a prolonged struggle in India and called for adequate measures to meet the emergency—calling up the militia and rapid dispatch of adequate reinforcements. The Conservatives were soon joined by the Irish nationalists, labour press and what I would like to call the 'moralists' in British society. Although at variance with the Tories on future British policy towards India, these three factions were with Disraeli in describing the outbreak as a national revolt. Their persistence in this view; the fulfilment of their prediction of the prolongation of the struggle; the difficulties which the Government of India had to face in suppressing the insurrection; the British government's earlier refusal to call the militia and its later decision to alter this stand; the extraordinarily large number of British troops sent to India;[44] and finally the abolition of the East India Company produced a trend in public opinion towards the Disraelian point of view.

CHAPTER 2

Causes of the Military Mutiny

The military mutiny school of thought was composed of those sections of British society, who, though liberal in their thinking at home and abroad, had a low opinion of Indians and Indian society. Consequently they had a radical zeal to 'purge' them. The government of the time, the Whig Party and its press, the independent but (insofar as the mutiny was concerned) invariably pro-government newspaper, *The Times*, majority of the shareholders of the East India Company, its Courts of Proprietors and Directors, a large number of the civil servants in India, and ardent Evangelicals like Lord Shaftesbury shared this view. As that majority of the components of the school reveal it was not in their interest to accept, let alone describe, the outbreak as a national rebellion caused by political, social, economic, or religious discontent in India.

From 1830 to 1857 Whigs held the majority in the Commons. During that fateful part of the nineteenth century they were invariably and deeply involved in the British imperial, colonial and foreign policies, and this was particularly true of policies pursued in India. To take one important event closely connected with the outbreak of the Indian mutiny, the annexation of Awadh, one finds that all the directives contemplated or issued for the incorporation of the state into the British dominions in India proceeded from the Whig administration. When, in 1831, Lord William Bentinck was asked to occupy Awadh, the secret despatch emanated from Earl Grey's administration. Again in 1835, when Lord Auckland was reminded of the secret despatch of 1831, Viscount Melbourne was in power. And finally when Lord Dalhousie occupied Awadh in 1856, Palmerston was the prime minister. Palmerston's presence in the two aforementioned administrations as foreign secretary, and the absorption of the state while he held the office of the prime minister, sufficiently indicate a definite continuity in Whig policies. Lord Dalhousie, who though a Conservative, embarked upon a career of vigorous imperial policy in India, was himself a Whig nominee. Under these circumstances, the fact of the outbreak and its intensity was no small reflection upon the British Indian administration. To have accepted the possibility of any grave political, social or economic discontent as the reason for the mutiny in India would have amounted to admitting the failure of government policies of the past decade or so and invited public wrath; more so when the Conservatives were demanding the application of the principle of ministerial responsibility over Awadh.[1]

As far as the liberal and independent press was concerned, i.e., *The Times*, the *Manchester Guardian* and others, it had, in the past, always supported and endorsed a 'forward' policy in India in fields both political and social. It is an admitted fact that the mutiny was also a reaction against the rapidity with which India was anglicized, and modernized. Since this part of the press had always advocated such policies, it naturally tried to discount the idea of any popular disaffection in India and avoided sharing any responsibility for the outbreak. Similarly, it was not in the interest of the East India Company or its civilian servants to recognize the existence of a general antipathy or popular alienation of public feelings towards their administration. Some of the Evangelicals, however, wanted to prove that since the army was the only part of Indian society not allowed to be penetrated by missionary activity, it had revolted—uncivilized and untaught as it was.[2]

Obviously, the thinking of the adherents of this school ran counter to the views of the proponents of the socio-political rebellion school of thought. Although the majority of the former pinpointed various defects in the organization of the army and in its management, many others emphasized the grievances of the sepoys—social, religious, military, political and financial. They explained the outbreak as a purely military uprising, which, it was argued, selfish interested parties took advantage of. Although it put forward strong and apparently convincing arguments, this school of thought was marked by a lack of cohesion and unity and were quite often contradictory. Their thinking based its case upon evaluation of the Indian character and people as lowly. Its most strenuous advocates based their thesis upon the contention that Dalhousie's modernized India did not contain simply one nation, but that the Indians comprised of a 'good score of native populations, far more distinct from each other in language, customs and religion than the nations of Europe.'[3]

The stress was upon the nationalities of India rather than upon the Indians as a nation. Regarding India as a mere 'geographical expression', the *Saturday Review* called the Indian subcontinent an 'untempered assemblage of tribes, races, classes, and sects, bound into a whole by the solitary tie of obedience to some strong master. National adversities, far more hopelessly irreconcilable than can be guessed at even by looking at the standing quarrel between Italians and Germans, or between Saxon and Celt, are eclipsed by yet more trenchant division in the society itself. Even if there were an India, there would be, we repeat, no people of India. The word is a foolish misnomer for a collection of stratified castes.'[4] They asserted that all nation-making ingredients, such as unity of feeling, of ideas, of blood, which could more or less harmonize Indian thinking and cause national unity, or could give the Indians a common purpose, were completely non-existent among the inhabitants of the Indian peninsula.[5]

To call the Indians a nation was, therefore, to this school of thought as erroneous a usage as the expression 'European', if the Europeans were to be thought of as one nation. India certainly was not to Indians, it was claimed, as England was to Englishmen or even Italy to Italians.[6] 'From the Himalayas to Cape Camorin', so contended the writer in *Blackwood's Edinburgh Magazine*, 'the use of the term "national"' is in India a 'mockery, a delusion and a snare'. In fact, India was an expression used only for the sake of convenience. Otherwise India never was, argued the same writer, a nation, not even a confederacy of nations and for that reason the Indians had nothing 'national within themselves.'[7] It was believed that the Indians had no internal bond of unity whatsoever and that they were, in reality, no better than 'a confused, disjointed collection of struggling races.'[8] The existence of any fusion among Indians was denied even at the village level. The only connecting link, thought one advocate of this thesis, was provided by the central police and the judicial system.[9]

Since the Indians did not fall into the category of a nation, there could be no question of 'national discontent' or for that reason of a 'national insurrection.'[10] A writer in the *Westminster Review* lashed out against John Bright when the latter called the outbreak a movement for independence. He observed, 'as to independence, it is the veriest chimera ever begotten by prejudice out of ignorance.... The people of India has no existence but in the brain of Mr Bright.'[11] *The Times* also expressed similar feelings but with regard to the Hindus alone. It maintained discreet silence as far as the presence of any national feeling among the Muslims was concerned.[12]

With nationality denied to the Indians and the idea of a national insurrection counted out, the mutiny school spent all its energies emphasizing the anomalies in the army administration of India and so tried to build, though with only partial success, its thesis of an army insurrection. Starting off with a discussion of the nature of the sepoy army they covered every conceivable aspect of military confusion and concluded that the sepoy was nothing less than a pent-up volcano. This group further stressed that time after time the government had been served with warnings and[13] on each such occasion it had behaved like an ostrich with its head in the sand. While these warnings went unheard, unseen and unnoticed and unchecked, the sepoy volcano built up pressure until it reached a point where an explosion was only a matter of time, and it came in May 1857.

Many interpreters deemed even the nature of the army upon which the continuation of the empire depended to be contradictory.[14] It was an organization composed of foreigners and mercenaries, from which the loyalty of a national army could not be expected. Its only link with the English was its pay and that was far from a steady bond.[15] This relationship was further enfeebled by the recognition of caste in the Bengal army.[16] The noxious practice of attending to caste at the time of enlistment quite frequently excluded not only the best material from the army but also resulted in 'enlisting the very worst.'[17] Under this system a man was not selected on account of the most important qualities in a soldier, i.e., physical fitness, willingness and strength, docility and courage, but because he belonged to a certain caste or sect. Where he failed to fulfil caste qualifications, whatever his other merits, he received no attention because the government was afraid of offending 'the lazy and insolent Brahmins.'[18] The result was that the Bengal army did not contain the same diversity of sects and caste as the armies of the Bombay and Madras presidencies. It was confined to Brahmans, Rajputs, and Muslims—the three dominant races.[19]

The *Manchester Guardian*, as did many other papers, periodicals, pamphlets and individuals, quoted liberally from Brigadier-General John Jacob of the famous Sind Irregular Horse,[20] who had earlier clearly underlined the perils and hazards hidden in the caste system. Jacob had observed:

> The effect of enlisting men of certain caste, or creed to the exclusion of others in the Indian army is to subject that army to the control, not of the Government and the Articles of War, but to that of Brahmins and Goseins, Moollahs [Mulla][21] and Fakheers [Faqirs][22].... The consequences are ruinous to discipline. By reason of this a native soldier in Bengal is far more afraid of an offence against caste than of an offence against the articles of war and by this means a degree of power rests with the private soldier which is entirely incompatible with healthy rule.[23]

The caste monopoly in the Bengal army was regarded as one of its major weaknesses. It led to the formation of caste and creed groups on regimental lines. Subsequently, the caste groups wielded real power in the regiments—a power to be reckoned with in several fields of army administration. While 'Treachery, Mutiny, Villainy of all kinds'[24] were rendered possible without much fear of detection because of caste, creed and family bonds, these orders (caste groups) became a sort of pressure group in the regiments. To support his contention, Jacob reported an instance of forced dismissal of 'an excellent sepoy because the other men had discovered him to be of inferior caste and demanded his dismissal.'[25] Moreover, if a low caste Hindu happened at all to fill a higher post, i.e., subedar in the army, he was invariably under the spiritual influence of the Brahmanical clique and would always show too great a reverence even to the rawest recruit of the priestly class.[26] This materially impaired discipline in the army. Even if he were to know of a conspiracy being hatched in the lines, he would not dare to divulge the secret for fear of excommunication—a penalty more dreadful than that of death.[27] Such a regimental composition was also dangerous from another point of view. Since the army had become a stronghold of caste and superstition, contended one, the soldiers could easily be made to believe the stories that man's ingenuity could invent.[28]

Furthermore, the Bengal sepoy being a high-caste man, took pride in his own person and soldierly qualities as against the Bombay and Madras sepoy, who, on the contrary, looked upon the European comrade as a model in 'all things pertaining to soldiership.'[29] As a result, it was argued, the latter was amenable to teaching, guidance, and discipline; the former was not. The Madras and Bombay sepoy was always prepared to execute any order from the cleaning of lines to the building of officers' houses and mess rooms as well as other odd jobs. This, however, was not applicable to his counterpart in the Bengal Presidency. The situation had become so deplorable there, complained Jacob, that a cavalry man would not picket, unsaddle or groom his horse until the arrival of 'Syces [Sa'is]' and grasscutters—sometimes several hours after the arrival of the regiment at its ground. A Bengal sentry was not prepared even to strike the gong at his own quarter-guard and men called 'gunta-panday [Ghanta Pande]'[30] were especially maintained and paid for that purpose.[31] To such a state of helplessness had the recognition of caste reduced the army, editorially complained the *Manchester Guardian*, that jobs became classified. A man who would dust his officer's furniture or trim his lamp would not sweep the floor; the personal attendant would not serve coffee; one who brought his officer's pipe would not light it; the groom who rubbed down his officer's horse would not make his bed or cut grass for him.[32] There was a general complaint that each duty required a person of separate caste to perform it. On 15 September 1857, the *Manchester Guardian* quoted Jacob who had severely criticized this rigid stratification in the army and the acceptance of caste in its ranks:

> ...in the army of Bombay, where in hundreds and thousands of men from Hindoostan, from the same villages, of the same caste, and even of the same families, brothers by the same fathers and mothers as the fine gentlemen of the Bengal army, are seen in the ranks, shoulder to shoulder, nay, even sleeping in the same tent with the Mahratta, the Dher and the Purwaree, without scruple or thought of objection. The one prides himself on being a Hindoo, the other on being a soldier. Which pride is best for our purpose? This system of regarding caste is the original cause of many other evils in the Bengal army;....[33]

Next day the paper editorially censured the army as uncomfortable, uneconomic and dangerous for discipline. It strongly advised the government that:

> We must not compel a high-caste man to do a duty below him, but there is no reason why we should not employ a low caste man to do a dozen above him. In Bombay this is done.... In Bombay ten low caste Hindoos, or the same number of Mussalmans, are taught to do the work of thirty Bengal servants; and as the same material is to be found in either presidency, we see no reason why what is done in the one, with economy and comfort, should not be followed out in the other, both in the army and domestic life.[34]

W. Sinclair, Rector of Pulborough in Sussex,[35] saw another clear advantage which could have accrued to the British, had they employed all different castes and sects in the Bengal army. Such a practice, if followed, would surely have bred mutual distrust and jealousy among the sepoys and would, naturally, have obstructed any unity of action among them against the government.[36] This 'castification' of the army produced the greatest damage. The Earl of Albemarle, earlier an MP in the interest of the Whigs, called the outbreak a caste affair in the army[37] and the *Manchester Guardian* critically remarked:

> It was by enlisting high-caste men on high-caste terms, and treating them on their own principles, that that disorganization was brought about which has been mediately the cause of such fearful calamities.[38]

In addition to the admission of caste, 'unequal enlistment of troops in the various provinces and principalities of India,' it was contended, also contributed towards the paralysis of discipline in the army.[39] Since a large section of it was recruited from Awadh, the opinions of Awadhian sepoys in the army governed the rest of it. This was regarded as a factor that bred greater possibilities of fellow-feelings and provided increased facilities for hatching conspiracy without being discovered—something dangerous for the continuation of British rule in India.[40]

The great disproportion between the native troops and their European counterparts was another factor. This imbalance in numbers was highly important and was naturally emphasized by many.[41] As the empire grew and as warlike and turbulent races of the Punjab, Sindh Awadh, Pegu, Nagpur, Berar and many other territories were added to the British empire of the east, so the problem in the imperial military machine was exacerbated. While the strength of European troops in India in 1857 was less than in 1835, the native army had increased by more than a 100,000 men.[42] Consequently, government demands upon the services of the European troops increased immensely.[43] The result was that hundreds of miles lay between places where British troops were stationed.[44] Awadh was left with only one regiment. The sepoys were quite conscious of their own numerical superiority and the weakness of the masters—a consciousness which, it was contended, was further enforced by the withdrawal of Anglo-Indian regiments for service in the Crimea, Persia and China.[45] The low tide, it was argued, was at its lowest ebb. The sepoys were now more willing to entertain the idea of a mutiny, and more reluctant to abandon it once they thought about it.[46] Thus it was that Martin R. Gubbins, afterwards a judge of the Supreme Court at Agra, strongly held:

> Religious alarm might have been excited; the native soldier might have been at the same time discontented and insubordinate; the talooqdars [Ta'alluqah dar][47] of Oudh and the royal families of Delhi and Lucknow might have plotted; yet had we possessed a few English regiments in the country, discontent would never have matured into rebellion.[48]

This might explain the ferocity of the outbreak in Awadh and the North-West Provinces as compared to the quiet (though Muslims were reportedly feeling uneasy everywhere) of the Punjab, which had several European regiments.

If the defective nature and composition of the Indian army had made the sepoys self-confident, it had also made the government conscious of the weakness in its large native army establishment. The government consequently adopted a weak and vacillating policy, which, it was contended, resulted in the ruin of army discipline. The sepoys were petted more and more into believing that they were indispensable.[49] This pampering had begin as early as 1827, when Lord Combermere, then Commander-in-Chief in India, limited the jurisdiction of court-martial and diminished the authority of the commanding officers. Finding power over their men seriously impaired, European officers were inevitably dissatisfied and disgruntled. Under the new regulations, they decided to pass over offences for which they could not take cognizance without exhibiting to the men their loss of authority over them. The sepoys, it was held, soon realized this and ceased to be as deferential and obedient as they had been in the past. Although Combermere's successor restored to the officers their partial authority, Lord William Bentinck, who was the Governor-General of India from 1828 to 1835, went one step further when, in defiance of all advice, warning and remonstrance, he abolished corporal punishment in the native army but retained it for the Europeans.[50] The result, in the words of a native subadhar addressed to Gubbins, was: 'the army no longer fears' *'fauj beydar hogeea'*, that is: 'the army had awoken.'[51] The *Manchester Guardian* called it 'a piece of moribund humanity and short-sighted policy',[52] an humanitarian error which the sepoys misinterpreted to be the result of the government's fear of their rebellious intentions. It very naturally rendered them more defiant and exacting.[53]

The new rule was allowed to work for ten years with all its consequences of disorder and mutiny until partially rescinded in 1845. The decade of its application, however, had already damaged army discipline.[54] Yet its restoration could not be welcomed by the sepoys. Robert J. Roy Campbell, M.P., and a resident of twenty-five years' experience in India, described it as an error in military legislation of which the sepoys took advantage.[55] In addition, it was further complained that Bentinck had also invited appeals against the decisions of army officers and had abolished night guards provided by native officers over the persons and properties of the Company's officers.[56] If the privilege of appeal, argued the same critic, had created a suspicion in the minds of sepoys regarding undue past exercise of authority by their officers the suspension of night guards removed what they had so far considered as the most sacred duty they performed. Both steps were regarded as sufficient to break the bond between officers and their men—a loss which could not be repaired.

To make matters worse, as expostulated by a military officer, the sepoys were at times asked to spy on the conduct of European officers—a step which was sure to bring the authority of these officers into contempt.[57] Although in 1857 European commanders were allowed to hold court-martial, the step failed to enhance them in the eyes of the soldiers for the act was described as no better than 'a mockery of justice and a curse to the army.' The court-martial was to be comprised of native officers. In order to enforce the performance of the smallest duty, or to punish the most flagrant delinquency, the commander was always obliged to appeal to the authority of the native officers, thus reducing the European officer to parity.[58] All these privileges or the 'Magna Carta of privileges'[59] as one of this school put it, had turned the sepoys' head and had led them to believe that the officers were only to superintend drill or show the way in battle, with no power to reward or punish.[60] It was this relaxation of discipline, believed Captain Oliver J. Jones, combined with the habit of 'giving in to all sepoy whims and fancies, reasonable or unreasonable' and the attempt to 'coax and cajole them to their duty by rewards often unmerited; instead of punishing the neglect of it,' which imparted to the sepoys an impression that the performance of their duty was a sort of favour rather than a necessity and in turn fostered the spirit of mutiny.[61] No wonder Lord Shaftesbury in his speech at Wimborne Town Hall categorically denied any semblance of civil support for the outbreak and decried it as entirely an army affair. Answering his own question as to who were the rebels, he exclaimed:

> It [the rebellion] arose from a monster of our own creation; it arose from an army pampered, flattered, overpaid and underworked. It arose from an army that we had raised by discipline into the attitude it had assumed...and by our neglect we allowed it to acquire a sense of its own importance and the conviction that it could act independently of its European officers, and that it was as capable as it was willing to take the empire into its own hands.[62]

The author of *India, the Revolt and the Home Government*, expressed similar sentiments (though he called it a Muslim inspired rebellion), and deplored that 'we have been bitten by the snake which we have nurtured in our bosom.'[63]

Apart from this, as editorially criticized by the *Manchester Guardian*, defect of a dangerous kind had gradually established itself in the army organization. It was the ever-growing tendency to exclude native talent from authority in the native regiments. This could not have augured well for the future. A cursory glance at the history of the sepoy army would at once reveal that the Company's army, though drilled in European fashion, was in the beginning primarily officered by natives,—'chiefs connected with the men by ties of consanguinity—and clientship.' European officers, well-versed in the use of native language, were only occasionally attached to very limited duties, confined to those of commissioner or field officer. The result, commented the paper, was that the service was very efficient. The first marked change, however, occurred in 1786 when, along with regularizing the size of each battalion to a thousand men, one European captain and two lieutenants were added to each unit. This addition of European officers, no doubt, led to undermining the authority of the natural leaders. Still it was done to a limited extent and the native subahdars and jama'dars continued to conduct their companies. So far so good. Then began a period in which increasing number of English applicants for commissions in the Indian army, coupled with British confidence in its complete supremacy in the subcontinent, resulted in a systematic disregard of the policy of enlisting the sympathies and interests of the Indian aristocracy in support of the British military organization. Soon, the Liberal organ complained, European personnel were introduced at a still lower level when a European subaltern was allotted to command each company. Though the feelings of native subahdars were spared as much as possible, this new element grew stronger and stronger in the 1790s. The native gentleman could no longer deny that his authority had become less and less.[64]

Such changes brought in its wake three evils:

a) It was no longer possible, the paper pointed out, to select European officers from the sepoy commands. As the vacancies arose, 'raw lads, fresh from England, with all their inexperiences and inborn prejudices in full flower were brought forward to supply them. Such boys could hardly avoid coming into constant and painful collision with the native officers.' The differences of colour and speech further enlarged the mutual aversion.

b) The increased number of English officers, it was argued, made them too familiar to be held at the same level of respect. Since the Englishman was seen holding no important position but was busy either in the performance of ordinary duties which any native officer or even a non-commissioned officer could do equally well, or was found trifling away his time in what was described as 'frivolous and vicious pursuits,' the 'prestige of the superior race' was thus destroyed and the officer too lost 'somewhat of his own self-respect.' At times also a young boy was placed in command of an old native subahdar, from whom, whenever anything was to be done, he had 'to crave instructions.'[65]

c) The effect, it was contended, of European appointments upon native officers and finally upon the whole military service was no less damaging. It not only deprived native officers of all their influence and authority in the corps, but soon their very character started to degenerate. In fact, the service 'may be said to have changed its very nature altogether.' Formerly, the elite of the native gentry was enlisted in the ranks of the Company's army. Now, no native gentleman would even think of donning the uniform of the regular army. Earlier, since each native officer was educated, he would keep the accounts of his company, would write orders and dispatches and, at times, act as an interpreter, 'where his European comrades would have been otherwise at fault.' All this had changed. The soldiers of India, it was pointed out, became the most unsettled men in the country.[66]

The tragedy was that the changeover from native to European officers was not complete. While more and more European officers were introduced, it was complained, native officers were also retained. This was a great anomaly. It resulted in the government gradually losing its hold upon the native army. It was, in fact, in imminent danger of falling 'between two stools.'[67] Either the government, it was suggested, should have made the European element much larger and more efficient than it did or it should have, if it thought fit to deprive the native officer of all real authority and patronage, completely discontinued the class of native commissioned officers. The fact, however, was that it did neither. My opinion is that power divorced from responsibility or responsibility divorced from power are both dangerous, but the absence of both power and responsibility is still worse. It is exactly the situation in which the native officers seem to have found themselves, holding office and rank without proportionate power and responsibility. Their position in the army had become tenuous. 'It was no longer,' editorially, argued the *Manchester Guardian* 'an honoured or honourable calling to wear the English uniform. The natural leaders of the people had been driven from the service with bitterness in their hearts and their place has not been adequately supplied in point either of numbers or respectability by the substitution of English officers. The controlling and directing power of the army had sunk into the hands of a low, ill-educated and unrespected class of natives, reinforced by the weakest part of the talent, and the least credible part of the ambitious annually exported from England.'[68] The net result was that when the mutinous spirit took root in the army—

something completely absent previous to these changes—these native officers for obvious reasons either could not or would not do anything. In referring to an article published in the *Edinburgh Review* on the subject of army organization some years before the outbreak and the subsequent neglect of the government in paying any attention to it, the very vocal *Manchester Guardian* critically remarked:

> ...the foreboding which they [allegations and reasoning] were calculated to suggest appear to be in the course of fulfilment with terrible minuteness and precision.[69]

While native commissioned officers were reduced to nonentities, European commanders fared no better.[70] It was contended, that Lord Dalhousie not only did not let the control of the army pass to the lieutenant-governor of Bengal, now that Bengal had been constituted into a distinct government by the Charter Act of 1854, he also embarked upon an ambitious course to centralize all power in his own hands.[71] What Bentinck had done out of humanitarian motives, Dalhousie did to satisfy his excessive desire for more power. This not only weakened the dignity of the commander-in-chief but also largely minimized the influence of commanding officers in their regiments.[72] This time around English officers were shorn of all powers to punish or reward their native wards and prior permission of the central government was needed for all such actions.[73] The most pernicious change, earnestly protested by many, was that in several instances sepoys were allowed and indeed even encouraged to forward complaints against their commanders direct to army headquarters.[74]

The disadvantages of the governor-general trying to exercise immediate and direct control over the army of Bengal were obvious to several contemporaries. In spite of his disposition to supervise the most minute details of even ordinary routine work, it was physically impossible for him to do so, especially when he had to attend to the countless civil concerns of the great Indian empire.[75] In such circumstances the inevitable result was easily predictable. The military administration of India, it was argued, instead of becoming simple, became 'complicated, disjointed and confused'; instead of becoming vigorous, it became 'weak, vacillating and ill informed even in general matters and lamentably ignorant in those minute details in which the Central Government so unwisely meddles.'[76] The excessive centralization, these people averred, had doubly harmed the army administration.[77]

Firstly, it sapped the strong feelings of personal attachment of the soldier to his officer which, earlier was the result of a feeling of love for and fear of the officer, and was indeed very widespread forming the life-blood of the regiment. As the sepoys now had to look to the government or the new regulations for future advancement rather than to the immediate superiors, love, attachment, and fear of the officers also disappeared..[78]

Secondly, excessive centralization of power and policy eliminated independence both of thought and action among the superiors cadre. Honest and efficient army officers resentful of this lack of confidence, were driven to aloofness and 'moody silence.'[79] Henceforward, they soundly slept on their difficulties, even when action was necessary. Communication of valuable information began to be ignored leading to the neglect of essential measures or conversely to the introduction of trivial or abortive ones, based on either ignorance or half truths. A little knowledge is a dangerous thing, and it was so true in the handling of the native army by the Central Government of India.[80] A correspondent from New Brighton asserted in *The Times* that centralization was dangerous to experiment with, especially when the native army was mercenary in character and its uninformed patriotism was likely to array itself against the British.[81]

To aggravate the situation further the Government of India had fallen into the habit of withdrawing army officers from military service for civil employment. This rendered the strength of British army officers highly disproportionate to the strength of the native army.[82] The Indian administration was scathingly attacked on this point by critics of all shades of public opinion.[83] The meteoric expansion of territories and the increasing demand for more and more civil administrators and engineers, coupled with the East India Company's desire to economize, led to new demands needed to be met at the expense of the army; more and more officers were pulled out of active regimental service and employed in the Company's civil and political service, the public works department, irregular corps or in staff and other appointments. The result was that in April 1857, 1215 officers of the Bengal army were absent from their regiments.[84] What were essentially loans of personnel, really became long term commitments.[85] The cumulative effect of all this was disastrous in many ways:

a) Such an anomalous practice, it was asserted, deprived the army of officers well acquainted with Hindustani. Those left knew little of the language and eventually the army administration was deprived of a healthy degree of communication with the soldiers. No doubt, in some regiments there were some linguists, but such regiments, it was further argued, did not revolt.[86]

b) It took away pride in military service and the civil service began to be more valued and highly thought of. The army was deprived of its most experienced hands. It was left either with young, inexperienced ensigns—fresh from England, haughty and arrogant in their approach to the problems of the soldiers, or else incapable and discontented officers caring less of anything other than the cut and dried routine of military duty.[87] In fact, regimental service came to be looked upon as 'a sort of penal servitude,'[88] and increasingly regarded as a 'stepping stone to dignified civil employment.'[89] If perchance, it was argued, a capable officer was left in the regiment, he felt hurt at his ambition being thwarted. Since such officers always tried to gain civil appointments, they invariably found themself busy manoeuvring to get rid of the regimental shackles and so very much tended to forget the needs of the regiment.[90]

c) Thirdly, civil employment of army officers and its negative effects reduced contact between the individual soldier and his officer to the detriment of English interests.[91] The officers, henceforth, failed to identify with the sepoys under their command.[92] 'Naturally', observed J.L. Archer, late of Lucknow,

> the influence of European officers over their men seriously declined, and eventually too great facilities were created either for designing persons to delude the men, or for men themselves to form and mature a conspiracy against the Government. Hence it was that the conspiracy which we now deplore spread secretly from corps to corps and steadily and gradually matured, while the Europeans in the country remained in their dangerous security and carelessness of ignorance.[9]

The indifference of European officers put power into the hands of native commissioned officers, who, because of advanced age, were either silent spectators of what the sepoys did or were tools in their hands.[94]

It was this inadequacy of English officers, their inexperience, incapacity and indifference which, it was thought, bred the opportunity for revolt.[95] The East India Company tried to save the 'almighty' pound and later had to pay the price with compound interest.[96]

There were many other factors which, it was held, led to the loss of contact between the European officer and the native sepoy and lowered regard for the former in the eyes of the latter:

a) The companies drew their salary directly from the divisional paymaster. This was done independently and often times without the knowledge of the regimental commanders. This tended to reduce the power of the commanders, curtailed their contact and influence with the regiments and brought them not only into contempt with their men but made 'them be despised'.[97]

b) Further improvement in the means of communications between England and India too was not regarded as an unmixed blessing.[98] While immensely reducing the time distance between mother country and colony to the advantage of Indian administration, it concurrently lessened the dependence of English officers in India upon India. Thenceforth, military officers could easily bring their wives or families with them comparatively inexpensively or could visit England more frequently than earlier.[99] The eased furlough regulations provided further stimulus to such a tendency.[100] Increased interaction with England as well as the increased number of European women in India were regarded as two factors largely responsible for the development of a spirit of indifference between officers and their men.[101] Fifty years before the outbreak, it was contended, there was no European society to draw the officer away from his camp duties. In 1810 there were only 250 European ladies in India.[102] Naturally, European officers maintained large local harems. In fact, in the same year, claimed an anonymous writer in the *Dublin University Magazine*, a work by one Captain Williamson, dedicated to the Court of Directors was published for the guidance of cadets in this matter. It contained minute details on how to keep native mistresses. One elderly officer kept as many as sixteen. In 1813, however, things started to change and 'English women and English morals began to be imported, together with the renewal of the Charter in 1813.' This improved morality, believed the same writer, of European society in India had an adverse effect upon the state of the army. The camp and the *'zenana'*[103] gave 'place to the compound, with an English wife and the monthly magazines.' The writer in the *Dublin University Magazine* went on to observe:

> The officer is now a refined European. The sepoy remains still a prejudiced Hindu. The time has passed when the Europeans can with decency Hinduize. The time has not yet come when the Hindu will Europeanize and so there remains a gulf fixed between officers and men; they have no interests in common—the *esprit de corps* is a tie too frail to bind men together who have no common national glories and consequently there is nothing to check a mutinuous spirit, should it unhappily break out among the men.[104]

It was this indifference produced by the enlargement of European society which, according to Thomas C. Robertson, late member of the

Supreme Council of India and lieutenant-governor of the North-Western Provinces, later prejudiced the sepoys towards the lives of their officers.[105]

c) After the great augmentation of the native army in 1824, old officers were transferred to new regiments and their places were filled either by men unknown to the regiments or by men who were new even to the service. This severed long standing connections between the officers and their corps.[106] New people with different attitudes, manners, habits and outlooks joined the regiments. The onus of building up understanding and assimilation anew became an uphill task especially when several of the officers were fresh from England. This must have rankled the soldiers. The following pertinent question posed by a sepoy to an officer who had succeeded in keeping the confidence of his men, 'Are the gentlemen who now come out to India of a different caste from those of the former days?' sufficiently reflected to the *Manchester Guardian* the seriousness of the situation.[107] Joachim H. Stocqueler, past editor of a couple of Indian journals and author of several books and articles on India, asserted:

> From that moment may be dated the discontent and alienation of the sepoy. He now looked upon himself as the paid servant of only foreign master, bound to him simply by a compact, of which the essence was pounds, shillings and pence.[108]

d) The 'bad example' in the Queen's service that a soldier could not address his officer unless in full dress and accompanied by a non-commissioned officer was emulated by the European officers of the East India Company. This, it was thought, completely separated them from their men.[109]

e) Still another factor which was thought to have prevented free interaction between the European officer and his men was the former's deficiency in 'ready knowledge of the colloquial language of the sepoy.' This deprived the officer of a much needed opportunity to win over the affections of the men under his command.[110]

The regimental mess system too, according to Jacob, was highly defective. While in certain cases no messes existed at all, in those regiments with the privilege of having them, the advantages were negated by the freedom allowed to their officers in joining them. Such an option did not augur well for regimental discipline. This inevitably broke the regiments into separate parties and gave 'rise to all manner of ill feeling.' It lessened the power and good influence of commanding officers immeasurably and deprived them of much of the support which they could otherwise quietly and imperceptibly command.[111]

The system of promotion by seniority in the Bengal army was also described as no less injurious in casting a shadow upon the already dubious authority of English commanders. Naturally it came under heavy criticism.[112] According to the system any native recruit who kept himself clear of actual crime and lived long enough, was sure to don the uniform of a commissioned officer, however unfit he might be for the promotion. Under this arrangement the soldier always felt himself 'entirely independent of his officers.'[113] He clearly understood that they could neither hasten nor retard his advance in the service. Listless performance of duty or timely shows of courage, fidelity and good conduct made no difference whatsoever in promotion. Also, since promotion to commissioned rank was independent of qualifications of fitness, pride in promotion did not exist.[114] So, while the arrangement constituted a great injustice to really deserving men, it held out 'the greatest possible encouragement to the lazy, the idle and the good for nothing.'[115] Evidently, this not only cut down the prestige of the commanders, bereft as they were of all power of promotion or demotion, but it also struck a sharp blow at the efficiency of the Company's military machine. The *Manchester Guardian* ruefully quoted Jacob as having observed:

> The whole of the native commissioned officers are entirely useless; the amount of their pay is a dead loss to the state. Everyone of them is unfit for service by reason of imbecility produced by old age, or, where in rare instances the man may not be altogether in his second childhood, he is entirely useless from having been educated in a bad school. All should have been pensioned off long ago.... It is astonishing, and says much for the good of the raw material of the Bengal Army, that under such arrangements the whole fabric has not entirely fallen to pieces. The things are rotten throughout, and discipline there is none; but it is wonderful that even the outward semblance of an army has been still maintained.[116]

The indiscriminate adoption of 'Asiatic habits, manners and feelings' by English officers had not only partly merged them with the Hindus, but this had, it was complained, the baneful effect of lowering their character. From the day of arrival in the Bengal Presidency, an officer was constantly reminded that everything English was sure sign of a 'griffin'. He was told not to go out in the sun; always to travel in a *palki*[117] instead of on horseback; to get '*punkaed* [fanned][118] and *tattied*';[119] to keep a *khidmatgar*,[120] a '*sirdar* [head][121] bearer and bearers', a servant for his pipe, another for his umbrella, one for his bottle; still another for his chair and so on. These external luxuries and lazy habits of India, it was contended, gradually eroded the manliness of the Anglo-Saxon character.[122] The *Manchester Guardian*, commenting on this, added that after lowering themselves to the level of the natives, European officers still tried to assume the superiority which a 'natural activity of disposition and strength of body and mind' alone could entitle them to exercise. The result was, reasoned the paper, that they became 'an imposter, trading upon a capital that he has lost.' Now that the English were no better than the Indians themselves, they could no longer command the usual respect from them.[123] No wonder Jacob strongly advised his compatriot officers:

> All our power in India rests on this. We may lay it down as an absolute certainty that the millions of natives which a handful of Englishmen govern in this vast continent will not consent to be governed by a handful of their equals. Our power consists in our being essentially different and their belief in our moral superiority only. The only thing which can endanger the existence of this power is the destruction or weakening of that belief.[124]

Here it is of importance to note that V.A. Smith, then President of the Board of Control for India and among the leading proponents of the mutiny theory, blamed, along with others, the officers for their changing attitude towards sepoys—a change that called a halt to the creation of better relations and understanding with the men. He emphasized that earlier the officers used to win over their men by such trifling things as joining in their pastimes, playing with their children, arranging their lawsuits or settling their quarrels.[125] Writing in the *Dublin University Magazine* he argued that fifty years before it had been the fashion among European officers to Hinduize, for the Hindus could scarcely be expected to Europeanize. He wrote:

> We attended their heathen festivals, and made offerings at the shrines of their gods. Colonel Stewart went even so far as to bring back with him his idols to Europe, for the purpose of continuing his worship at home.[126]

Not only had these friendly gestures disappeared, even the tone and temper displayed by the officers was far from friendly. A strong aversion to sepoys had gotten hold of the European officers. The former came to be 'esteemed an inferior creature'; was sworn at; spoken of as a 'nigger'; addressed as a '*soor* or pig,' an epithet most opprobious to a respectable native, especially Muslims. In addition to all this they were very harshly treated. At times the officials even struck them. Such conduct, it was stated, was not an exception, was not confined to one or two officers of a regiment, but was the rule of the day.[127] However, there could be found among elderly officers respect for the sepoys and to them they remained closely attached and did their best to save them.[128] All this surely isolated the men from their commanders and cooled the warmth of affections towards them.[129] The terrible disasters and troubles which later broke out, so contended the *Manchester Guardian*, were 'not wholly devoid of a character of reasonable retribution.'[130]

Alongside all these factors, the sepoys had a fairly long list of important grievances of their own. Continued existence of some of these, and indeed the addition of others, had become strong irritants. While this was the need of the hour, immediate attention was seldom forthcoming. With a few noble exceptions the general body of officers, as well as the government, had begun to take the sepoys for granted. Their calls for redress of their grievances were ignored and the frequent outbursts of displeasure either went unattended or were lightly regarded. This, it seems to the present writer, was a dangerous neglect, which led to serious consequences.

The major grievance of the sepoys stemmed from religion. If religious grievance was a universal cry among the rebel soldiers in India, significantly it was universally admitted in England as a major cause of the outbreak. Whatever controversy there was, it centered round the question of responsibility. A cursory glance at the history of the rise to power of the East India Company would reveal an extremely cautious and conservative policy followed by them with regard to native religions, customs and conventions. There was a time when the Company's government would not let a missionary set foot on their territory, obviously for fear of offending native religious beliefs. Every conquest, every annexation and every occupation was invariably followed by a solemn pledge of non-interference and observance of complete neutrality in religious affairs. This was applicable to the sepoy army in a still greater and stricter degree. At the time of enlistment every sepoy was given an imposing promise of non-interference in his religious worship. While the sepoys were delighted with this security and jealously guarded it, the ranks of European army officers began, slowly but surely, to be infiltrated by the rising tide of the evangelical spirit in England. As the army was the only section of Indian society 'off limits' to the missionary, quite a few English officers entered its ranks with a missionary spirit to rectify the error allowed to exist by the government. It was the development and progressive nourishment of this spirit which, if the critics of this trend are to be believed, really began to change the face of things.

Quite a few of the British army officers had, it was reported, come to believe in their 'double commission'—'double commission of rendering unto Caesar the things that are Caesar's and unto God the things that are God's.'[131] This was what Colonel Wheler, Commander of the 34th NI at Barrackpore, said in his defence to the charge of wrongly using his position in the army for proselytizing.[132] Wheler openly preached the gospel to all classes, inside and outside of the army, and made no secret of his zeal for conversion of natives. Officers of Colonel Wheler's stamp[133] were described by Hargrave Jennings, the anonymous author of *The Indian Religions; or, Results of Mysterious Buddhism* by an 'Indian Missionary', as 'missionary colonels' and 'Padree Lieutenants'.[134] 'Forgetting their allegiance in their piety',[135] such officers actively indulged in missionary activity in their regiments. Their wives too did not stand aside, and helped them in carrying out what they thought was the right thing to do. Lectures were arranged and tracts and Bibles distributed among the soldiers.[136] At times promotions were also given out of religious considerations.[137] Jennings wrote:

> Of course, the sepoys could hardly connect these day and night preachings, these earnest solicitations, these ceaseless efforts, this enormous expenditure of money in books and tracts, with mere private enterprise.[138]

The result was that such officers lost even the ordinary respect of their men. Colonel Wheler confessed that 'if his regiment were ordered on field service, he could not place himself at their head, in full reliance upon their loyalty and good conduct.'[139] Sir Bengamin C. Brodie,[140] who regarded the outbreak as a mere military mutiny, but assigned to it a long list of socio-political-military causes, observed:

> There can be little doubt that a proselytizing spirit has long manifested itself amid a portion of the Company's servants. They have sought to effect through the means of their official authority, that which missionary zeal unaided has been unable to perform.... No one dreams of a missionary collecting revenue, administering justice or commanding a regiment; yet collectors of revenue, administrators of justice and military officers have attempted this.[141]

The *Saturday Review* described Mrs Colin Mackenzie's book, *Delhi, the City of the Great Mogul*, as a 'missionary record in the guise of a military tour.' It also strongly criticized the proselytizing activities of Colonel Wheler and his ilk as producing disaffection among the sepoys.[142] Jennings observed that such things were, in the beginning, tolerated by native sepoys 'sometimes with distaste; sometimes with indifference; sometimes, even, with respect for mistaken zeal.' But a persistent effort in that direction did eventually alarm soldiers of both persuasions.[143] This certainly, argued the author of the *Mutiny in the Bengal Army*, led to a loss of cordiality between the officers and their men and decreased intercourse between them.[144] It also tended, commented *The Illustrated London News*, to strengthen the suspicion that 'Great Britain, not content with destroying the political independence of India, had determined to subvert its religion.'[145] *The Scotsman* could not swallow its anger when, referring to the atrocities perpetrated by the sepoys, it forcefully reasoned that 'Colonel Wheler is but the type of a class out of whose spiritual conceit and mental weakness have been bred these horrors at which the whole civilized world stands amazed and affrighted.' Not feeling content with this observation, the paper went on to call the Colonel 'silly' and a 'foolish person.'[146] A large portion of the people and the press ventilated their wariness and disapproval at the activities of the army commander by making a unanimous call for his punishment.

Religious fear created by missionary zeal of misplaced officers was believed to be the major cause of the outbreak. It was questioned why such a revolt did not take place when British authority in India was feeble; when the powerful Indian chiefs continuously threatened its existence? Why did the sepoys remain loyal then? Why, more recently, did they not waver during the Afghan disasters? Why did they choose the year 1857 when the British were strongly entrenched on the soil of India; when the independent princes were few and far between and were languid and listless? So what brought them together, in spite of their extreme and unbridgeable differences? Was it not the fear that their forefathers' religion would be wiped out? Was this fear not clearly rooted in the proselytizing fervour of the officers in the army?[147] One Edward Smith Mercer regarded official religious interference by the government and its servants, as a major cause of the outbreak. He warned that evangelicals of the day would ruin the empire.[148]

Thus while the *Illustrated London News* fervently urged that missionaries be allowed to go to India to spread the gospel, they should not wear state livery or have any connection, pecuniary or official, with the state.[149] The *Manchester Guardian*, proposing condign punishments for the offending officers, reminded the government of its solemn obligation to protect the faith and the prejudices of its subjects against all 'proposed or accidental outrage.'[150] It further exhorted that the government should be as tender to the superstitions of the natives as if it shared them; that it should put down all attempts which might cause affront or alarm for their religious feelings; that the government should suppress such attempts as promptly as England would 'an anti-popery demonstration in Tipperary, or an attempt to thrust episcopal ordinances into the pulpit of the free kirk, nay even more vigorously.'[151]

Still another cause for grievance was provided by the Company's changed manner, strictness and greater scrutiny in granting pensions to old and disabled soldiers.[152] According to old regulations a sepoy, disabled after fifteen years of service, retired on a monthly pension of four rupees. Henceforth the system was changed and a sepoy declared unfit was to be retained for odd cantonment duties.[153] Several invalided sepoys whose cases were strongly recommended by the regimental committees were turned down by the general invaliding committee. The result was that they had to go home 'to wear out their dregs of life in hopeless despondency.' Consequently the sepoys came to believe that government had 'broken faith' and so could no longer be trusted.[154]

Low salaries of army personnel, sepoys and officers, were described as another reason for disenchantment with the government.[155] The salaries, expenses and duties of the soldiers were spoken of as highly incompatible with one another.[156] Gubbins firmly supported Henry Lawrence on this question, when the latter compared the status and emoluments which a native gentleman could attain under native governments with those obtainable in the British Indian army. To him the disparity appeared to be too great.[157] In this regard the European soldier, argued the author of the *Mutiny in the Bengal Army*, was an indulged person compared with the sepoy.[158] 'My father used to receive five hundred rupees a month in command of a company of Ranjit Singh's horse,' reported a Sikh Na'ib, Risaldar Sher Singh, to Gubbins, 'I receive but fifty.'[159]

Earlier, soldiers' mail would pass freely under the frank of the commanding officer. Later, this privilege was suspended and letters were subjected to postage charges. This, it was reported, naturally became a big grievance with the sepoys.[160]

Another action that was reported greatly to have disturbed the Bengal sepoys was a government decision to enlist 200 Sikhs and Punjabi recruits for each regiment.[161] This was highly distressing to the sepoys for two reasons: firstly, they feared a gradual domination in the army by the Punjabis and, secondly, they felt that foreign military service would not end with the addition of these 200 Sikh recruits.[162] The latter was a fear, contended Gubbins, highly intensified by further extensions of territory and the projected invasions of the Crimea and Persia.[163] The sepoys were convinced that in future, because of the introduction of this new and diversified element in their ranks, they would no longer be able to say no to foreign deployment. Coupled with this, of course, was the realization that this reduced weight would deprive them of bargaining power and that they would no longer be able to play the 'cocks of the walk.'[164]

The sepoys' fear of foreign service became a reality with the passage of the General Service Enlistment Act of Lord Canning in 1856. A part of the sepoy-government covenant was that sepoys were not to be sent on extra-territorial service. This was to assure the high-caste man of the government's regard for his caste. According to tradition, if a caste man crossed the borders of India he lost his caste. No penalty could be severer than this loss. With the passage of time and the development of imperial policy such a contract was difficult to fulfill. Just as the East India Company was sure to require the services of its native Bengal army for extra-territorial service, the sepoys were sure to resist such a call. The first test came at the time of the First Burmese War, when in 1824, the 47th Regiment refused to serve in Burma, mutinied at Barrackpore and was suppressed with the help of artillery. The name of the regiment was subsequently erased from the army list.

This was just the start of the quarrel, and government victory, though inevitable, was not going to be easy. While Lord Amherst was able to suppress this show of disobedience and resistance, in an exactly similar case Lord Dalhousie had to give way when in 1852 the 38th Bengal Native Infantry refused to serve in Burma as the 47th had done in 1824. Referring to this failure of Dalhousie, William Witherspoon Ireland pointed out that the sepoys were now 'beginning to know their power.'[165] Every new step was sure to add to sepoy dissatisfaction. Even the sepoy's traditional regard for money was not as strong as his fear of losing his caste. This was especially experienced during the First Afghan war. When the sepoys refused to go even to Peshawar, sufficient extra-allowances had to be offered as a bribe. Still it was found, reported a writer in *Fraser's Magazine*, that sepoys' attachment to Mammon was less than his hatred of Peshawar. The writer further stated that regiments were known to break into jubilation after crossing the Indus on their return journey. He declared that it all resembled the ecstatic state of Prussian soldiers on seeing the Rhine. The sepoys always thanked God for letting them leave Peshawar.[166]

It was in the face of this abhorrence of leaving Indian soil that Lord Canning, shortly after his assumption of office in India, introduced the General Service Enlistment Act. The Act enjoined compulsory foreign service for all new recruits, if and when necessary. Not only was the

Act uncalled for, asserted John Bruce Norton,[167] since eighty-one regiments of the Madras and Bombay presidencies were ready for service abroad, but that it was too hazardous to rush in where even Dalhousie had feared to tread. He pointed out that such a step should not have been taken unless the government felt quite sure of itself; unless it felt convinced that it was in a strong position promptly to crush any sign of disaffection which such an unpalatable order 'was certain to call forth.' To have decided upon such a course of action, when there was only 'a miserably small European force in the country', was to Norton an act of 'blind infatuation and inflated self-sufficiency.'[168]

Turning to the annexation of territories as a cause of the sepoy mutiny, the holders of the mutiny school of thought were divided among themselves. An overwhelming majority of these who held this interpretation, led by *The Times*, the *Manchester Guardian* and prominent individuals like Palmerston and V.A. Smith, then president of the Board of Control, as well as government benches in the Commons and other pro-government elements, vehemently argued against any such contention. Since all of them belonged to the 'forward' school and, as such, had in the past either justified annexations, endorsed them or advocated such a course of action, it was, very obviously, difficult for them to admit the political excitement of the sepoys and thereby shoulder the responsibility. For example, the *Manchester Guardian* repeatedly in its editorials and general writings denied any connection whatsoever between the annexations and the mutiny, not even the annexation of Awadh. In its editorial of 16 October 1857, it at once rejected Norton's argument that 40,000 sepoys from Awadh had taken part in the revolt because their feelings were bitterly wounded by the deposition of their native sovereign, as being 'childish and dishonest.'[169]

The *Guardian* feebly emphasized that the very fact and motive for which every native of Awadh enlisted one or more members of his family in the British army was to obtain British protection for themselves and their families from the grinding oppression of their own sovereign. Since the British occupation of Awadh had taken the sheltering umbrella to their very doorsteps, it should have, the paper argued, satisfied them rather than precipitated rebellion.[170] Any such admission would naturally have looked self-contradictory. The paper was so steadfast in rejecting such a theory that it was prepared even to accept the presence of a Muslim intrigue in Awadh rather than admit of any connection between the annexations and what it called 'the professional revolt of the Bengal army.'[171] In fact the paper had earlier elaborated its point of view by arguing that to accept annexations as a cause of the outbreak would be to regard the inhabitants of India as a single nation[172]—a thesis which the advocates of the present theme were loath to accept. *The Times*, on the other hand, had, on the first receipt of the news of the mutiny in Britain, at once called for a complete extinction of all native states.[173] Smith, however, was less rigid in this respect and he accepted the annexation of Awadh as a cause only insofar as it affected the sepoys in the loss of exclusive privileges of redress which they formerly enjoyed.[174]

Quite a few of the same school, on the contrary, refused to hold to such an opinion. In their view the policy of annexation had deeply aroused the sepoys and had stirred them into action. They asserted that the Awadh sepoys were highly perturbed over the developments in their country and questioned the justification for the deposition of Wajid Ali Shah and the subsequent annexation of his state.[175] It was pointed out that to give an answer to this frequently asked question had become difficult for the army officers.[176] The preferred reasons of misgovernment and mismanagement put forth had failed to convince the soldiers. The sepoys knew that both of these had existed for a long time and that the British government in full knowledge of this had crowned king after king on the throne of Awadh. Therefore misgovernment and mismanagement failed to accredit themselves as plausible excuses in their eyes. The reason, they thought, was to be found somewhere else. Earlier the hands of the British government were full and so it could not act, even if it wanted to. All along, reported Archer, the sepoys thought that the government followed a 'time-serving policy rather than an honest and upright' one. And when all else was subdued, it struck against Awadh.[177]

The 19th and 34th Regiments of the native infantry were among the first three regiments to revolt months before the Meerut outbreak. Both of them were reported to be present on parade at Lucknow when the annexation of the state was announced. A writer in *Fraser's Magazine* saw a definite connection between their mutiny and the annexation. He called the cartridge incident only a hypothetical cause.[178]

Armed with these grievances, the sepoys received further encouragement from the contemporary scene. Beginning in 1841–2 they had intermittently heard of British troubles and losses, and by 1857 the myth of British invincibility had turned into fiction. The disasters in Afghanistan in the early 1840s and the news that English officers were prisoners in the hands of Afghans, made a powerful impression upon the armies of the three presidencies. The tales of the miseries of those who returned further shattered the halo that hitherto surrounded England's power in their minds.[179] Added to the retreat from Afghanistan were the battles of Sutlej and the repulse of Chilianwala during the Anglo-Sikh wars. These events, it was held, clearly indicated to the sepoys that even a single tribe among the several Indian races was sufficient to hold the English in check.[180] The Crimean War, the fall of Kars, and the withdrawal of troops for the wars in Asia Minor and Persia further strengthened the impression of growing English weakness.[181] The 'Persian war, though a success, was universally believed in Upper India to have been an utter failure,' reported the *Saturday Review*. The false news circulated about the victories of the 'invincible Shah of Persia' had become a common topic of conversation.[182] The tide was now at its lowest ebb. The native sepoy establishment, conscious of its numbers[183] and irritated by grievances, was already waiting for an opportune moment. The sepoys had started to foresee the impending nature of the forthcoming opportunity. Lord Portman in his address in answer to the Queen's speech on 3 December 1857, expressed similar feelings when he said:

> Might not the military revolt in India have arisen...from an opinion among the sepoys that we were much occupied elsewhere, that our army was small, that, in short 'their time was come.'[184]

'It was only a question of time with the sepoys,' asserted Charles Raikes, a judge of the Sadar Court at Agra and late Civil Commissioner with Sir Colin Campbell, 'when they should make Bengal as was Cabool, the grave of the Whiteman.'[185]

In fact, the sepoys, it was reported, had already started to test English control. One regiment was disbanded for refusing to serve in Burma during the First Burmese War. The sepoys next defied authority during the siege of Bharatpor. So great was this defiance that the commanding officers had to resort to wholesale use of court-martial. As a result the use of corporal punishments became so extensive that the commander-in-chief found it necessary to intervene and restrict the powers of commanding officers. The sepoys saw this as a triumph, were exultant and became more insolent.[186] Here, this writer would like to add that at the time of the annexation of Sindh, there was some trouble over the issue of allowances. Though the regiment was disbanded, it was not sufficient punishment. Whatever little impression the punishment might have produced upon the sepoys, it must have been spoiled by the fate that Charles Napier met at the hands of Dalhousie. Napier had to resign because of the former's military policies.

Dalhousie, the last of the British empire-builders in India, though strong and stern in his dealings with the princes of India and his own commander-in-chief, had, strangely enough, shown a weak heart when called upon to face the army. At the time of the Second Burmese War when the 38th Regiment refused to serve in Burma, Dalhousie easily yielded. The native army, it was pointed out, must have been flushed with this victory.[187] Another important army *emeute* had taken place at Bolarum in the Nizam's territory. Here, during the Muharram mourning,[188] one Colonel Mackenzie was wounded and several English men and women assaulted. Von Olrich, whose pamphlet had reportedly gained wide popularity on the continent and was soon anonymously translated in England for the benefit of Britons, argued that this should have served to arouse the British government to dispatch 20,000 extra soldiers to India. When nothing occurred, the native army was further emboldened.[189]

Not long after this followed the incident of the greased cartridges. The new measure took effect despite all warning[190] and bitter experiences of the past. It appears to the present writer as if the government was bent upon testing the anti-government feelings of its native army. The cartridge news spread like wildfire throughout the length and breadth of the country. Aware of the after-effects of using the new bullet,[191] the sepoy, it was reported, felt increasingly convinced of the government's intention to tamper with his religious and caste beliefs, especially so when enough material for suspicion was already present in the matters of laws for widow remarriage, the abolition of *sati* and encouragement of female education.[192] They believed, it was stated, that the government intended to convert them to Christianity by a ruse—the pollution of their caste and by rendering them alien among their own people and 'loathesome and worthless' persons in their own eyes and those of their fellows,—thus leaving them no choice but to enter the fold of Christianity.[193]

It seems that the history of sepoy mutinies in the preceding fifty years and their success was sufficient to inspire them to further action. This time again they decided to challenge the government rather than give way. The rumour of the greased cartridge started at Dum-Dum, near Calcutta, in January 1857. The 19th Native Infantry mutinied at Burhanpur on 25 February and its disbandment followed a month and five days later (30 March 1857) at Barrackpore. In April there was unrest and incendiarism in Ambala. On 3 May, a mutiny in Lucknow was prevented by Sir Henry Lawrence. The regiment involved, the 7th Irregular Cavalry, was, however, disbanded. Three days later (6 May) the 34th Native Infantry was also disbanded at Barrackpore.

So far the government had signally failed in the trial for acts of mutiny as disbandment was criticized as being no punishment at all. In fact, it was perhaps a reward. According to Dr Edward Henry Nolan, who had rejected the mutiny thesis, regiments which were already desirous of such a retrenchment, when let off so easily, felt encouraged rather than discouraged.[194] Henry Beveridge, who regarded the mutiny to be the result of Muslim conspiracy, similarly described the punishment as inadequate and one which rather provoked 'than suppressed the crime against which it was directed.'[195] The *Manchester Guardian* described it as a source of further discontent, disaffection and revolt in the ranks of the army.[196] George Crawshay, the Mayor of Gateshead, in his lecture on 4 November 1857, strongly criticized the disbandment of the 19th Regiment, the first of the series at the time of the mutiny. He argued that such a punishment raised them from disbanded soldiers to 'martyrs of their faith in the eyes of the Hindoos,' and so enabled them to spread 'disaffection from station to station, wherever they went. The first effect of the disbandment of the 19th was to destroy the 34th Regiment.'[197] Later on, the *Manchester Guardian* felt so strongly about the disbandment affair that it ranked it higher than the so far most-emphasized caste and cartridge causes. It believed that the latter causes had nothing to do with later insurrections, and that they had ceased to exist immediately after the outbreak. Now the cause was the incitement by emissaries of the disbanded 19th and 34th regiments combined with probably extra military sources, the paper shyly admitted.[198] Moreover, it was contended, that when the sepoys saw one regiment after another being disbanded without committing any overt act of mutiny at all, they naturally felt apprehensive about their own fate. Under these circumstances they considered it a better part of wisdom to join their comrades and thus deserve the punishment which they otherwise were afraid to incur.[199] Crawshay, in his later address to a special general court of the East India Company at the India House on 25 August 1858, further asserted:

It must be remembered, that if no disaffection pre-existed, the act of disarming was certain to create it; if disaffection did exist among any it was certain to extend to all.[200]

Thus it seems to this writer that the government and sepoys were engaged in a perilous game. Each tried to outdo the other. The impression so far was that the sepoys were on the winning side. Conscious of this, Major Hewitt, the commander at Meerut, decided to strike hard. This fact was reported universally. On 6th May, eighty-three sepoys of the 3rd Cavalry at Meerut refused to use the new cartridge while on parade. On 9th May all of them were sentenced to rigorous imprisonment, ranging from five to ten years, by a court martial composed of native officers. This was a serious challenge to the sepoys. The cartridges were a common grievance with a large part of the sepoy establishment. There were only two alternatives left with the soldiers; either to submit to a similar punishment of 'ten years in irons', or else get rid of the people responsible for the introduction of the cartridge.[201] The choice was not hard to make. The sepoys, it seems, were in no mood to yield. They picked up the gauntlet. The strike rebounded and what was called the 'epoch making mutiny of 1857' began its heavy course.

CHAPTER 3

Variations on the Mutiny Theme

What really caused the outbreak on 10 May 1857? Was it the cartridge incident or was it a general religious upheaval? What was its character? Was it an army *émeute* first and last or was it a mutiny which developed into a national struggle—limited or general? Was it inspired from outside? What were the motives behind it? Was it just a Praetorian struggle of the army or was it aimed at the re-establishment of native rule, especially that of the Muslims? These were the questions vociferously debated by the advocates of the mutiny school of thought. The debate led to major differences of opinion and consequent divisions among the adherents of this school of thought. It soon lost its focus, however, made major exceptions to its thesis and weakened its own point of view.

There was almost unanimous agreement among all sections of the British public regarding religious panic as the prime cause of the outbreak. But, at the same time, there existed a large difference of opinion as to the cartridge incident's share in causing the uprising. *The Times* thought of the cartridge as a mere pretext designed to shield the real intentions of the sepoys,[1] and the *Saturday Review* regarded it as a minor cause of the mutiny deserving to be 'placed last in order.'[2] Several of this school of thought believed that religious apprehension was already there and that the cartridge incident came only as a last spark. Even the opponents of this view admitted the immediate significance of the cartridge affair.[3] Still an overwhelming majority of this school considered the cartridge grievance as the prime mover.[4] This section launched a virulent attack upon those who completely refused to admit the strength of the cartridge argument, chief among them being Disraeli. The *Manchester Guardian* called them 'men of limited experience and narrow views,'—people with an infantile imagination, incapable of appreciating a national character different from their own. It branded them as a people deficient in philosophic care and accuracy, not observing how, in all human affairs, the greatest events sometimes appear to hinge upon the most inadequate causes.

To drive home the strength of its argument, the paper emphatically controverted, 'What should we expect if a regiment of Irish Roman Catholics were ordered to trample under foot the consecrated host.'[5] The attack was clearly directed against Disraeli and his followers.

The Examiner was still more open in directing its fury; it attributed the mutiny primarily to the cartridge affair and repeatedly called the author of the opposite theory 'D'Israeli'.[6] Upon Lord Ellenborough, the ex-Governor-General of India, it bestowed the honorific title of the 'Eastern Oracle', contriving 'to make his tinsel sometimes pass for gold.' The paper added that he should no more be judged 'by his words but his worth.'[7] In fact, Disraeli, Ellenborough and other members of the opposite school were all targets for serious criticism by the 'hardline' section of the mutiny school. Colonel William Henry Sykes, MP in the liberal interest and a director of the East India Company, holding that the cartridges were the main grievance—a grievance that left only two alternatives for the sepoys—argued that from that time an outbreak in the army became inevitable.[8] Answering those who rejected the cartridge idea on the grounds that the same cartridge was used by the soldiers against their rulers, J.L. Archer argued that the end justified the use. He pointed out the well accepted maxim:

> ...it is meet and proper, ay, meritorious, to do evil with the intent that good may therefrom ensue.[9]

The fact, however, remains that it was the religious fear generated by so many factors put together, cartridge included, which had contributed to the strength of the outburst. No wonder T.C. Chambers, the Common Sergeant of the city of London called it 'a religious mutiny.'[10] A writer in the *Missionary Herald* observed:

> During the extraordinary troubles from which we are now emerging, nothing has so cheered our minds as the fact, which appears to be now well established, that the disaffection of the native troops has originated in their dread of the growing power of Christianity. Most strangely have they erred in believing that the Government was endeavouring to entrap them into the sacrifice of their caste, yet we believe they are right in apprehending that their idols and superstitions are decaying and will be speedily overthrown not by might nor by power.[11]

Another writer writing in the same magazine as late as June 1859 admitted:

> I am persuaded that its immediate cause was religious panic, produced to a large extent by the inconsistencies of our rule. Professing to be indifferent to all religions,

we have yet in spite of ourselves been destroying heathenism and advancing truth; and as one important element of Hinduism after another had disappeared, the people have felt that some secret power was at work which they could not understand, and thus their fears have gradually become excited until all confidence was gone.[12]

Turning to the character of the mutiny, one is at once faced with a major group of thought in the school comprised of 'hardline' individuals. To them the 'entire affair was nothing but a mad military outbreak,'[13] which had no background cause whatsoever, military or civil, and had started spontaneously.[14] Existence of a conspiracy or of any combination was thought highly unlikely.[15] Had this been the case, it was argued, Barrackpore or 'the great European stations' of the North-West of India would not have been chosen for raising the banner of rebellion. In that case the central stations of Dinapore, Banaras, Allahabad, Nimach and Mhow, where there were few or no European regiments, would have better served the aims of conspirators.[16]

For this and other reasons, soon to be discussed, the outbreak was thought to be sudden. Had it not been, the mutineers, though illiterate, were, it was held, not so simple as to have thrown all precaution to the winds by not selecting a safe place instead of Meerut[17]—a place where, but for the pitiful incapacity and inaction of the commanders, the outbreak 'could instantly have been crushed by the total destruction of the mutineers.'[18] It was, therefore, looked upon as an act of desperation rather than one of premeditated treason.[19]

The choice of Delhi too, it was thought, was accidental rather than planned. It was regarded as a choice dictated by the proximity of that city to Meerut rather than by its imperial character. Perhaps, not even one man, it was emphasized, turned his face towards Delhi with the idea that it was the home of the king. It was stressed that the mutineers would have gone there all the same. On the contrary, it 'would have been a marvel if they had not made their way to Delhi.'[20] It was further reasoned that a previous general conspiracy would have resulted, after the takeover of Delhi, in the seizure of Allahabad, Banaras and other places. The absence of such attacks, argued a writer in the National Review, went far to prove the absence of any premeditated plan.

A long range conspiracy, he thought, should have availed itself of the years 1854–5, when the British Army was busy in the Crimea. Even in 1857, why did it wait until the Persian war was over?[21] Haphazard risings of the sepoys were offered as another proof of this point of view.[22] Absence of definite leadership was to Sir Benjamin Colin

Brodie, as it was to many others, further evidence of the truth of their thesis.[23] The author of the 'Military Revolt in India' (published in the *National Review*) contended that the 'puppet king' of Delhi was not at the head of any party and that he was not prepared to 'assume the functions of the mimic royalty.'[24] The *Saturday Review* believed that the king 'Became a political personage in spite of himself,' who 'dreamt as little, a few months ago, of the new honours thrust upon him, as of fitting out an expedition at Calcutta for the conquest of the British Isles.'[25] Just because the mutiny was widespread, it should not be assumed that its organization must have been of commensurate magnitude.[26] The *Manchester Guardian* explained away even the extent of the mutiny to the presence of *esprit de corps* among the sepoys. In many cases, argued the paper, the mutinous regiments just followed the example of their comrades [following like a flock sheep] doing it partly out of sympathy and partly from a vague idea that the government had fallen.[27]

Similarly, it was thought that the mutinous sepoys had no auxiliaries and that they were only joined by the 'rabble from the bazars [Bazars],' such as London or any other great European town would produce 'when murder, robbery and incendiarism were afoot.'[28] It was believed that the sepoys were fighting just for themselves; that they had nothing in common with the people; that they did not rally round the throne of Delhi; had no attachment to the king; no admiration for the princes; no national objective before them, and last of all they lacked the presence of a master spirit in their ranks—a spirit, which could bring together the heterogeneous elements in the rebel army and 'elevate the sepoy mutiny...into a great national movement.'[29] It was emphasized that there was not even an atom of patriotism in the movement and that it was just a sepoy fight for loaves and fish.[30] The *Manchester Guardian* pointed out that the sepoys were not even sparing their own people. The paper took comfort in the fact that this would do much in making the agricultural population of India loyal towards the government and in increasing their hatred of the rebels.[31] *The Times* arguing that sepoys had only one personality—that of the soldier, chastised the British Parliament and editorially observed:

> It is no part of the duty of the English House of Commons to elevate mutineers into malcontents or to recognize them as representatives of their race and religion.[32]

It was because of this thinking that one adherent of the mutiny school asserted that the 'cruel stab was from the hand of Brutus,'[33] implying thereby that the blow came from the most unexpected quarter, i.e., the sepoy army, whose loyalty to the government was seldom doubted.

The mutiny, it was further contended, though all-embracing, and inclusive of 'all tribes and all arms' in the Bengal army, the masses were with the government.[34] The writer in the *National Review*, cheerful at the military character of the catastrophe, pointed out that every 'fresh piece of authentic information' received from India further elucidated the argument in hand. It showed, he stressed, that from first to last the outbreak was a mutiny and not an insurrection; that the peasantry and civil population had abstained from any participation in the mutiny; that the animosity exhibited towards the European fugitives was confined only to 'a few villages'; that the indifference shown 'in several' was due to 'craven terror of the mutineers' which deterred the inhabitants 'from harbouring or aiding Europeans' and, above all, the fact remained that 'in many others' they had concealed them and displayed kindness towards them.[35] In this way, not only the public was singularly passive and apathetic, but, insofar as the Hindus were concerned, contended the same writer, they certainly opposed the revolt rather than support it.[36] To another of this school even the civil population of Delhi seemed to be siding with the English against the mutineers.[37]

Having expressed similar opinions, the *Manchester Guardian* saw no reason why the natives should be sympathetic towards the army. It felt that the people had everything to fear from the rebels and everything to hope from the re-establishment of British authority in India. In addition to this, the paper also saw race differences causing active hostilities between the army and the populations among whom the army was stationed.[38] Under these circumstances, it was reasoned that the outbreak, far from being a civil rebellion was not even a mixture of civil and military revolt. Gigantic mutiny as it was, emphasized a writer in the *National Review*, the mischief was wholly initiated and carried out by the mutineers themselves. Their only associates in this work, he asserted, represented nothing but criminal elements.[39] Such a conviction enabled *The Examiner* and many others of the same mind to forecast confidently an early suppression of the outbreak. This paper observed:

A mutiny of this sort, a servile military war, cannot drag on; the first blow it receives will be decisive.[40]

It is no wonder that one W.B. Adams, in his letter to *The Spectator*, held the sepoys guilty of heinous crime and called for their 'utter extinction' as 'complete as that of Sodom and Gomorah.'[41] This strongly-argued thesis, however, fell to the ground when Martin Richard Gubbins, a staunch supporter of the military mutiny theory, was forced to concede to the objections of others. He accepted the fact that the people, instead of helping the government had rapidly fallen away from their rulers; had broken into acts of violence and robbery; had shown no goodwill even when the cause of the mutineers was failing, and had not only withheld much needed information, but had even misled the English troops. Though Gubbins offered a strong plea for the last default in the severities of the mutineers, he ended up admitting that:

> ...affection is a feeling which we have no right to challenge from our native subjects in India. Aliens as we are from them in blood, in feeling, in religion; nowise mingling with them in social intercourse, and interchanging few kindly offices, we have no right to expect from them love and sympathy; least of all, active assistance and support.[42]

The mutiny's views were also the opinions which, at one time or another, were strongly maintained by the Palmerston government, i.e., Earl Granville, President of the Council, rebutting Ellenborough's point of view in the Lords, stressed that the revolt had not 'extended beyond the army.'[43] Sir G.C. Lewis, Chancellor of the Exchequer, took the outbreak very lightly and ardently hoped that the whole affair might have failed.[44] Ross Donnelly Mangles, MP in the liberal interest and chairman of the East India Company, refusing to admit Disraeli's point of view in the Commons, emphasized that 'so far from being a national revolt, the simple truth was that where there were no troops there had been no revolt.'[45] The government emphatically denied the role of the princes in any conspiracy whatsoever. Instances of the loyalty of Patiala and Gwalior were quoted.[46] With the exception of one or two *zamindars*, it was argued, all were helping the government.[47] The loyalty of the Punjab was offered as another instance. The Punjabis were, remarked Mangles, even enlisting themselves in English regiments.[48] Thus it was that the *Manchester Guardian* admonished Disraeli and the Conservative Party's organs for regarding the mutiny of the Bengal army as a national protest on behalf of the entire people of Bengal against the domination of the foreigners. Calling such a thesis an 'evident fiction,' it hopefully observed:

But we do not suppose that even Mr Disraeli will consider the adhesion of the rabble of the towns or the banditti, who avail themselves of so tempting an opportunity to rob the fugitives and to plunder villages, a proof of national sympathy with the mutineers.[49]

Here it is interesting to quote a couple of strong opinions in full. Lord Shaftesbury confidently declared:

And who were they that perpetrated these atrocities? Was this a nation rising in a sense of its wrong—writhing under torture, plunder, oppression and cruelty—writhing under the violation of every sacred and social right—rising to recover their lost liberties, rising as one man to assert their independence and the integrity of their religion? No such thing. Has any proclamation been put out by the rebels that they have a single wrong to complain of? Have you found in any one instance a national or even the symptom of a national rising? Has not the whole country, with a very few exceptions, been perfectly tranquil and quiescent? Have not the greater part of the villagers assisted the Royal troops and attempted to discomfit the mutineers? Wherever an exception occurred, it may be traced to brigands and those wild lawless hordes that always will be found on the continent of India, wandering from one village to another. The villagers themselves in no instance have arisen against the British power; on the contrary, they have known that their security consisted in the vigour, and permanence of Her Majesty's dominion. Who then were the mutineers and from whom arose the frightful rebellion?

It arose, he asserted, from a 'monster' of British creation, the army.[50] Three days later the *Manchester Guardian* wholeheartedly endorsed this view of Lord Shaftesbury,[51] but had to contradict itself later on, when it admitted the presence of a civil rebellion worthy of notice in Awadh as well as the participation of the Company's native civil servants in the revolt at other places.[52] Rejecting the parallels drawn by the European press between Austrian rule in Italy and British rule in India, and denouncing their justification of the sepoy revolt as a consequence of the tyrannical rule of the British, of their wilful treachery and spoilation of the princes of India and gross oppression of the agricultural population, the paper desperately cried:

But we repeat perhaps the hundred thousandth time, there has been no national rebellion in Hindostan. There has been none and could have been none, because there exists no such thing as a nation. More than this there has been no civil rebellion deserving of notice except in Oudh....[53]

In line with Lord Shaftesbury, the *Illustrated London News* observed:

No one seems to have entertained the idea that the rebellion was a national movement. None of the thousand and one races spread over the vast continent have arisen against us.... As a rule the rural population in every part of India have stood aloof and watched the contest between the sepoys and the English.... Of the hundred and fifty millions of Asiatics over whom our rule has been extended not more than two hundred thousand have arisen in arms against us, including the criminals liberated from the gaols and the regular robber population, who have become the secret allies of the soldiery.... Of the Rajahs, Nizams...only three or four have declared against us and they are among the very minor dignitaries of their class—the King of Delhi being the most conspicuous name, although he has long been without territory; and as to Nana Sahib, he is not a monarch at all.[54]

As it is always difficult to hold fast to and be consistent with strong opinions, the *Illustrated London News* also found itself confronted by the same difficulty when it contradicted itself in the next breath. This part of the above editorial needs to be especially noted in view of the opinion regarding the loyalty of the people and princes. The editorial commented that 'on the other hand, the most powerful of the native princes have done their best to keep their subjects in hand.'[55]

Others of this school of thought were more flexible and accommodating towards the rebels in India than were those whose opinions are described in the preceding pages. Although the opinions expressed by its members cut across the unity and strength of the 'parent school', and that these opinions themselves were quite divergent, still one finds them more responsive to the tide of events in India than the ones expressed by the 'hardline' group. That is why the first group (the 'hardline' one) soon found itself indulging in serious self-contradictions and exceptions, as will be seen in the following pages. These other opinions ranged from voices suggesting that the outbreak was a Muslim inspired military mutiny, to more frequently heard cries of a military mutiny taken advantage of and used by others, especially the Muslims; from the outbreak as 'something beyond mere military mutinies'[56] covering all areas, to a war or a national movement in Awadh.

If the author of *India, the Revolt and the Home Government* thought of the outbreak as 'a military rebellion fomented by Mahomedan conspirators', which was 'not to be traced to a discontented people',[57] that of *India and the Mutiny* called it 'purely a military rebellion', the true cause of which was a 'long-planned and a well laid Mahomedan conspiracy for their restoration to power.'[58] Sharply pointing out the known hatred of the Muslims for British rule; the choice of a Muslim city and a Muslim King; the annexation of the Muslim state of Awadh and its Queen's representation to the British crown; the Awadh King's attempted escape to Calcutta and his later imprisonment there, a writer in the *British Controversialist* found it difficult to 'escape the conclusion that the ultimate object of the mutiny was the re-establishment of [Muslim] power in India.' Himself a firm believer in the military character of the outbreak, he argued that the scheme to mutiny, however, did not originate in the ranks of the army. He inclined to believe that Muslims hatched the plot and that sepoys were merely instruments in their hands. He thought that since the latter were imperfectly informed on the details of the plot, they had only learnt the signal of the revolt without learning when it was to be acted upon. As a result, he emphasized, the revolt miscarried.[59]

Others held that the Muslim conspiracy was the 'chronic disease' and the 'cartridge excitement' just an 'inflammatory' cause of the uprising.[60] Similarly the Rev. Richard Kidd, M.A., Vicar of Potter Heigham in Norfolk, ridiculed the importance that was being attached to the greased cartridge; to him it was just a 'colourable pretext for the mutiny.' Behind the cartridge pretence, he contended, was cloaked years of anti-government plotting by the 'proud Mohometans, who gladly seized the opportunity, which the employment of the greased cartridge gave, for inflaming the passions of their comrades of the Hindoo superstition.' This, he thought, was amply proved by the sepoys' later using the same cartridge to kill their own officers—a clear indication of the fact that they had no 'insuperable objection' to its introduction.[61]

The Rev. James Wallace of the General Assembly's India Mission further connected the military outbreak with Muslim propaganda about the Persian War. Such propaganda, by presenting the defeats of the Persians as victories, had convinced native sepoys that they could sweep the small number of Europeans before them. In this way, Wallace thought, the sepoys were rendered 'the more willing to entertain the idea of mutiny, and the more reluctant to abandon it when once entertained.'[62] The Rev. J.D. Massingham, M.A., of St. Paul's Church, Derby, in his effort to trace the rebellion of the sepoys to its true source, endeavoured to bring home to his congregation that the mutiny was an 'attempt to make Mahometanism supreme by the power of the sword...by the annihilation of all those who worship the One True God.'[63] It was this widely shared conviction among the members of this school regarding the nature of the mutiny which made Captain Mowbray Thomson feel relieved at the absence of an Aurangzeb, a Haider or a Tipu in the ranks of the sepoys. The appearance of any such general or leader among the rebel soldiers, Thomson felt sure, would have required 'in all probability,' a reconquest of India.[64]

There were others of the mutiny school who, however, refused to accept the idea of a conspiracy previous to the outbreak, (including 'The Military Revolt in India',—published in *The National Review*, who contradicted his earlier stand that it was purely a military mutiny). On the contrary, they added that the mutinies had 'encouraged many individuals to plot against the government at Calcutta, Banaras, Poona, Bombay, Satara, Hyderabad and several other places.'[65] They further thought it probable that 'in these, as in most Indian conspiracies, Mahommedans were the chief actors.' This was so because it was regarded as their habit to 'talk secret treason' all over India.[66] In addition to fomenting rebellion, the Muslims were also believed to have influenced the press.[67] Charles Raikes argued that the catastrophe was looked at differently by different sections of what he called 'quondam' British subjects. He contended that the mutiny was taken advantage of by the predatory class of Gujars, the Mewatis (who, finding an opportunity, resorted 'to their hereditary vocation of plunder') and, above all, by those whom he preferred to call, 'the followers of the...prophet.' To quote Raikes:

> The green flag of Mahommed too had been unfurled. The mass of the followers of the...prophet rejoicing to believe that under the auspices of the great Mogul at Delhi, their lost ascendancy was to be recovered, their deep hatred to the Christian got vent and they rushed forth to kill and destroy.[68]

He maintained that outside of these three classes, the sepoys, the Gujar plunderers and the Muslims, 'the great agricultural communities, the Jat, the Brahmin, the Rajpoot' looked on the English race, under whose reign they had so long tasted peace and security, with undisguised compassion.'[69] Even *The Times* and the *Manchester Guardian* occasionally indulged in self-contradiction by admitting the strength of Muslim animosity towards the British and their participation in the outbreak.

Within six weeks of the arrival of the news of the uprising in India, the Palmerstonian liberal Manchester daily observed that 'except among the discontented Mussulmans there exists no hostility towards us on the part of our non-military subjects.' It went on to warn the government against any secret machinations of 'Mahometan conspirators and partisans of the mutineers,' since the press law prevented them from open action.[70] Less than a month later, the paper editorially quoted excerpts of a letter from India, which called the mutiny a definite result of a 'cunningly contrived political conspiracy on the part of Mahometans' for the 'extermination' of British rule in India. The paper commented that it had no reason to disbelieve that opinion, especially in view of Muslim behaviour, choice of the city, and proclamation of a descendent of the Mughal dynasty as the emperor.[71] Thus the mutiny school of thought punched a strong hole in its own thesis by considerably altering its analysis of the events in India.

There were others who thought that the convulsion ceased to be a mere military mutiny. Acknowledging large civil participation, they stressed slow government action had allowed the mutiny to grow into a massive civil rebellion. This was a clear and unequivocal recognition of a large scale civil disaffection among the people of India. The writer of the article 'Extent of the Indian Mutinies', held that, excluding Awadh, the mutiny spread over a space of 500 miles in length from Meerut to Banaras and 200 miles in breadth from Fatehgarh on the borders of Awadh to Banda on the right bank of the Jumna.[72] (an area of approximately 100,000 square miles). Calling the region 'an Alsatia or a battle field,' he argued, 'It is here that the atrocities have been most numerous, the cruelties most refined, the damage most wanton, the loss of property, private and public, most irreparable and the wreck of our institutions the most complete.' With these facts he found it 'impossible to deny that the disturbances were something beyond mere military mutinies. Where we have had to burn villages, to hang plunderers by scores on the nearest tree, and to execute justice summarily on sundry petty chiefs and landholders, it is clear that a very large portion of the Hindostani population of the Daob, has been more or less against us.'[73] (This was equally true in several parts of the Punjab province, especially Sahiwal, Chichawatni, Mianchanu, and Khanewal. This entire region was ablaze in revolt and village after village was razed to the ground). Similarly, Massingham admitted, that though the outbreak sprang from the soldiers and not from the people, yet the people were sympathetic towards it and desired 'to establish their independence and religion.' However, he took care to emphasize that such a spirit was confined to those men and areas which were 'most exempt from missionary efforts.' Among these men and areas Massingham listed: 1) The native army and places where the native army was stationed; 2) Awadh, the districts of Hansi, Hissar, Moradabad, Bareilly, Shahjahanpur, Bithur, Azamgarh—as regions and places where there were no missionaries, and Delhi, where one was stationed, but only recently.[74]

Several others voiced similar feelings, important among them being the Mayor of Gateshead,[75] Charles Raikes, Julius George Medley and an Anglo-Indian writing in *Fraser's Magazine*. The last one pointed out that the habitual sight of overturned British authority contributed towards giving the uprising a national character.[76] Medley held that what undoubtedly had started as a revolt of the Bengal army had become something between a national rebellion and a mutiny. In addition to the interested parties, he admitted that the revolt of the Purbiya army had also drawn into its vortex the whole of that class from which the army itself was enlisted.[77] Judge Raikes, who emphasized the revolt as a mutiny with broad-based Muslim participation, also accepted the changed nature of the revolt when he emphatically held that 'we have in many parts of the country drifted from mutiny into rebellion, is too true; but I repeat my assertion, that we have to deal now with a revolt caused by a mutiny, not a mutiny growing out of a national discontent.'[78] Even the *Manchester Guardian*, though persistent in its refusal to admit of anything like a civil revolt in North and Central India had, with the passage of time and because of the difficulties faced by the government in the suppression of the revolt, changed its attitude. Four months after the start of the outbreak the paper editorially accepted the fact of a 'popular rising' at Hyderabad[79] and the existence of civil disturbances in the districts of Saugor and Indore in the Madras Presidency.[80] Earlier, all these places claimed to be very loyal.

This section of the military theory school of thought was further reinforced and strengthened when it came to discussing Awadh. Here even some of the 'hardline' school like the *Saturday Review*,[81] the *Manchester Guardian*,[82] *The Examiner*,[83] the *Illustrated London News*[84] and many others admitted the truth of the marked civil or national character of the revolt in Awadh. Thus even civil assistance to sepoys was reported and accepted.[85] *The Examiner*, vigorously maintaining that the outbreak was military in character, admitted at the same time, its different character in Awadh. Casting aside all reservations it boldly agreed that the entire state of Awadh was in flames—was up in arms against the rulers, the Lucknow Residency being the only place under British control. The paper felt anguished at this unpopularity of British rule in the whole state of Awadh and strongly doubted the wisdom of its annexation. Though any previous complicity on the part of native gentry, noblemen or chiefs in a possible conspiracy for the overthrow of British administration was doubted, it was confessed that all of them had shown no attachment to their rulers. The defection of the upper classes was reported to be universal.[86] No wonder in January 1858, the *Illustrated London News* was constrained to observe:

> The situation of affairs in India has assumed a new character. It is no longer an insurrectionary movement in the Bengal army which we have to face—it is a war in Oude.

Again:

> We no longer give ear to pratings about triumphal marches throughout India, and sudden exterminations of the mutineers, but we know that we have got a task to perform, the difficulty of which will be greater or less just in proportion to the estimate which we form of it. One thing is clear, if we have not to reconquer the whole of India, we have to conquer Oude; and we have in fact to found a new empire in the East.[87]

Such thinking on the part of the *Illustrated London News* and others was especially significant as it came after the fall of Delhi and the relief of Lucknow. This displayed a clear veering round to the Disraelian point of view.

As noted above, a large majority of the school under present discussion asserted with the help of forceful reasons that the mutiny was a sudden affair with no characteristic background at all. There was, however, a powerful group of dissidents to this proposition. Calling the outbreak a mutiny, the group admitted the existence of outside interference and aid to the sepoys soon after the cartridge incident and months before the final outbreak. Prominent among them were Gubbins, Medley,[88] Henry Mead, Archer, some anonymous writers in *Blackwood's Edinburgh Magazine,* the author of 'The Military Revolt in India' in the *National Review,* the *Westminster Review*[89] and many others. Each one of them came forward with his own explanation. The writer in the *National Review*—a stout opponent of the civil and political rebellion point of view, admitted:

> We yet see little reason to doubt that about this time the cartridge affair was followed by several, perhaps many, conspiracies.[90]

As proofs leading to a conspiracy theory this writer emphatically alluded to several advance indicators foretelling a visible change in the air: a) the mutiny of the 19th Regiment at Barrackpore in January; b) General Hearsey's conviction on how the regiment was tampered by outside forces; c) confessions made by soldiers after their disbandment; d) disbandment of the 34th Regiment and discovery of secret correspondence leading to it; e) the distribution of flour cakes in the countryside; f) the distribution of lotus flowers among the regiments earlier in the year; and g) the conduct of the mutineers themselves.[91] Likewise, a writer in *Blackwood's Edinburgh Magazine,* while maintaining that the outbreak was a military mutiny, and that the civil population was incapable of any conspiracy, accepted the fact that sepoy cupidity was fired by the Dharma Sabha (a Calcutta society) and the native press. General Hearsey blamed Dharma Sabha for inventing the greased cartridge story and effectively disseminating it among the native soldiers. He believed that all disaffection was introduced from Calcutta and that every detachment sent on duty there came back imbued with suspicions never exhibited before.[92] Advising the government to impose similar restraints upon the society as the ones imposed upon the press, he critically upheld that:

> It is a caricature of constitutional Government to allow a nest of ignorant and malicious traitors to slander its intentions under its very nose, and hamper every design for the improvement of the country by an incessant appeal to the darkest and wildest passions of human nature.[93]

Similarly Gubbins, who firmly believed in the military nature of the rising, also believed in the exploiting hand of an outside agency, especially in fanning religious disaffection. As to the agents of disaffection, he pointed to the Brahmans, discontented followers of Wajid 'Ali Shah the deposed ruler of Awadh, and his minister 'Ali Naqi Khan. According to Gubbins the 'most absurd rumours were circulated and believed,' i.e., it was rumoured that carts or boatloads of bone dust were reaching cities and cantonments to be mixed up with flour; that the government intended to cause the spread of Christianity by importing English Crimean War widows to the subcontinent and by forcing the principal landlords of the country to marry them, declare their children heirs to their estates thus supplant Hindu proprietors.[94]

Mead, on the contrary, emphasized the part played by the Royal House of Delhi in tampering with the loyalties of Muslim elements in the army. In anger he called Bahadur Shah Zafar 'the sepoy King of Delhi.'[95] Even the *Manchester Guardian,* while admonishing Disraeli for persisting in his national rebellion thesis, slipped into an angry mood and grudgingly admitted the presence of what it called, the hand of 'factious conspirators' on a limited scale.[96] *The Times* also intermittently contradicted itself when, while persisting in its mutiny thesis, it frequently described the outbreak, in its moments of anxiety and anger, as 'an atrocious, sanguinary conspiracy' and called its leaders 'monsters.'[97]

With all these differing opinions in this school, however, almost all agreed on one point. This concerned the role played by the native press—as an independent agency or as a tool in the hands of the conspirators. Although it was not regarded as representative of the Indian people, the proponents of the mutiny school of thought unanimously upheld Canning's Press Act, insofar as its suppression of the native press was concerned.[98] If one member of this school believed that the Indian Fourth Estate was influenced by fanatic Muslim conspirators,[99] another blamed Muslims and the Dharma Sabha (*vide supra*) for exploiting the cartridge issue and 'exciting the jealousy of the sepoys.'[100] It was admitted that the circulation of native newspapers was very small, but then it was pointed out that that deficiency was made up by devotees, both Muslim and Hindu, who passed as agents and read the papers in regimental lines.[101] Lieutenant Edward King, supporting the Press Act, quoted from the *Life of Sir Thomas Munro*.[102] The latter, in his minutes written on 12 April 1822, had observed:

> ...owing to the unnatural position in which India will be placed under a foreign Government, with a free press, and a native army, the spirit of independence will spring up in this army long before it is ever thought of among the people.
>
> The army will not wait for the slow operation of instruction of the people, and the growth of liberty among them, but will hasten to execute their own measures for the overthrow of the Government.[103]

The author of *India, the Revolt and the Home Government*, likewise quoted and agreed with another prophecy of the same sage. Holding that the British Empire in India was evidence of the awe and respect with which the rulers were regarded by the natives, Munro argued that a free press would surely destroy such a foundation. He thought that native troops, because of the influence of the native press and their close contact with European officers were doubly vulnerable, exposed as they were to the doctrines circulated by the press and the freedom of discussion enjoyed by their officers. From both of these they tended to learn to compare their own low allowances and humble rank with their European officers;' to examine the grounds on which those differences rested; to calculate their strength and resources, and to believe that it was 'their duty to shake off a foreign yoke and to secure for themselves the honour and emoluments which their country yields'. 'If the press be free,' contended Munro, 'they must immediately learn all this and much more. Their assemblage in garrison, and cantonments will render it easy for them to consult together regarding their plans; they will have no great difficulty in finding leaders qualified to direct them; their patience, their habit of discipline and their experience in war, will hold out the fairest prospect of success; they will be stimulated by the love of power and independence and by ambition and avarice to carry their designs into execution.'[104]

Similarly, all supporters of the mutiny theory, the 'hardline' group included, whether individuals, or newspapers, i.e., *The Times*, the *Manchester Guardian*, the *Saturday Review*, *The Examiner*, the government and the government benches in the two Houses or the members of the courts of Proprietors and Directors of the East India Company, one and all looked askance at the freedom of the native press and praised the curbs imposed upon it by the government. Holding the native press responsible for 'disgraceful and mischievous use of the liberty it enjoyed' for a long time before the outbreak of the mutiny, the *Manchester Guardian* argued that the government would have been guilty of frightful irresponsibility had it failed to act in this regard.[105] The paper not only dated the attacks of the native press in India upon the government to the year 1856, but also strongly suspected the political control and motives behind it.[106] *The Examiner* described the native newspapers as 'edged tools' in the hands of infants.[107]

Thus the advocates of the mutiny theory, while holding fast to the idea of a military uprising in one shape or another, either differed from each other or indulged in remarkable self-contradictions. These schismatic tendencies not only took away even the outward semblance of congruity and consistency from their ranks, but each differing voice and each new argument tended to weaken their main theme as against the view which held the uprising to have resulted from social and political factors. Those holding the latter view may be conveniently referred to as the revolution school of thought. The strength of the mutiny school was undermined by its internal discord; it soon succumbed to its own inconsistencies rather than to the adverse forces of the opposing school.

CHAPTER 4

Causes of the Revolution

A very large section of the British public reacted sympathetically towards the Indians and the outbreak as a socio-political rebellion or a revolution. Thus some of the many strong sentiments expressed depicted the uprising as: 'political'[1] in origin, a 'social rebellion miscalled a military mutiny',[2] a 'servile war and a sort of Jacquerie combined',[3] a 'patriotic war',[4] and a 'national movement in the fullest sense'.[5] Although the words were different, the theme was the same. All the different currents of opinion issued forth from widely separated sources and channelled themselves into one course. Thus, with added strength and greater direction the current continued forward until it emptied into one great ocean. These diverse voices were of the unanimous opinion that the revolt was a vigorous endeavour to repatriate the native authority.

This school of thought was composed of a much wider variety of Britons than the one already discussed. It was made up of the Conservative Party, its Party press—with Disraeli and *The Press* most vocal among them respectively; a great majority of British military servants, General Sir Robert William Gardiner[6] being their chief spokesman; a large number of missionaries stationed in the subcontinent, chief among them being Dr Alexander Duff;[7] the Irish nationalists, with *The Nation* as their principal mouthpiece;[8] the Chartists, with Ernest Charles Jones[9] as the moving spirit among them and, finally, those whom one might call the 'moralists' in the British society.

Military servants and the missionaries were directly involved in the Indian question; one for allowing lax discipline in the army and the other for allegedly causing religious alarm in India. In their case, therefore, it could be argued that both of them came in for a share in the responsibility for the outbreak and as such had reason to stand in self-defence as well as attempt to shift responsibility on to their counterparts among advocates of the opposite theme. Naturally, they made vigorous and sometimes successful attempts to expose the acts of omission and commission of the Indian civil administration, and to challenge the validity and prudence of imperial policy prior to the Indian mutiny.

In the case of Irish nationalists it could similarly be argued that they had their own interests to safeguard. Irish experiences of English rule had, in the face of the strong ever-present nationalist element in Irish politics, made foreign rule distasteful, not only for their own country, but also for other countries. Apart from this consideration and the fact that the India of 1857 offered to the Irish nationalists a strong parallel to their own country and called for their sympathetic attitude. Also England's difficulty was Ireland's opportunity. Naturally the Irish wanted to make political capital out of the Indian outbreak. All these factors combined, led *The Nation* and others to call the outbreak a revolution in India whereby the people of a subjugated colony strove to overthrow foreign rule.[10]

The Chartists and 'moralists' were the two sections of this school of interpretation most uninvolved personally in the Indian question. Their reactions, therefore, avoided particular, collective, or general party policy motives. They stood for liberty, equality, freedom and fair play at home, and honestly advocated the same for the Queen's subjects in India. As will be evident in the course of the three chapters devoted to this aspect of British reactions towards the Indian crisis of 1857, these groups advocated freedom for India before the outbreak, during the uprising, and even after it was crushed. In fact, Ernest Jones, the editor of the Chartist news medium the *People's Paper*, felt so sympathetic towards the Indians that his heart literally wept for them. While in prison in the late forties, he had depicted the condition of Indians in verse written using his own blood—pen and ink having been denied him.[11]

Turning to the Conservative Party, it appears to the present writer that their reactions were based upon their convictions. The history of this party, as well as the development of the East India Company, reveals that it was always, more or less, the Tories who tried to restrict the activities of the Company. Starting from Pitt's India Act of 1784 down to the Charter Act of 1854, the Conservatives invariably either tried to impose further restrictions upon the Company to limit its powers, or even to strive for its complete extinction. Not only that, they even opposed, by words or by deeds, the policy of territorial expansion in that far-off part of the empire. As at home, they were for the maintenance of the *status quo* abroad and India was no exception to this rule.

This does not, however, mean that there were no wars waged during Conservative administrations. There were many, but these were, generally speaking, wars of necessity and were usually followed by hesitation to occupy territories. A survey of British imperial history in India shows that whenever wars were waged in India during Conservative administrations, victory was generally followed by a partial, if not full restoration of territories. In this way an attempt was made not only to retain a semblance of native rule but also to keep the interest of the ruling princes alive in the continuity of the British rule in India. This also meant to avoid suspicion in the native mind and the possibility of an early confederacy among Indian princes.[12] Similarly, Conservatives advocated a cautious approach in the fields of social and administrative reforms.

Thus it was that all these sections of the British public, with little in common in their political thinking, rejected the mutiny theory. Although there were longstanding predictions of a possible revolt in India by various experts in Indian affairs, and indeed the poetic imagination of Lord Byron,[13] Ernest Jones[14] and a nephew of Canning[15] had long sensed the unmistakeable direction of adverse winds blowing in India, and had forecast an insurrection and a war of vengeance in that far-off part of the British Empire, yet vigorous leadership in the present trend of thought seems to have been provided by Disraeli. It was Disraeli who first demanded a discussion on Indian affairs in the House of Commons—a demand to which the government had reluctantly agreed. Unlike many other past and contemporary critics, Disraeli was close to the centre of power. His concern for Indian affairs therefore, was more likely to influence Imperial policy. It appears that Disraeli sincerely believed that an honest and objective analysis of the whole situation in India was badly needed; otherwise all remedies might easily fall short of the mark.[16] He seems to have been convinced that if such an attempt was in the interest of India, it was also in the deepest interest of Great Britain.[17] The sincerity of his conviction is proven by his non-committal attitude towards the outbreak for around a month after the first news of the disasters in India. He maintained this attitude even though on 19 May a highly important member of the Conservative Party and one of their most experienced India men, Lord Ellenborough,[18] had warned the government of the military situation in India.[19] Ellenborough's concern was so great that on 21 May he addressed a letter to the secretary for the War Department in which he emphasized the Indian situation *de novo* and earnestly inquired about the steps taken by the government.[20] Still Disraeli was reluctant to draw conclusions soon after the receipt of the news from India, as he easily might have done, had he been inspired by party motives alone. On the contrary, the Conservatives appreciated some of the steps taken by the administration after the mutiny had started.[21] Another factor which proves the strength of his convictions on the Indian situation is that he carried them into office in February 1858, with the formation of the Derby-Disraeli ministry.

Thus it was that Disraeli, who claimed to have been inspired by his profound study of the Indian subject, finally broke through his earlier non-committal stand, and made a dramatic statement in the Commons. Having opened the debate on 'India–State of Affairs' on 27 July 1857, he remarked:

> The decline and fall of empires are not affairs of greased cartridges. Such results are occasioned by adequate causes, and by an accumulation of adequate causes.[22]

Quoting instances of street riots in Boston and in Paris which had respectively ushered in the two greatest revolutions of modern times, he strongly emphasized that significant events always started in an insignificant manner. This might be the case with the Indian outbreak.[23] It was, therefore, incumbent upon the British people to make a realistic approach to the problem so as to be able to devise an effective cure.[24]

This statement quickened the public mood. While many strongly criticized it, many more found in it sufficient food for thought. It had necessitated a searching inquiry by the people for what Disraeli called 'adequate causes.' All those reports, books, pamphlets, memoirs, observations and warnings which had earlier received little or no notice at all at the hands of the British public, were carefully read, analysed and reappraised. People like Sir Henry Lawrence,[25] John Malcolm,[26] Sir Henry Russell,[27] Sir Charles Metcalfe,[28] Lord Ellenborough,[29] The Duke of Wellington,[30] Bishop Heber,[31] Sir Thomes Munro,[32] Charles Napier,[33] Mountstuart Elphinstone,[34] and some other British Indian celebrities became the most frequently quoted personages. Their diagnosis revealed that it was not simply an army outbreak with the cartridge affair as its immediate cause. Social, religious and political discontent had been the driving forces and the sepoys were just pawns. Thus it was that Edward Henry Nolan was able to assert that to call the outbreak a 'disturbance created by a pampered sepoy and some of the vagabond population of the cities would be tantamount to deliberately shutting eyes to the realities of the matter.[35]

Similarly a reviewer in the *Eclectic Review* called the greased cartridges and the bone-dust 'as diagnosis of the disease and not the disease itself.'[36]

The weaknesses of the British Empire in India

It was argued that the very foundation on which the superstructure of the British Indian Empire was built up was unsound. No two characters could be more incompatible than those of the trader and the sovereign. If the commercial interests of the East India Company rendered them 'very bad sovereigns', the spirit of the sovereignty made them equally bad traders. In their former situation the servants of the Company 'considered themselves as the clerks of the merchants', but in the latter case, the same servants came to regard 'themselves as masters of sovereigns.'[37] Apart from this, it was argued, it was inconceivable for the Indians to see 'a small band of traders—peddlars with their packs— who, at their first coming, bowed humbly at their *musnuds* (seat of power/authority; throne) and licked the dust at the feet of the Rajahs and Omrahs.'[38] building up a magnificent empire.[39] This was the anomaly of history.

The dilemma of the Indians becomes easily understandable when one reads about the type of questions often put to the members of the ruling class. Referring to the imperative necessity of the transfer of government from the Company to the Crown, the author of the 'Crisis of the Sepoy Rebellion', argued:

> Fancy the efforts of a native to get an idea what the Company is! 'Is it a King?' 'No.' 'An army?' 'No.' 'A Religion?' 'No.' 'It is a *sabé* [sic].' 'Ah, a society?' 'Yes.' 'Of Padrees (i.e., parsons)?' 'No.' 'Of Kings?' 'No.' 'Of officers?' 'No.' 'Of Pundits (i.e., learned doctors)?' 'No.': 'Of merchants!' 'Of merchants! Ah, a society of merchants! And does the society of merchants do the *sirkar* business (the Government) of England?' 'No, the Queen does that!' 'And does the Queen do the *sirkar* business of Ceylon?' 'Yes.' 'Not the Company! And who is the highest, Queen or Company?'

This was true, reported the author, not only of the common man but also kings and princes.[40] To this writer it appears that the answer to the last questions regarding the nature of the two governments in England and Ceylon (Sri Lanka) must always have given real anguish to the inquiring natives.

Now if it was hard for the natives of India to reconcile themselves to the rule of a body of merchants, it was equally hard for the merchants of London to lay aside the ledger and manipulate the sword successfully,[41] that too in the interest of the ruled. Merchants they were by nature and so they remained throughout. It was the sheer force of circumstances, it was pointed out, which raised them to the pedestal of political power.[42] Since their chief interest lay in commerce, mercantile pursuits dominated their political moves. Their desire for profit and gain could not comfortably harmonize with the interests of the governed. The fact of the matter was, criticized Gardiner, that the character of the sovereign was regarded 'as an appendix to that of the merchant, as something which ought to be made subservient to it or by means of which they may be enabled to buy cheaper in India, and thereby to sell with a better profit in Europe.'[43]

The 'dividends and not the millions of India', argued one, were their chief concern.[44] Naturally the policies they pursued were aimed at selfish commercial aggrandizement which branded them as unwelcome rulers to the natives of India. This was not the end of the anomaly. There was still another accompanying evil. A company of merchants acquiring political power had still to look after the interests of the shareholders and directors. Thus it was that the right of patronage in the civil, military and educational services of India took deep root in the body politic of the East India Company.[45] India began to be exploited for the 'benefit of the civil service.'[46] Who gained? The British! Who suffered? The Indians! 'A Resident in the North-Western Provinces of India' lamented:

> One of the false principles is that India exists for the benefit of Great Britain and not for the benefit of India itself.[47]

Henry Drummond, MP, a Tory of the old school, and one paternally regarded by Pitt in his early boyhood, addressing the Committee on the Government of India on 7 June 1858, observed still more strongly:

> If we were going to look upon India as we had looked upon it hitherto, as a mere place of plunder for English officials, we should surely lose it, and we deserve to lose it![48]

W.H. Russell, *The Times*' special correspondent in India, held exactly the same opinion when he wrote that as long as 'we regard India as a mere cotton-field, as an indigo-garden, as a plantation for the growth of five-percents and for enriching of younger sons, or as the *arida nutrix* of the civil and military services', the tenure of the British rule in India was going to rest on weak and uncertain foundations.[49] On the contrary, had the protests and selfish advice of the civilian service been ignored and settlement of Europeans encouraged, an independent body of loyal nobility would have arisen in the land. The numerarity of this class of landholders, it was contended, would not only have given a better organization to the Europeans in India, but would also have provided an endurable and wholesome link between the government and the natives. It was in the absence of such an arrangement, however, that Britain failed to enlist the interests and the sympathies of the natives on her side.[50]

Furthermore, the British Indian empire was not only an empire of merchants, it was also an empire of conquest. It was an empire held by truly foreign rulers—foreigners by origin and foreigners also by inclination. They were different from their Muslim predecessors. The latter were foreigners by origin but not so by disposition. After the conquest, pointed out the writer in the *Quarterly Review*, they made India their home and adopted Indian customs and manners and so ceased to be, at least in this respect, foreigners.[51]

It was, however, different with the new merchant masters of the country. Not only were the sacred doors of the Company's India closed to European settlers and missionaries for a long time, but even the British civil and military servants did not like to settle there, for despite their service in India, England remained their home. Their affections, their loyalty, their love and wealth were all for Great Britain and not for India. Their Indian allegiance, it was stressed, was meant only to suit the interests of the East India Company.[52] In very rare cases would a Briton decide to settle in India after his retirement. They always regarded themselves, alleged one critic, as Englishmen in India, and so kept themselves aloof from Indian society.[53] Every civil and military station had separate European quarters, which were veritable ghettos.[54] This it was felt, very naturally fostered loss of contact.[55] Feeling despondent about the situation, Russell was compelled to observe that Belgravia was 'not so much removed from Hounds-ditch in feeling, modes of life, and thought' as were the Europeans from the natives. He went on to say:

> There is no bond of union between the two.... The West rules, collects taxes, gives balls, drives carriages, attends races, goes to church, improves roads, builds theatres, forms masonic lodges, holds cutchery [court], and drinks pale ale. The East pays taxes on what it eats grown on taxed lands, grumbles, propagates, squabbles, sits in its decaying temples, haunts its rotting shrines, washes in its failing tanks, and drinks its semi-putrid water. Between the two there is a great gulf fixed....[56]

Evidently the European population of India remained very sparse. If the Europeans and the Indians did not intermarry, they did not dine together either.[57] In fact, it was forcefully maintained, there was nothing in common between the Europeans and the natives.[58] Both were 'aliens in birth, soil, climate, manners, language, and religion.'[59] There was no common social instinct which could bring the two together. This absence of a common ground was emphasized and re-emphasized by several men of experience.[60] As a result, it was argued, the relationship between the British and the natives could not take any other form save that of governors and the governed.[61]

The net result was, it was asserted, that British rule in India could not become national and therefore could not claim the affections of the native subjects. They were, in fact, looked upon as its 'internal enemies.'[62] Internal insurrection thus, firmly believed Gardiner, was one of the greatest threats from which the British Indian administration always suffered.[63] Naturally the empire was basically one of conquest, maintained solely by a strong British military machine.[64] It was with this realization that, on 7 June 1857 Gladstone profoundly observed before the Committee on the Government of India:

> Great conquests have been made by races of superior energy, who have gone in among inferior races, who have incorporated themselves with those inferior races, naturalized themselves in the country, associated probably with their religion and institutions, and at last amalgamated in one consistent and homogenous body, so as to become essentially the same in all the particulars which go to make up national existence. That is not our case. We go into the Indian peninsula with no such purpose. We go to take power out of the hands of those who formerly exercised it.[65]

John Bruce Norton, then a member of the Madras judiciary, quoted Metcalfe who had, long before the outbreak, observed:

> We are still a handful of Europeans governing an immense empire *without any firm hold on the country,* having warlike and powerful enemies on all our frontiers, and the spirit of disaffection dormant, but rooted universally among all our subjects.[66]

From the constitutional point of view too, the rule of the East India Company was described as a major irregularity. It was defined as 'absentee sovereigntyship', and so all the more anomalous. The experiment of 'absentee proprietorship' in Ireland alone, it was argued, should have been a sufficient lesson to prevent its further application in India, which was more remote, vaster, and far more difficult to control.[67]

Turning to Indians, the argument looked very simple. British rule in India was far from national in character. Though it did succeed in enlisting the loyalty and affection of interested and selfish people, true loyalty was always wanting. Henry Beveridge argued that since it was the rule of a completely alien people, it was, therefore, 'submitted to as a galling yoke to be endured so long as there was no hope of being able to shake it off, but not a day longer.'[68] The present writer is of the opinion that it was the division among the Indians themselves which encouraged the English to aspire to political power in India. Actually India with its millions had always been its own worst enemy. Earlier political rivalry among the congeries of Indian states facilitated the invasions of the Persians, the Greeks, the Kushins, the Huns and, later, of the various waves of Muslims invaders. The arrival of the Muslims, while it gave comparative political oneness to strife-torn India, injected duality of religion instead. Islam and Hinduism in its various forms had nothing in common. To the Reverend Henry S. Polehampton, an Anglican priest at Lucknow, it was Hindu-Muslim disunity in its very acute form on the one hand and Shi'ah-Sunni differences on the other which enabled a small band of Britons to set themselves up as the rulers of the land.[69]

The ground indeed looked quite fertile. In spite of the original weaknesses of the British themselves, they could conveniently build what looked like a weatherproof superstructure. The Government of the Company was well aware of the differences between the two communities and their internal schismatic tendencies, and it did use them. What Disraeli called the 'spontaneous circumstances of the country' were, in fact, profitably employed under the principle of divide and rule.[70] This writer is of the opinion that while the existence of such a situation did provide the English an opportunity to spread their roots around, it could not enable them to send these deep into the soil of India. The ground of communal differences was itself too slippery or sandy to tread on or to dig sound foundations upon; while the Hindus and the Muslims remained at heart the enemies of the Company's rule, the game of divide and rule must also have proved highly demanding. It always required several experts to handle the situation tactfully. The incapacity of one individual could spoil the hard work of many. That was why the *Manchester Guardian*, in spite of its strict adherence to the mutiny theory, metaphorically described the two communities 'as charcoal, to which sulphur and saltpetre have only to be added, in the shape of arms and discipline, to complete the manufacture of a very dangerous' substance.[71] The fact remains however that the Company rule was not acceptable to people in general. According to Beveridge it never was popular.[72] Even the sepoys were said to have accepted it only as a *fait accompli*.[73] The reasons for such antipathy were not far to seek. They could easily be detected in the native spirit of patriotism—a spirit which, according to the 'British Resident in the North-Western Provinces of India', never dies.[74] Before long, another factor was added to the already existing weaknesses of British rule in India—the excessive confidence which the Company had acquired as a result of its successes. It started to overrate the situation in its favour and embarked upon a set of policies which soon caused cracks in the already weak structure. The cracks grew wider and ultimately threatened the very existence of the edifice in 1857.

While Disraeli voiced his strong doubts and challenged the government's contention that the outbreak was a mere military mutiny, Ernest Jones had long expected such an occurrence in India. Almost all the members of this school unanimously ascribed the outbreak to various economic, social, political, religious and administrative grievances of the people. These grievances, they believed, produced a strong sense of disaffection in the country. While many started to plot, many considered it their duty to spread disaffection. The majority of the aggrieved and disgruntled, however, kept silent but sullen, and continued to live in an alternating world of hope and despair.

Economic Grievance

The first list of grievances was set forth as partly economic and partly political. Imposition of foreign rule naturally excluded a large number of natives from offices of trust and responsibility. Starting under Warren Hastings, the process of de-Indianization of services reached its zenith under Lord Cornwallis. His contempt of native talent as inefficient and corrupt and his simultaneous desire to Europeanize the services produced both irritation and estranged feelings; it also severed a healthy and much needed connection between the ruler and the ruled. From that time onward the distance between the two, it was contended, grew wider and wider.[75] A writer in the *Westminster Review*, severely criticized this aspect of the administration. He wrote:

There has never been anything like it in the Mussulman kingdom of India. Under Mogul kings, Hindoos have frequently been prime ministers, and from every rank persons have risen into high office.... We can look nowhere for a parallel to the English rule, except to the Roman empire, where none but Roman citizens could hold office in the provinces. Notoriously this degraded the provincials into a sort of tame cattle...liable to be slaughtered by barbarians the moment the trained troops were withdrawn. Out of this came the ruin of the empire.[76]

Even Sir Benjamin Colin Brodie, who called the outbreak a mere military mutiny, agreed that the shutting out of the natives from participation 'in the government of their own country' injured the feelings of the Hindus and the Muslims.[77] The native states, in spite of their disorders, had presented, he held, an opportunity to the Indians for competition, restless enterprise and for advancement in life.[78] This opportunity was now denied to them. The exclusion of the natives from the services of their country had taken place in spite of audible complaints of humanitarians like Munro. He had earlier observed:

The consequence, therefore, of the conquest of India, by the British arms would be, in place of raising, to debase the whole people. There is, perhaps, no example of any conquest, in which the natives have been so completely excluded from all share of the government of their country as British India.[79]

The liberalization affected by the Charter Act of 1833, which abolished all distinctions of caste, colour and creed in the recruitment of the Company's services, and promised to afford equal opportunity to all was, it was contended, at once negated by the introduction of the English language as a passport for any such employment. Apart from this, the inclusion of examination questions in the Greek and Latin languages (neither of which was taught in India), as well as the insertion of questions on subjects of Christian theology, it was further stressed, were sufficient to keep prospective candidates out of service.[80] Malcolm Lewin, late Second Judge of the Sadar Court of Madras, virulently attacked the assumption of all the offices by Britons—offices which were otherwise the due of the natives. He regretfully noted:

Our rule has been that of the robber and the bandit and we are suffering from the natural result—insurrection.[81]

Simultaneously, it was made clear that the present grievance was more than merely politico-economic. It was social at the same time. The Englishmen who took the place of the natives were, generally speaking, men of youthful years. This surely added insult to injury. The natives considered it degrading to have to submit to inexperienced youths who had no great sympathy with them and were unaware of their interests and problems.[82]

Socio-Religious Reasons

The social and religious grievances occurred partly under pressure from the Evangelicals and public opinion at home,[83] and partly out of its own benevolent intentions when the government of the East India Company decided to purge Hindu society of its various weaknesses. Now these weaknesses had acquired religious significance, and were matters of pride and prejudice among a very large and influential section of the Hindu population. An attempt to suppress them was at once construed as uncalled for interference in their religion. A writer in *Blackwood's Edinburgh Magazine* complained that this was being done in the face of a prophetic warning by Reginald Heber, Bishop of Calcutta, in 1824 against any meddling with the religious prejudices of the people of Upper India.[84] Thus it was that the suppression of female infanticide[85] and *sati*,[86] allowing of widow remarriage[87] and interference in the Hindu system of adoption,[88] one and all, quickened the pace of anti-British thinking in Hindu society. Just to take the case of *sati*, Ludlow, who himself was highly appreciative of its abolition, informed his countrymen that even this much-needed reform failed to evoke approval among the Hindus, 'except in the minds of a few thinking men, one or two perhaps in a million.' In fact, *sati* was a matter of so deep a conviction with the people who practised it that they even went to the extent of fighting out their case in the Privy Council.[89] *The London Journal and Weekly Record of Literature, Science and Arts,* criticizing this interference of the government in Hindu observances, remarked:

> It is more than probable that the present outbreak in the East is more the result of some blind, precipitate attempt to meddle with the religious sympathies and antipathies of the people than from another cause.

It further went on to advise the government strongly when it observed:

> We cannot govern Calcutta as we govern London; we must respect the hereditary sentiments of two thousand years; and as inhabitants of the North, it would be folly on our part to disdain the ceremonies, even of pleasure which, in the East, unnumbered ages have invested with traditional sanctity.[90]

A vague fear regarding the safety of their religion had already begun to pervade Hindu society. There came another reason for it in the introduction of the Religious Disabilities Act. The Act removed earlier customary law disinheriting apostate Hindus. While it opened the gates for litigation,[91] it also went a long way in further confirming Hindu apprehensions regarding religious policies of the government.[92] Even before the Act could be passed, the Hindus of Calcutta and Madras lodged protests and addressed petitions and memorials to the government about their apprehensions. One of the Bengal Memorials read:

> Your memorialists will not conceal that from the moment the proposed Act becomes a part of the law applicable to Hindoos, that confidence which they have hitherto felt in the paternal character of their British rulers will be most materially shaken. No outbreak of course is to be dreaded; but the active spirit of fervent loyalty to their sovereign and of pride in their rulers will be changed into sullen submission to their will and obedience to their power.[93]

The Madras Memorialists, on the other hand, called it 'a direct Act of tyranny' and were supported by English lawyers in their denunciation.[94] The government, however, moved by a counter-petition of Bengal Christian converts, passed the law in April 1850. This, according to Sir John William Kaye[95] fomented growing discontent in the country.[96] The strenght of Hindu feelings on this subject can be easily seen from a perusal of the thirteenth grievance of the Madras Memorial. Fearing a reversal in the religious policy of the Company, it read:

> On their first arrival the British behaved kindly, securing to the natives of the Carnatic, by Proclamation, under date of 31 July 1801, the immunity of their religion, laws and privileges: for this the Hindoos willingly engaged in the Military Service of the Honourable Company; and wherever the British standard has been victorious in India, down to the last perilous engagement, on the banks of Sutlej, their Hindoo blood has freely flowed to secure the East India Company's dominion over their native land; because they have preferred it to Mohammedan; and now that the British Government has become consolidated by the assistance of the Hindoos, the country is inundated with missionaries, who bring their creed in the one hand and the sword of persecution in the other—bidding the Hindoo to take their choice between conversion and extermination. British and Christian policy thus delineated, is far more oppressive and unjustifiable than that of the Mohammedans, for it adds ingratitude to partiality and injustice, and creates a belief that in weakness they are friends to the oppressed, and in power the perpetrators of oppression and wrong.[97]

That was not all. The government had also stopped the worship of Kali[98] or Durga[99] and the Charkh Puja,[100] The latter step aroused strong feelings and so had to be withdrawn.[101] Concurrent with this had developed what Lewin called the 'missionary mania' in the chief departments of the government. Many high ranking civil and military officers had started taking an active interest in missionary activity in India. Some had even gone to the extent of assuming the role of preachers of the gospel.[102] So great had become their zeal that the civil and military servants were reported to be vying with each other.[103] This bred the fear that the government 'entertained the idea of compulsory conversions.'[104] Even the courts of justice were reported to have shown partiality to Christian converts. If they failed, they were, at times, overturned and the judges dismissed 'for refusing to side with the Christian convert against his adversary.'[105] The result was a complete lack of confidence even in the administration of justice. Thus referring to the contemporary situation, Lewin, himself a judge of the Madras Presidency, who was relieved of his duties for having tried to maintain the independence of his court,[106] ruefully observed:

> Our morality is now accounted for hypocrisy, our Christianity a passport to licentiousness.

He went on the quote Sydney Smith, the well-known canon of St. Paul's, who had advised his countrymen in these words:

> If you wish to convert the heathen, you must first burn your Bibles, which instead of exhibiting you as Christians, will merely prove you to be imposters.[107]

The situation became so precarious that the Court of Directors decided to control the proselytizing zeal of its employees in the far-off colony. In a dispatch to the Government of India, the Court made it clear that the British government in India was known by its officers and that the latter were identified with the former. The dispatch, therefore, made the officers cognizant of the fact that while 'invested with public authority their acts cannot be regarded as those of private individuals.'[108] These orders, reported V.A. Smith in the Commons, had gradually fallen into abeyance, and official efforts had since been carried on with renewed vigour.[109] So much so that even the governor-general, Lord Canning, was reported to be greatly enthusiastic. Some of his critics firmly believed that his contributions to missionary societies and his reply to a Missionary Memorial, in which he commended their past labours and exhorted them to further efforts, caused much alarm among the Hindus. The Hindus, it was thought, now came to believe in the official nature of the missionary programme.[110]

Government interference in the field of education also, it was believed, stirred up strong doubts in India. Long years of controversy between the Orientalists and the Anglicists, known as the Macaulay-Wilson controversy, resulted in the adoption of the Western system of education in India in 1833. This brought about several changes in the educational set-up of the country, i.e., almost complete withdrawal of state support for the teaching of Hinduism and Islam and transfer of all funds to British institutions, both government and missionary,[111] adoption of a new curriculum based on Western philosophy at school, college and university levels, and grants-in-aid to the missionary schools. Missionary teachers began to be appointed as inspectors of schools. Norton complained that the appointment of clergymen to such offices was sure to alarm the natives in the provinces and feared that it would be thought of as 'covert attempts upon their religion.'[112] The result was, it was pointed out, that even the missionaries came to be looked upon as government servants. A writer in *Fraser's Magazine* affirmed that these measures of the government acted as a triple-edged blade against British rule in India; they came to be regarded as concealed attempts on the part of the government to Christianize the people and, as such, were strongly resented.[113] Government attempts to assure people of its good intentions, unsupported as they were by example, were said to have further aggravated the situation.[114] Holding religious neutrality impracticable, Lieut.-Col. Sir H. Edwardes accused the government of saying one thing and doing another. He believed that in this attitude of the government lay the 'secret of disturbances in British India.'[115]

The new educational system, it was emphasized, was not completely in the interest of British rule either. It had its own hidden disadvantages, which were far from conducive to the continuity of a foreign rule. For example: The study of Roman and Greek history was believed to have made strong nationalists of Indians. These studies provided a 'glorious example of ridding one's country of her tyrants and of shedding one's blood in her cause.'[116] The *Edinburgh Review* shared the opinion of Lord Ellenborough, who described the European system of education in India as incompatible with the existence of British rule in that country.[117] In fact, some young Hindu philosophers, it was reported, had already held public meetings under the unavoidable impact of the new system of education. In them they described the government as tyrannical and called upon their people 'to defend their liberties and claim their privileges of a free nation.'[118]

Moreover, Western education was stated to have brought home to the natives one great weakness of their rulers. Now they knew the immense distance from which their country was ruled; now they were aware of the long journey which British men and munitions had to undertake before reaching India. In short, education had opened up 'a vast field of practical knowledge and has thus diminished the great superiority once possessed by the Englishman.'[119]

Administrative provocations

The administrative grievances of the country presented a very grim picture as well. These largely contributed towards disaffection which ultimately led to the outbreak. The Company's revenue system was described as very oppressive.[120] If 'every mode of exaction and extortion was adopted'[121] in its arbitrary collection before Cornwallis, the Permanent Settlement had fixed the state share still higher. No leniency whatsoever was shown at the time of collection, no matter what the situation. The rigour of the system included the extreme measure of sale of a *zamindars*' property to clear up any arrears, and quite frequently this resulted in his ultimate ejection.[122] The report of the Torture Commission[123] revealed that the instrument of torture in its different forms was frequently resorted to by native employees of the Revenue Administration. Even women were not spared and were, in fact, subjected to most indecent and indescribable forms of torture.[124] Henry Mead, a British-Indian journalist of long experience, felt strongly the indifference exhibited by the people of England at the disclosures made by this revealing document and complained that they needed the 'occurrence of a rebellion to induce them to give even a passing thought to the subject.'[125]

The Press editorially drew attention to one of Charles Napier's letters to a friend (written perhaps on 31 May 1850), in which the then commander-in-chief of India attempted to expose the horrors of Indian maladministration. He had pointed out that porters by the thousands were pressed into carrying the governor-general's baggage and then left for a year and a half unpaid. In some cases cultivators who were dragged out of their fields with their carts to carry the baggage and stores of the army and were taken hundreds of miles away from their homes, often without payment finding on their return their carts broken, bullocks dead, their wives dishonoured and in the keep of officials. He knew of a judge, who openly bragged that 'when either of the parties before him was a woman, and a pretty one, he always made the sacrifice of her honour the price of his decree.' He pointed out a district where a regiment composed of low-caste men was openly encouraged by the commander in schemes of systematic seduction and abduction. When challenged by police authorities, the commander hurled abusive language upon them. Napier complained that in spite of all this the culprit had escaped because of the governor's interest in him.[126] Having communicated all this to his Calcutta friend, Napier disagreed with him for having described the British Indian administration a blessing for India. He observed to his friend:

> The high compliment you pay the Indian Government makes me laugh, because I know that while you believe in it, it is not correct. No! no! I will neither concede to you that 'we are strong, just or regular'; or that 'we take no more from the people than the law declares', or that we 'pay every mouth.' Ourselves, yes! but not others. My dear Sir, you live in an enchanted circle at Calcutta; you know nothing of the Indian Government beyond its theories—no more than if you were Governor-General. The atrocities which go on are beyond description. You, in your library at Calcutta, could not know anything of them, but I, on my horse, passing through all countries saw and learnt them on the spot; and very indignant I am at them, and have been for many years.[127]

With all these revelations *The Press* ceased to wonder why Lord Canning had, under the advice of his advisers, muzzled the press.[128]

The administration of justice fared no better than that of revenue. Naturally it fell under heavy criticism. In this respect the critics appeared to be realistic. Starting with F.J. Halliday, the Lieutenant Governor of Bengal,[129] down through the Commons and with many other writers in England down to the 'Resident in the North-Western Provinces of India',[130] all could see the anomalies of the system. The whole system was described as defective and unsuitable to Indian circumstances and an irritant to the natives. The British system of jurisprudence, it was reported, introduced either young judges from England[131] or senior officials of the Indian political and revenue departments.[132] In both instances they were, to a large extent, devoid of the skill required for meeting the basic needs of Indian society. The tragedy of the whole system lay in the great venality of native subordinates, the web woven by them around the European judge,[133] the latter's virtual inaccessibility to the natives and his lack of familiarity with native affairs and the use of regional languages, not to speak of the local dialects. The last one was a major deficiency as it must have incapacitated him from communicating directly with the plaintiff and the defendant. Naturally a British tribunal often found itself paralysed in 'cases where the experience of a native would have at once unravelled the truth.'[134] If the cases brought to the notice of the court ended up in inordinate delays, the method of presenting petitions to the courts was no less cumbersome. All this resulted in an accumulation of civil and criminal cases, 'amounting', it was said, 'almost to a denial of justice.'[135] Naturally it disheartened and discouraged even the most determined. *Blackwood's Edinburgh Magazine* critically observed:

> Our courts of justice were little adapted to the usage of the land. They were too slow, too expensive. Their process or principles were not understood or comprehended. They promoted litigation. Consequently these courts were viewed as grievances by the higher classes and not considered as blessings by the low. To the latter they were hardly accessible from their expense and nearly useless from their delays.[136]

The *Westminster Review*, agreeing with Halliday, termed the system as 'little better than lottery',[137] and the 'Resident in the North-Western Provinces' called it a system of 'justice falsely so called.'[138] At times the whims of European judges also made a farce of justice. The Marquess of Clanricarde deplored the fabrication in 1854–5 by a certain Jones, a collector and magistrate in one of the Indian districts, against Bhawani Lala—a resident of the same district. It was a clear case of harrassment, social insult, use of force and false conviction.[139] Later, when the Supreme Court upheld Lala's contention of innocence and granted him a compensation of 1000 rupees, he could not get the sum, as the authority of the Supreme Court to question the acts of a magistrate was questioned.[140] C.L. Cumming Bruce, MP, reported another case in which a native officer was convicted on false evidence. He, however, was able to redress his grievances as a result of his appeal to the Court of Directors.[141]

Discontented Nobility

No less acute was the economic distress of a very large section of agriculturalists and landed nobility. The agrarian outrages committed first in the time of Bentinck under financial distress and later repeated under Dalhousie 'as proof of a powerful Government, a vigorous executive, and a most fruitful source of public revenue', brought poverty to the doorsteps of thousands of landholders in India.[142] Inquiries were instituted into the titles of the rent-free tenures, ending up in the confiscation of thousands of estates, either because the title-deeds had been lost, or because the land was held by a long prescriptive right. Another writer in *Blackwood's Edinburgh Magazine* stressed:

> No plea was considered too weak to justify a resumption. Grants stamped with the approval of Warren Hastings, Clive and Sir Hector Munro in the Lower Provinces, were pronounced insufficient; while in the Upper India, even the fact of a tenure having been conferred at the instance of Lord Lake, could barely rescue it from confiscation. At last resumption became a passion; hundreds of decisions in favour of Government were passed in a single day; and the principle was broadly proclaimed, that the very existence of a rent-free tenure was a nuisance and ought to be abated.[143]

Though this scrutiny had yielded, it was thought, £500,000 and £370,000 a year respectively in the presidencies of Bengal and Bombay,[144] this 'clumsy expedient'[145] had not only cost the British their 'name for good faith, humanity and justice'[146] but had also left thousands of nobility and their dependants without any means of subsistence. This was sure to earn the government active ill will and hostility from the deprived landlords and their adherents.[147] Since they had lost their '*Jan se azeez*' hereditary land holdings,[148] all of them, it was argued, prayed for the overthrow of British rule in India.[149] William Edwards, as collector of Budaun, had publicly warned the government on this subject but was regarded as an alarmist.[150] 'Even in England,' argued Disraeli in the Commons, 'the process if carried on, would produce a revolution, as the menace of it once did.'[151] It was further believed that while the investigations had benefited the tenantry, it had removed the only hand that could keep it loyal to the state.[152]

Other irritants

In addition to the above major causes of social, religious, economic, and political unrest in India, there were many other equally important irritants which further enhanced local disenchantment with the British. For instance: Dalhousie's unilateral lowering of five per cent rate of interest on loans given by natives to the government to four per cent highly dissatisfied its native creditors. This was viewed as a serious act of high-handedness and bad faith.[153]

The system of taxation too was regarded as inconsiderate and productive of bad blood. The Company's government, it was claimed, thought more of Indian revenue than happiness of Indians.[154] L.E. Ruutz Rees wrote:

> There was a duty on stamps, on petitions, on food, on houses, on eatables, on ferries. There was an opium contractor, a contractor for supply of corn and provisions, a salt and spirit contractor,—and, in fact, contracts were given for everything that in Paris would come under the name of octroi.[155]

In reality, criticized Lewin, the Company enjoyed monopolies in opium, salt, arrack and ferry and naturally derived exorbitant profits.[156]

Quite a few emphasized the Europeanization and modernization of India as contributing factors to the whole mass of suspicion and disaffection.[157] It was not a question of one or two European influences at work but many of them. In fact, Christian civilization was said to exercise its influence in all different directions.[158] The introduction of steamship, railway, telegraph, the canals, it was argued, had further 'filled the imagination of Hindus with vague apprehensions',[159] and had led them to misconstrue benevolent measures as a 'design to Europeanize their country, and to overthrow the whole system of their cherished superstitions.'[160] If the high caste priests felt chagrined at the introduction of railways it was because in them they saw the approaching doom of the caste system;[161] the start of telegraph had, on the other hand, alarmed the whole of Hindu society. Lieut.-Colonel Edwardes told his audience at the Town Hall, Cambridge, that it was generally held that after the poles and wires had been set up all over India, the governor-general would pull a string and that would convert the whole of India in one telegraphic shock.[162] In short, Hindus resented this encroachment upon their civilization. They realized that a stand had to be made somewhere, and so, pointed out a writer in the *Dublin University Magazine*, 'Hinduism has taken its stand here.'[163]

The department of police, the real guardian of public security, was reported to have become 'the bane and pest of society, the terror of the community.'[164] *The Press* charged the British Indian Police system with inefficiency and corruption. The paper editorially argued that the system could not afford even as much protection to the natives as they enjoyed under the earlier Hindu and Muslim rulers.[165]

On top of all this, it was pointed out, the insolent behaviour of the English residents and officers in India went a long way to alienate the people from their rule.[166] They 'stalked as conquerors' in the country.[167] The language of 'Billingsgate' was frequently practised towards respectable native servants.[168] Private conversations and correspondence aside, even in their official records, it was reported, they branded the natives as 'heathens.'[169] At times, their treatment of domestic servants was rather harsh and severe.[170] In view of this Richard Congreve, a nineteenth-century positivist, in his pamphlet *India*, in which he pleaded for Britain's abandonment of her Eastern dominions, wrote:

> Men must reap the things they sow; Force from force must ever flow.[171]

The British, it was stated, rejected all notions of equality between them and their Indian wards.[172] Since they were caught up with the idea of maintaining their dignity, complained the 'Resident in the North-Western Provinces of India', they were, with the exception of missionaries, 'critical, overbearing and fault-finding' of the natives.[173] This trend had become so alarming that even persons in the rank of governor-general were no exception to it. John Bright regretfully informed the Commons that one of the governors-general had in his letter to an Indian prince, 'ruler over many millions of men', described him as 'dust' under his 'feet'.[174] The fact of the matter was that while the Indian lower and middle classes found the Britons 'cold and disdainful', the upper bourgeoisie and the nobility found their behaviour intolerable.[175] Reporting the case of a magistrate who insisted that the natives of all ranks should dismount from their horses or other conveyances to salute him, Drummond went on to observe before the Commons:

> Now, if we were proud of our aristocracy and mindful of their dignity, how could we think that these things did not rankle in the breasts of men who could trace their hereditary rank and their possessions up to a period anterior to the commencement of our history—in some cases, indeed, up to the time of Alexander the Great? Were we so foolish as to imagine that because they did not retort an insult upon the instant, they did not feel it? We might depend upon it that the Italian proverb was true in India as everywhere else—'Vengeance sleeps long, but never dies.'[176]

In short, every individual in India had a cause to complain: either his land was resumed; or he was ruined by a lawsuit; or was tortured by the police; or harassed by a trumped up case; victimized by a spiteful magistrate; forced into *corvee*; or constrained to part with his bullocks and carts to facilitate the movement of the army; compelled to wait for the money payment of materials supplied, and what not. The budget of complaints was full. Norton was prepared to produce a hundred such cases out of his own experience.[177] If some wondered at the delay in the occurrence of the outbreak, Drummond asserted that there was sufficient ground for the Indians to hate the English and causes enough for half a dozen rebellions.[178] Such calamities, however, did not occur due to acute schismatic tendencies in the Indian society caused by the caste system as well as different Indian religions. These did not let them unite against what Norton described as the common enemy, the British.[179]

Political grievances

The most acute grievance, however, was political in nature. The annexation policy of the Company, it was contended, cut the ground from under its rule both directly and indirectly and hastened the revolt of the Bengal army. While it weakened the European force by spreading it over a larger part of India, it also excited the animosity of influential sections of society all over India.[180] John Malcolm Ludlow, barrister-at-law and author of several books on India, emphatically reproduced the carefully considered opinion of the Duke of Wellington on the subject of the extension of territories. The latter had profoundly observed:

> ...wherever we spread ourselves...[we make] additional enemies, at the same time that by the extension of our territory, our means of supporting our government, and of defending ourselves, are proportionately decreased.[181]

In fact, it was the government's grasping hand which perturbed some of the major political elements in the country and led them to unite to rid the land of its foreign ruler.[182]

The native states of India and their populations had completely lost faith in the promises and pledges of what was called the 'paramount power.' This suspicion and distrust was not at all new. Brodie in his *English Tenure of India* pointed out the lack of confidence expressed by the Amirs of Sind in reply to the friendly overtures of Lord Auckland. The plea offered was that 'every state which had begun with an alliance with the English Government, had ended with falling under their domination.'[183] This distrust reached its climax under Lord Dalhousie, the last of the Company's great imperialists and empire builders. His strong ambition and imperial instinct led him to launch an aggressive policy of conquest, annexations, confiscations and abolition or curtailment of pensions.[184] The means adopted seldom bothered Dalhousie who was called the creator of modern India, for the end justified them. All this was done against advice rendered by men of experience in the civil, military and diplomatic services of the East India Company.[185] While each one of these steps meant an additional blow and an additional loss to the Indian society,[186] the English suffered as well—to being regarded as '*be-eeman*' (faithless) in the observance of their treaties.[187] A writer in the *Westminster Review* ruefully observed:

> Conceive the famishing ruin, first, to the respectable families, next, to crowds of their dependents, which would be produced in England by ejecting all the Queen's servants of the rank of gentry, all the judges, magistrates, with all officers of the army, and replacing them by foreigners of opposite habits, who spend their money in quite new channels. Such is the financial convulsion in every native State when it is annexed by the East India Company, to say nothing of the natural displeasure which must always attach to the face of new and foreign rulers.[188]

Furthermore, the annexations were described as a source of weakness to the English in more ways than one. Every new annexation, it was stated, deprived the British government of a favourable contrast which the two administrations presented to the people on both sides of the border before the act of incorporation.[189] They not only made the situation explosive locally but also tended strongly to augment the sense of collective loss. A headlong pursuit of this policy went a long way to deprive the Company of the essential basis of Hindu-Muslim disunity upon which the empire was raised. If the British annexation of various Hindu states and their abolition of Nana's pension had alarmed the Hindus, it was very largely held, their annexation of Awadh had equally galled the Muslims.[190] They saw common ground to get together. The need for solving their differences could not be more apparent than at that time as any further delay would mean complete absorption and near ruin of both communities. Early united action was immediately needed. Norton, as did a few others, significantly quoted the last address of a Marahtah rebel to the people of India as a specimen of the 'spirit which might have animated a South Marahtah outbreak, had it not been checked in time.' This Satara conspirator shouted at his countrymen from the gallows on 19 June 1857:

Listen all! *As the English people hurled the Rajah* [of Satara] *from his throne, in like manner do you drive them out of the country.* This is murder. I am illegally condemned.... This example is made to frighten you, but be not alarmed. Sons of Brahmins, Mahrattas, and Mussulmen, revolt! Sons of Christians, look to yourselves![191]

Thus it was that Hindu-Muslim unity was nearly achieved and the dissatisfaction and disaffection of the two communities took on a national character.[192]

Contemporary situation as a cause

The contemporary situation too was understood to have added its share in unsettling the minds of the Indians. Great Britain in the 1850s seemed to be an utterly exhausted power. This must have added to the confidence of the people of the subcontinent.[193] Azimullah had, [194] on his way back to India, purposely visited the actual battlefield in Crimea,[195] to see with his own eyes 'those great Roostums [Rustams],[196] the Russians', who had beaten the French and the English together. He carried home, it was pointed out, a highly unfavourable opinion of the English army.[197] The Crimean war was quickly followed by another in Persia. Quite a few regiments were sent from India to participate against the Persians. While the Persian war was still in its concluding stages, war clouds were gathering over Canton. Again Britain was compelled to depend upon the sepoys. Two native regiments were sent out from the Madras Presidency. This British dependence upon the native troops for carrying out the wars of England must have further lowered the military prestige of rulers among the ruled. To them Great Britain must have looked like an over-extended and exhausted power; the time was ripe for an uprising. Answering V.A. Smith's argument that the number of troops sent out of India was not large enough to have encouraged the natives to embark upon a rebellion, Disraeli contended:

Do you think that the nations of India count you troops upon their fingers? They know that your troops are going away; they hope that you may have to send more; and, deciding broadly upon these facts, they do not inquire how many are going or how many are coming back; it is sufficient for them to know that you have war in Persia and China, and that your European troops are gradually leaving the great Peninsula.[198]

Thus it was argued that the defective nature of the empire, a degenerate and delinquent administration, disenchanted Hindus and dispossessed Muslims, deprived nobility and deposed royalty etc., provided sufficient causes to the various parties to be active, to conspire and overthrow the foreign ruler.

CHAPTER 5

The Conspiracy Theory: A Recurring Theme

It was against the background described in the preceding chapter—of popular discontent, social, religious, political and economic,[1] as well as a favourable contemporary scene,[2]—that the adherents of the conspiracy theory began to develop their ideas. If the soil looked fertile, the time seemed to be no less auspicious. The advocates of the conspiracy theory argued that the mutiny was the result of an organized, vast and well prepared plan that was meant to be simultaneous, but misfired as a united uprising.[3] The material to support this theory was abundant. Its proponents had no faith in the argument that caste and cartridge were the only two causes of the Meerut *emeute* and that once the army broke out into open mutiny, it was exploited by disgruntled parties. Pointing to the long list of grievances, they contended that disaffection was much more widespread than was believed; that the conspiracy preceded rather than succeeded the outbreak, and that the army outbreak was the result, and not the cause, of that machination. The events immediately preceding, as well as those which occurred during the outbreak convinced them of its conspiratorial and national character.

This school of thought eventually put the rulers of Delhi and Lucknow at the head of the list of plotters. The initiative having been taken by the king of Delhi[4] it was believed that the two houses were reported to have buried their differences and decided to work conjointly against a common foe. The grand motive behind this combination was described as political—the restoration of the native rule, the sovereignty of the ruler of Delhi and under him that of the subordinate states.[5] Different measures were taken to maintain secrecy to avoid detection. To avert the attention of the government, the ruler of Awadh resorted to subtle diplomacy. He changed his quarters from Lucknow to Calcutta and sent his mother and brother to London. In this manner the government was thrown off guard and Wajid 'Ali, the deposed ruler of Awadh, was able to keep sending his emissaries to Lucknow.[6]

Slowly and gradually the ranks of the conspirators began to enlarge. 'Ali Naqi Khan, the Prime Minister of Awadh, was reported to have assumed an increasingly important role.[7] The Nana's tone and demeanour towards Europeans were also said to have assumed an insolent and haughty character.[8] That he was a party to the whole affair, considered George Bruce Malleson, then an assistant military auditor-general at Calcutta and a well-known military writer, was evident from the fact that ever since the annexation of Awadh, the Nana had been disposing of his investments in government securities. He did it so secretly that it could not be known until afterwards when the securities had already dwindled from £500,000 down to £30,000.[9] For the time being, however, he bided his time by 'concealing his enmity under the mask of an admiration for the European civilization and a taste for English manners', as well as by entertaining English civil and military officials at his palace.[10]

These and other conspirators soon realised the importance of the role which the native army could play in the fulfilment of their scheme and so decided to undermine its loyalty—perhaps the easiest thing to do, since the sepoys were already said to be serving 'with willing limbs' but 'not willing hearts.'[11] It was at this moment that the cartridge incident occurred as a heaven-sent tool to be usefully and effectively employed.[12] Here the present writer feels that against the background of causes which led to this outbreak as described in the second, fourth and seventh chapters of this book, the cartridge incident appears to be as hollow a cause for the outbreak of the revolt of 1857 as was the murder of Archduke Ferdinand of Austria for the First World War. However, the mention of the two kinds of fat used in the cartridge grease was argued as essentially a part of the same game.[13] Agents were employed in the guise of faqirs in many garbs and hues,[14] and rumours of all sorts were spread.[15]

It was given out that the grease in the cartridges was used as a result of a petition to the Queen by the missionaries in India, who obtained her subsequent concurrence and blessings.[16] It was to contradict these rumours that the governor-general in Council had to issue, albeit in vain, a proclamation on 16 May 1857—a proclamation which admitted the work of designing and evil-minded men and warned the civil and military populations to beware of the traitors.[17] The army, however, had already fallen victim to the machination of the plotters. The two arch-conspirators were even said to have offered to give service to the disbanded soldiers at a higher salary.[18] Hence the punishment of disbandment, it was argued, only served as an inducement to revolt to get into what was described as the 'national service.'[19] One or two sepoys, it was thought, were enlisted in each one of the regiments for the purpose of working upon their fellow troopers and for maintaining secrecy.[20] The Nana himself, it was reported, in the company of 'Azimullah, had toured some of the cantonment stations before the outbreak, where the 'worthy couple' was said to have successfully meddled with sepoy loyalty.[21] One of Nana's emissaries was mentioned as having penetrated as far south as Mysore, and was reported to have singly tampered with forty regiments.[22] In addition, the mysterious instrument of lotus flowers was reported to have been employed—an instrument which equally mysteriously travelled from regiment to regiment, and finally drew the sepoys into the 'vortex of that conspiracy which had long been secretly' brewing.[23] One of this school felt very sure of the message conveyed by them and believed that no student of religion and anthropology could fail to discern the revolutionary plan which they contained.[24]

While instances of civil emissaries sapping the loyalty of the army during the outbreak were stated to be many, there was evidence of prior warning of its coming as well.[25] J.M. Ludlow quoted from the Eighteenth Report of the German Evangelical Mission of the Western coast of India. It read:

> Long before the outbreak in the North-West, hints were received by silk mercers at Bagulcote from mercantile connexions in the north, to limit their engagements for the next year and call in their debts - gloomy rumours then gained ground from day to day threatening Europeans and native Christians with ruin and death.

Again:

> At this festival which took place some time before the mutines in the north broke out, Brother Kies' addresses were met with the assertion, that the British rule would cease within a year.[26]

General Hearsey, described by V.A. Smith as a man of integrity and resourcefulness,[27] wrote on 28 January 1857, to inform the deputy adjutant-general of the Bengal Army about the disaffection created in the ranks of the army 'by some designing persons.'[28] He reported that agents of the Hindu party in Calcutta were using the widow remarriage grievance as a means of exploiting religious prejudices of the sepoys.[29]

On 8 February 1857, twelve days after communicating his first warning, Hearsey wrote to complain of the successful activities of the emissaries of Delhi and Awadh in corrupting the loyalty of the 19th Regiment.[30] On the 11th of the same month he further wrote to inform the government about the precarious nature of the situation at Barrackpore. 'We have,' he wrote, 'at Barrackpore been dwelling upon a mine ready for explosion.'[31] Similarly the Ghonda Raja was reported to have been diligently meddling with the loyalty of the 52nd Regiment stationed at Jubbulpore.[32] The mutiny at Sialkot was reported to have been caused in all likelihood by the arrival of a messenger from Delhi with a letter from the king.[33] Three of the Mughal king's emissaries were caught in action at Lucknow and one at Kanpur.[34] The *Illustrated London News* reported the hanging of a Mawlawi caught in the act of abetting the 70th Native Infantry, then stationed at Calcutta, to revolt.[35] Moreover, Mathew A. Sherring, a missionary of the London Missionary Society, also reported on the work of civilians trying to subvert the loyalty of the army at Allahabad and Aligarh, as did many others at several other places.[36] Sir Charles Edward Trevelyan, who preferred to style himself as an 'Indophilus', perhaps rightly believed when he argued that the army was only a 'pitiable' dupe to be employed for political purposes.[37]

If all this is to be credited, it would seem as though the task of preparing the civilian population for a revolutionary movement had progressed hand in hand with that of the army. The national sentiments of the literary sections of Indian society were said to have been aroused by the evidence of British weakness. England's involvement on the continent and parliamentary debates on the estimates of war were said to have been printed and reprinted at Calcutta in native languages and circulated all through the country. Similarly, maintained William Sinclair, the retrenchment of Britain's militia, her fleets and her army following the establishment of peace on the continent, were not unknown to the educated people of India.[38] For the rural areas, however, the well-known medium of pancakes was believed to have been employed.[39] This was described as nothing new in the history of mankind. The *Notes and Queries* and *Blackwood's Edinburgh Magazine* found a corresponding movement in Chinese history, which had resulted in the overthrow of the Tartars. The Chinese had, it was stated, not only adopted the pancake medium to achieve revolution, but since then had celebrated the day under the name, 'Feast of the Moon Loaves.'[40] E.H. Nolan reported that the outbreak had its parallels at home in Scotland and Ireland. The Scottish occurrences took place in

Celtic times, while the Irish experience was reported as recent. At the time of agrarian disturbance they had reportedly adopted 'the holy straws' and 'the holy turf' as their signs.[41] The *Edinburgh Review* came up with an analogous occurrence in India at the time of the Vellore mutiny in 1805, when some form of sugar changed hands.[42] If this be true, its repetition, though in a different shape, seems significant. However, the movement went on for several months.[43] Many felt convinced of its sure connections with the conspirators, including possibly the ruler of Awadh.[44]

The irony of the whole affair was that the cakes, variously described in size[45] and number, travelled from village to village through the agency of the police. Since these 'storm signs', as the *chapatis* were described, carried 'significant but enigmatical expressions', they were regarded as all the more dangerous.[46] It was thought that these carried some form of secret communication 'only to be comprehended by the faithful of either creed allied for the destruction of the foreigner.'[47] No wonder the government was charged with serious neglect for its failure to institute a full scale investigation into the whole affair. A rigorous inquiry, it was believed, could have yielded useful information. Disraeli, calling the cakes 'outward visible signs of confederacy', chided the government for its culpable negligence. He argued that had such a thing happened in Russia, the Czar would surely have regarded it as something highly dangerous for the state and would have instituted a searching inquiry.[48] The *Notes and Queries,* attributing the outbreak to the pancake movement, was still bitter when it wrote that for twelve months [sic] the cakes kept changing hands, 'and yet, so far it appears, not one functionary in India found it within his scope, one scholar within his knowledge, one native within his duty, to explain the meaning of this direful symbol.'[49] *Blackwood's Edinburgh Magazine,* calling it 'an Eastern symbol of portentous import', described it (on the basis of a district officer's inquiry) as an old custom whereby the king or chief in need of the services of his people would circulate the *chapatis* in advance in order to prepare the country for receiving his orders.[50] The undeniable fact, however, remains that the cakes did traverse the land with the rapidity of a 'fiery cross', as in the *Lady of the Lake,*[51] and the natives must surely have looked upon the movement 'as a forerunner of some universal popular outbreak.'[52]

Apart from this, prophecies were said to have been circulated all over India, stating that the British rule in the country was destined to come to a close on completing its first centenary, i.e., 23 June 1857.[53] This historic day was, therefore, reportedly fixed as the day for a simultaneous rising from the Himalayas to the Hooghly.[54] According to the scheme, it was believed, all Europeans were either to be expelled or massacred.[55] Luckily, however, for the English, so argued several of this school, the Meerut incident misfired on 10 May 1857, before the united plan was fully ready.[56] Having rebelled prematurely, the Meerut sepoys then made for Delhi, described by the *People's Paper* as the long pre-arranged centre of operations.[57] There, in combination with the already corrupted Delhi force, Bahadur Shah Zafar was installed as the king of India, it was stated, to the boom of a twenty-one gun salute on 11 May 1857. On 12 May, he reportedly seated himself upon the silver throne for the first time since 1842, received homage of the chiefs, and at once settled down to the job of transacting the affairs of the state.[58] Coins, another sign of royalty, were said to have been immediately issued in the name of the Mughal ruler, bearing a sign of victory.[59] Proclamations were issued to the people and the army, and letters were addressed to the rulers of various states demanding their loyalty and allegiance.[60] Hindus and Muslims were exhorted to get together for the expulsion of the foreign ruler.[61] The response was encouraging in every case. From that day until its fall, Delhi became the rendezvous of the rebellion. While almost all the regional rebel leaders declared themselves loyal to Delhi and its king,[62] the alienated sepoy army, regardless of the distance, invariably made for the centre of the insurrection. The report of *The Times'* correspondent stationed at Ambala is worthy of serious notice. It read:

> It is to be remarked throughout the rebellion that all the mutinous troops within several hundred miles of Delhi seem to have made for that place as the centre and nucleus of the rebellion. They have established no local posts, indulged in none of the cares of districts on their own, but have marched to the point where a common stand was to be made against the common enemy–the Feringhee. Still more strange, they have generally not divided the plundered treasure; no man has been permitted to act for himself.... They have, almost all in the regular order, marched to Delhi with the treasure, as public treasure. Indeed, the quiet, orderly and peculiar character of the sepoy has been throughout the rebellion our greatest difficulty.[63]

Having already described the city of Delhi as the pre-arranged centre of operations,[64] still later the *People's Paper* editorially called Delhi the capital 'of the patriotic power.'[65]

It seemed to the adherents of this school that the object and purpose of all these activities was rebellion. It surely was the restoration of native rule which prompted such a big conflagration. Nolan called it the 'grand motive' of the rebellion.[66] Rebel leaders, big and small, in Rohilkhand, in the North-Western Provinces, at Lucknow, at Kanpur and several other places declared themselves as Na'ibs of Delhi. A spirit of cooperation and accommodation pervaded the ranks of the two communities—the Hindu and the Muslim. Bahadur Shah, in order to infuse a spirit of unity and oneness among the two peoples, issued proclamations calling upon them to join against the foreigner, and the 'famous' Nana did not lag behind. He not only declared himself for Delhi; had the standard of the Mughal overlord unfurled at Kanpur; issued a similar proclamation, but even dated his proclamation of Kanpur according to the Muslim calendar rather than the Christian or Hindu.[67] Speaking of the unity of the people, the *Morning Herald* wrote:

> The Hindoos and Mohammedans have at last coalesced. The priests acted upon the minds both of soldiery and civilians, and the three classes animated by the fiercest hatred and foulest passions, are leagued in opposition to our rule.[68]

The *London Quarterly Review* agreed with a Hindu observer when the latter said that the 'people have joined thinking they would clear the English out of the way and have the country to themselves.'[69] This unity among the two peoples and their animosity towards the English, it seems, was not confined to the leaders alone; it was also reflected quite clearly among the masses. The proclamations of Delhi were stated to have spread at an extraordinary speed throughout the length and breadth of the country, disseminated with equal zeal by dervishes,[70] brahmans and faqirs.[71] A writer from Nimach reported that daily prayers were offered for the success of the Mughal ruler.[72] Even the adamant *Examiner* veered round to admitting the presence of a spirit of unity, though it argued that plunder was the primary motive behind it.[73]

If all this is to be accepted, it appears that the revolt was guided by the subtle machinations of the conspirators. Once the conspiracy was launched it received the support of the army and the united efforts of the two peoples.

CHAPTER 6

Unity of the Revolution Theme

Having provided themselves with a sound foundation in the socio-political and economo-religious causes of the outbreak to build up their thesis, advocates of the revolution theory found still more believable materials in the actual events of the revolt to back up their contention as to its civil and political character. In fact, every time the mail arrived from India, it further drove home their point of view. If anything could firmly support and prove their line of thought, it was the attitude of the Indian people towards (a) the outbreak, and (b) their afflicted rulers. There was an overwhelming amount of evidence which supported the holders of the civil rebellion theory.

The Press editorially pointed to the 1853 petition of 1800 Bengal Christians, which called for a parliamentary inquiry into the state of affairs in Bengal.[1] The *Quarterly Review*, on the other hand, referred to the forewarning of the Protestant missionaries of all denominations. In a petition to the parliament in December 1856, they outlined the sullen discontent which prevailed among the rural population of the Presidency. The petition emphasized that discontent and bitterness were daily on the increase and warned that relief measures 'could with safety be no longer delayed.'[2] Similarly several revenue collectors reported the same phenomenon.[3] Clearly enough, it was believed, the attitudes of the people of India had started to change much before the outbreak. What was it, it was asked, that persuaded Henry Lawrence to prepare himself for the eventuality beforehand?[4] An anonymous writer drew attention, on the authority of Macaulay, to the great decline in the prestige of an Englishman in India in the past sixty years. Six decades before the uprising an English traveller was sufficient to cause awe in the countryside. Even twenty years before though fear had given way to respect, a native would dismount his horse or vehicle, respectfully salute the English traveller, let him pass for a distance of a hundred yards, and then remount and proceed with his journey. But the situation was reported to have changed entirely on the eve of the outbreak. During the convulsion, however, the sight of a Briton was reported to have become a source of 'amusement.' He was jeered at; even children, who earlier would fly away at his approach, participated in it.[5] W.H. Russell, *The Times'* mutiny correspondent in India, complained of the same thing on the basis of his own experience.[6]

In fact, everybody was reported to be aggrieved; everyone was said to be disaffected.[7] Even those who had benefitted at the hands of the British were not loyal to them.[8] No wonder, it was argued, the revolt enjoyed near simultaneity in widespread parts of India; no wonder all those who could, actually did participate in the uprising.[9] The reports coming from all the disaffected areas were far from happy. The villagers and citizens were reported to be taking an active part everywhere. Virtually the entire regions of Bengal, Bihar, Assam, Awadh, Rohilkhand and the North-Western Provinces were either reported to be seething with a spirit of discontent and looking for an opportunity to revolt, or were actually up in arms. The major cities of Delhi, Lucknow, Allahabad, Banaras, Kanpur, Agra, Patna and many others were reported as thoroughly disaffected.[10] Delhi was described as 'one leavened mass of disaffection',[11] while the cities of Kanpur, Lucknow, Meerut and Patna were reported to be no better.[12] If 'hatred sat on the averted faces of Mohamedans' at Allahabad,[13] the Hindus of Banaras were described as praying and waiting for their chance.[14] Some wealthy merchants of Banaras and Lucknow actively plotted against the British; were found guilty of providing sepoys with monetary assistance and a dozen of them were hanged at Lucknow on 15 June 1857.[15] Nightly conferences were reportedly held in complete secrecy in mosques and private houses in the city of Patna.[16] A Muslim, who maintained a European style hotel in Kanpur cantonments, 'raised a troop of horse, and served against his old customers.'[17] The events of the outbreak, it was contended, clearly proved how little Hindus and the Muslims could be relied upon. Native Christians were thought to be the only people who could be safely trusted.[18]

That was not all; various other extreme measures had to be taken. The four districts of Meerut, Muzaffarnagar, Bulandshahr and Delhi was clamped under martial law by the lieut.-governor of Agra.[19] The city of Patna was disarmed altogether and the movement of people was severely restricted by William Taylor, the Chief Commissioner of the Patna Division.[20] Fearing the safety of his British officials, Taylor recalled all of them from district headquarters in his division.[21] In addition to these, other difficulties were also to be faced. Dr William Brock, later on the President of the Baptist Union of Great Britain and Ireland, and others emphasized the difficulties of Havelock's march from Allahabad to Kanpur and from Kanpur to Lucknow.[22] Nolan did the same thing for an earlier passage of Major Renaud along the same route.[23] In fact, both of them had to fight their way through because the whole population was described as hostile. One John Henry Temple who styled himself as a 'Plain Speaker' reported on the authority of Havelock himself that he found 'every cottage turned into a place of arms and defended by the villagers with a resolution which showed that their hearts were in the cause for which they were fighting.'[24] An 'Irishman' stressed the fact that popular participation in the slaughter of Europeans was larger than that of the soldiery.[25] In the Jubbulpore territory the old Raja Shankar of Ghonda's invocation of the goddess Kali was quoted as a clear indication of the amount of hatred and enmity he entertained towards the rulers of the country.[28]

Instances of active participation of villagers and maltreatment of their masters were also reported in plenty.[29] The British fugitives were not only deprived of their belongings, but were beaten, mocked at and even starved. Whenever they were pitied, treated gently, or provided for, it was said to be not out of love, or any sense of fidelity or duty towards them, but out of human feelings or self-interest. Again, it was, generally speaking, a kindness that was exhibited either in the darkness of the night, or in complete secrecy. True, Indians were also killed; but were they not generally, it was contended, plundered or killed for their association with the rulers, and were not the latter, at the same time, plundered with peculiar zest?[30]

In fact, there were numerous reports of people's participation and their subsequent liquidation. Villages were also burnt wholesale. Some people asked why, if the outbreak was just a mutiny, was such action considered necessary.[31] In short, the entire people were reported to be disaffected. Only individual cases of loyalty were reported—individual natives attached to individual Britons.[32] The Reverend Alexander Duff and another Englishman from Agra firmly believed that the Muslims to a man and three-fourths of the Hindus were against the British. Duff ridiculed as 'utterly erroneous and misleading' the oft repeated assertions of *The Times* and some other journals, such as: 'It is a *military* revolt and nothing more'; the 'entire non-military population, from Cape Comorin to Himalayas, have stood aloof from the movement'; 'not a man has stirred'; the 'chiefs of Upper India vie with each other in tendering to the Government their assurances of support and attachment?' as far from the truth. He went on to warn his countrymen that such statements 'by lulling the rulers and the people of Great Britain into a false security—a security as fatal as it is false'—could prove highly mischievous.[33]

Naturally, the difficulties of the rulers were great. The outbreak looked like a revolution which affected all classes. It seemed as if a powerful combination had been formed against the authority of the British. It became a war that was to be waged on many fronts. The native civil officers of long-standing had defected to the rebels.[34] The contractors of supplies and carriages backed out of their commitments. Malcolm Lewin could find only one exception in this general wave of defection in the person of Joti Prasad—'among the faithless, faithful only he.'[35] Many Britons, both government officers and civilians, complained about the desertion of their household servants.[36] Referring to the situation at Agra, Mathew A. Sherring, a missionary of the London Missionary Society, reported that all the 'heathen and Mussulman servants had fled from the fort...and the applications from the most respectable parties in the fort, the Lieutenant-Governor not excluded, for Christian servants were far more than could be procured.'[37] There were others who were indignant at the insolence and maltreatment offered by their servants, or at their betraying them.[38] New servants were not available even at double the salary.[39] Highly placed English men and women were compelled to do their own domestic work.[40] The procurement of labour for transportation purposes became equally difficult.[41] While old or regular porters would defect at the earliest opportunity, new ones were difficult to hire. Captain Oliver J. Jones faced a similar quandary; his *qulis* having bolted, new ones were forced into the job. And on their refusal to carry the goods Captain Jones stated that:

> ...I did what I dare say my philanthropists will blame me for; in fact, I took a big stick and gave the miscreants a good licking all around; after receiving which in every good part they took traps and carried them to the end of that day's journey.[42]

Such boycott by the natives had rendered the job of obtaining information an uphill task. At times troops were misled by informants into ambushes of the sepoys;[43] at times they misinformed the English of the strength of the rebels,[44] and still at others they maintained a favourable silence about the movements of rebel troops.[45] The intelligence department of the Company badly failed to secure information.[46] L.E. Ruutz Rees reported that while the enemy could obtain information about what was going on inside the Lucknow Residency, it was difficult for the English to obtain information even at a distance of 20 yards.[47] The result was, it was reported, that the companies of soldiers were often under the guns of the enemy before they could be aware of their presence. Sir Colin Campbell, the Commander-in-Chief of India, himself bitterly complained about situations of this nature.[48] Communications were also affected when post-runners and boatmen in fairly large numbers joined the rebels. The result was that different stations were almost completely cut off from each other. 'Little is known for certain of what is going on, as there is no communication with or from below,' wrote Major Hodson on 16 May 1857.[49] This became one of Hodson's standing complaints, as it was with James Outram and many others. While one of the letters of General Inglis, the Commander at Lucknow, took 35 days to reach Kanpur, twenty-two of his letters written in 45 days could fetch only one reply.[50]

Quite ingenious methods had to be adopted to send bits and pieces of information through *qasids*. In spite of all precautions, messengers, who were generally natives, were caught and killed on many occasions.[51] This and the enmity of the people also made the procurement of provisions a highly difficult task. Lieut.-Col. McIntyre bitterly complained of such a situation when he was at Alambagh. He reported that provisions could be made available only by foraging parties, or under the shelter of guns.[52] Indeed, so great was the hostility that even mammon failed to solve the difficulties. The best of Hodson's efforts to get the Jumna bridge blown up failed.[53] The *People's Paper*, emphasizing native antipathy towards the British, stressed that their lack of cooperation was obvious from their inability to help them. While British troops found bridges broken and boats missing, these mysteriously reappeared the moment native troops arrived.[54] All this was attributed to a complete collapse of civil authority, which, to function at all, was forced to shelter behind British bayonets. An Ambala officer, making a historical review of the events in India, remarked:

> Thus it was that early in June the whole of the North-West Provinces had become, we may say, completely revolutionized—the British rule was confined to a very few insulated stations held by European troops; in the country generally it had ceased to exist. Entire anarchy had taken its place.[55]

The extent of disaffection and rebellion was not confined to the Bengal Presidency and parts of the governor-general's territories alone. It was described as all-pervading. The two presidencies of Bombay and Madras, the chief commissioner's province of the Punjab and a good many other princely states were not free either.[56] The only difference was that in these territories either the two elements of disaffection and rebellion could not combine themselves or else, if they did, the combination could not assume an active form. The *People's Paper* in its editorial, the 'Revolt in Hindostan', strongly belied the assertions that Bombay and Madras were loyal. 'If the soldiers and the populations were faithful,' it forcefully argued, 'the former would assuredly be marched on Delhi, and crush the centre of insurrection. Why are they not marched thither? Either they are not faithful themselves, or else the population would rise if the soldiers were removed.'[57]

Numerous conspiracies reported in the Bombay Presidency indicated that the situation there was quite explosive.[58] Hindus and Muslims were said to be equally active in tampering with the loyalty of the army.[59] The head of the Wahabi sect at Poona,[60] and Rangu Bapuji, one time *wakil* in London of the deposed ruler of Satara, had become the leading conspirators in Western India.[61] One of the followers of the Wahabi leader, a munshi, was found guilty of active treasonable correspondence with the regiment at Kolapur; he was executed.[62] The intercepted letters, it was said, revealed the wide extent of the conspiracy and the readiness for a general uprising. The disaffection really was extensive. Nobody, it was thought, could be safely depended upon.[63] If the Chief of Nargund[64] and the Raja of Shorapur[65] taxed the resources of the state, the collusion of Chimah Sahib, the younger brother of the ruler of Kolapur and younger Raja at the same time, was also proved by the discovery of a sword sent to him by the Lucknow Darbar.[66] The forethought and the secrecy with which the conspiracy was shaped, the caution with which each group of conspirators worked apart to conceal the connecting links, the care used in entrusting just sufficient information for the purpose in view, and the fidelity with which the conspirators adhered to each other surprised and baffled Maj.-Gen. Sir G. Le G. Jacob, the Political Commissioner of the Southern Marahtah Country. So loyal were the participants that they preferred death to betrayal.[67]

How great the extent of the danger was clearly indicated by the government decision to disarm the people and by the subsequent fate suffered by a small disarming party under Lieut.-Col. George Malcolm at the hands of the inhabitants of Hulgully village. Several of the party were murdered. Referring to the incident, Sir Jacob observed:

> The affair showed the inflamable state of the people and the danger that might accrue from the Forts, when a comparatively defenceless village could thus venture to oppose a Government force, however small.[68]

The exemplary punishments, however, prevented 'further open resistance to the demand for arms.'[69] One hundred and seventy villagers were reported to have been killed.[70] The Sawunt rebels along the Goa frontier, however, remained in the field as late as November 1858, and could only be suppressed with the active cooperation of the Portuguess Government in Goa.[71] In spite of all this, the revolt could not assume as threatening proportions as the one in the Bengal Presidency. The *Quarterly Review* attributed this to the 'energy, foresight and judgment' of Lord Elphinstone, the Governor of the Presidency.[72]

In the Madras Presidency, the comparative tranquility was attributed not to any love of the government, but to the heterogeneous character of its people; the remoteness of the Presidency from the centre of the rebellion; the existence of a large native Christian population interspersed all over the Presidency; the presence of native Christians in the army, and, above all, the comparative weakness of the Hindus and the Muslims in a large but 'poverty striken and long oppressed class' of the aboriginal races.[73] Despite all this, it was reported, the government still did not feel confident of itself. It was sufficiently concerned to keep a vigilant European guard at Queen Victoria's birthday ball in the city of Madras. In addition to the above mentioned weaknesses, the major handicap to the Hindus and the Muslims, it was argued, came from the presence of the European force. But for their presence, held J.B. Norton, no European would have been left in the city of Bangalore, so hostile was the population.[74]

Though the Punjab was made the base of operations against Delhi and practically saved India for the British, still the situation there was said to be far from satisfactory. In spite of the fact that fighting potential in the province had already been crushed as a result of the two Sikh Wars; in spite of the fact that inimical elements in the province had already been wiped out of existence as a result of the vigorous measures adopted by the government consequent upon the conquest of the province, i.e., disbandment of the Sikh army, complete disarming of the population; demolition of the forts, resumption of the rent-free tenures in order to curb the power of the landlords, the establishment of strict civil and criminal courts, the conviction of over 8000 hostile elements in the province during the very first year of British administration; and, in spite of the extraordinary and harsh measures taken by the administration of Sir John Lawrence to control the province (George Crawshay, Mayor of Gateshead, compared these measures with the reign of terror in Paris during the French

Revolution), and, above all, the introduction of a large European force in the province,[75] civil discontent was still reported at Lahore, Amritsar, Sialkot, Ludhiana, Sirsa, Hansi, Hissar, Firozpur, Kangra, and Karnal. If the people of Ludhiana, it was pointed out, petitioned the restored monarch at Delhi to rescue them from the iron rule of G. Ricketts,[76] the Gujar population of Sialkot actively participated in the task of rapine and plunder.[77] A writer in *Blackwood's Edinburgh Magazine* described them as 'vultures' flocking upon their prey. The domestic servants at the station were mentioned as 'privy to the whole plot.'[78]

The districts of Hariana, Sirsa, Hansi and Hissar were also up in arms. All of them had declared loyalty to Delhi, and General Von Cortlandt was deployed for their suppression. So great was the aversion of the people of Sirsa that they were said to have gone to the extent of ravaging the Christian cemetery there.[79] Even the south-east of Punjab was not regarded as safe and restrictions were imposed upon the travels of officers down the river Sutlej.[80] The people of Panipat in Karnal were disarmed.[81] At Ferozpur the 45th Regiment was reportedly incited into action 'by the fanatic Moulvies [Mawlawis] and disaffected Bunnias [Banyas] of the Bazar [Bazar].'[82] However, the timely fall of Delhi, with which the safety and loyalty of the Punjab was closely linked, and the stern measures adopted by the vigilant administration of 'Christian militants', like John Lawrence and others, were said to have forced the disaffected elements to retreat.[83] Frederick Henry Cooper, the Deputy Commissioner of Amritsar, therefore wrote in his book:

> Thus no half measures were adopted. Moreover, the principle that he who is not for us is against us was strictly followed. There was no pause. Treason and sedition were dogged into the very privacy of the Harem [Haram] and up to the sacred sanctuaries of mosques and shrines. Learned moulvies [Mawlawis] were seized in the midst of a crowd of fanatic worshippers and men of distinction and note were wanted at dead of night. Like selugh-hounds, the district police, on the first scent of treason, and egged on by certainty of reward, fastened on the track, and left it not until the astonished intriguer was grounded in his lair.[84]

Another important reason for the easy control of the situation in the Punjab was to be found in the Sikh dislike of Hindustanis, especially sepoys[85] and Muslims.[86] They hated the former for helping the British into power in Ranjit Singh's kingdom, and with the latter they had old scores to settle.

Outside the Company's territories the contrast between native and British rule failed to charm the civil and military populations of the quasi-independent states. While several princes and their courts were loyal, or at least sympathetic, their subjects were not. This, in fact, posed a serious problem for many princes. In order to be loyal to the British they had to contend with their own people. In reality, the English name was said to have become a source of weakness for them rather than of strength. Holkar, Sindhiya, the Skinder Begum of Bhopal, the Nizam of Deccan, the Raja of Rewah, that of Jodhpur, all had to, at one time or another, face a hostile population or an insurgent army because of their sympathetic leanings towards the British.[87] They could not even guarantee protection to European fugitives. While the Europeans had to flee for their safety from the states of Holkar and Sindhiya, the Begum of Bhopal, in spite of her loyal intentions, failed to provide shelter to the Indore fugitives within her territories. Welcoming the refugees from Indore, the Begum clearly but respectfully pointed out the difficulties in which she was involved. She informed Colonel Durand that all India was turning against the British; that 'instead of being a support as hitherto,' the English 'were now a source of weakness to her; that if Colonel Durand and the British officers would retire for a time to Hashungabad, within the British territories, she might be better able to stem the torrent; but if, on the other hand, they decided upon remaining in Bhopal, so be it—their safety would be her care; her lot and their's should be one.' Colonel Durand, sensing the delicate nature of the situation, left for Hashungabad, escorted by the Begum's carefully chosen loyal troops.[88] The 'Plain Speaker', pointing to the defection of Holkar's army, asked:

> Is it possible, then, to believe that the popular feelings in the provinces from which these contingents have been drawn is not strongly averse to our rule.[89]

Hyderabad, the metropolitan city of the South Indian state of the same name, was the scene of 'a popular (not military) rising.'[90] However normalcy was soon restored by the strenuous efforts of the British Resident to the court of Hyderabad and the cooperation offered by Salar Jang, Prime Minister of the state. *The Press* and others described Salar Jang as the only hope of the British, as even the Nizam had wavered and had reclaimed the districts he had ceded to Lord Dalhousie in 1853.[91]

This, however, does not mean that all other princes were loyal to the British. Several instances of open and at times masked hostilities were reported. Apart from the rulers of Delhi and Awadh, the Rajas of Bhartpur,[92] Jaunpore,[93] Mainpuri,[94] Baudpore,[95] Jubbulpore[96] and Pachete,[97] the Nawabs of Murshidabad,[98] Jujjhur and Ballabgarh,[99] the rulers of Kulu[100]—a state in the Himalayas—and Bhitoor [sic],[101] the Ra'o of Burtorolee [sic][102] and many other minor chiefs[103] were reported to be actively hostile to the government. Some even doubted the loyalty of the Marahtah ruler of Gwalior.[104] On 4 October 1857, Hodson reported that he had defeated 'several rebel rajas', captured their strongholds, and treasure amounting to £70,000.[105] Referring to the much boasted loyalty of Hindu chiefs, a writer who described himself as a 'friend of the Muslims' taunted that Russia too enjoyed strong adherents in Poland.[106] In fact, the government was so scared that Meadows Taylor, Deputy Commissioner of the Ceded Districts in Deccan, reported that it had to compromise with Torra Borg Khan, the Rohila Zamindar, who had led the attack upon the Residency.[107]

A writer in the *Dublin University Magazine* appeared to be quite pessimistic about the whole situation in India, when he observed:

> A few of the rajas seemed disposed to remain neutral; none dared to assist us. Many of them had armed retainers to the number of thousands, and might have quenched the rebellion in their districts, had they been so minded. There is too much reason to conclude that the majority was closely mixed up with the plot.... Even the mahrajahs and shopkeepers seemed to care less for the safety of their property than the success of the revolt.[108]

In short, the whole of India was described as being against the British. Even the loyalty of the 'loyal' princes was attributed not to their love or liking for the foreign ruler, but to their strong suspicion regarding the success of the outbreak.[109] Several of them offered pseudo-loyalty and tried to keep both sides happy.[110] It was this dismal picture which compelled men of courage and perseverance—like Havelock and Hodson, to make frequent utterances of 'a nation in arms',[111] 'a continent in arms',[112] or else 'all India is up in arms against us.'[113] Quite frequently such utterances came from as widely distant places as Banaras and Mhow. If an officer from Banaras wrote that, 'the whole country has risen as one man', another from the latter place did not write differently when he said, 'the whole country has risen up against the Government.'[114]

Along with the First, Second and Third Estates, the Fourth Estate of India, the native press, was also mentioned as notoriously disaffected. It continuously discussed the propriety of various government measures, assailed them in the severest language, pointed out the grievances of the people and called upon them jealously to guard and defend their caste and religions.[115] It was believed that the native press had not only made the Hindus aware of their powers, it also made them conscious of the weaknesses of the rulers who had earlier been regarded as invincible.[116] For months before the outbreak the press preached sedition and warned the government of the writing on the wall.[117] Ironically enough, a native newspaper was said to have published in Meerut on 20 February 1857, that 'all the Mahomedans and Hindoos were agitated in mind, that the natives would not obey the Government and that the fire of mischief and the flame of disaffection would be kindled in the Western Provinces.'[118] In fact, it was the native press that was said to have taken to every home the news of: a) Dalip Singh's conversion; b) the baptism of the daughter of the Raja of Coorg,[119] and c) the parliamentary attacks on the rulers of India.[120] The *Manchester Guardian* blamed the local Indian press for making a 'disgraceful and mischievous use of the liberty it enjoyed.'[121] Referring to the small circulation and their commercial viability, the *Guardian* felt sure there were political motives behind the existence of the native press. It regarded these as instruments in the hands of the least well-disposed persons—all the more dangerous when the Company, the *Guardian* admitted in this case, had no friends, but only servants and foes in India.[122]

The power and influence of the native press, however, was duly recognized by all shades of public opinion. When dealing with it and its share in bringing about the revolt, similar feelings were expressed by everybody. Even the *Manchester Guardian,* a paper rather averse to the idea of calling the outbreak a civil revolt, described the Indian Fourth Estate as disloyal, disreputable and scurrilous, playing into the hands of either 'those who would employ it as an engine of sedition and disaffection, or of men who would simply pander to the passions and prejudices of the populace.'[123] A military officer in his letter home called it 'unrestrained and licentious.'[124] It was unanimously held responsible for a share in the outbreak; Lord Canning's Gagging Act was highly approved insofar as it covered the native press.[125] It was argued that its continued freedom might further have sapped the loyalty of the so far faithful princes upon whose support the government was then depending. The *Guardian* naturally proclaimed the Press Act as 'a measure clearly dictated by the law of self-preservation' and so needing no defence.[126]

Armed with these facts, the exponents of the revolution school of thought vigorously took issue with those who called the outbreak only a military mutiny, used and exploited by outside interests. They suggested that this was the reaction of interested parties among the British—interested in diverting the attention of the public from their own responsibility. Duff called it a feeble attempt at self-deception on the part of those officials to whom truth was unpalatable, humiliating and discreditable. They preferred to seek shelter behind 'isolated snatches of loyalty.' Moreover, he argued, it was also expediency of self-interest, promotions and efficiency mark, which dictated to them not only not to report the explosive situation but to make it a matter of policy to belittle the outbreak.[127] It was in pursuit of this deliberate policy that the leaders of the civilian service had decided to carry out at all risks, that restrictions were imposed upon the Anglo-Indian press, which alone was in a position to expose their shortcomings.[128] Duff, therefore, asserted that to call it a military mutiny 'is an egregious mistake and as mischievous as it is egregious.'[129] Lewin also seriously disputed the thesis of the opposite school and called it 'a convenient plea for those who were concerned in annexing the territories of the native princes—for others who insulted them by advertising or selling by public auction the jewels and paraphernalia of their families and for those who attempted to force the gospel on the natives of the country.'[130]

N.A. Chick ridiculed the notion that a few regiments at Meerut and Delhi could conceive the idea of overthrowing British rule and that too over the issue of cartridges.[131] *The Press* made a double charge first of self-induced blindness earlier, and of an attempt later on to blind the people.[132] Arguing it to be 'essentially a social revolt'[133] rather than a military outbreak, General Gardiner assailed advocates of the military theory as people trying to hide from themselves the reality— a reality which was the inevitable result of their long practised misrule, misgovernance and injudicious legislation.[134] To invest civil insurrection with a military character was to Gardiner poor praise for the brightest achievements of British officials and native soldiery, both of whom were already honoured with the recorded approbation of their monarchs and the British Parliament.[135] *The Nation*, on the other hand, thought that to characterize the Indian outbreak as a military mutiny was no more reasonable than calling the French Revolution, with the national guards in possession of Paris, as another military uprising.[136]

It was emphasized that the outbreak was a rebellion caused by national alarm. If it was a mere military mutiny then why were the 'natives hung by fours and fives on the trees by the roadside?'[137] Why were the rebel districts being asked to pay for their pacification?[138] Duff took the argument from the mouth of the opposing school by telling them that a mere military uprising in the midst of an unaiding and unsympathetic public could have been crushed after a 'few decisive victories, such as we have already had.'[139] The outspoken Irish nationalist paper, *The Nation*, added that in such a case 30,000 British soldiers should have been sufficient to make short work of the mutineers.[140] On the contrary, Duff pointed out, as several others did, that the enemy appeared time and again in spite of repeated crushing defeats, and its loss of guns. 'No sooner', he argued, 'is one city taken or another relieved, than some other one is threatened. No sooner is one district pronounced safe through the influx of British troops, than another is disturbed and convulsed. No sooner is a highway re-opened between places of importance, than it is closed again and all communications, for a season, cut off.'[141]

If *The Press* complained of the inexhaustible number of rebels,[142] the *Quarterly Review*, reporting that the whole of North-Western Provinces and Central India were against the British to a man, observed:

> ...like a field of corn stricken by the wind, the population bends as we pass but to rise again.[143]

It is no wonder that the *People's Paper* emphatically described the outbreak as an 'itinerant insurrection–a walking revolt–a moving mutiny–a travelling war.' Referring to the fortunes of the insurgents, the paper remarked:

> ...conquer them [insurgents] at Delhi, they go to Lucknow; conquer them at Lucknow, they go to Bareilly...they carry the war to new scenes, without abandoning the old, and while you [the British] think you have got the hydra in your grasp, lo! it divides its body, the one half still confronts you–the other glides off to a fresh arena, and there grows–grows larger than the entire form was before....[144]

It was pointed out that sepoys were the most favoured of all classes, with all facilities available, and with secure prospects for the future.[145] They were described as the only part of the Indian society which was loyal previous to the outbreak, while everybody else detested the British.[146] In spite of the fact that Hindu and Muslim tamperers of the army loyalty, described by Capt. G. Hutchinson, Military Secretary to the chief commissioner of Awadh, as hissing serpents, jumped into the field early in 1857, the army remained steadfastly loyal throughout the months of March and April. Apart from loyalty, the native soldiers and officers even went to the extent of aiding the government in the arrest of offenders. Soon, however, the tide had turned; the cartridge incident was profitably employed to sap their allegiance to the government. Even the most loyal could not escape falling prey to the tactics of the plotters. Hutchinson reported an instance in which a native officer who had received 'a handsome present for conspicuous loyalty, was hanged for as conspicuous mutiny six weeks afterwards.'[147] Further still, it was reported that the troops on escort duty were scattered all over the country and 'were in hourly intercourse with the priesthood at the villages,' and that the priests never lost any opportunity of 'sowing the seeds of disloyalty among them.'[148] Under these circumstances it is not surprising if Gardiner attempted to dispel all wishful thinking regarding the loyalty of the native subjects by quoting from Adam Smith's *Wealth of Nations* and from Lord Metcalfe. He quoted the latter as having written in 1814:

> Whatever delusions may prevail in England respecting the security to be derived from the affections of our Indian subjects...it will probably be admitted in India that our power depends solely upon our military superiority.[149]

This school unhesitatingly confessed the fact that British rule was not acceptable to the people at all and that they were happier under native rulers.[150] Russell, after having visited Patiala, contended that had that state been annexed as it could have been on one pretext or another, the British would have experienced a rising in that state as well. There too the natives would have risen to restore their deposed prince to his full rights and powers as they had done, he stressed, in all those states annexed by the British government.[151] He perhaps exaggerated the state of affairs in India when he said that even the cattle seemed to hate the English.[152] J.B. Norton, quoting the last stirring exhortation of a Satara rebel to his compatriots, pointed to the diametrically opposite reactions shown by the British and the natives. To the former he was just a traitor, to the latter a hero and a martyr.[153] Lewin ridiculed as nonsense the notion that India was tranquil before the outbreak. He sarcastically noted that the same was also boasted about a day before the disastrous retreat from Kabul.[154] At best, it was asserted, the British rule in India was no better than that of Napoleon's in Spain.[155] In an attempt to convince the people of Britain of the true nature of the rising, Duff went on to quote a thirty-year old statement of Sir John Malcolm.[156] The latter had stated:

> My attention has been, during the last five-and-twenty years, particularly directed to this dangerous species of secret war carried on against our authority, which is

always carried on by numerous though unseen hands. The spirit is kept up by letters, by exaggerated reports, and by pretended prophecies. When the time appears favourable, from the occurrence of misfortune to our arms, or from mutiny in our troops, circular letters and proclamations are dispersed over the country with a celerity that is incredible. Such documents are read with avidity. The English are depicted as usurpers of low caste, and as tyrants, who have sought India only to degrade them, or to rob them of their wealth, and subvert their usages and religion. The native soldiers are always appealed to, and the advice to them is, in all instances, I have met with, the same–'Your European tyrants are few in number– murder them!'[157]

The fact of the matter was, asserted Lewin, that whenever an opportunity presented itself for striking a blow against the rulers, Indians never missed it. He could not find any period of five years during which they had not attempted an uprising.[158]

To bear misrule silently, it was argued, was a special trait of the natives of India. They would certainly not expose themselves to bolder risks when helpless to act and would rather prefer to ponder over their lot and wait for the opportune moment. If there was one thing over which they were united, it was in their hatred of the English rule, 'which was never more deeply felt and never more openly expressed.'[159] The universal cry, it was reported, was for the destruction of everything English, including the British themselves—the idea being completely to obliterate the past.[160]

The Athenaeum, holding that a revolt was long brewing in India, and that the English were sitting upon a powder keg, came up with a review of the verses of a nephew of George Canning. A score of years before the outbreak, the composer, summing up his experiences at Delhi, Bareilly and Kanpur prophesied a vengeful revolt in India:

> There needs but some surpassing act of wrong
> To break the patience that has bent so long;
> There needs but some short sudden burst of ire
> May chance to get the general thought on fire;
> There needs but some fair prospect of relief
> Enough to seize the general belief,
> *Some holy juggle, some absurd caprice*
> To raise one common struggle of release.

Again:

> Think not that prodigies must rule a state,
> That great revulsions spring from something great;
> Out breaks at once the far resounding cry,

The standard of revolt is raised on high,
The murky cloud has glided from the sun,
The tale of English tyranny is done,
And torturing vengeance grinds as she destroys,
Till Sicil's vespers seem the game of boys.[161]

In short, it was the universal dislike of the English, combined with political discontent, which, many thought, had led to the projected rebellion.

The proponents of the civil rebellion point of view drew further support from the special nature of the sepoy army. Lewin called it 'unsafe' and 'absurd' to think of the sepoys differently from other people of India.[162] They were in fact one of the people before enlisting in the army. They became their representative after joining the ranks, and ultimately went back to them after retirement. Perhaps they were to be thought of as with the people, of the people and by the people.[163] The army was described as the 'Magna Carta', 'the Constitution', and 'the Bill of Rights' of the people of India.[164] The grievances of the people were the grievances of the army and *vice versa*. Both belonged to the same organism; injury to one limb pained the whole. With this thought in mind, Lewin asserted that the 'soldiers and citizens of India have all things in common, and the wrongs done to one will be avenged by the other.'[165]

The *Quarterly Review*, admitting the laxity of discipline in the ranks of the army and its faulty distribution, pinpointed the same fact:

> But the real causes of the rebellion must be sought for elsewhere. The sepoy army was a part of the people, its grievances were those of the population from which it had been drawn, and with which it still maintained the most intimate social ties.[166]

'Well paid and well cared' for, the nature of the native army's grievances was described as national and religious rather than military. Actually the sepoys, it was pointed out, never did put forward any military grievance. Intercepted letters bespoke the kindness of officers, but emphasized the wounds of their country and their religions.[167] The fact was that they could not reconcile their love of India with their military allegiance. The latter was stated to be like 'feathers' when put in balance against the former. Again, the sepoy army was the only educated, well-knit and well-equipped body which could help the people to strike effectively for deliverance.[168]

The people of India, it was claimed, knew this very well. That was why the army was always appealed to over a period of decades. Of late the appeals had changed into biting taunts and sarcasms. Capt. Thomas Evans Bell of the 2nd Madras European Light Infantry wrote to inform that for the last fifteen years the sepoys had been hearing 'loud execrations in every place of public resort against the grasping and greedy policy of their foreign rulers.' They were sneered at and held responsible for the ruin of the motherland. It was pointed out to them that their bayonets had enabled a group of merchants to efface the name of the 'most illustrious native monarchies' and 'extinguish the last remains of the Indian glory.' The sepoys were told that at that pace in a short time no Indian prince would be left to be 'deposed and plundered', and that the British government would then either discharge them or send them on extra-territorial service to 'conquer the countries of Burmah, Persia, Arabia and Russia'. After all this they were painfully reminded of the absence of any reward for their numerous services. Not even one of them had attained any 'exalted rank, wealth or dignity'. No doubt they were paid regularly; no doubt some of them might rise by seniority to the rank of a jama'dar or subahdar, then what! None of them, they were further told to their anguish, could ever hope to obtain even one quarter of the pay of a freshly arrived ensign from England, or for that matter rise to the rank and authority of the youngest ensign.[169]

In this way the sepoys were made increasingly aware of national neglects in the past. They were informed of their duties and obligations to the motherland and, above all, shown the possible way for atonement. They were alternately flattered and reproached. Naturally when the higher call came, their 'uninformed patriotism' was reported to have ranged itself against the British.[170] The sepoys arose to redress the national afflictions and became the first exponent of the people's grievances.[171] *The Tablet* seems to have been carried away by its pro-Irish sentiments, when it observed:

> The sepoys after a hundred years of submission, have begun to retaliate upon us the wrongs which their countrymen suffered. They can tell stories of torture, of fraud, of violence and of rapine. Their grandfathers suffered what we are suffering now. The wheel has turned now and the conqueror submits to the law of the conquered. The tortured Indian tortures in turn and the robbers are robbed.[172]

In this way the native soldiery shook their allegiance to the English; 'declared for the legitimate king of Delhi'— the 'national sovereign' of the country, and as a 'national army' revolted at the head of the people.[173]

Sir De Lacy Evans, MP, strongly endorsed the opinion of an Englishman in India, who described the sepoy participation in the revolt as 'one side of a great national insurrection'—an insurrection for freedom.[174] The Indian people, however, played their role by actively supplying the national army, by enlisting themselves in it, keeping open its lines of communications and cutting off those of the 'enemy'.[175]

Sure in their convictions, the advocates of the present theme severely criticized their opponents for not comprehending the outbreak in its proper perspective and blamed them for playing down the Indian news. They censured the government and what *The Press* called 'the ministerial journals' for underestimating the situation in India, for confiding high hopes in the fall of Delhi as well as for deriving false satisfaction from the belief that the worst was over.[176] They contended that neither the fall of Delhi nor that of Lucknow was going to end the rebellion so easily. It might have been true, they emphasized, had the rebellion been just military. 'Since it neither was nor is confined to the sepoys' ranks,'[177] the fall of Delhi, on the contrary, would signal only the start of the real struggle.[178] The *People's Paper*, earlier having cautioned its readers against the one-sided character of the news coming from the government,[179] convincingly prophesied as late as October 1858, six months after the fall even of Lucknow, that the enemy would still fight 'from town to town–village to village, city to city and hill to hill', and so drain the British resources.[180] Comparing Lucknow with Prague and Moscow, *The Nation* contended that the fall of 'Indian Prague' was just as profitable 'as Moscow was to the Great Napoleon.'[181] Gladstone though a Liberal voiced similar feelings when he admitted before the Government of India Committee in June 1858:

> We are landed again in the hot season, and, I apprehend, the most sanguine man among us does not believe it possible that a war which, unfortunately, has assumed so much more formidable character since we were accustomed to regard it as a mere military mutiny, can be terminated during the present Session of the Parliament.[182]

A general amnesty was eventually suggested as one of the possible ways to end the struggle. John Bright and others took issue with those who favoured amnesty to all those who had done nothing, for, it was strongly argued, there was no such person.[183]

1. Bahadur Shah Zafar, 24 October 1774 – 7 November 1862, the octogenarian King of Delhi in his royal regalia.

2. Zeenat Mahal, wife of Bahadur Shah Zafar, d. 1886.

3. The King's Palace at Delhi

4. View of Delhi from the Palace Gate

5. Repulse of a Sortie from Delhi

6. Penetrating Delhi's defences: Blowing up the Cashmere (sic) Gate

7. British re-entry into Delhi: Assault on Delhi—Capture of Cashmere (sic) Gate

8. Contingent Force of Sikh Irregular Cavalry (See appendix 2 for detailed comments)

9. Blowing Mutinous Sepoys from the Guns (See appendix 3 for detailed comments)

10. Capture of the King of Delhi by Captain Hodson

جنگ آزادی کے مجاہد اعظم
بہادر شاہ ظفر خلد آشیاں

11. Bahadur Shah Zafar's permanent abode, Rangoon, Burma (Myanmar)
The Plaque on the grave reads: 'Great warrior of the War of Independence'.
(See appendix 4 for detailed comments)

کتنا ہے بدنصیب ظفر دفن کے لیے   دو گز زمین بھی نہ ملی کوئے یار میں

How more unfortunate could Zafar be that he was not even allowed a haggardly
burial spot in his beloved homeland.

12. The Palace at Agra

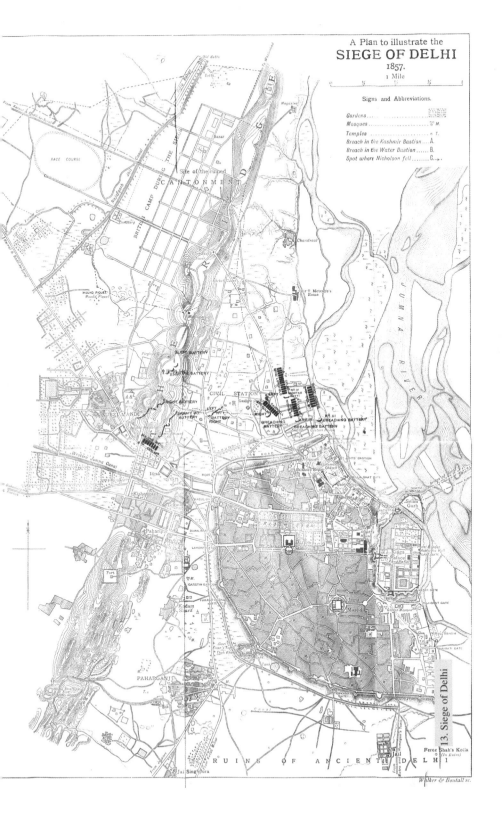

A Plan to illustrate the
SIEGE OF DELHI
1857.
1 Mile

Signs and Abbreviations.

Gardens............................
Mosques........................ᵒ M.
Temples .... ᵒ T.
Breach in the Kashmir Bastion.... A.
Breach in the Water Bastion...... B.
Spot where Nicholson fell .... C.

RACE COURSE

Walker & Boutall sc.

13. Siege of Delhi

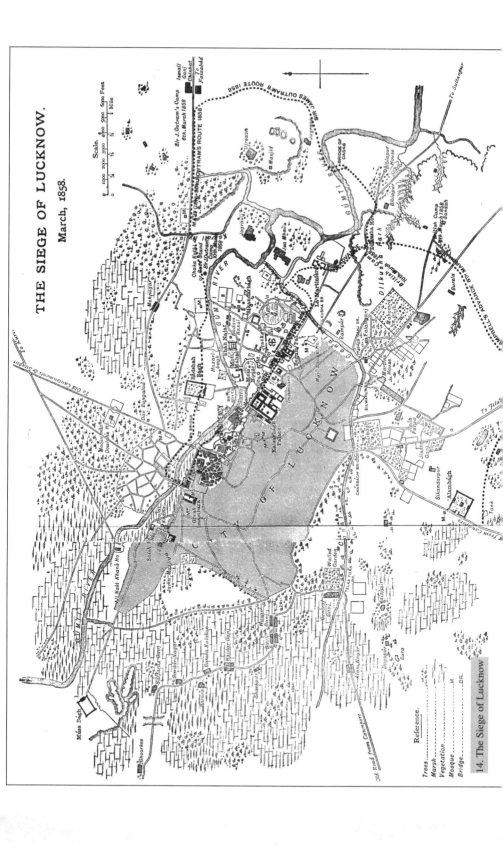

THE SIEGE OF LUCKNOW.

March, 1858.

14. The Siege of Lucknow

Reference.

Trees............................
Marsh............................
Vegetation..................M.
Mosque..........................M.
Bridge........................BR.

Scale.

0 1000 2000 3000 4500 5500 6500 Feet
                                    1 Mile

So sure was Ernest Jones about the nature of the revolt that he and his newspaper termed it as one of the noblest movements, in which the people were fighting for a very sacred cause—just, holy and glorious, as genuine as that of the Poles, the Hungarians, or the Italians. He not only prayed for the success of the rebels and at times expressed satisfaction and joy over it, but he also invoked the sympathies of the people of Britain for India and unhesitatingly told them that their blood was shed in a bad cause. Appealing to the democratic sense of his countrymen, Jones attempted to bring home to them the idea that the cause of the Indians was theirs and the success of the Indians was, indirectly, theirs as well.[184] The Irish nationalists went even a step further; not feeling satisfied with verbal sympathy, they called upon the Irish youth not to enlist themselves for an unjust cause.[185]

From the above discussion, if anything is evident in the present school of thought it is the increasing strength it gained as a result of the different arguments and different points of view put forward by its diverse components. In the case of the military mutiny school of thought, each additional argument detracted from or weakened the main theme. It was, however, different with the revolution school. Here every new reason either ratified or added to and so strongly built up the main thesis. Whatever doubts the British public may have had about the national revolutionary character of the revolt, the frequent appeals for national unity to meet the challenge to British prestige make it evident that the outbreak constituted a national crisis for Great Britain.[186] In a sense Palmerston's government itself gave tacit recognition to the national revolutionary character of the mutiny. By appointing Wednesday, 7 October 1857, a working day, as a 'Day of National Humiliation, Fasting and Prayer', it acted contrary to its own convictions, and successfully endorsed the broad impression that the outbreak in India was certainly more than a mere military uprising. The lingering doubts in the minds of Britons in this regard, however, were further removed by the Queen's Indian Proclamation, issued by the Derby-Disraeli government. The Proclamation had 'frankly and manfully' admitted that ambitious men had led their countrymen into 'open rebellion'; and that the Queen's power 'has been shown by the suppression of that rebellion'.[187]

CHAPTER 7

Muslim Conspiracy

The beginnings of Muslim rule in India coincided with their overrunning of Spain in AD 711. With the start made by the Arabs the thread, only much later on, was picked up by Mahmud of Ghazna and Muhammad Ghuri. Qutbu-d-Din Aybak, with his capital at Delhi, laid the foundation of Muslim rule in India in 1206. They came as invaders; they conquered and settled down in India. Thenceforward India became their home. Various dynasties rose and fell, but the Muslims continued to hold sway over most of the subcontinent. Centuries of uninterrupted rule gave them a strong vested interest in India. They were rulers, courtiers, nobility, civil servants and the military aristocracy—the 'thanes' of the Muslim monarchs. Even though Muslim rule in India was quite tolerant and Hindus achieved high positions in the state; there were inter-faith marriages at the highest level; Akbar established the first royal inter-faith temple in the world at Fatehpur where inter-faith dialogue among major religions became the hallmark of his administration, the fact remains Muslims enjoyed all the advantages which could, generally speaking, fall to the share of a ruling community.

The arrival of the English and subsequent establishment of the British empire in India changed the whole situation, especially for the Muslims. The Muslims of the Indo-Pakistani subcontinent were, in fact, placed in an unusual position. Earlier they had dispossessed the natives of India, the Hindus, of their inheritance and the fruits of power. As a result the Hindus disliked Muslims, and the latter distrusted the former. The tensions arising from this situation were compounded by their religious differences; Islam and Hinduism as religious and social systems had virtually nothing in common. Centuries of living together and the strenuous efforts of those Hindu and Muslim preachers who were able to rise above individual affectation and communal strife, and who tried to bring about more harmonious relations between the two communities, had considerably softened their acute differences without removing the basic causes so that the underlying suspicion and hatred was still prone to flaring up.

It was in this situation that the English put aside the ledger and unsheathed the sword. Now it was the turn of the Muslims to be dispossessed, disliked and distrusted. They had an anomalous position—disliked by an overwhelming majority of the Indian population, the Hindus, and distrusted by the new masters of the land. Now the gain of the English was to be the loss of the Muslims. All that the latter had acquired over a period of eleven centuries was at stake. Naturally, there would be a very strong reaction among them at the establishment of British rule in India. Such at least appears to have been the British experience and hence it coloured their interpretation of events. The Christian-Muslim clash through the ages, especially the Crusades, so-called 'scholarly' European writings on Islam and Muslims, European aversion to Islam, in general, and British hostility towards Muslims and their faith, in particular, were a dangerous mix, which inevitably effected the British view of the events in the South Asian colony. No wonder then that in every uprising, in every serious movement, the British suspected active Muslim involvement.

In these circumstances, when the mutiny broke out in India, the Christian missionaries—virtually one and all—several of the Company's civil and military servants, and an overwhelming number of the British population in India lost no time in declaring the outbreak to be a war between the Cross and the Crescent in India.[1] Many of these guides of public opinion claimed to speak on the basis of their personal experiences; many echoed the experiences of others and many more dwelt on hearsay. Of all these, the missionaries, however, were the most agitated and vocal in this regard. It seemed as if they were possessed with only one thought: 'Islam', 'Muhammadanism' or the 'Mussulman'. Naturally they headed the above school of thought; laymen joined them in large numbers but with still stronger reactions.

The Rev. W. Carey, a Baptist missionary, with several decades of experience in India, hurriedly edited a book in India, its *The Mahomedan Rebellion; its Premonitory Symptoms, the Outbreak and Suppression,* in the very first year of the mutiny. Without a doubt the book was inspired by Carey's deep conviction. He was so sure of his thesis that his opinion never wavered. In his subsequent work, *The Good Old Days of the Honourable John Company,* published twenty-five years later, he again styled it as the 'Mahomedan Rebellion of 1857.'[2]

Almost every letter from the missionaries which touched the nature of the revolt had something to say on Muslim hostility. This hostility became more obviously true in the eyes of the British public when around half a dozen incidents of Muslim bigotry were published by most of the newspapers, periodicals, books and pamphlets. As the reaction went on mounting, an overwhelming section of the public in Britain felt convinced that it was a Muslim affair, and that all other causes were of secondary importance. In their view the Muslims because of their religious hostility to Christianity should logically wish to re-establish their own House upon the throne of India.[3] On this assumption many opinion-makers in Britain built their theory of Muslim conspiracy.

It was a first proposition that Islam was ambitious and bloodthirsty in its very nature and bore active and unmitigated religio-political hostility towards Christianity.[4] Every Muslim, it was boldly asserted, was sure to be an enemy of the professors of Christianity, however much he might pretend otherwise. The antagonism was believed to be so ingrained that no amount of affection, kindness or benefit could change it. This, combined with the Muslim past in India, it was argued, produced a dangerous situation.[5] Here it is interesting to note what a writer in *Blackwood's Edinburgh Magazine* had to say around ten months before the outbreak of the mutiny. Referring to the descendants of Muslim conquerors, he quoted from the 'First Punjab Report'. The quote read:

> They look upon the empire as their heritage, and consider themselves as foreigners settled in the land for the purpose of ruling it. They hate every dynasty except their own, and regard the British as the worst because they are the most powerful of all usurpers.[6]

Many made references to Muslim religious bigotry and fanaticism— what they called the animosity of Islam towards Christianity.[7] One of the papers on India, published by the Church Missionary Society, argued that the Muslims had chafed 'under the British dynasty, not only on mere religious grounds, but also as conquered conquerors, whose rule has been immediately suppressed by Nazarenes from the west.'[8] A writer in the *Quarterly Review* pointed out that no 'Moslem people, before our conquest of India, were ever long subject to the Christian yoke, while their whole history is full of their triumphs over the sons of Nazareth.'[9] This, it was argued, gave the Muslims a feeling of pride and this was especially true of the Muslims of India. The Indian Muslim had long ruled over the subcontinent. He could never be expected to accept the yoke of an alien people. His Indian past and its glories were too recent, and the glimmers of it were still living. The memory of his past dominion, it was asserted, had acquired a permanent abode in his breast.[10] The belief was that at heart the Muslims had always looked to the King of Delhi as their real sovereign.[11] This was regarded as a dangerous phenomena because it added religious hatred to resentment of past defeat.[12] In fact, British power was considered to act as an open wound to the Muslims, a constant reminder to them of their vanished glory, and the result was a sullen animosity towards the British. This was even more so since the Muslims were a warrior 'race' and a people who, it was argued, could intrigue as well.[13] The 'Resident in the North-Western Provinces of India' held that the Muslim 'hostility to the conquerors of India is deadly. It is a fire always burning. Proud, vengeful, and fanatical, they look upon the British as a lawful prey, to be slaughtered and exterminated by every means that cunning and cruelty could devise.'[14] The Muslims would clench their fists but feel helpless. The British might made them realize their impotence. The editor of the *Delhi Gazette* wrote in his 'Indian Mutiny to the Fall of Delhi':

> Instead of being the dominant race, the friends and kinsmen of the mighty emperors of Hindustan, they found themselves reduced to the miserable alternative of engaging in trade and agriculture, or accepting subordinate situations in our law courts.... The unwonted humiliation rankled sorely in their hearts, but they felt their impotence and were constrained to abide their time.[15]

Even the *Manchester Guardian*, a newspaper most insistent upon calling the outbreak a sepoy mutiny, editorially remarked:

> [That] the Mohammedans should be ill disposed is natural enough. When the English first landed in India, they were the rulers of the country; they have been dispossessed, and they have not yet forgotten or forgiven.[16]

The Rev. Alexander Duff and several others expressed similar views. The author of 'The Revolt of the Bengal Army' expressed strong opinions on the subject, which were put forward as either his personal observations, or those of a friend. Holding that it was the fierce hand of Islam that worked behind the outbreak, he gave instances of Muslim malevolence and bigotry. He pointed out that at the time of the Kabul disaster many officers had the opportunity of discovering this truth. One of General Nott's staff, on his return from Kabul, continued to wear his Afghan dress as he passed through the North-Western Provinces. His knowledge of the native languages and customs enabled him to pass through Delhi and its neighbouring districts without causing any suspicion. As he visited 'the chief places of resort, the mosques' and other spots of travellers' interest, everywhere he 'heard the same avowal of rancorous hate from the lips of Mussulmans.' Around the same period the author himself had a similar experience near the British Indian capital of Calcutta, when he attended a large gathering of 2000 high-class Muslims. As the European visitor passed unnoticed in the guise of a Mughal, he had the opportunity of hearing from all sides the eager and oft-repeated hope that the star of the *Farangi* had set. In that 'secure assemblage of the faithful', all native officers of the government had taken off the smiling mask and come out in their true colours—each having a 'scowl of hatred and defiance' for the British. The author complained that they did not even remember the salt they were eating. It appeared as if it had completely lost its savour. He went on to observe:

> This being the leaven which leavens the whole mass of Muhammadan population in India, it cannot be a matter of surprise that at the great cities, Delhi, Meerut, Agra, Cawnpore, Benares, and Lucknow, there has been a decided movement against us.... At Hyderabad, in the Dekhan, the stronghold of Muhammadism in the south of India, there has been a violent outburst, quenched only in blood and quenched but for a time. 'Tell us', cried an impatient listener to the Friday sermon at the capital of the Nizam, 'tell us how we may slaughter the infidel Feringis. This is the only thing to preach about and all we care to listen to.'[17]

The loss of political power meant serious economic setback for the Muslims. Day by day the Europeans were stepping into their shoes in the field of higher civil and military services and other allied opportunities. Only subordinate ranks were left open to the Muslims or else they were compelled to take to 'the miserable alternative of engaging in trade and agriculture.'[18] As such they could not stand the sight of alien masters holding positions which they had once enjoyed and administering territories which they had earlier administered. Even in the subordinate ranks, it was contended, Muslims of 'High birth and illustrious antecedents were compelled to jostle with reprobates and outcasts.' Every new annexation meant an additional loss, and the already 'narrow field of employment was still further contracted.'[19] Advancement was denied to the Muslims, and aspiration was daily becoming more and more impossible for the 'once dominant race.' As the desire for money and social status are the roots of all evils, so this ever increasing deprivation of socio-economic opportunities was sure to make for irritable and disgruntled elements in the Muslim population—ever brooding upon their losses. A writer in the *Edinburgh*

Review contended that it 'was a necessity that the descendants of Mahomedan conquerors of India should hate us, and that mingled with this hatred there should be an undying hope of recovering the supremacy they had lost.'[20] Such a state of affairs was bound to reverberate; a calamity, contended the same writer, was long predicted by the more intelligent and keen sighted of the Company's civil servants in India.

For these reasons Muslim submission to British rule was regarded as a purely perfunctory one. It was pointed out that the submission of the Hindus was sincere but that of the Muslims was not. The latter tendered fealty because there was no other way out. And when they yielded, they did so 'with a painful recollection of their fallen greatness and with the hope of the restoration of their power.'[21] Many of the Muslims, it was believed, had to pacify their conscience for serving the English. In so doing they either transferred the 'reproach to destiny' or repeated the old maxim '*Jeska deg uska tegh*,' meaning 'Whose the purse, his the sword.'[22] Even this, thought the *Manchester Guardian*, they did with curses on their lips and vengeance in their hearts.[23] Thus it was firmly believed on the basis of experience that Muslim political as well as religious spirit had survived in India 'in all its active and unmitigated hostility to Christianity.'[24] In such circumstances the question arises, why did the Muslims not make an earlier attempt, a wholehearted one, at the overthrow of the British? The answer appears to be quite simple; earlier the situation was not as bad as after 1856. Formerly the titular sovereignty of Delhi was still intact and the house of Awadh was still in power. This was no small consolation. The Muslims had something to call their own; something to stand upon. It was better than nothing. They were, however, reported to be passing time in the hope of a better future.

The enmity of the Muslims toward the British was not political alone. Added to their loss of power was their reported aversion to Christianity, and their hatred of the *Farangi*.[25] Such an opinion was shared by a very large portion of the present school, chiefly the missionaries and the clergymen. The Rev. Edward Storrow, of the London Missionary Society, contended that 'Christianity has no foe in India, so fierce, unyielding and formidable as Mohamedanism.'[26] It was reported that all Europeans were regarded as 'infidels and unclean' by the Muslims in India. One major reason for the Muslim intolerance of Christianity was said to be the success of Christians in depriving the followers of Islam of their centuries of supremacy in India. A Muslim, it was believed, could never be satisfied with any government other than that of Islam.[27] In spite of the fact that Islam, doctrinally speaking, was nearer to Christianity than the idolatrous religions of India, still, it was argued, its followers hated Christianity most. While their attitude towards Hinduism was reported to be that of 'dislike and contempt', their feelings towards Christianity were said to be those of 'unmixed hate and fear.'[28] Henry Mead in his *Sepoy Revolt* argued:

> The bitter hatred with which Orangemen and Roman Catholics used to regard each other in Ireland had its intensified type in the feeling entertained towards us by the whole Mussulman race. Fierce antipathy to our creed, intense loathing of our persons, and never-ceasing dread of English valour and ability, make up the impression which is stamped on the minds of their children in early infancy, and deepens with every year of growth.[29]

In fact, the Muslim, it was thought, dreaded the spread of the Christian truth and so employed all possible means to check it.[30]

In the opinion of this writer, behaviour and attitude are always the best indicators of a people's disposition and temperament. At least the outward show of fidelity, attachment, fear, respect, or regard could only be lacking when the inner fountain was either wholly non-existent or dried up. If contemporary British writers are to be credited, the apparent behaviour and attitude of the majority of Muslims in the pre-mutiny period toward their foreign rulers left no doubt about their true feelings. It was certainly not favourable to the new governors of the subcontinent, who were Christians at the same time. Virtually the entire stream of Muslim thought flowed against the British.

Starting with education, a powerful base for profitable employment as well for human progress, the Muslims of the mainland of South Asia almost completely boycotted the educational system introduced by their new rulers. They knew the consequences of not sending their children to the schools established by the British. Although threat of economic impairment, loss of influence in government circles combined with loss of social status stared them in the face; although the risk of Hindu advancement at their expense was present as a very real incentive, still the Muslims would not, or could not, reconcile themselves to the idea of placing their children in schools run by their rulers—schools run by both missionary and government. If the Bible was taught at the missionary schools, what about the English language? It was taught at both agencies of education.[31] As both the study of English literature and philosophy formed the main items in the curriculum, the Muslim fear and aversion to these was as strong.[32]

This could not have been shown more clearly than from the attitude adopted by the Muslims towards schools run by government in general and missionaries in particular. The number of Muslim children attending these schools was very small. The Rev. M.A. Sherring, referring to the Kanpur School, points out in his *Indian Church and the Great Rebellion*:

> Those who attended were chiefly Hindoos of the surrounding villages, with a sprinkling of Christian boys resident on the premises. The number of names on the rolls seldom fell under a hundred. Parents and children all seemed eager to avail themselves of the opportunities of improvement afforded them. The Bible was a constant class-book, and Christian works were freely used; yet there was no murmuring, no apprehension, apparently, on the part of the heathen. Mohammedans, it is true, were scarcely seen in school; and no wonder, when one considers the bitter contempt for Christianity which Mohammed's... religion instils into its votaries.[33]

So great seems to have been the Muslim dread or hatred of missionary teachers that even native initiatives failed to produce any results. For example, the Raja of Mysore established an English school in 1840. Since he employed a missionary teacher, and allowed the teaching of the Bible, that was sufficient to hold Muslim children back from the school. Of a total of ninety-four students, there were sixty-nine Hindus, and three Muslims. They too acquiesced in the reading of the Bible after some initial difficulty.[34] This was perhaps quite generous in the circumstances, for parents were reluctant to send their children even to a class instructed by a Muslim teacher where he was either in touch with or receiving aid (books in this case) from Christian missionaries.[35]

In fact, every government effort to gain support among the younger generation was described as having failed badly insofar as the Muslims were concerned. *Chambers's Journal*, referring to the new class of Indian students and teachers, educated in the Western style in the English schools and colleges, thus bitterly commented:

> Not one Mussulman, not a single follower of the Prophet of Mecca is to be found in their ranks. Those stiff-necked, stubborn disciples of the Koran remain as they were a thousand years ago, and as they will be found a thousand years hence. They never change or progress; they are neither softened nor civilised; they have still the same undying hate for every 'dog of a Christian', for every unbelieving Feringhee, as of old....[36]

The result was not much different from what could be expected in such circumstances. The Hindus, though described as inferior to Muslims in 'point of energy and intelligence', showed greater desire for receiving English education and conveniently stole a march upon their former rulers. Muslim pride in their past; their inability to reconcile themselves to British rule; their aversion to Christianity; their strong attachment to their literature; and, above all, their national prejudices, were the reasons that kept them at a distance from the new system of education.[37] No wonder, as a community, they were losers, economically and socially. The 'Resident of the North Western Provinces' observed:

> For a long time a remarkable change has been going on in the courts of law and Government offices throughout India, whereby the Mussulmans have to a very considerable extent been supplanted by Hindus. Formerly the great majority of the employees were Mussulmans. Now the Hindus outnumber them in the ratio of three to one. This startling difference has arisen mainly through the pride of the Mussulmans, who have refused to give proper education to their children in those subjects which would eventually qualify them for Government situations.[38]

Muslim sensitivity about Christian missionary activity was quite in keeping with their misgivings regarding English education. It was known that the missionaries could seldom make any headway in the Muslim districts.[39] The Rev. John Mackay in his letters home invariably admitted frankly the difficulty of approaching the followers of Islam for their conversion to Christianity. Always admitting the superiority of their race, intelligence, valour and civilization, but blaming them for their bigotry, the Baptist missionary confessed to the dilemma posed by the Muslims. As compared with the Hindus, the intelligent among the Muslims were reported to be well acquainted with the rudiments of Christian doctrine. Though not very familiar with the general contents of the Christian Scriptures, they were described as especially well versed 'with most of those difficult passages' which referred to the Trinity. Muslim knowledge of the arguments used by the Unitarians in England, and their critical faculty often led them to challenge the arguments used by the missionaries. Even attempts to avoid getting involved in discussion on complex subjects like the Trinity were not always successful.[40] The Muslim mind was said to be obsessed with the force of the idea of 'Divine unity', and firmly believed that the Christian doctrine of the Trinity was inconsistent with it.[41] The skilful among them would often use their 'Socratical mode of disputation', and lead the missionary 'into a subtle and profitless discussion', even before the latter could be aware of the inner meaning of the trend of argument.[42] To make the argument comprehensible, Mackay reported one of his personal experiences. He observed:

> Take a single example. Some time ago a Mohammedan came to me, and in a very simple manner put the question, Does God know all things? Of course I was bound to answer, Yes. And is Jesus Christ God? Yes, I again replied. Then Jesus Christ must know all things? As I did not know what the man was driving at, I again answered, with some hesitation, Yes. Upon which, with an air of triumph, he quoted Mark XIII, 32, 'But of that day and that hour knoweth no man, no, not the angels which are in heaven, neither the Son, but the Father.'[43]

The followers of Islam were invariably described as bigots. Instances of obstructive activity by Muslims against English evangelical activity were also given.[44] It was further thought that the Muslim hatred of Englishmen had driven them to exclusiveness.[45] 'Like a relentless and stubborn foe he shuts himself up in the fortress of his faith, refuses every overture and stands ready to repel every advance.'[46] The result was evident: missionary work became an uphill task. The Muslim 'moulvies [Mawlawis] and fanatics', much to the chagrin of the missionaries, jealously watched their activities and watched them with 'the greatest suspicion.'[47] Christian missionary activity was naturally then confined to the Hindus.[48] Even that was not safe. It was reported that the fear of a Muslim *zamindar* acted strongly upon many Hindus. At times even the arrival of a Muslim landlord's servant was sufficient to deprive a missionary of a fair part of his listeners.[49] Consequently, Islam was described as the most violent, determined and implacable foe of Christianity.[50] The *London Journal and Weekly Record of Literature, Science and Arts* called it fruitless even to think of Christianization of the subcontinent unless 'Mohamedan passion for rule in India was tamed and broken.' This, the periodical argued, was a prerequisite. Once that was done, it asserted, Christian voice would reach the Hindus more easily and successfully.[51]

It was argued that the spirit of independence is part of human nature. No people ever like to be ruled by another. Once yoked to foreign domination, they always strive for the cherished goal of liberty and freedom.[52] This was, indeed, reported to be the case with the Muslims. R.H.W. Dunlop, the Deputy Commissioner at Meerut, argued that, like a conquered nation, they naturally discussed ways to achieve their independence. Born to intrigue, and enjoying greater unity of action among themselves than the Hindus, the Muslims of

India, he contended, had always been 'engaged in plotting our destruction.'[53]

Muslim acceptance of the British rule was universally described as very reluctant. The result was they were 'incurably disaffected to the British Government.'[54] Theirs was regarded as a double hatred—religious aversion,[55] combined with hatred generated by their loss of political power.[56] It was a double force marching in the same direction, operating towards the same goal—the overthrow of the foreigner and the restoration of the Muslim rule.[57] The Muslims always considered themselves a 'wronged' people—'wronged', it was said, 'by the hateful infidel force.'[58] Their glorious past stuck fast in their dreams. That was why, believed many of this school of thought, they were in a state of permanent ferment. Whenever they were not, it was not for lack of hostility towards their rulers, or because they had reconciled themselves with the situation, but because it was not feasible to launch an anti-government movement.[59] A writer in the *London Quarterly Review* angrily pointed out that the Muslims regarded India as the 'spoil of their forefathers' valour' and that their deep rooted feeling was 'that they will

Spoil the spoiler as they may,
And from the robber rend the prey.[60]

They were, in fact, waiting for a safe and propitious opportunity.

To establish their point of view still further, the members of this school profusely quoted instances of past Muslim hostility. The Muslim hand was clearly seen in the Vellore Mutiny of 1805.[61] Taylor, the Chief Commissioner of the Patna Division, referred to the Patna conspiracy of 1846 which, he argued, not only involved several Muslims of Patna and the neighbouring districts but was regarded as a branch of a more general plot. At that time too, attempts were made to tamper with sepoy loyalty, the objective being the overthrow of the British government in India and re-establishment of Muslim rule; that since then Bihar had been the '*Bete noire*' of Indian statesmen, and that Patna had become the most dreaded place in India.[62] Capt. G. Hutchinson pointing to the revolt of Mawlawi Ahmad 'Ali Shah at Faizabad in February 1857, reported that the Shah, (a native of Arcot in the Madras Presidency), before his arrival at Faizabad in 1857, had visited a 'vast number of cities and stations' under British rule; had everywhere preached *jihad* against the Europeans and had established his disciples everywhere.[63]

The author of 'The English in India' also referred to the existence of a plot for the murder of all Europeans in January 1857, and believed that the ministers of the ex-King of Awadh in concert with the sons of the King of Delhi were the chief conspirators.[64] A writer in the *Dublin University Magazine*, who stoutly believed in the Muslim character of the rebellion, referred to Mawlawi Skandar Shah, who with his armed followers had publicly preached holy war upon the English on 17 February 1857, in Awadh, and had called upon the Muslims to throw off the English yoke. He also referred to the murder of Mr Boileau, Assistant Commissioner at Ghonda (near Lucknow), on the 8th of March by a Muslim 'desperado' named Fadl 'Ali.[65]

Six months before the outbreak, the Rev. W.H. Haycock of the Society for the Propagation of the Gospel was informed by a Mawlawi that the British 'will soon feel the sharpness of the Mussulman's sword.'[66] That was why a writer in the *Church of England Magazine* argued that the outbreak would have taken place even without any religious apprehension, 'for it would not be difficult', he argued, 'to show that the Muslims had laid their plans for years.'[67] If the 'Resident of the North-Western Provinces in India' dated the Muslim conspiracy 'as far back as the termination of the last Cabul campaign',[68] another of this school thought that the Awadh annexation exploded the mine laid up for years.[69] Even the most mutiny-minded Sir Benjamin C. Brodie complained that the Muslims had prompted every disorder which had occurred since the establishment of the Empire. He argued that in the present mutiny, as well, the Muslim hand could be seen clearly. Brodie maintained that since the follower of Islam had long brooded over the loss of his power, he 'eagerly pounced upon the cartridge grievance as a subject affording him an excuse for insubordination and as one likely to excite the superstitious Hindu.'[70]

Even a cursory reading of contemporary writings on the mutiny leaves one in no doubt that the entire Muslim population was dangerously disposed towards the British. The Muslims were said to be ever in a state of readiness to revolt.[71] They had no solicitude for their rulers, and hated them with the hatred of a dispossessed race. Always intent upon revolt, the Muslims were reported to be hesitating because of the Hindus—the Hindu majority of the country not being with them. The worshippers of Brahma were the friends of the British. They looked upon them as emancipators and not tyrants as the Muslims did.[72] The former, it was said, still had painful memories of Muslim domination. It was in recognition of this deliverance of theirs that the Hindus gave the new rulers their wholehearted fealty and respect, and reposed full confidence in them.[73] In these circumstances, if the Muslims could not rely upon the Hindus, the latter too were not prepared 'to rally round the standard of a Mohamedan revolt', and thereby reinvite the once hated rule.[74] Moreover, the native army as well, it was pointed out, was dominated by the Brahmans—something very discouraging.[75] The Hindus were thus described as the Achilles' heel of the Muslims. They 'feared to be crushed by the Hindu legions of the Government.' They were well familiar with the fact that any untimely action would mean disaster and so were not prepared to translate their feelings into the language of hasty action.[76]

Fearful of the might of their rulers, apprehensive of possible Hindu treachery, the Muslims were reported to have taken recourse in God. They believed in the efficacy of prayers. The followers of Islam felt that actions joined by prayers had perhaps a greater chance of success—all the more so, because India was believed to have been snatched from them by God for the sins of their forefathers.[77] The atonement for past omissions and ungodliness called for long and genuine prayers. As the national spirit of the Muslims was also to be kept alive and since they could not always remain in action, prayers were perhaps the safest way to pursue that end. No wonder, ever since the dawn of British rule in India, prayers were held in mosques all over India at daily, weekly and annual congregational services, as well as at religious festivals. Allah's mercies and help were earnestly invoked 'for the restoration of ancient Mahomettan princes…and for the final expulsion of the stranger from the land.'[78] If this was so of public prayers, it was no less true of private ones. This, in fact, was said to have become the beat of the Muslim pulse,—their hourly wish; their permanent longing. The *Missionary Magazine* thus reported the conclusions of Major-General W.H. Sleeman, late British Resident to the court of Lucknow, formed on the basis of his personal observation:

> The Muslims in India sigh for the restoration of the old Mohamedan regime. 'We pray', said they, 'every night for the emperor and his family, because our forefathers ate the salt of their forefathers.' As a result of personal inquiry, I am enabled to state positively that for nearly the last hundred years daily prayers have been offered in the mosques throughout India for the House of Timur and the re-establishment of the King of Delhi on the throne of his ancestors—a fact probably, which at this moment is wholly unknown to the British rulers of this land.[79]

To keep the Muslim mind in a state of constant agitation and expectancy, soothsayers and sufis among them also circulated prophecies, stating that the British rule in India was to last only a hundred years after the battle of Plassey.[80] These were thought to be of divine origin by natives of all creeds. It was 'blindly and confidently' believed, reported *The Press*, that the prophecies would be accomplished with the help of 'God and Mahomet, his prophet.'[81] The result was, complained *The Press*, that every Muslim found himself bound to respond to the call now made upon him to fight for the recovery of the kingdoms given as an inheritance to the faithful.[82]

It was in the context of the above situation that the Indian social, political and religious scene started to change. While the entire Muslim population was disaffected, was even desirous of overthrowing the foreign and Christian ruler in India; while they had almost unanimously shown their indifference, verging upon enmity, towards receiving English education; while they had expressed their united disapproval of the Christian missionary activity; while they were resorting to prayers mixed with feeble actions to overthrow the British rule—in brief, during the time when the Muslim mind was in a furious state and was looking for a chance, just then the rulers themselves had begun to alienate the sympathies of the Hindu majority. The Legislative Council in India had started issuing laws 'bearing in the strongest manner on Hindu superstitions.'[83] It was a change of policy that certainly tended to help Muslim designs. Perhaps their prayers were in the process of being heard. The East India Company had started to interfere with the customs and usages of Hindu society having religious significance. The changes, generally speaking, were benevolent, humanitarian, and civilizing in their nature, and in certain cases they were approved by a large section of Hindu society. But other reforms, it was contended, completely antagonized an equally large section and, in quite a few instances, the entire Hindu society.[84] Hindus were full of murmurings and complaints. This, it was argued, provided the Muslims with a long sought opportunity indeed, one not to be missed.[85] Upon successful achievement in this field depended their future success. The Muslims decided to play upon Hindu feelings.

Tempers of the followers of Islam were said to be running high. Full of desperation, they were on the verge of explosion. Still something more was needed to raise the storm, and it was not long in coming. In February 1856, a singular event took place, which proved to be the last straw. Awadh was annexed in spite of its treaties. This annexation drove a knife into the Muslim heart.[86] The last hope of the Muslims was, it was said, being washed away. The belief was that the deposed monarch of Awadh, as the last remaining independent Muslim sovereign, 'commanded veneration and regard of all the members of Mussulman persuasion.'[87] To strike him down, it was held, was sure to excite further discontentment among a very powerful class of the British Indian subjects.[88] That was why the act of settlement was heavily criticized by a large segment of the British people. If it was described as 'a measure as ungrateful as it was impolitic',[89] an act of outright 'political robbery',[90] 'burglary',[91] and 'atrocious machiavellism'[92] by the rulers themselves, the deposition of Wajid 'Ali Shah was taken as a 'personal misfortune' by every Muslim. The act of annexation was regarded as 'a terrible disgrace' to the whole Muslim community in India.[93] The sudden nature of the blow, argued one Briton, not only hurt the Muslims most, but it also shook their trust and faith in the rulers. No one could imagine that the English nation could be guilty of 'such slyness and secrecy.' The followers of Islam, it was thought, saw in the occupation an approaching doom for them in India. In the future their royalty in India was to be a symbol rather than a reality.[94] They now desired eagerly to pay back.[95] The *Illustrated London News* called the incorporation of Awadh into the British Indian dominion a signal for the Muslim conspiracy to extend itself.[96]

The Awadh affair made the Muslims so angry that they would not even discuss the pros and cons of the annexation. The anarchical state of affairs in the state, the debauchery and dissoluteness of the king, argued the author of the investigation into some of the causes which had produced the rebellion in India, and his incapacity to rule, were all immaterial to them.[97] After their experience of Kashmir, contended W.W. Ireland, the people were not prepared to believe in the good intentions of the British government. Looking back into the recent record of the actions of the East India Company, Ireland observed:

> It was not forgotten, how a few years before, we had sold the beautiful valley of Cashmire for a sum of money to Golab Singh, one of the most odious tyrants that ever desolated Central Asia and had lent our troops to force the people to submit to his hated away. The Mohamedans have a close sympathy with one another; to degrade a prince of their religion is to put out one light of Islam. The King of Oudh had long been our friendliest and truest ally. The country might be ill governed; most eastern countries are so; but one thing is clear, they preferred the rule of their native princes to ours.[98]

Muslim thinking now channelled itself into a dangerous path. A very alarming and explosive ingredient of national consciousness was said to have added itself to their politico-religio-economic grievances. 'We have lost our King and our country was their only thought.' They felt that their foreign masters had, slowly and gradually, 'denationalized' them and that they were 'no longer a society which could boast of a monarch who was one of themselves, but a scattered people, without a head, without glory, without power.' The present grievance, it was pointed out, drove the entire Muslim community mad, and consequently endangered the lives of Englishmen. Wherever the Muslims were in India, revolt had become a matter of time.[99] Even then their resentment was so strong that several Muslim cities, reported the author of the 'Revolt of the Bengal Army', could not contain their anger. In many there were outbursts of hatred and violence. In some of these incidents Europeans were injured and even killed.[100] This was a dangerous trend, and certainly augured ill for the British.

The annexation of Awadh was followed by another event of great significance—an event that was calculated further to arouse Muslim hostility towards their Christian rulers. The event was the war with the Kingdom of Persia. The *Free Press* argued that it served only to unite in India 'the most opposite creeds and races against us',[101] and a correspondent, in his letter to the Honourable Secretary of the Church Missionary Society, pointed to the inflammable ingredient in the war. He wrote to say:

A war with Persia, the Shah of which is, to our Shiah's here, something like the Pope to our Romanists. Can you wonder that we now discover that this is a Mussulman movement.[102]

The Muslims of India at this time, it appears, were undergoing an intense process of reviewing their past and present. Once rulers of a great Indian nation, they were brought down to a lowly status. Every inch of Indian territory bore mute witness to their glory but that glory was rapidly becoming a thing of the past. They realized, pointed out a writer in the *Eclectic Review,* that the splendid 'pageant of the empire at Delhi was fast fading away, and the Kingdom of Oude had recently been extinguished.' Now they had virtually nothing to call their own. If their present looked dark to them, their future looked darker still. They 'thought their time had come.'[103] 'Now or never', suddenly became their desperate cry. Whatever be the hazards, they must make a last bid to recover their old supremacy.[104] In 'their opinion', argued the 'Resident in North Western Provinces', 'they had nothing to lose, for all had been already lost. Whereas there was everything to gain.' While success might bring them back their past glory, failure would cost nothing. There was a shining ray of hope in the gamble. The only important ingredients they needed to make the eventual outbreak successful were: a) unity in their own ranks, b) the assistance of the Hindus—only if they could get it 'by some device.' Then, they felt sure, the game was going to be theirs.[105]

To the delight of Muslims the internal as well as external situation *vis-à-vis* Great Britain seemed to be quite favourable to them. Hindus had already started feeling discontented and could be profitably exploited. The Muslims believed, it was thought, that the might of England had already been strained in the Crimean War. Now it was busy squandering resources in Persia. While the empire in India had greatly expanded, a part of the existing European force—the true guardian of the British interest in India—was withdrawn for service in the Crimean and Persian Wars. The Chinese danger was looming large on the horizon.[106] Leopold Von Olrich believed that the news of the martyrdom of two Englishmen, Colonel Stoddart and Captain Connolly, in Bokhara, and Britain's failure to rescue them, had gained currency, and 'had produced an averse influence upon the minds of Mussulman princes.'[107] It was thought that the journals of England had also contributed towards strengthening native belief in the weakened power of Britain by publishing stories 'about the wretched condition of our army at home, and the miserable feebleness of our Government.'[108]

There was another flaw in the situation; a major portion of the native regular army came from the ex-state of Awadh. These soldiers were all in favour of the state as a separate entity. In fact, the Awadh sepoys in the British army had lost a good deal of prestige as a result of the annexation. The social esteem in which they were held in their village, and the privileges they used to enjoy as a soldier in the British army, had ceased to exist with the extinction of Awadh as an independent state. They now felt, it was firmly held, disgruntled, and this provided fertile ground to exasperated Muslims to breed anti-government activities.[109] Furthermore, the Indian administration, believed the 'Resident in the North-Western Provinces', was new in office. Lord Canning had arrived only recently; he had still to acquaint himself with the Indian scene. Such an opportunity might never come again and 'the Mussulmans thus decided not to let it slip.'[110] The two houses of Delhi and Lucknow assumed the leadership of the movement.

At Delhi, either the king or his council, it was thought, had started carrying out their designs.[111] Ever since General Lake's deliverance of Shah 'Alam from the Marahtahs in 1803, the kings of Delhi, it was believed, had never given up their pretensions to the throne of Delhi.[112]

In fact, they had, it was said, asserted their right occasionally, though in 'an artful and cautious manner.'[113] Muhammad Bahadur Shah Zafar, the octogenarian Mughal emperor at the time of the outbreak, and the princes of his house were reported to have been long disaffected with the British. The princes felt especially chagrined over the prospects of a dismal future lying in wait for them—debarred as they were from receiving even a particle of the shadowy dignity and pomp of their father, after the latter's death. If the heir to Bahadur was precluded from inheriting the royal title of King, the whole house was asked to quit the royal palace in Delhi (after the death of the old king), and find some other place outside Delhi for their residence. Thus they were all eager for a rebellion.[114] One Sidi Qambar was said to have been sent to Persia and the Porte as early as 1855 to solicit aid from the sovereigns of those two countries. The idea behind this mission was to help restore the house of Delhi. Sidi had promised to be back with succour in 1857—a year fixed, it was held by Muslim soothsayers, as the last year of British rule in India.[115]

It would seem from reports that Bahadur Shah's strong desire to restore his house to power had made him a very credulous person. His courtiers took advantage of his weakness. In order both to gain their prince's good will and to stiffen his attitude towards the British, they played upon his credulity. On 27 March 1857, one Muhammad Darwesh wrote to inform Colvin, the Lieutenant-Governor at Agra, that Hasan 'Askari (through whose agency Sidi Qambar had been sent to Persia)'[116] had convinced the king on the basis of a divine revelation that:

> ...the dominion of the King of Persia will to a certainty extend to Delhi, or rather over the whole of Hindoostan, and that the splendour of the sovereignty of Delhi will again revive, as the sovereign of Persia will bestow the Crown on the King.[117]

That was not all. Receptive as Bahadur Shah was to any news which augured ill for the British, he seems, as was reported at the trial of the king, easily to have accepted Hasan 'Askari's version of a resounding Persian victory over the British. The unfortunate king was further brought to believe that the King of Persia had occupied Bushire and planned to invade India through Afghanistan, ostensibly to facilitate his task of overthrowing the foreign rulers.[118] Such a conviction ushered in a period of rejoicing in the palace at Delhi. Prayers were offered and vows taken. Hasan 'Askari himself was reported to have 'entered upon a daily performance of an hour and a half before sunset course of propitiatory ceremonies to expedite the arrival of the Persians and the expulsion of the Christians.' Every Thursday alms began to be distributed by the king, obviously to please God, so as to hasten the course of events.[119]

Active in seeking foreign assistance, the Delhi conspirators did not remain inactive at home. They launched, it was argued, a well prepared scheme to turn the minds of the people from their Anglo-Saxon masters. The end was described as twofold: a) to make the Indians ready for the change; and b) to prepare them for their participation in the work of overthrowing the English by means of a well prepared insurrection.[120] All possible means were said to have been adopted to put false but ingenious and effective rumours into circulation. Here too the conspirators were faced with the double problem of dealing with two widely divergent communities: a) Muslims—the ever sympathetic people of their own faith; b) Hindus—a people they had to win over at any cost in order to achieve their end. If the latter were ensnared through the medium of *chapatis*, bone-dust and cartridges, the former, strongly maintained the advocate judge at the Delhi trial, were worked upon through the agency of the press.[121] The *Authentic News* was reported to have started promoting Delhi as early as 1856. News of Persian assistance, of fully equipped Russian armies on the alert to back the Persians, and even of expected Turko-French assistance, were played up. Once the paper was said to have observed:

Let the readers of the Authentic News, be prepared to see what the veil of futurity will disclose.[122]

In its issue of 19 March (probably 1856) it reported that 500 Persian troops were staying in Delhi and that 900 more were on their way. At another time it said that the King of Persia had assigned even the governorships of different provinces to his courtiers—one was to get Bombay, another Calcutta and a third Poona, while the Crown of India was 'plainly spoken of as reserved for bestowal on the King of Delhi.' Sir Theophilus Metcalfe, a joint-magistrate at Meerut at the time of the outbreak, was mentioned by the advocate judge as having admitted the wide currency which the rumours of Russian help to Persia had gained. Even Dost Muhammad was publicized as having been in league with the Persians. Having established all that at the trial, he argued:

Are we then to suppose that in all this there was no connection between the palace and the press? Were all these concurrences fortuitous? Can it be that the dreams of the priest, the plots of the Court, and the fabrications of the newspapers worked accidentally together?[123]

That was why Dr Daniel Wilson, the Bishop of Calcutta, called it a 'secret conspiracy of the court of Delhi and other Mahometan princes'[124]—a conspiracy which, he told his congregation, spread over a 'number of years.'[125]

Moving south-east to Lucknow, the annexation of Awadh had made a Simon de Monfort of Wajid 'Ali Shah, the ruler of the state—up until now a staunch ally of the East India Company. Truly the Company had sowed the harvest in this case and shortly had to reap the inevitable. Earlier described as if soaked in wine and sunk in debauchery, Wajid 'Ali behaved very sensibly at the time of annexation. Perhaps the great shock had awakened his so far dormant faculties. Quietly setting his plans, he was reported to have politely turned down all offers of an annual family allowance made by the Governor-General. He decided to hit back, and hit back with compound interest. It was firmly believed that Wajid was a party to the conspiracy and the rebellion.[126] Ireland held that to compel the British government to abandon the state of Awadh, as it had been done in the case of Afghanistan, some leading men of the state started a series of intrigues.[127]

To disarm suspicion among the rulers Wajid 'Ali was reported to have taken a few clever and competent steps. To convince the government of his harmlessness, his gentle demeanour, and of his good intentions, he was said to have turned down overtures of assistance made by the people and sepoys of Awadh.[128] Next he changed his quarters from Lucknow to British India's metropolitan city of Calcutta. Thirdly, he lost no time in dispatching his mother, brother and son to England in order to plead his case before the Queen. In this way, argued some, the stage for a counterstroke was set and the English were caught off their guard.[129] The cities of Calcutta and London were said to have become centres of numerous subtle stories. These were attributed to the Awadh royal family which was then divided between these two cities. Rumours of the government intentions of occupying Udaipur in Rajesthan; of making drastic reductions in the stipends of all native princes; of transferring His Highness the Nawab of Murshidabad to Dum Dum; of converting his palace into an engineering college, and the like, emanated from these two headquarters.[130]

Wajid Ali, reported Carey on the basis of documentary evidence found bearing his signature, lost no time in entering into correspondence with the ruler of Delhi. Therein he proposed to: a) corrupt the entire native army; b) invite all native princes to join in the plot; c) fix a day for the uprising; d) revolt as a single unit against the British and massacre all Europeans and Christians, and e) repatriate the native rule as it existed before the advent of the 'hated' British rule. This he suggested was to be achieved 'under the general sovereignty of the King of Kings at Delhi.'[131] Their common grievance had, it was argued, brought about a conciliation between the Shi'ah and Sunni houses of Awadh and Delhi.[132] The fact remained that they were all Muslims. And the Muslims, as indicated by the British, had come to acquire a common grievance and a common cause against their rulers. By its sale of the Muslim-dominated state of Kashmir to a Hindu, Maharaja Gulab Singh, the government, it was argued, had earlier forfeited their trust and confidence.[133] The misdemeanour in Awadh, and the changing attitude towards the ruler of Delhi, had now compelled them to forget their differences and foster unity within their ranks. To galvanize the rank and file of the movement, placards, 'some ambiguously hinting at a general rebellion, others openly calling on the followers of the Prophet to exterminate the unbelievers' were reportedly circulated.[134]

Apparently Nana Sahib had, in one of his proclamations, invoked the authority of the 'Sultan of Roum' against the British in India. Pointing this out, a writer in the *Edinburgh Review* complained that 'even the Mahrattas appear to recognize the superior force and ferocity of their Muslim conquerors.'[135] The fact of the matter was that of late Hindus had been badly disenchanted by the attitude adopted by the administration. Now, they too were an aggrieved party. The Muslims, aware of this, did their best, it was repeatedly and forcefully pointed out, to play upon the Hindu feelings, and draw them closer to themselves. This was to be done at the cost of Hindu relations with their British masters. All possible ways and means were adopted to draw the former away from the latter. The Indian princes were invited to join in the task of overthrowing the British. A return to pre-British days was promised. Re-establishment of all Hindu and Muslim principalities, which existed before the advent of the British rule, was pledged under the overlordship of the ruler of Delhi.[136] It was at this development that W.H. Russell of *The Times* remarked in his diary:

...the heart of every Mussalman was moved within him, and Hindoos were naturally agitated by the prospect of regaining their independence in their old States.[137]

Every effort, it was widely reported and held, was made by the wily Muslims to dupe harmless Hindus into their net.[138] A writer in the *Dublin University Magazine,* describing Hinduism as 'a frozen serpent in the fable...grasped as a whip in the hands of the blind man', angrily held that it 'needed the hot breath of Muhammadan fanaticism to give it life and energy to wound the arm that wielded it.'[139] Capt. R.P. Anderson reported that a garlanded head of 'a half grown buffalo' was found on the gate near the king's palace in Lucknow. Calling it a Muslim device to hurt the Hindus, he observed, 'I fancy it was as much to say, "see the Europeans kill buffaloes in your very streets."'[140] The Muslim spies were said to have told their Hindu audiences that, like Islam, Hinduism too would be disrespected; the Hindus would all be Christianized and compelled not only to handle cow fat, but also to eat beef. As the Hindus were already against the government, they were easily led into believing all this.[141]

Bishop Wilson felt so sure of Muslim antagonism and their machinations, that he told his congregation that 30 million 'ruthless Mussulmans' were engaged in conspiracies against their rulers; that they had worked 'with too much success' upon the feeble minds of 150 million Hindus for a number of years and, as such, had ultimately broken out into open rebellion against a small number of Europeans.[142] It was because of these reasons that the *Illustrated London News* was able to assert that 'as the drama develops and unfolds itself, it seems to become evident that the [the ruler of Delhi] and the dethroned King of Oudh—both of them Mahommedans and not Hindoos—were the prime instigators of the plot; that the conspiracy was Mahommedan; and that the Hindoos have been made the instruments of villains more crafty and more savage than themselves. ...The religion of the Hindoos, which is not in its nature aggressive, is the instrument, and not the cause, of the explosion.'[143]

It was simultaneously decided to undermine the loyalty of the army.[144] It was contended that agents, well provided with money, were sent to every army station in India. Their main duty was to prepare the native army for an insurrection and in doing so they were instructed to adopt all possible means to 'bring about the revolt without the cognizance of the authorities.'[145] Here again, insofar as the Muslims in the army were concerned, it was argued that there would not be much difficulty. Like their brethren outside the army, the Muslim soldiers were reported to be always in a state of readiness to revolt. It was claimed that their views were wider and more dangerous than those of their Hindu neighbours and that they never cherished any affection for their Anglo-Saxon rulers—'not a spark.' Hence there was no need to buy or corrupt them; they were already rebels.[146]

With the Hindus it was, however, very different. Hindu sepoys were described as 'friends of the English', who, it was said, 'looked upon them with confidence and respect.' Naturally, any effort to corrupt them was a highly delicate affair. All difficulties, however, had to be overcome because Hindu support to the Muslim cause was described as very essential.[147] It was all the more imperative since the army was virtually in the hands of Brahmans. But for the help of Hindu soldiers, the Muslims, it was contended, realized that they would not be able to achieve their objective out of sheer numerical weakness.[148] Again, if the Hindus were a weakness in the Muslim plan for revolt, the latter had their own to cover up as well, argued the author of the 'Poorbeah Mutiny.' These consisted in what he called past tyrannical rule of Muslims and their present objectives.[149] A small miscalculation would have led to a complete fiasco of the whole insurrectionary movement even before it could have started. Hence the wooing had to be done with utmost caution.

The work of corrupting Hindu sepoys, though difficult and delicate, did not turn out to be an uphill task. The whole affair, it was argued, was facilitated by the Hindus themselves. Hindu sepoys, though friends of the English, had their own weaknesses. Avarice was described as a master passion with them—a passion stronger than their friendship with the English. Their weakness was that a sepoy 'could be bought' and 'he was bought.'[150] In addition to putting in strenuous efforts to lure them from their allegiance, the emissaries of Delhi and Awadh used bribery to seduce Hindu sepoys.[151] But this was not all. The Hindu sepoys had another weakness and it consisted of their caste and religion—things for which they had always been quite willing to make any sacrifice.[152] Along with the exploitation of their 'master passion', the Muslim conspirators, in order to assure their success, decided to touch this most delicate chord of religion and caste.[153] Hence the religious feelings of the sepoys were worked upon. It was at this time that the government erred. The error was of great magnitude, and led to fatal consequences, and this was the introduction of greased cartridges in the army. The ingredients used in greasing the cartridge were said to have been cow and hog fat—both detrimental to Hindu bias, and the latter drastically impure in Muslim eyes. The cartridge

affair provided the Muslims with a long-sought opportunity. The
incident, it was widely believed, was at once profitably seized upon by
the 'watchful and exasperated' enemy,[154] and shown as evidence of the
government's intentions of Christianizing India.[155] The crafty Muslims,
it was argued, used it as an effective handle to stir up Hindu
prejudice.[156] It served both of their purposes; it supposedly enabled
them successfully to play up the Hindu weakness of religion and caste
and play down, as well as cover up, the Muslim weaknesses due to past
tyranny and present ulterior motives. One from this school
observed:

> Thus under the idea that an attack was being meditated on their religious
> prejudices, the great mass of Hindoo sepoys were caught in the trap laid for them
> by wily Mohammedan, who himself also could find, or pretend to find, in the same
> cartridge with its fancied odour of forbidden pig's fat, a religious motive for
> rebellion, under which the real political motive was cunningly kept out of
> sight.[147]

The *Christian Spectator* had something similar to say when it
remarked:

> It is now pretty generally acknowledged by the more independent portion of the
> press that the causes of the mutiny are anything but mysterious. Our own bad and
> blundering Government had furnished the fuel to which Mohammedan ambition
> has applied the torch.[158]

A writer in the *British Quarterly Review* summed up this debate when
he argued that in this way it was 'determined that the Hindu and the
Mussulman should combine and rise together to expel and massacre
the Christian.' Firmly believing in the existence of a Muslim conspiracy,
and definitely dating it back to the annexation of Awadh, he further
tried to convince readers by telling them that weeks before the
outbreak Lucknow had become 'the hotbed of intrigue and the scene
of nightly meetings and conflagrations.' He pointed out that soon after
the disbandment of the 19th Regiment, the deposed king's brother
informed the native troops that he was 'prepared to give service, at an
increased rate of pay, to all who might be discharged by the
Company.'[159]

To disguise their intentions from the government, the conspirators
of Delhi and Lucknow were reported to have employed the subtle,
effective and dangerous agency of disguised faqirs to go about the
country to loosen the discipline and corrupt native sepoys and the civil
population.[160] Nur Muhammad Khan, a *Sarishtahdar* of Canal was sent

from Delhi to Amritsar 'to inaugurate a crusade' at that place. When apprehended by Frederick Cooper, the Deputy Commissioner of Amritsar, he found 'suits of Fakeers' [Faqirs'] clothes and disguises for further emergencies.' Holding that the faqirs were mostly Muslims, Cooper argued, 'Had all the suspected been pursued, the number of Mussulmans involved would have become embarrassing to the Government.'[161] Reporting similarly the case of an itinerant faqir who was sentenced to receive a hundred lashes for preaching universal war against the British, L.E. Ruutz Rees went on to inform his readers that it was not a solitary case. He perhaps exaggerated when he stated that thousands of such ill-looking wretches could 'daily be seen passing under the gallows, registering vows of vengeance against us.'[162]

The Advocate Judge of the Army at the Delhi trial, attributing the circulation of *chapatis* to the 'wiles of Mohammedan conspiracy', argued that the Muslims resorted to these means in order to prepare the minds of the people for the forthcoming rising and to create among them a feeling of standing by one another. Or else it was intended to show to the people 'that in future there should be but one food and one faith.'[163] Carey also regarded them as the most powerful and the most successful contrivance that could be devised for 'combining all classes of Mahometans in the general cause.' He told his readers that the Muslims, in order to avoid detection, let it be known that the government had given orders for their distribution.[164] The cake movement, having been found out and stopped by the government, the Muslim schemers, it was pointed out, hurriedly took to flour. The bone-dust idea replaced the circulation of cakes. It was firmly believed that this was a continuation of the *chapati* matter—a continuation of the same symbol of 'one food and one faith.'[165]

The Muslim or the Muslim-inspired rebellion, it was contended, did not come like a bolt from the blue. The government had received a couple of warnings long before the outbreak, but it had preferred either to laugh at or just ignore them. Gulab Singh, the well-known ruler of Kashmir, pointed out one, had written to Canning in November 1856, warning the Governor-General of Muslim intentions to rise and overthrow the government. Gulab also mentioned that the Muslims had even offered him the 'direction of the projected movement.' But he had refused. Again, Hamilton, a merchant at Kanpur and Allahabad, was requested by his native dealer friends to send his family away within six months—an advice which the former was reported to have accepted with some hesitation. Hamilton, however, did not fail in his duty but passed the information on to the Governor-General and offered still further to assist in the matter. His letter failed to evoke even the courtesy of a formal reply. One Thomas Johnson approached the President of the Board of Control, the Earl of Clarendon (the Foreign Secretary), and finally the Court of Directors, one after the other, in order to inquire into the above mentioned charges, but failed. To his letters, though acknowledged, the replies were either discreetly silent or else the recipients declined to answer the specific inquiry.[166] No wonder, Sherring, in his letter home, appeared quite perplexed and astonished when he wrote this:

> I think little doubt exists in the minds of Europeans in India, that Mussulmans and they alone, have originated this foul conspiracy to upset the Government and massacre all white faces. The papers in the hands of the Government implicate several of the chief Mussulman families in India, including the Great Mogul and the King of Oude. The Hindus have been gulled by them into rising against their rulers and have been too infatuated to perceive, until too late, the fatal mistake they have made. How it is the authorities were not acquainted with this conspiracy—which was so widespread that I suspect there was scarcely a Mussulman of influence in North and Central India who was ignorant of it—is a mystery as great as the conspiracy itself.[167]

In fact, the British seem to have felt themselves so secure and entrenched that when Mrs H.H. Greathed, the Commissioner and Political Agent of Delhi, told her husband and his colleagues, Colonels Constance and Finnis, on 9 May 1857, at Meerut, that 'placards had been seen about the city calling upon all true Mussulmans to rise and slaughter the English', they treated the 'threat with indignant disbelief.'[169] The very next day the outbreak started at the same station and ravaged the land.

CHAPTER 8

Muslim Rebellion

After having established on the basis of past evidence that there were reasons enough among almost the entire Muslim community of India for them to feel dissatisfied with the political, social, religious and economic situation in the country, the advocates of the Muslim rebellion theory went on to strengthen their contention by drawing further testimony from actual events of the outbreak in India. From the conspiracy, they now shifted their attention to the rebellion itself. In fact, the best demonstration of their thesis was the hearty reception the Muslim masses gave to the news of the outbreak, and their subsequent participation in the ensuing struggle. This was the observation of the numerous British reporters on the spot. The present writer believes that the mere prospect of the crescent rising once again over the horizon of India made the Muslims of India cheerful and exuberant. Their dreams and prayers must have appeared to be taking the shape of reality, hence their joy and jubilation.

The reports of the day to day progress of the uprising convinced an overwhelmingly large section of the British public of its Muslim genesis. The adherents of this school came from all shades of public opinion. Indeed, if there was anything on which a large majority of the first two groups, the civil and the military, as well as others, agreed, it was in calling the outbreak a long-planned Muslim conspiracy for the overthrow of the British and restoration of Muslim rule in India. The result was that participation of the Muslims was emphasized, and their attitude towards fugitive members of the ruling community, their treatment of the few converts from their faith to Christianity and the sullen, insolent and dismayed expressions worn by them when powerless to act, were especially marked and brought to the notice of the masses in Britain.

The missionary and the Church of England press actively stressed the Muslim role in the crisis. These were followed by secular newspapers, periodicals, pamphleteers and public speakers. It was strongly argued that if the catastrophe was India-wide, it was so only insofar as the Muslim resentment of the British rule and their sympathies for the rebels were concerned.[1] To the *Saturday Review* all Muslims appeared to be excited and it argued that their enthusiasm would never subside into 'repose so long as the king of Delhi is really king, though his dominions may be bounded by the limits of his ancient capital'.[2] This was perhaps because of the fact, as Henry Mead pointed out, that the Muslims of India had always regarded the Mughal ruler, in spite of the long subjection under which he had lived for around a hundred years, as 'being the fountain of honour' and 'the rightful monarch of Hindostan'.[3] In short, from the *Church of England Magazine* through the *Manchester Guardian*, *The Scotsman* down to *The Free Press*—popularly known as an organ of the 'mystery monger'[4] David Urquhart; from the pulpit down to the completely secular platform, all agreed in pronouncing it as a Muslim rebellion.

The first thing that attracted the attention, nay, struck the imagination of the press and consequently of the people, was the centre and the leadership of the revolt. Delhi, the pivot of the revolt, was a Muslim city and had been the chief Muslim capital for centuries in the past.[5] Muhammad Bahadur Shah, who was described as its leader, was a Muslim. An old Indian in his letter to *The Times* emphasized this aspect of the uprising,[6] and the *Manchester Guardian* in its issue of 3 September 1857, brought out an editorial on the same subject.[7] Soon, the inclusion of Lucknow—another Muslim city—plus the suspicions entertained regarding the part played by the deposed ruler of Awadh left no doubt in British minds regarding the role of the crescent in the insurrection.[8]

On the basis of what was reported to have followed the outbreak, this analysis seems to be justified. It was believed that Bahadur Shah had long been preparing for revolt and soon was said to have assumed the leadership of the uprising (although feebly because of his age and temperament). Once having shown himself in his true colours, Bahadur was reported to have lost no time in issuing proclamations to the army and the people invoking their assistance in ousting the foreign rulers.[9] He was also said to have addressed letters to various princely states impressing upon their rulers the magnitude of the situation and the value of their help.[10] His messengers even talked of a letter written to Sir Robert Montgomery, the revenue Commissioner at Lahore. Condescendingly thanking him 'for his excellent arrangements hitherto on his behalf for the affairs of India', Bahadur was reported not only to have dispensed with the services of the

Revenue Commissioner, but also accorded him 'his royal permission' to retire via Bombay.[11]

After the start of the outbreak, emissaries of Delhi and Lucknow were reported to have penetrated and tried, at times very successfully, to disrupt the army and civil establishments of the East India Company. Every department seems to have been invaded. All sections of the Indian population were approached to join the movement. Perhaps no part of India was safe from their operations. The turbulence and disaffection at Bareilly, the capital of Gwalior, a Marahtah state, both in the city and the cantonment, was attributed to the machinations of the emissaries from Delhi.[12] Frederick Cooper, Deputy Commissioner of Amritsar, referring to the situation in the hills of Kasauli and Sanaur, thus quoted the Governor of Lawrence Asylum:

> Before and during these troubles, faqueers [Faqirs] were everywhere seen about the neighborhood; and I have since learnt that the emissaries from Oude and Delhi were empowered to offer seven rupees per man to anyone willing to enter the service of the respective pretenders to sovereignty. About a hundred coolies [Qulis] employed at the Asylum went off to Oude in consequence, and small drafts of Poorbeas have been continually leaving the hills during the whole period for Oude and Delhi.[13]

Even the newest recruits to the Company's service, the Sikhs, were approached, albeit in vain, to join the standard of Islam with promises of land endowments.[14]

If the chief leaders of the revolt—the king, the prime minister and the commander-in-chief at Delhi[15]—were described as Muslims, the great centre of rebellion was the city of Delhi itself.[16] A lady writing from Gwalior to *The Scotsman* described it as the 'stronghold of Mohammedanism,'[17] and Beveridge called it a notorious 'centre of Mohammedan intrigue'.[18] Mawlawis were reported to be flocking to this pivotal point of the movement to become *ghazis*, and the green flag was said to have been unfurled from the Jami'Masjid.[19] Even *The Examiner*, a newspaper which persistently called it an army *emeute*, repeatedly emphasized the Muslim character of the city of Delhi. It feared the fact that the mutiny was backed in the city 'by a fanatic Mohammedan population of 80,000.'[20] That was why 'A Volunteer' in his *Journal* recorded:

> There is no doubt that as long as there was a king of Delhi, acknowledged though in ever so small a way, and so long as there remained a Delhi for that King to live in, so long would the Mohammedans all over India hope and pray to see him once more seated in state on the throne.[21]

It was believed that the entire mass of the Muslim population was disaffected.[22] Even Muslim women were reported to be participating in the actual war.[23] The fidelity to the British even of the most loyal Muslims was doubted. If they were loyal at all, it was argued, they were not so from the core of their hearts but on account of selfish and worldly reasons.[24] An Englishman, writing from Meerut, observed that among 'our enemies are thousands of the worst sort of people, viz.,

Goojjurs [Gujars], and I believe every Mussulman in the country. We have found many here whom everyone would have supposed incapable of it [enmity], and they have been some of the principal leaders in the riots. The sepoys have lost all spirit (if they ever had any when opposed to us). The Hindoos and Mussulmans quarrel, and the Hindoos reproach them and say, 'This is all your fault'.[25]

The Muslim civil servants in the employ of the Company were no exceptions to this general Muslim hatred of the British. The *Chambers's Journal*, referring to the enlistment of Muslims in the civil service, 'even to the exclusion of Christians', bitterly remonstrated:

Well, the Government have sown the storm, and they have reaped the whirlwind. The foremost men in the present murderous rebellion are Mohammedans. Every Mussulman official in Upper Bengal and in the North-West provinces has turned against us, has obeyed the dictates of his faith, and drawn his sword upon us 'dogs of unbelievers'.[26]

The fact remained that two among the top three leaders of the outbreak at Delhi, the Commander-in-Chief and the Prime Minister, and several others, occupying ministerial and lower ranks in the rebel government, came from among the Muslim civil servants.[27]

If the Muslims of Delhi and Lucknow were either hostile, disaffected, intriguing, excited or up in arms, so it was reported were the Muslims all over India. Muslims of all three presidencies, Bombay,[28] Bengal[29] and Madras,[30] were given out to be equally strong in their anti-British sentiments. The Muslim populations of the cities and towns of Agra, Allahabad, Amritsar, Banaras, Belgaum, Bakarganj, Bahagalpur, Bombay, Budaun, Calcutta, Chittagong, Dacca, Firozpur, Faizabad, Fatehgarh, Fatehpur, Gorakhpur, Hyderabad (Deccan), Jessore, Jaunpur, Lahore, Ludhiana, Monghyr, Moradabad, Mymensingh, Madras, Nagpur, Patna, Peshawar, Poona, Rampur, Ratnagiri and Sawantwadi were either reported to be in actual revolt or eagerly awaiting a suitable opportunity.[31] Plots by Muslims, it was largely reported, were discovered everywhere and they seemed to be at the bottom of everything.

The countryside was no exception· to this. Far in the North-West, the Khyber Pass[32] and Swat state[33] were reported to have become centres of Muslim intrigue. So great was Muslim zeal that at some places voluntary subscriptions were raised, men were hired and arms provided.[34] Seditious letters written by private Muslim individuals were intercepted.[35] Stores owned by Muslims were reported to have become centres of revolutionary talk. Cooper thus observed:

> The shops of Elahi and Nubee Buksh (Amritsar) as familiar in India as Moses and Son in England…became arenas of political discussion. The Delhi, Bareilly and Shajahanpur massacres were freely discussed and the necessity of imitation became a matter of commonplace talk.[36]

The participation and the joy and jubilation of the followers of Islam was reported to know no bounds. Even long-standing Muslim domestic servants in the employ of the Company's officials, if not actually implicated, were ecstatic at the news of the convulsion. Cooper tells us of the rapturous notes into which the Muslim *khansaman* of General Hewitt had fallen after he had heard of the uprising; forgetting his twenty years' service, he at once started 'flinging all the plates from the dining room into the air, dancing with joy', when General Hewitt's aide-de-camp, Captain Hogg, 'suddenly allayed his transports' by killing him on the spot.[37] The Muslim household servants at Muree were said to have gone a step further—they were actually implicated in a plot.[38] Even Charles Raikes, the judge of the Sadar Court at Agra, who was inclined to believe that the outbreak was a mutiny, had a similar complaint to make against the Muslim servants.[39]

Nothing could better illustrate the nature of the uprising than the attitude adopted by Muslims towards the British during the outbreak. As rulers, as foreigners, and as Christians, the British had to undergo all types of experiences. If there were a few instances of Muslim generosity, there were many more of Muslim bigotry. The instances of generosity were quite insufficient to balance acts which went against their own Muslim vision of moral law. These were the experiences, past and present, from which the advocates of the Muslim rebellion school of thought drew their support. If the fact of Muslim rule over the subcontinent; earlier Muslim reactions towards the establishment of British rule in India; towards Christian missionary activity; towards the English educational system; one and all provided the strong foundation on which to build the superstructure; the material for the superstructure itself was deduced from some of the practical experiences of the mutiny. In fact, the Muslims were driven mad by their pent-up feelings towards their *farangi* rulers and their missionary activity. Many were only endeavouring to protect Islam from what they thought were the threats of Christian encroachment. Many thought a *jihad* (holy war) had started.[40] W.H. Russell even tells us of *ghazis* taking part in the battle of Bareilly. They wore green turbans, *kamarbands* and silver signet rings with verses of the Qur'an engraved on them. Raising cries of 'the Faith!', 'the Faith!', they were said to have courted death in the bravest manner.[41] We also hear of a Muslim lady leading a sortie out of the city of Delhi. Calling her a *jihadan*, H.H. Greathed, the Commissioner and Political Agent at Delhi, described her as another 'Joan of Arc'. Dressed in male attire, her head covered with a green turban, this lady was said to have fought like a 'satan' until she was captured.[42] With many Muslims, however, the outbreak became simply an opportunity for passing all limits of religious legality and traditional behaviour.

Quite a few incidents of religious fanaticism and bigotry were reported in which the Muslims were either actors or suspects. If Dr Batson secured his escape because of his knowledge of the native language and by making an appeal in the name of the Prophet Muhammad (PBUH),[43] Wilayat Ali, a Muslim convert to Christianity, died a 'martyr's' death.[44] Referring to the Muslim activity outside of Agra, Dawarkanath Lahori, a Hindu convert to Christianity, wrote that 'fanatical...followers of the prophet armed to the teeth, like so many hungry wild beasts sucking the forlorn and inoffensive followers of the lamb for their prey, and with the...war cry 'Allah! Allah!' breathing bloody vengeance against them and those who moved by compassion, would dare shelter them'.[45] Marcus, an English soldier, was reported to have been offered a choice between Islam and death.[46] Carnillious, a native Christian, had to embrace Islam twice.[47] Robert Tucker, the judge at Fatehpur,[48] and Timothy Luther, another native Christian,[49] underwent similar experiences. Dhokul Parasad, the headmaster of the City School at Fatehgarh, his wife, four children and twenty-eight other Christians were reportedly killed by the Nawab of Farrukhabad.[50] The native Christians of Gorakhpur were said to have suffered almost as badly; they were compelled to abandon their houses and take refuge at Aliganj. Not only that, seven of them were stated to have escaped only after their pretended acceptance of Islam.[51]

All these incidents were looked upon as a manifestation of the general enmity of Islam towards Christianity. The result was that pathetic and at times highly moving verses were composed on several of these cruel and unfortunate happenings. These reflected the strength of public opinion on the subject. The Honourable and Reverend Baptist Wriothlesley Noel, MA, thus referred to the plight of Gopinath Nandi whom he described as a Muslim convert to Christianity (he had never been a Muslim as his name clearly indicates). This is how Nandi was said to have suffered at the hands of the people of his supposed former faith.[52]

> But who is he that elderman,
> Bound, beaten, fearing worse,
> On whom each fierce Mohammedan
> Is pointing out his curse?
>
> Why are those guards around him set?
> Those chords upon his wrist?
> He was the slave of Mahomet,
> And now he preaches Christ.
>
> 'Repent!' exclaimed the sepoy crew
> 'Or Allah's vengeance taste!'
> 'Repent!' exclaimed their captain too,
> 'or this day is thy last!'
>
> 'Seek then the prophet's aid by prayer.
> Abjure the Christian lie
> Or by his sacred name I swear
> Apostate thou shalt die!'[53]

In short, bitterness on the part of Muslims was reported from all parts of India. The letter of almost every missionary had something to say on this subject.[54] The Rev. Robinson, the Baptist pastor at Johnnugger,[55] complained of Muslim malignity when he wrote to say that the Muslims 'in our neighbourhood gave expressions to feelings no less bitter than their brethren elsewhere'.[56] Almost everywhere their slogan was that the Company's rule had come to an end and that the Muslims were to have supremacy in its stead.[57]

Such opinions, already strongly held, tended to become stronger still when the attitude of the Muslims was contrasted with the behaviour of Hindus. There were occasions when the Muslims attacked Europeans or native Christians and Hindus rescued them.[58] The Reverend W. Buyers, a missionary, in his letter home wrote of how the native Christians in Banaras were protected by 'a heathen'—a job rendered difficult the next day by Muslims 'some of whom said, that if they got a chance they would kill all Christians'.[59] Gopinath Nandi, an evangelist of the American mission at Fatehpur, when attacked by a group of Muslims, was saved by a Hindu goldsmith.[60] Nathanial, a native

Christian of Agra, along with nine others, while hunted by Muslims, was saved by some Hindus.[61] The Reverend W. Beynon, an evangelist of the London Missionary Society at Belgaum, informed his people in England how the Christians there were saved by a Hindu friend, Mooto Comar [Muttu Kumar], and how Mooto's employment of very trusted servants led to the discovery of a plot among the Muslims. The plot had as its objective the murder of all Europeans at and between Belgaum and Poona.[62] Several other Britons in India had similar complaints or experiences.[63] Major-General W.O. Swanston, who wrote under the pseudonym 'Volunteer,' emphatically noted in his *Journal*:

> That the villainous and barbarous deeds committed have, with few exceptions, been perpetrated by the Mohammedans there is little doubt: and however guilty the Hindoo soldiery may be, the Hindoos as a race have generally been the people to save and protect the Christian.[64]

And an officer from Naini Tal had this to say:

> Since I wrote yesterday news has come that Hindoos have arisen against the Mohammedans and seized Moradabad and the guns there, and that they have also split and are ready to go at one another's throats at Bareilly. The Mohammedans have been oppressing the Hindoos terribly, and the worm has turned. The Hindoos are numerous enough to win the day if they are staunch.
>
> They are also very well affected to us (at least in this neighbourhood), and have been sending us constant messages to come back again, which we should have done if we had had any force here at all....[65]

Those who held the Muslim rebellion thesis were convinced that the outbreak was entirely a Muslim movement, in which Hindus had no part. They had reasons to offer, on the basis of which they tried to rationalize their arguments. It was contended that: Firstly, it was centuries ago that Hindus were deprived of their domination in India—practically a millennium. During such a long period it was unlikely that the art of government would be retained by them. In fact, they had come to believe in their status; they had ceased to be aspiring; ambition had become foreign to them. In the future too, maintained the *London Journal and Weekly Record of Literature, Science and Arts*, it 'would be a matter of indifference to them who were their rulers.'[66] Secondly, the Hindus had, it was contended, not yet forgotten the tyranny of Muslim rule. They hated them from the core of their being. As such, it was maintained, they would not be prepared to restore the past and so cause their own doom.[67]

Thirdly, the rich merchants in the Indian community came from among the Hindus. The establishment of peace and security was in their interest. This was what, it was thought, they knew they could only get from the British administration. The *Missionary Magazine* wrote that 'notwithstanding the critical state of the country, there is much to excite our confidence and gratitude, and to fill our hearts with thanksgivings to our heavenly Father. The whole country, including all its wealth and respectability is with us—that is, the mass of the Hindus'.[68] The wealthy landowners and bankers, happily reported a lady from Gwalior, were feeling as concerned as did the British about the law and order situation. They openly said that if once the Muslims gained power in the subcontinent, they would snatch their lands and riches from them.[69]

Finally, it was believed that Hinduism was not an aggressive religion. Aggressiveness was thought only to be in the nature of Islam.[70] Unlike Muslims, the Hindus had no religion to preach—nothing to propagate. Politically as well, it was affirmed, while the Muslims had a tradition of almost a thousand years to impel them to action and while they had a ruler to reinstate, the Hindus had no king to rally around.[71] Nationally speaking, the Muslims were represented as a homogeneous body. They, it was stressed, viewed themselves as a conquered nation, and a vanquished people. Naturally, they wanted to be free of the British yoke. It was pointed out that in order to overthrow the British and achieve their goal of freedom, the Muslims enjoyed greater unity of action through their faith. This unity, however, was said to be wanting among the Hindus.[72] It was reported that not only did the Hindus not conspire against the British, but the most significant fact about them was that they even reproached the Muslims for misleading them.[73] In these circumstances the advocate judge was able to assert at the Delhi trial:

> ...it is a most significant fact, that though we come upon traces of Mussulman intrigue, wherever our investigation has carried us, yet not one paper has been found to show that the Hindus, as a body, had been conspiring against us, or that their Brahmins or priests had been preaching a crusade against Christians. In their case there has been no king to set up, no religion to be propagated by the sword. To attribute to them, under such circumstances, the circulation of these chapaties or the fabrications about ground-bones in the flour, would be to ascribe to them acts without a meaning, and a criminal deception without any adequate motive.[74]

In brief, it was claimed that it was not in the political, religious, social or commercial interests of the Hindus to take up arms against the

British, and as such the outbreak could not be attributed to them. It was purely a religious war waged by the followers of Islam. Archer took issue with those who called it just a political affair and alleged:

> ...I would say that when the Hindoos had once been induced to cross the Rubicon, the Mohammedans would not fail, as their assistance became valuable, and indeed indispensable, to turn the religious war to political account.[75]

To prove this further still, the Hindus were represented as cheerily reconciled to the falling fortunes of the rebels, while the Muslims were gloomy and sad.[76] The Rev. Williamson, a missionary, reported from Sewry that while all Muslims had believed that the English would either be all killed or driven out of India and were now crestfallen, the Hindus did not share such beliefs or feelings. The latter neither wished nor believed in the expulsion of the British.[77] That was why, argued the Reverend Lawrence, the Baptist missionary at Monghyr, the Hindus, whenever they were asked to condemn the mutineers, always joined in, but it was not so with the Muslims.[78] Even after the backbone of the rebellion had been crushed, the missionaries could not resume their activities in the predominantly Muslim areas.[79] On the contrary, it was reported, in Hindu regions the evangelistic work had either continued through the insurrection or was resumed shortly thereafter. In such regions, while the number of Hindu audiences had gone up considerably, the expression worn by a casual Muslim listener, it was stated, betrayed his injured pride—his recent defeat was writ large on his face.[80]

The depth of the feeling of the Muslim rebellion theorists is evidenced further by the retaliatory steps and punishments, especially their implementation, that some members of this school proposed for the Muslims. Such an attitude was based upon their conviction that Islam or its followers were the only enemies of both the British rule in India and the spread of Christianity in the subcontinent. The result was that even a religious-minded person like General Outram failed to mention the Muslims when he advocated lenient treatment for the Hindus to the Lieutenant-Governor of the North-Western Provinces.[81] The omission looks deliberate when one considers a fruitless attempt by Outram to separate the Hindus from the Muslims to weaken the latter's position. Raikes, who regarded the uprising as a sepoy mutiny, plus a Muslim and Gujar affair, with an emphasis upon the Muslim role, completely concurred with Philip Egerton, the Magistrate of Delhi, when the latter proposed the conversion of the Delhi Masjid into a church with each brick named after a Christian martyr. Raikes went so far as to write to Sir John Lawrence, the chief commissioner of the Punjab, urging him to attend to this proposition.[82] An Anglo-Indian ardently advocated through the agency of *Calcutta Englishman* the reintroduction of torture for the Muslims of Delhi. He recommended that 'respectable' Muslims should be subjected to the thumbscrew or the rack.[83] The author of 'A Few Words from the Khyber', while advocating memorable punishment for the 'murderers of women and infants', gave vent to his wrath against the city of Delhi. Especially emphasizing the Muslim character of the city, he observed:

> ...the city which has been for centuries the stronghold of Islamism in India, and in which was hatched this last great conspiracy against the Christian religion should be utterly destroyed; and that on its site should be built another city, to be the centre from which victorious Christianity should radiate to every point from North to South, from East to West, from Bombay to Calcutta, from the Himalayas to the Cape Camorin.[84]

Thus the treatment of the Muslim population of Delhi was especially harsh. They were all regarded as unfaithful. Every Muslim house was reportedly ransacked and every Muslim inhabitant was turned out of the city to remain in banishment for six months. The treatment given to the Hindus was far more lenient.[85] Fifteen months after the fall of Delhi, the *Missionary Herald* of January 1859 had this to report on the authority of the Rev. James Smith from Delhi:

> As yet Mohammedans have not been admitted to the city. There are about sixty thousand Hindoos, a third of the former inhabitants. The beautiful musjids [sic] are all occupied as barracks by the Sikhs, and there can be no doubt that the humiliation of Mohammedans is complete.[86]

A writer in *Fraser's Magazine* proudly remarked:

> ...the unfriendly race of Mahomedans was put on its defence, and banished for the time from that city which had so long been the pestilent focus of Mahomedan intrigues....[87]

Later on, however, those Muslims who were allowed to return to their homes had to give proof of their good intentions before gaining entrance into Delhi.[88]

There were many others who could not contain their happiness at what they thought to be the declining fortunes of Islam—'its violent overthrow and humiliation'.[89] A writer in *Blackwood's Edinburgh Magazine* thus observed:

> While believing that the insurrection was meant as a lesson to us, I also believe that by it a great blow has been struck at the Mohammedan religion—a blow from which it will never recover in India. Tens of thousands of its most bigoted supporters will lose their lives; the King of Delhi, the head of the religion, will infallibly be hung; and the city itself, the great stronghold of the faith, will be utterly destroyed. This mutiny, I believe, will be the death blow to Islamism, and from its ashes will spring up and flourish, that only true religion which is destined to overshadow the whole earth.[90]

CHAPTER 9

Worldwide Jihad or a Clash of Civilizations?

A sizeable section of the British public looked at the uprising in India as if it were a jihad waged by worldwide Islam against worldwide Christianity—a modern day name change would make it clash of civilizations. Of course, this view was based on Islamophobia of the British and had no real basis. It was largely drawn from Britons' own memory of the Third Crusade, two European crusades before 1187, as well as several crusades thereafter. European and British hostility against Islam and Muslims was so intense that the Fifth Crusade was a children's crusade—teenage soldiers of Christ. Pope Urban II called Muslims, 'infidels'. All popes thereafter were inimical and hostile to Islam. This Anglo-Saxon view of Islam and Muslims continued unabated in time. As a result, British perception of the revolt in India as a global jihad was also based on a European view of Islam and Muslims which was non-factual, polemical, hostile, demeaning, and dehumanizing. It also rested on Britons' self-perception of themselves as possessors of the best Christian tradition.[1]

From the very beginning, the Christian church was faced with internal self-questioning which gave birth to the movement of heresy. The Church at Rome took drastic steps to control deviations from the mainstream teachings of the church. Any infringement would lead to severe punishments, such as excommunication, crucifixion, and even burning alive. During this time Islam came to the fore; it accepted Jesus in almost all Christian precepts except his divinity. In the environment of the time this was a monumental heresy. Muhammad (PBUH), the prophet of Islam, was not in the jurisdiction of the church. He could not be pulled in and excommunicated or given any other prevailing punishments. Helpless in apprehending Muhammad (PBUH), Christian hostility toward Islam took the form of venomous writings on the new religion. Instead of doing a rational analysis of Islam, comparing it with Jewish and Christian traditions, European writings on Islam and its prophet were accusative, insulting, and characterless.

These writings were mostly produced at monasteries and church-related institutions by ignorant Europeans who did not know much about Islam, its prophet, Muslim traditions, or the Arab world. Most had never travelled to the Middle East, did not know the Arabic language and yet they were the earliest European writers on Islam. In the climate of the time, their writings were viewed as definitive and used by later writers to develop their own theses on Islam. Ignorance multiplied was like compound interest, usurious in nature, in which interest quickly far outweighed the principal. All kinds of unbelievable stories verging on the ridiculous were invented about Muhammad (PBUH).[2] Large scale conversions to Islam, both in the Middle East and Europe, added fury to European invectives and misrepresentations of Islam. To 'stem this tide of conversions' by convincing 'Christians not to convert,' leaders of the Christian communities needed to logically explain to the faithful 'the dramatic successes' of Islam and do so in such a way that an average Christian would easily comprehend the situation. This certainly needed to be done 'in the context of a (Christian) divine plan.' Therefore, one of the important weapons used was initiation of Christian polemics against Islam: Muhammad (PBUH) was declared as the antichrist and Islam a 'form of diabolical error.'[3]

This tide of Christian polemics against Islam took the form of personal attacks on the prophet and Muslims as a whole. Facts were distorted to the degree that they could no longer be recognized; history was rewritten in an unhistorical manner. These misrepresentations were so gross that they had no resemblance with reality. A prophet who, in the tradition of Abraham/Ibrahim, forbade idolatry, who eliminated hundreds of idols from the Kaa'ba, who forbade imagery including his own likeness, and whose followers took pride in being the most focused Unitarians, was himself presented by British writers as a deity and as an idol worshipped by Muslims. At times one finds an entire church service devoted to this Christian perspective of Muhammad.

The Qur'an was also depicted as an object of worship. European imagination surely ran wild when Muslims were portrayed as an idol-worshipping people who blew brass horns in elaborate rituals to worship idols. Apollo was depicted as another Muslim idol. Roland, a French poet, and Arthur S. Sway, an English writer and translator, described Arabs as Apollo worshippers; therefore, after their defeat at Saragossa in 778 by Charlemagne, Muslims ran 'to their god Apollo' and threw themselves upon his statue.[4] World famous Elizabethan philosopher-scholar, Francis Bacon, referred to the Prophet of Islam as a 'miracle-monger.' In his essay entitled 'Of Boldness,' Bacon revealed both the depth of his hostility to Islam and the clarity of his inventive mind when he fabricated the proverbial hill story. Bacon wrote:

> Mahomet made the people believe that he would call a hill to him and from the top of it offer up his prayers for the observers of his law. The people assembled. Mahomet called the hill to come to him again and again and when the hill stood still, he was never a bit abashed, but said, 'If the hill will not come to Mahomet, Mahomet will go to the hill'.[5]

This alleged quotation from the Prophet of Islam became an axiomatic proverb in the English literature, while it has no existence in the Islamic or Arabic literature whatsoever.

The following titles of works on Muhammad (PBUH) and Islam are indicative of the depth of British hatred of Islam and its prophet. Lancelot Addison, an English chaplain at Algiers, anonymously published in 1679 his famous book on Islam: *The First State of Mahumedanism: Or, An Account of the Author and the Doctrines of that Impostor*. His contemporary Dr Humphrey Prideaux, Dean of Norwich, wrote the first complete biography of Muhammad (PBUH). It was entitled: *The True Nature of Imposture Displayed in the Life of Mahomet*. This book went through dozens of editions and remained a standard book of readings on the Prophet and Islam well into nineteenth century Britain. The theme of this book was that Islam was a perfect example of a fraudulent religion.[6] On the other hand, the title of the book written by John Lydgate, a fifteenth century poet and scholar, is not worthy of reproduction in this work. It will hurt the feelings alike of all Muslim as well as unbiased non-Muslim readers.[7] Sir William Muir, a well-known nineteenth century British civil servant and scholar, author of 'much celebrated' works: *Life of Muhammad* and The *Caliphate, Its Rise, Decline and Fall*, helped develop the myth that Muslims always carried the sword in one hand and the Qur'an in the other.[8]

Indeed, this ignorance and hostility toward Islam and Muslims continued unabated into the eighteenth and nineteenth centuries. The first British translation of the Qur'an was done by George Sale in November 1734. An attorney by profession, Sale was a narrow-minded, self-righteous, arrogant Christian scholar. On the first unnumbered page of his translation, this is how he dedicated his effort to educate his countrymen about the Muslim holy book:

> ... the most authentic and truthful translation of the al Koran, written by the...prophet Mohamed, whose religion subjugated more millions of mankind than Christianity ever liberated.

In dedicating his translation of the Qur'an to John Lord Carteret, a member of the King's Privy Council, he described the Prophet of Islam to be 'an impsture' and 'a most abandoned vallain [*sic*]'.[9] For more than a century Sale enjoyed a profound influence among his countrymen as well as in Europe. Robert D. Richardson, Jr. of Denver University, who wrote the introduction to the 1984 edition of Sale's *The Koran*, observes:

> Sale's edition is…the single most influential source of English knowledge of Islam for the last two-thirds of the eighteenth century and the first two-thirds of the nineteenth. Sale's work was also translated into German, Polish, and twice into French.
>
> It would seem that nearly all writers—between 1750 and 1850 who dealt with Islam used Sale's Koran. Beckford drew on it for *Vathek*, Gibbon used it, Byron's *Bride Of Abydos* and Shelley's *Queen Mab* owe something to it. Southey, Moore, Carlyle, and Bulwer-Lytton all drew on it, and in America Poe made repeated use of it beginning with 'Al Aaraaf.' This is only a sampling.[10]

This bias and hatred of Islam and Muslims was carried right into India by British civil and military servants who went to rule the colony. In order to join the Indian civil service, these Britons needed to graduate from Hailebury College. Here, the required history textbook on India was written by James Mill, a famous Benthamite philosopher. As soon as he finished his *History Of British India*, James Mill was taken into the service of the East India Company. In no time, he became secretary of state for India, even though he had never been to India, had no first-hand experience of Indian culture and traditions, and did not know a single language of India. His only qualification was that he wrote a six-volume history of India, which was based more on hearsay and second-hand knowledge than scholarship. It was designed to fit the imperial thinking of Britons. Even though the book is full of errors and assumptions, its negative influence upon British thinking about India could hardly be underestimated. Mill conveniently excluded India from his political philosophy of greatest happiness of the greatest number. Like a chameleon, he changed his colours; indeed he was a subtle pioneer or a companion of Rudyard Kipling—greatest happiness of the greatest number of Europe but not for Asia and certainly not for India. He was an imperialist who did not find much good in India. He stressed that India needed British imperial guidance, governance and enlightenment. His work, an updated fifth edition of which was published in 1848, was highly esteemed by less informed

Britons and it quickly established a firm hold on the minds of a large majority of so-called 'Indophiles.' No wonder C.H. Philips, the well-known editor of *Historians Of India, Pakistan, And Ceylon*, stresses that Mill's book established a 'James Millian tradition' in the historical accounts of India.[11]

Apart from the above ignorance, Britons were deep into a new age of evangelism. They were convinced that India, the second largest country in the world, was given to them by God as a gift to spread Anglican Christianity among the 'heathens' of India.[12] A new passion took hold of the British public. Brainwashed by James Mill through his book, Britons were convinced of their mission in the South Asian colony.[13] If that were not the case, why would God snatch India from 'Romish' Portugal and endow it upon an Anglican nation. Indeed, many Britons asserted, already much precious time was lost due to the un-Christian and obstructionist policies of the East India Company. God was angry and He was visiting Britain through a punitive revolt in India.[14] Such views were held firmly and broadly, and shared by such prominent personalities as W.E. Gladstone, who later became the British prime minister, members of the House of Lords, members of the British parliament, directors of the East India Company, members of the Court of Directors, almost all clergymen, and many British citizens.[15] While Reverend Hoare stressed that India 'was placed in British hands by God Himself,'[16] the Reverend J. Cairns asserted that the 'man who does not see the hand of God in this, does not believe in God at all'.[17] The Reverend John Hampdon Gurney, Prebendary of St. Paul's, London, went a step further when like a clerical Rudyard Kipling, he unequivocally stressed that it was 'the will of God that Indians should be a subject race to the British, unless the latter had given the former their faith.'[18] R.C. Mather was even more decisive when he declared that to Christianize India the hold of 'the three surviving systems of error, Hinduism, Buddhism, and Muhammadanism' upon the people of India has to be broken.[19] And Edward Hoare faithfully concluded that the Lord chose to give India to England 'in order that England's light might shine in India's darkness'.[20] Indeed, this feeling had become the heartbeat of the British; with few exceptions they had become a nation of Rudyards. As discussed in Chapter One, even *The Times* stressed, 'We cannot now refuse our part or change our destiny.' A clash of civilizations was in the making: a determination by the British to Christianize South Asia and a counter-determination by the South Asians to resist all such efforts. Little wonder, Dr Ian W. Brown in his Master's and Ph.D. dissertations, both entitled 'English

Evangelicals in British Politics, 1780–1833; correctly entitled his chapter on Britain's South Asian colony, 'Crusade to Christianize India'.[21]

Consequently, convinced of this mission, many British civil and military servants of the East India Company took it upon themselves to preach the Gospel to Indians, both Hindu and Muslim—in and out of the army.[22] The Church of England establishment in India began to be supported by Indian revenues; bishops were provided 'royal' protocol with military escorts.[23] Missionaries began to be appointed as inspectors of schools and the Bible was introduced as a classroom book. However, in their evangelical endeavours the British found Indian Muslims not only hard to penetrate but somewhat obstructionists to their public preaching. At times Muslims would successfully debate them on Christian theology and this would drive a good part of the audience away.[24] Indeed, British missionaries always complained about Muslim intransigence in receiving the Gospel.[25]

This was the mindset of Britons when the news of the revolt in the South Asian colony arrived in London on 28 June 1857. Since the two centres of the revolt, Delhi and Lucknow, were Muslim cities, as were the two top leaders of the revolt, Islamophobes among the British started to look for a broader meaning behind the events in India. In its article 'Delhi and the Muhammedan Rebellion in India', *The New Monthly Magazine* readily and confidently observed:

> It is not only that Islamism has raised the standard of revolt in the old capital of India—the seat of Patan [Pathan] and Mogul [Mughal] dynasties, and the centre of Muhammadan rule in Asia—against Great Britain, that it has, by misrepresentations and falsehoods, seduced the plain and superstitious Hindoos, and by a mongrel hybrid proclamation, after the style of those of Hannuk [Nanak], the founder of the Seiks [Sikhs] attempted to identify paganism of the Hindoo with the iconoclasm of the Muhammadan,—it is that by reviving the sway of the Mussulman in India and central Asia, the long-dormant ambition of fanaticism of Islamism is aroused throughout the world.
>
> The hopes of better days, the promises of success and triumphs, have been once more brought home to the impulsive imagination of the followers of the Prophet, and have caused the pulse of Islamism to vibrate from Delhi to Tehran and Bokhara and from Constantinople to Cairo, to Algiers and to Morocco.[26]

People in Britain immediately started to pick at isolated incidents in the Muslim world which occurred more as a reaction to British imperial policies in Arabia, Persia, or the Ottoman Empire than anything else, and projected them as a global Muslim endeavour to fight global Christianity.[27] These Britons did not pause to think that it was the British who made provocative and strong military, political, economic, educational, and spiritual inroads into Muslim lands. It would be foolhardy for analytical minds not to expect resistance and opposition. Red carpet treatment was simply out of the question. To translate various local incidents against British interference in local affairs, to be a global movement was a far-fetched idea. So, as there was very little factual basis for such a point of view except intense British dislike of Islam, this view neither gained the strength nor the depth of the mutiny, revolution, or Muslim rebellion theses. In sum, the British confused their imperialist exploits with their Christian faith—making it sound like 'imperialism of faith'—and wrongly viewed Muslim resistance to it as an Islamic response; they were looking at Islam and Muslims in their own image.

Clearly, therefore, the worldwide jihad perception of the Indian revolt was born of: a) Britons' self-perception as a Christian nation 'enjoined by God' with a distinct task of spreading Christianity among the 'heathens' of the world, in general, and the 'heathens' of India, in particular; b) their biased perception of Islam; c) their belief that Islam was a religion of the sword;[28] d) the discovery of a document at Khurramshahr (then called Mohamara)[29] in Persia during British invasion of Iran; e) Allied treatment of Turkey after the Crimean War and its possible repercussions in the Muslim world; f) stray incidents in the Turkish empire and, finally, massacre of twenty-one individuals—mostly Christians—at Jeddah on 15 June 1858.

This interesting attitude received a major boost all over Britain after the last-mentioned event in Arabia, but it started to dissipate shortly thereafter leaving not much of a trace behind. Like the Muslim rebellion school of thought, this group gained its adherents from all different levels of British society, irrespective of their political, social, or denominational affiliations. One thing was evident, however, with significant exceptions this attitude largely remained confined to the British press. It would be hard for the present writer to assign any definite reasons to their conclusions, except that they were based upon their advocates' understanding of Islam, the contemporary situation, biased British scholarship and journalistic flavour in writings on Islam.

It was believed by advocates of this thesis that Allied help to Turkey to meet the Russian threat in the 1850s was regarded as an affront to Turkish power. The Allies, by sending their armies, had slighted the

Turks—a slight which the latter had not forgotten. In fact, it was believed that Allied assistance in the Crimean War had humiliated the entire Muslim world. The conditions attached to military assistance and the consequences thereof appeared to the 'faithful' as a menace to the 'doctrine of Islamism' in the region. The supposition was that Muslims viewed it as a blow to four centuries of their hegemony on the banks of Bosphorus.[30] Allied insistence that the Porte introduce reforms gave the Muslim states, especially the Muslims of Persia and South Asia, an impression that the Allies helped Turkey to betray her.[31] More significantly, Muslims all over the world were reported to have felt indignant at the Tanzimat.[32]

Muslims feared, it was stressed, that the Allies by entering into a treacherous alliance with Turkey had destroyed 'the ascendancy of the religion of Muhammad and of the grand Padishah.' Thus, it was asserted, 'the war in Turkey prepared the way for a Mohammedan struggle in India, in Persia—everywhere.'[33] It was stated that the Christians had never been more detested, persecuted or abused than since the 'Christian states declared themselves the protectors of Mahometanism.'[34] A writer in the *Edinburgh Review* contended that all this was 'attributed to the sinister influence of Great Britain.'[35] The result was, it was stressed, that the Muslims made no secret of their feelings; they broke out everywhere, whenever a pretext presented itself for the 'explosion of their suppressed hatred.'[36]

A further development of this spirit took place, it was contended, when Persia, already aroused, was itself threatened with hostilities from England. Emissaries were dispatched to the states of central Asia to call upon Muslims 'to reject the alliance with a nation whose friendship was more dangerous to Islamism, than its enmity could be.' The author of the article 'India', published in the *Edinburgh Review*, went on to argue that the emissaries, having been sent to India with the idea of playing upon the religious fears of the Muslims of India, had thus incited the soldiery to revolt, but the train of powder could not be ignited in time to aid Persian designs. The only reason for this failure was, he maintained, that England struck Persia too quickly and effectively, and was even able to relieve the invading armies in time for them to aid in the suppression of the revolt in India.[37] W.H. Carey, however, dealt with the Persian machination elaborately and emphatically, when he referred to the proclamation of the king of Persia found at Delhi. To him this document was sufficient indication of a Persian-backed Muslim scheme for an uprising, plan to murder Europeans indiscriminately and restore the house of Timur at Delhi.[38]

He attached so great an importance to this paper that he came to regard the late events in India as the immediate cause of the outbreak, and the machinations of Tehran as the ultimate one. The well-known missionary believed that it was the Persian proclamation that 'had already unsettled the minds of good Mussulmans throughout the length and breadth of the land, and laid them open to the reception of any well devised plan whereby they might regain that ascendancy which they had lost for so many years.' Otherwise, he thought, Muslim disaffection in the presidencies of Bombay and Madras could not possibly have been due to the influence of Delhi and Lucknow alone. To emphasize this aspect of the revolt he went on to observe:

> And we are rather confirmed in opinion from the circumstance that when intelligence of the rebellion reached Teheran [sic] the ulemas preached up the righteousness of the cause in all their mosques, and supplicated the divine blessing on the efforts of the insurgents.[39]

So sure was Carey of the Persian machination that he dated Muslim conspiracy back only to the Anglo-Persian war. The basis of such a view with Carey was the discovery of a 'manifesto of the Shah of Persia', found in the camp of a prince after the Battle of Khurramshahr. The evidence quoted in full by Carey provides, if an authentic document, an insight into the Persian feelings, verging on conviction, of common wrongs of the Muslims at the hands of the British in particular and the *farangi* in general. It also gives a vivid pen-picture of Persian efforts to put up a common front against a common enemy.[40] The manifesto was indeed a strong exhortation to the Muslims of Persia as well as of Afghanistan to 'arise in the defence of the Orthodox faith of the Prophet.'[41] After having referred to various army commands and the dispatch of various troops, the manifesto alluded to India and read:

> ...and in the direction of Cutch and Mekran towards Scinde [Sindh], and from the direction of Affghanistan [sic] the Nawab Ahsham Ooh Sultanut with 30,000 men and 40 guns, abundantly supplied and equipped; and the Affghan [sic] Sirdars (viz). Sirdar Sultan Ahmed Khan, Sirdar Shah Doolah Khan, Sirdar Sultan Ali Khan and Sirdar Mahomed Allum Khan, who have been appointed by his Majesty, *have been ordered towards India*, and they are hopeful that by the blessing of divine aid they may be victorious.[42]

The manifesto, urging 'all true believers' to unite, fervently invoked their help against the British. In fact, it gave a call far jihad, which read:

And it is necessary that the Affghan [sic] tribes and the inhabitants of that country, who are co-religionists of the Persians, and who possess the same Kuran [sic] and kiblah [Qiblah, meaning direction of prayer: i.e., toward Mecca and the ka'bah] and laws of the prophet should also take part in the Jahad [Jihad] and extend the hand of brotherhood, and on receiving these glad tidings act according to the words of the prophet...*and for the purpose of settling the quarrel it is necessary that not only a small number of true believers should stand forth in the defence of the faith, but that the whole should answer our call*...and we are hopeful that after the publication of this proclamation, Dost Mahomed Khan, Ameer of Cabool [sic]...should also unite with us against the tribe of wanderers from the path of righteousness, and that he should become one of the leaders of the faithful in this Jahad, and that he should become a 'Ghazi' in Hindostan.... *And this proclamation is published for the information of all true believers, and to please God the followers of Islam in India and Scinde will also unite with us and take vengeance upon that tribe (the British) for all the injuries which the holy faith has suffered from them, and will not withhold any sacrifices in the holy cause.*[43]

This manifesto and the clauses which it contained were to Carey a clue to the 'formidable rebellion' which plagued the British Indian administration for quite some time. Frederick Cooper and a few others also emphasized the influence of the Persian proclamation.[44]

Similarly, Reverend G.P. Badger, a chaplain in the diocese of Bombay, had another piece of evidence to offer on Persian complicity in the conspiracy. He referred to what he called 'a singular proof', a Persian Government Farman,[45] which appeared in the *Tehran Gazette* in March 1857. The object of this decree, contended Badger, was to 'excite a jihad or religious war against the infidel British.' According to this clergyman, the decree, after severely commenting on the British Indian financial and taxation systems, charged the British Government in India with an attempt to: a) subvert the religion of the natives of India; b) force the wives of the 'faithful' to walk abroad unveiled; c) compel them to 'violate another precept of the holy Koran, by commanding them to drink'; and, d) above all, to 'crown the nefarious and profane designs', force Muslim children into English schools at a 'very young' age and keep them there until eighteen years—an age at which the youth would not submit to the initiatory rite of circumcision, thus enabling the rulers to convert them from Islam.[46]

The advocate judge of the Army at the trial of Bahadur Shah, and quite a few others, referred to the discovery of 'a traitorous correspondence', which, according to the *Annual Register* was kept up between the courts of Delhi and Persia.[47] The *Register* reported that efforts were being made to allure Dost Muhammad of Afghanistan into the conspiracy. The belief was that Dost was being asked to invade Punjab after the Bengal army had revolted and after the north-west frontier had been left defenceless. A concomitant object of this plot was to spread disaffection in the ranks of the native army. But as the sepoy army was not easy to penetrate, and because it took longer to bring the soldiers into the plot, this absence of a timely civilian-sepoy combination prevented an earlier uprising as originally envisaged by the plotters.[48] Dr Alexander Duff likewise feared that Persian agents had long been present among the Muslim princes of India. In his letter of 26 August 1857, addressed to Dr Tweedie in Scotland, the Scottish missionary further informed the latter:

> And to-day one of our best-informed journals positively announces that the 'Government of Bombay has transmitted to the supreme Government of India, certain Persian document addressed to the khan of Kelat [Kalat], asking him to give his assistance to the mutineers in expelling the British power'.

Duff attached great significance to it because of the Shi'ah ties between India and Persia.[49]

All this becomes more meaningful when one reads about the Indian government's efforts to shroud the Persian war with complete secrecy as well as the rumours spread by the allegedly Muslim-backed press about the presence of Persian troops at Delhi. Twenty-five days before the actual outbreak at Meerut, the Calcutta correspondent of *The Times* bitterly complained of what he called the government's 'rigid and most injurious secrecy' regarding the operations of war in Persia. Referring to the attempts made at concealing even the 'smallest facts', he wondered 'if the Persian court were in communication with the Indian press.' To him such an inexplicable attitude was symptomatic of weakness 'beginning to be felt by every department of the Government', as well as indicative of 'want of courage' and 'of audacity' in every resolution of the supreme authority.[50] Compared with this was the news item in the *Authentic News* of 19 March (most probably 1856), as pointed out by the advocate judge of the Army at the Delhi trial, about the presence of Persian troops in India.[51]

It was reported that the outbreak, though little more than a military revolt in India, was not viewed as such in the Muslim countries stretching beyond the British Indian frontier. Instead of merely regarding it as a contest between the master and the servant—'between a discontented or excited army and the Government, they regarded it as a war between Mahomedanism and Christianity, upon the issue of which the very existence of Islamism was staked.' The outbreak had, it was believed, caused much hope and jubilation among the 'faithful' in all the countries in which the word of the Prophet was 'preached to the many or to the few'—a feeling which, it was thought, was sure to continue so long as the Muslim city of Delhi remained the centre of the outbreak and Bahadur Shah its leader.[52]

Such opinion was not shared by certain sections of the British society alone, but also seems to have been held by the European press. Under the title, 'The Coming Struggle', the *Free Press* quoted from and agreed with the *Neue Preussische Zeitung*. It was believed that the struggle of Islam against Christianity was not confined to India alone, but that Muslims were 'standing to their arms...throughout Asia Minor, Syria and Egypt.' The *Neue Preussische Zeitung* reported that the trade in arms in all these countries had enormously increased; that there was a massive movement of arms to the above mentioned Middle Eastern countries and that the gunsmiths' stores everywhere were full of customers. No doubt, Birmingham and Liege were 'reaping a golden harvest' from this arms traffic. The paper maintained that this was a matter of concern to the 'Franks and Christians'. Wherever there were Muslims and Christians living together—be it Calcutta or be it Smyrna, Acre or Alexandria, everywhere, the paper stated, the Muslims were showing signs of distrust and hatred towards the Christians. If the Governor-General at Calcutta witnessed them buying arms, so did the consuls in Egypt, Syria and Turkey. If this account is to be accredited, Muslim anxiety and feverishness seems to have reached its highest pitch at this time. It was reported that even the most peace-loving among the Muslims, and even villages and towns were working towards an organization of communal defence. To the paper it appeared as if the entire Muslim population of Asia was preparing itself for the kind of struggle that had already manifested itself in the Indian subcontinent.[53] Finally, the paper rounded up its discussion of the East with a warning to the people of Europe as well as the countries championing the cause of Turkey, of the incredible amount of antipathy and hostility that existed against them broadcast among the Muslims. The paper went on to observe:

> Whether these intense feelings will be allayed without bloodshed, we cannot tell; but it is quite necessary for Europe to be on its guard.[54]

It was against this state of public thinking that around a year later news of the gruesome massacre of twenty-one individuals—mostly Christians—in Jeddah arrived in Britain in middle of July 1858. On 15 June 1858, a mob of 5000[55] to 8000[56] infuriated Arabs was reported to have attacked the British and the French consulates at Jeddah, killing the consuls of the two leading nations of Europe. Fourteen to nineteen other Christians, mostly Greek, who attempted to protect the English, were among those slain.[57] The cause of this bloody event, as reported by the Earl of Malmesbury in the House of Lords, was a dispute over the nationality of an Indian ship. Its owner, obviously a Muslim, desired to change the nationality of his ship from Anglo-Indian to a Turkish flagship. The British turned the matter over to a 'legal tribunal'. Surprisingly, while the French Consul was invited to sit on it, the tribunal had no Turkish, Arab, or Muslim representation. As expected, it returned an adverse verdict. The ship's owner changed the flag anyway. British effort to take the Turkish flag down and re-hoist the Union Jack in a Muslim land infuriated the citizens of Jeddah to such a degree that several thousand of them charged on the British and French consulates and let loose a day of horror.

That the above flare-up was unplanned and sudden in nature is clearly established by a letter from a correspondent of *The Times*. Writing from Alexandria, Egypt, on 6 July 1858, he informed his readers that the crew of the Cyclops toured the neighbourhoods of Jeddah on 14 June 1858 late into the evening. Not only was there no hostile incident, they were well received. Yet 15 June experienced a bloody uprising. What brought about this change? Of course, the flag incident. It was native nationalism versus encroaching British imperialism in a Muslim land clashing with each other. The Earl of Malmesbury further reported that the Ottoman government did its best to protect Christian lives and that five Turkish soldiers were also killed in the performance of their duty.[58] It is highly significant to note that the flag issue in Jeddah had been very sensitive for nearly two decades or more. In a letter to *The Times*, Antoine D'Abbadie, who identified himself as a correspondent of *l' Institute*, reported that in his personal experience the Union Jack was previously trampled under foot at Jeddah twice in 1839 and 1840. Once D'Abadie's own brother was forced to walk on the Union Jack in 1840.[59] Under these circumstances for the British to have insisted on the nationality of the Indian ship and the flag it flew in another sovereign state was not only impolitic but also quite provocative.

Additionally, several other plausible causes were offered for the Jeddah uprising; that it was: (a) caused by trading jealousies, which it was stressed, lay at the bottom of the sanguinary affair;[60] (b) instigated by a Muslim messenger from India who described the rebels at Delhi and other places to be triumphant; (c) provoked by deep-seated Muslim hatred and distrust of Europeans;[61] (d) caused by what *The Nation* described as the real explanation of the incident—the excitement produced in the Muslim mind by the continued slaughter of their brethren in India by England. This paper forcefully asserted that England was engaged in raising a blood-cloud in the East, which might one day engulf the whole world.[62] However, Antoine D'Abbadie rejected all of the above reasons for the Jeddah calamity and unequivocally attributed it to unpredictable Muslim malevolence against Christianity and Christian powers. Instead of analysing the background of the Arab national sentiment, D'Abbadie listed several instances of Arab hostility against the British and the French in 1839–40 in Jeddah, and irrationally asserted that he had never had the 'good fortune of meeting a Mussulman who was not a liar'; for him, therefore, it was inconsequential to assign any reasons to the Jeddah revolt of 15 June 1858.[63] In the opinion of this author, however, the real cause of the tragedy at Jeddah was the arrogance of the captain of the British ship, Cyclops, who would not tolerate the hoisting of a Turkish flag on a Muslim ship at a Turkish port. This lack of tolerance, diplomacy, and statesmanship by Captain Pullen quickened the pace of events in Jeddah. A large number of the local population responded suddenly and the mob mentality could not be brought under control by the local authorities.

Whatever the true cause of the bloody tragedy in Jeddah, it stirred the already excited British people and their press to new heights. It was firmly believed that Muslim ill will was of long standing and widespread all over Arabia. D'Abbadie attested to it on the basis of his personal experiences and those of others.[64] Hence, it was thought that the flag issue was merely a pretext, hurriedly seized upon to execute 'a long concocted scheme',[65] which had as its ultimate end the expulsion of all Christians from the Muslim 'Holy land'.[66] For further proof, it was reported that public thanksgivings were offered at Mecca for the extermination of Christians in the neighbourhood of the city.[67] The real cause, therefore, was fancied to be the Muslim fanaticism and their 'national' hatred of Christians.[68] Various other incidents, i.e., the alleged treatment of the British embassy in Persia and the attempted assassination of the British consul at Belgrade, were at once lined up one after the other.[69] It was also recorded on the basis of intelligence from Athens that a terrible reaction against Christians had set in among the Muslims in Candia and that attacks upon European consulates and the Catholic Church at that place had compelled its Christian population to leave the city.[70] Further rumours of belligerent attitudes assumed by Muslims at other places in order to intimidate Christians were also reported.[71] Having held England indirectly responsible for the Jeddah massacre, *The Nation* feared that the incident appeared to be the beginning of a larger movement. The paper denounced the Muslims and observed:

> The religious fanaticism of the Mohammedans is analogous to the patriotic enthusiasm of the western nations. Islamism is the nationality of the East.[72]

In short, the press and the people refused to regard the Jeddah massacre as an isolated incident. They at once looked at it as a supplement to the Indian revolt—a monstrosity that had visited England on its 'high road' to India in the Red Sea.[73] From the sober Church of England press to such popular publications as the *Illustrated London News*, including highly informed papers like *The Times, The Manchester Guardian,* and *The Spectator,* strong editorials were written condemning the brutal massacre, as well as what was called 'Islamism' as the driving force behind it.[74] The Muslims of Turkey, Arabia, Persia, Egypt, Syria and India, one and all, were seen in a state of ferment, and their religion and 'race' were chiefly blamed for the late occurrences.[75] Since the centre of the present tragedy was Jeddah, the port town of Mecca, the whole thing was viewed with still greater apprehension. The *Church of England Quarterly Review* believed that the latent spirit of intolerance among the Muslims had been stirred to its depths. The periodical observed:

> From Candia in the Mediterranean to Jeddah on the Red Sea, the old hatred of Islamism to Christianity is in full activity. Wherever the followers of the... Prophet are strong enough to express their real convictions, the hatred against the Giaours breaks forth and there is reason to believe that that hatred, especially in the more Eastern domain of Islamism, vague rumours of which have found their way to all parts of the Mussulman world.[76]

The Spectator seems to have been much more appalled, and the paper candidly warned the entire Muslim world of the definite consequences—

another crusade—which could follow such an attitude, as the challenge would have to be accepted. It observed:

> ...it would appear that the Mussulmans, following the instinct of their lower race...are spoiling their own alliances by acts which must array against them, not only England, not only Western powers, but whole of Christendom, for all Europe must be aroused against warfare carried on as it has been at Jeddah and against the gross superstition which asserts its religious rivals in such shapes.[77]

As no oppression or outrage was believed to have been offered to Islam or the Shari'ah, the Church of England *Quarterly Review* saw no reason to account for the late events in India and the Arab world, except that the outrage was the outcome of a 'conscious weakness' on the part of the followers of Islam. Regarding the entire system of this religion as 'moribund', the Church magazine looked at the whole chain of events as a result of sheer desperation on the part of 'more sincere' or 'fanatical' spirits among the Muslims, who wanted to prove the vitality of their religion. It was confidently believed that like all 'such paroxysms of violence', the present outbursts in the Muslim world were sure to hasten the destruction of Islam.[78]

It was this very important aspect of the outbreak in India which led to its inclusion in a series of talks on the 'Signs of Time'.[79] The uprising began to be viewed in the much larger context of Islam. Efforts were even made to find the event in Biblical apocalyptic prophecies in the hope of discovering its 'bearing...on prospects of Mahometanism'.[80] Having been requested to do so, the Reverend Edward Hoare told his congregation about the futility of such an attempt. The 'prophecy', he declared, 'deals more with great systems than minute details.' No doubt, the mutinies had caused a lot of suffering, yet the event, he thought, was not big enough to find an independent mention in biblical writings. The occurrences in India were, therefore, to be treated as 'mere drops in the great ocean of world's troubles—a mere link in the long chain of world's history'. He exhorted his audience to concern themselves with the chain—'the great plan' and behold the 'sad events' in India as 'passing incidents in the gigantic purpose, whereby God is preparing the word for the glorious appearance of its coming King'.[81]

Hoare drew a crude analogy between the 'rise and spread' of what he termed 'the most extraordinary power, having its origin at Baghdad near the banks of the Euphrates'—the Ottoman empire and the rise and overflow of the Euphrates. He firmly believed that this symbolism held just as true when applied in reverse. To convince his audience of what he had said, Hoare further emphasized that it was no mere theory, but that history itself was evidence for this phenomenon. Thus if the overflow of the Euphrates was a sign of the rise and spread of the Ottoman Empire over Asia, Africa and Europe, the recess, he stressed, was surely a 'symbol of the loss of it'. As the waters of the Euphrates advanced, so did they recede. Similarly, the Turks, who had experienced a rapid rise to power, had already, he pointed out, lost their hold in North Africa, Persia and India. All this, he adduced, was happening according to the divine plan. Just as the waters were returning to their original channel as designed,[82] similarly the Turks would have to quit Constantinople and go back to Asia. It seemed as if the Turks were also conscious of their impending doom. Otherwise 'why', queried Hoare, 'to this day [do] they bury their dead on the other [i.e., Asiatic] side of the Bosphorus?'[83] This, he stressed, the Turks were doing because they themselves knew that they had no tenure on the European side of the strait; 'we shall see', he continued, 'the living soon following the dead. We shall see the great Euphrates beaten back again to Baghdad from which it originally took its rise.' The Indian mutiny, he claimed, provided further evidence of the same phenomenon. Although there was no mention of the revolt in the prophecy, still he could easily see the great loss of power that Islam had suffered in India during the last twelve months—a loss 'that was never supposed possible before.'[84] He observed:

> And thus it seems to me that the mutiny will just be an additional blow to weaken the Mahometan power, or another link in the mysterious chain which is drying down the great Ottoman empire.[85]

To Hoare the decline of Islam was not purposeless. The fresh defeat of Islam was another indication of God's will for an accelerated effort in the field of missions. The most important duty of the Church of Christ at a time when the Euphrates was drying up (or when the Turks were in the process of decline) was to assist in the work of Eastern missions; to exert itself more than ever in order to 'pour forth the Gospel amongst the kings of the East.' In the first instance India was not given to England just for acquiring wealth. There was a different purpose behind this acquisition—it was that 'England may carry the glorious Gospel to the 170 million people under her sceptre.' Now, he emphasized, there was a still greater reason to achieve the same end because of the 'fresh opportunities' offered by the remarkable breakdown of the Muslim power in India.[86] Hoare thus exhorted his audience and concluded:

> ...we are encouraged by prophecy to believe that it is our special duty to act in obedience to the Divine signal, and to pay peculiar attention to missions in the East.[87]

It was in deference to this divine call that the Church of England and all the missionary societies in Britain stepped up their fund-raising efforts considerably, so as to enable them to send more missionaries to India to civilize the people with 'the Christian light.'

Before closing, however, it seems desirable to comment on the observations made by the British public. The revolt of 1857 in India was anything but a worldwide movement among the followers of Islam against Christianity. At least the presumed head of the Muslim world, the Turkish Sultan or the Khalifah, certainly does not seem to have been a part of any such movement. On the contrary, instead of giving aid to the Muslim rebels in the India–Pakistan subcontinent or even sympathizing with their cause, the Ottoman sovereign subscribed £1000 towards the relief fund set up by Britain to aid British sufferers in the rebel colony. The amount is especially significant as it equalled the contribution of Napoleon III, head of one of the largest Christian nations of Europe.

In the case of the Jeddah massacre too, the attitude of the Turkish government at all levels was rather stern towards the insurgents. Local authorities at Jeddah tried hard to stem the tide of events and five Turkish soldiers lost their lives in the attempt. Soon after his return to Jeddah on 19 June 1858, Namik Pasha, the Governor of Hijaz, allowed re-hoisting of the British and French flags 'under a salute of twenty-one guns.'[88] At Constantinople as well, the Government of the Sublime Porte not only expressed deep regret and annoyance at the untoward events in Jeddah, but also took practical steps to dispense justice. Mr Fitzgerald, British Undersecretary of State for Foreign Affairs, informed the House of Commons that the Sultan:

> ...placed a million Piastres at the disposal of the British Government, to be disposed of among the sufferers, and has signified his intention of giving an allowance of 400 pounds to the daughter of the French Vice-Consul, and a similar annuity to the next representative of our own unfortunate Consul.[89]

Additionally, government investigation revealed eleven citizens of Jeddah to be 'deeply implicated' in inciting the rioting on 15 June 1858. On 2 August 1858, they were all put to death near Jeddah in the presence of sailors from Cyclops, the British ship that was actively involved in the Jeddah incident.[90] In brief, justice was dispensed in less than seven weeks of the tragic events in Jeddah, something difficult to match.

From other Muslim countries as well no material help seems to have crossed borders into the rebellion-torn subcontinent. Ever increasing and assertive speculations were made about the existence of such aid, but none of the adherents of the global jihad thesis could produce credible evidence. Support in kind nor token sympathy, at least at the official level, did not seem to have existed. Of all the Muslim rulers, Dost Muhammad of Afghanistan was the only one who could have helped fellow-Muslims in India. The fear of such a help coming from Afghanistan was so real that Sir John Lawrence, Chief Commissioner of the Punjab, and the most eulogized saviour of India for the British, anticipated an Afghan move not only to help the rebels but also to reclaim Peshawar, formerly an Afghan city. To avoid a second war front, Lawrence ordered Frontier Command to withdraw from Peshawar and concentrate on recovering Delhi. Dost Muhammad disappointed the British; he did not take advantage of an apparent British weakness, he did not try to help fellow-Muslims in India, nor did he try to recover Peshawar. An advance by Dost Muhammad across Punjab to Delhi squeezing the besieging British force there between his troops and the rebels in the city would clearly have jeopardized the British empire in India.

Likewise, no material help or even an official word of sympathy seems to have come from Persia, even though the excited British did visualize such a development. But what of that! The British had always been expecting a Russian thrust through Afghanistan into India. Indeed, Persia had a genuine reason to act—to settle scores; the British had just come back after invading their country and there was no love lost between the two. Obviously, there was no conspiracy and no plan of action to take advantage of British problems in India.

In light of the above analysis of the situations in Turkey, Afghanistan, and Persia, the three most likely sources of help to the rebels in India, it is very easy to determine that the theory of a worldwide jihad waged by global Islam against global Christianity was entirely a figment of the excited British mind. It was a groundless speculation based on animus and lack of clear vision.

Conclusion

The Indian mutiny left its traces forever upon the Indo-Pakistan subcontinent, and the year 1857 is recognized today as the turning point in its history. Also, the intensity of public reaction in Britain radically changed the trend of the British Indian policy. Public debate among the parties concerned as to what groups should be held responsible for the sanguinary outbreak led to successful attempts to expose each other. The participation in the debate by the conservatives, the Chartists, the Irish nationalists and the 'moralists' brought to light the acts of omission and commission in the British ranks and revealed the weaknesses of the British Indian administration. While there could be no poll of the reactions of British public opinion, it would seem that these reactions produced a commensurate impact upon all those aspects of future British thinking—especially political, imperial, military and religious—which had anything to do with British relations with India. When legislating for India, the Government of Britain now had to take into account the interest and the demands of the British people. This was amply manifested in the Act for the Better Government of India as well as Queen Victoria's India proclamation of October 1858. The once often concealing mantle of dual government was thrown off; henceforth, the Government of India was to become the special care of a responsible minister.

Before the insurrection, the average Briton accustomed to the daily perusal of newspapers could, like the Indian, not understand the relations between the East India Company and the crown. He asked questions as to who was responsible for the disastrous campaign in Afghanistan in the late 1830s? Were those operations conducted by and for the Queen or by and for the Company? If for the Queen, then why was the Company made to bear the expenses of war? He also wondered whether the Punjab was taken possession of by the Company or by the Queen? Similarly questions were asked about various other operations, i.e., the annexation of Awadh, the war in Persia, the Burmese war and the like. This confusion was not confined to the people at large; even their representatives in the Parliament, and members of the cabinets, disagreed with one another. Still the anomaly of the East India Company—a governing body whose governing powers no one rightly understood—continued to exist. The revolt of 1857, however, altered the whole tenor of public reaction; it led to almost universal dissatisfaction with the Company. In spite of the petitions and protests of the once mighty merchant corporation, which had survived over a dozen British monarchs and fifty Parliaments, the Company passed into history on 1 September 1858, by a Parliamentary Act for the better government of India. A new era in Anglo-Indian history began.

In the imperial field the reactions of the anti-annexationists, who were for the most part men familiar with Indian affairs, were respected. Although the advocates of the mutiny theory virtually refused to admit any connections between the outbreak and Lord Dalhousie's policy of annexations; although they argued that each annexation brought the oppressive native rule to an end and introduced instead enlightened British reign, and thus provided its subjects the cherished protection of the British, their argument failed to carry weight. The contrary view—that the policy of conquests and annexations had caused politico-religious and socio-economic resentment in India—was much more widely accepted and appreciated.

It came to be believed that the breach of treaties with the native states (particularly in the case of Awadh) had cost the British their good name—a name which needed to be re-established in the interest of the British Empire in India. The co-operation, support, and help rendered by Holkar, Sindhiya, several rulers of Rajputana, the ruler of Nepal and the Prime Minister of Deccan were highly regarded. In fact, their loyalty had provided a breakwater to the storm which otherwise would surely have swept away the British in one great wave. The belief grew that but for their valuable help the British would have had to leave India. They also began to realize that had Wajid 'Ali still been on the throne of Awadh, the revolt might never have occurred; had the Doctrine of Lapse not been applied to the state of Jhansi, its Rani would not have joined in the rebellion; and had more consideration been shown to the Nana regarding his pension, the massacre of Kanpur would not have taken place. The British people and the government were now convinced of the hold which the rebel princes enjoyed over their subjects.

It was due to this widely held belief which the government of the time shared with the people, that the Queen's Indian proclamation carried eloquent pledges of honouring past treaties with the princes of India. The proclamation declared that henceforth the British government would not annex Indian states. The whole policy towards the princely states of India was brought under complete review. In the future, instead of subordinate isolation, a new policy of subordinate union was inaugurated. In affirmation of the new policy, Lord Canning granted *sanads* and certificates to all important ruling chiefs in recognition of their status. These documents assured native princes of Queen Victoria's ardent desire to see their rule perpetuated. Henceforth all Indian princes were assured of their right of adoption and succession; the result was that the post-mutiny era saw no more annexations.

The changed British Imperial policy in India had its parallel in the reorganization of the Indian army. Though there were sharp differences among the British on the nature of the revolt, no one disputed the fact that the sepoy army had taken the lead in it; whether on its own or after having been incited into action by an outside agency was a different matter. Naturally the army administration came under heavy attack. As the basic weaknesses of the army administration were revealed, it became evident that the Company's method of recruiting and enforcing discipline had proved a failure. Earlier the principle of 'divide and rule' in the army had been applied to a limited extent and had, in fact, misfired. The three major orders in the sepoy army, composed as they were of Brahamans, Rajputs and Muslims, had become pressure groups. They formed not only close caste and creed circles but a geographical identity also existed among them. As they all came from almost the same regions, it was relatively easy for them to arrive at an understanding among themselves. In fact, frequent alliances among these three factions became a common phenomenon. Above all, the number of British army personnel in India were out of proportions to their native counterparts: the ratio was one to five.

Several radical proposals were made. It was recommended that Britain should disband the native army and garrison the country with a European force. Opponents of this view insisted that it was financially impossible and suggested that in the future Britain should recruit its Indian army from different parts of the British Empire, especially from among the negroid people. This was also declared a highly impracticable proposal. The proposition that the government should do away with the high caste element too was not regarded as a perfect solution. However, men of experience contended that the government should increase the comparative strength of the European army, simultaneously diversifying the character of the native army by recruiting soldiers from all religions and races of India and maintaining only European artillery units.

The government response to these proposals was quite favourable and was amply evidenced in the reorganization of the army. In the new arrangement the strength of the European army was increased to 65,000, and that of the native was reduced to 140,000, the new ratio being four to nine. A carefully considered principle of balancing communities inside the army was introduced. A large number of regiments were disbanded; the reorganized army was drawn from a much wider range of castes and creed; it contained a very strong element of Sikhs, Gurkhas, Dogras and Jats, all of whom had proved their loyalty to the British Government during the uprising. At the same time the principle of retaining artillery in European hands was adopted and religiously followed. In this manner the instrument of the army was secured against any future military *coup d'etat* or participation in a possible civilian outbreak.

Religion, however, offered a more delicate problem. A large number of Britons regarded it as the powder keg which had brought about the revolt and blamed the Evangelicals for having created religious apprehension among the native populations of India. An equally large number of people, headed primarily by the missionaries and the Anglican clergy and with Lord Shaftsbury as their Parliamentary spokesman, refused to admit of any such incitement to the rebellion. The government in this case was in a difficult position. It knew that legislation affecting native religions, especially Hinduism, introduced under the pressure of the Evangelicals, as well as private missionary efforts (at times aided and urged by government officials) had contributed substantially to the discontent of the Indians. It also had to realize that the spread of exaggerated atrocity stories (largely by the Evangelicals) had caused extreme anger among the Britons, and increased rather than abated their desire to bring Christian light to their trustees in India. The public was already so convinced of the missionary point of view that the latter were able not only to absolve themselves of all blame in the eyes of the public, but were also able to raise upwards of a hundred thousand pounds for the purpose of expanding the missionary program in India.[1] Their meetings were largely attended by members both of the Lords and the Commons. The religious question, therefore, posed a delicate problem to the weak Derby-Disraeli ministry. In fact, there was a triangular conflict of the practical problems of the empire in India, the presence of an influential

Evangelical group in the House of Commons, and mounting public pressures.

All these considerations had to be weighed heavily before setting the tone of the government's religious policy in India. However weak the government might be, imperial issues demanded action. At the same time, popular support at home and in the Commons could not be sacrificed by placing restrictions on missionary activity in India, just as the empire could not be endangered by further government legislation on the 'superstitious beliefs' of the Hindus and the introduction of the Bible in government schools. Only the time-honoured expedient of a compromise policy would secure the empire, silence the critics of pre-mutiny religious policy and retain the good-will of the Evangelical group. Thus it was that the Queen's Indian proclamation carried the promise of complete religious protection to all creeds and strictly forbade any official interference in the native religions. The Evangelicals, at the same time, were in no way prevented from continuing their private efforts to 'redeem' the people of India from 'darkness'.

The only aspect of public opinion in which there was virtual unanimity among all schools of thought on the Indian uprising was that it was a Muslim rebellion. The Muslims were considered the main culprits, the spirit and the body of the whole movement. Slogans demanding severe punishment, destruction and even annihilation were issued from public platforms and by the press. The British government too had always apprehended strong hostility from the Muslim community of India. Naturally, in consonance with the trend of public thinking the followers of Islam came in for immediate and prolonged repression. The punishment took form in physical, political, economic, social and educational chastisements. Several Muslim leaders were either hanged or exiled. Twenty-four Muslim princes were hanged in Delhi on 18 November 1857. The heads of two earlier victims of Hodson's execution were displayed from the Kotwali in Delhi for three days. The eighty-year-old Mughal ruler, Muhammad Bahadur Shah Zafar, was exiled to Rangoon. The Muslim rulers of Jujjhur, Ballabgarh, Farrukhnager and Farrukhabad were similarly punished. Everywhere Muslim quarters became targets of the wrath of the rulers; their homes were searched, their property occupied, their belongings confiscated and, in innumerable instances, occupants banished. The doors of all government services were rapidly closed upon them. The Hindus were encouraged to receive higher education at the expense of Muslims, to benefit from the Western institutions and to occupy government jobs of trust and responsibility. This was specially true in the Bengal Presidency. The followers of Islam were crestfallen after the revolt; their future in India seemed to be dark, dismal and gloomy. It was, however, not until W.W. Hunter, the erudite civil servant, and Sir Sayyid Ahmed Khan, the pioneer Muslim educator, both of whom ardently wanted to cause better understanding between Muslims and the British, eloquently urged the former to give up their past hostility and pleaded with the latter to restudy their attitude toward the former rulers of India, that the Muslims started to slowly regain something of their share in subcontinental affairs.

Lastly, the British view that the revolt in India was a clash of civilizations between global Islam and global Christianity was devoid of facts on the ground. It was based entirely on Islam-phobia of the British and the chronic Christian fear that Islam was a serious threat to the spread of Christianity, regionally and globally. This led to an ever-increasing Christian intolerance of Islam and its Prophet in Europe; the name Muhammad (PBUH) was marked for the worst epithets. This writer does not know of any significant Hindu, Buddhist, Confucian, Shinto, or Muslim scholar or writer who puts down founders of other religions; but Christian Europe did so on a broad scale, and without finesse.

In the case of the revolt in India, the 'global-Jihad' school of thought was led by British Evangelicals, the Anglican Church, and their allies. Unlike the 'Muslim rebellion' school of thought, British Islam-phobes lacked concrete evidence to support their thesis. Prompt actions taken by the Turkish government to punish the culprits and help the victims took the wind out of British sails. Indeed, steps taken by the Sublime Porte and Namik Pasha, the Turkish governor of Hijaz, were a great show of generosity and magnanimity—possibly unmatched in the European environment of the time. If the Turks and the Arabs had a 'crusading' spirit against the British or Europeans, they would not have shown such sympathy, generosity, and understanding to the British, French, and Greek victims of the 15 June emeute in Jeddah.

Epilogue

Islam is the only religion outside of Christianity which recognizes Jesus as an act of faith. Jesus occupies an exalted position in the Qur'an, in the teachings of Muhammad (PBUH), and in Islamic literature The only chapter named after a woman in the Qur'an is after Mary, mother of Jesus. Muhammad and early Muslims tasted Christian open-mindedness and generosity at the hands of Warqa bin Naufal, a Christian monk in Makkah, and Najashi, the Christian king of Ethiopia. Christians are the followers of the prince of peace and Muslims are the followers of the religion of peace; their warring with each other is a contradiction in terms. Hostility and suspicion between the followers of the two religions is an ongoing tragedy even today . The deep-seated nature of this animosity manifested itself when Generals Allenby and Gouraud marched respectively into Jerusalem and Damascus after their victory against the Turks which was achieved with the help of the Arabs. Upon entering Jerusalem, Allenby rudely declared: 'The Crusades are over today.' His French counterpart, General Gouraud, was even more brutish when he went to the grave of Saladin, set aside all civilized etiquette, and with a kick pronounced to the over 700 year old remains of a generous Muslim hero, 'We are back.' In other words, in the Western psyche, the crusades continued through the centuries. Could this sit well with the Muslim psyche? Of course not.

Pope Benedict's remarks in Germany,[1] caricaturing Muhammad (PBUH) in Denmark, toilet-flushing the Qur'an in Guantanamo, the 1991 launching of a missile from a US ship during the First Gulf War with the inscription 'Saddam, here comes Jesus. Call on your Allah,' and an untold number of other similar incidents are further evidence of an ongoing assault by the West on Islam and Muslim institutions. There is no difference in the treatment given by the British to Muslims in Delhi in September 1857 and the one given by the US army to Iraqi prisoners at Abu Ghraib. The psyche behind all of them has been to shame and ridicule Muslims. Dr Akbar S. Ahmed's carefully considered thesis in his book: *Islam Under Siege. Living Dangerously in a Post-Honor World* is applicable to the Western treatment of Islam from its inception, but more particularly since 1092 when Pope Urban II initiated a Papal Age of Crusades against Islam. The Church-initiated brainwashing against Islam was so intense that one of the crusades was a children's crusade—child soldiers fighting for Jesus. In his initial response to 9/11, George Bush, Jr. also wanted to launch another crusade against the Muslim East. More importantly, using Muslim alliances and Muslim help against terrorism, the Bush-Blair duo have been unsparing in their terminology against Islam. This historic march of ignorance, malevolence, and bigotry against Islam has to stop; radical fringe groups, both in Christianity and Islam, have to be de-emphasized, sidelined and ignored.

Tracing the roots of 'Orientalism' in European imperialism, the late Dr Edward Said of Columbia University pleads for overcoming hostility and mistrust between Islam and the West, 'if conflict, discord, and violence are not to be humanity's permanent future.' Indeed, it is time that Christians and Muslims look at the CAUSE AND EFFECT of their relationship and develop strong national, regional, and global dialogue groups at the highest level so that they can truly become what the 'founders' of the two faiths wanted their followers to be: believers with kinder, gentler, perceptive, understanding, and forgiving demeanours.

The Spanish experience under Muslim rule needs to be replayed—when Jews, Christians, and Muslims happily coexisted and a new Spain emerged in a 'Golden Age' for Jews and Christians alike. It is time that after 9/11, Kabul, Baghdad, Beslan (Russia), the West Bank, Gaza, Kashmir, Beirut, Chechnya, Darfur, Congo, Cambodia, Sri Lanka, and the like, the three Abrahamic/Ibrahimic religions and other faiths create a *New Ornament of the World*[2]—a new age of cooperation and progress that benefits all mankind. On 22 August 2006, on board Northwest Airlines' Flight 343 from Detroit to San Francisco I saw the whole world—Chinese, Japanese, Pakistanis, Koreans, Indians, Thais, Hispanics, whites, blacks, Jews, Christians, Muslims, Hindus, and others—all travelling together. It was a joyful experience. The age of Osama bin Laden, George Bush, Ehud Olmert, and Pope Benedict XVI needs to be retired, and an age of peace and goodwill needs to be ushered in. Humankind is hungry for a new 'Ornament of the World'—a new al-Andalus with global dimensions so that the world tastes the peace, freedom, equality, plenty, justice, and progress that it has been denied for so long through selfishness and self-righteousness, through misrepresentations and outright lies, through dehumanization and denial of rights, and through usurpation and hatred.

The events surrounding 1857 in South Asia and the events which have betaken the world today have striking similarities: the same disregard for cause and effect in history; the same irresponsible and hateful rhetoric, the same exploitation and dehumanization and the same display of ruthless and relentless power against the powerless and the have-nots. Enough is enough. The past is the past and must be consigned to history books. Now the world has become more like a global village 'dangerously educated and dangerously equipped.' Continued human welfare depends on mutual recognition, respect, justice, equity, and fair play at the global level. With a broader understanding and cooperation between Christianity and Islam, the two religions certainly have the potential to solve half the problems of the world. Should that not be the case? This, indeed, is our survival kit.

NOTES

1. It is little compliment to Pope Benedict XVI to think that he was unmindful of what he said about Islam to his university audience in Germany on 12 September 2006. As a former academic who taught from 1951 to 1977 and who was a theological consultant at the Second Vatican Council (1962-5), he has to have known fully well historical sensitivities behind Christian-Muslim relations. However, as a Pope, Benedict is consumed by his concern for the increasing trend toward 'de-Christianization, secularization, as well as Islamization of the West.' He wants his flock to return to fundamental Christian values. He sees the spread of Islam in Europe as a major threat to his goals. Therefore, at Regensburg he attempted to raise alarm bells against Islam in a very suave way—aiming at Muslims from behind the shoulders of a 14th century Byzantine Emperor, Manuel Paleologus. Did not the mediaeval Christian leaders adopt the same approach in similar circumstances? (See above chapter IX).
2. Title of a well-acclaimed book published in 2002 by Little Brown Company of New York and Boston on Muslim Spain written by Maria Rosa Menocal.

Appendix 1

Sir Colin Campbell was recognized as a hero for his invaluable services in suppressing the revolt in India and was raised to the rank of a baron.

The above enigmatic signs of the revolt appeared in different parts of India six months to a year ahead of the rebellion and were verified by several sources. The British felt so secure in their power they paid little or no attention to these forebodings. Subsequently, they reinforced the conspiracy theory of the revolt.

Appendix 2

The Sikhs offered all kinds of help to the British to regain authority in India. Only a few years before (1852–1854) they had fought the British valiantly, but were defeated and their homeland occupied. The British were able to vanquish the Sikh army entirely with the help of their native 'Poorbeah' army. Evidently, this was a Sikh payback to the rebels.

Appendix 3

The British pathway to victory was by striking terror into the hearts of the civilian populations by blowing rebels out of cannons in different parts of India. Wholesale executions constituted a second tier policy to paralyze the Indian population into subjection and prevent them from joining the ranks of the rebels.

Frederick Henry Cooper, Deputy Commissioner of Amritsar, boasted of what 'a single Christian' and 'a solitary Anglo-Saxon' did in a single day that history took one hundred years to enact—a Black Hole and a well at Ajnala. The day was well-chosen— the Muslim holy day of the Festival of Pilgrimage and Sacrifice (1 August 1857) when the chief civil and judicial officer of the district dispensed an unusual kind of justice by performing, to use Cooper's own words, 'a ceremonial sacrifice of a different nature.' Aided by 'faithful Sikh' soldiers, Cooper executed in public view 237 rebels in batches of ten each. At least one executioner passed out while doing his 'duty'.

Cooper was hurriedly commended by his superiors, especially by Sir John Lawrence, Chief Commissioner of the Punjab (equivalent to a governor) and Robert Montgomery, Revenue Commissioner of the province. In fact, Lawrence asked for his share of this unique booty: 'You have had slaughter enough,' he wrote to Cooper. 'We want a few here [Lahore].'

The request was faithfully complied with and forty-one rebels were sent to Lahore where they were all blown from the cannon along with a severely wounded soldier who earlier could not walk to the place of execution at Ajnala. Forty-five others died of suffocation in the small room where Cooper had huddled 282 prisoners together in the blazing heat of July. (Normal temperatures in the area during this month range from 102 to 112 Fahrenheit.) To further humiliate the natives, the dead were shown no respect. As Cooper boasted their bodies were dragged and 'consigned in common… into one common pit (a dry well) by the hands of the village sweeper'.

Robert Montgomery, the Revenue Commissioner, used his purse strings to buy loyalty and further divide the Indians. He asked Cooper to immediately provide him with a list of men who performed their duties honestly. He stressed: 'Do this judiciously. I mean discriminate between the medium, the good, and the super excellent…You will have abundant money to reward all and the Sikhs should have a good round sum given to them.'

Many Britons believed that God specifically sent Sir John Lawrence to save India for their country. Apart from honouring Sir John with a vote of gratitude, the House of Commons also raised his salary from 7,500 pounds to 10,000 pounds a year and awarded him the Grand Cross of Bath. The Court of Directors of the East India Company, on the other hand, honoured him with an annuity of 2,000 pounds.

It should be noted that George Crawshay, a proprietor of the East India Company and Mayor of Gateshead, felt so indignant and embarrassed at what his countrymen did in the Punjab, that he called it 'a Reign of Terror' surpassed only by that of Robespierre in Paris. He further voted against the grant of the 2,000 pound annuity to Sir John Lawrence.

Later on, thirty Mughal princes were shot to death in and around Delhi. Bodies of two who were killed by Captain Hodson after a promise of safe conduct were suspended in front of the Kotwali (central police station) in Delhi for several days to humiliate Muslims as well as to please Sikh soldiers for the alleged mistreatment of Guru Teg Bahadur by Aurangzeb, the Mughal Emperor of India, almost two hundred years before the revolt.

Appendix 4

Poet, philosopher, and eighty-two-year-old Emperor of India, Bahadur Shah Zafar instantly assumed leadership of the rebellion. There was no hesitation or pause; it was as if he was awaiting the moment. He acted more like a Cavour and a Garibaldi; unity of all Indians against the British was paramount in his political thinking. He quickly called for national unity and urged Hindus and Muslims to join the revolt. To win them over, he forbade cow slaughter on the Muslim Festival of Sacrifice (1 August 1857) and dated his *Firmans* (decrees) in the Hindu calendar. He wrote letters to several rulers—Hindu, Sikh, and Muslim—asking them to join in the struggle against the British. He assured his subjects a better future under his suzerainty. He asked the British to submit and offered them safe passage.

NOTES

Chapter 1: Background of British Reactions

1. The total number of European settlers in India in 1857 was reported to be at 10,006. Of these 9689 resided in the three presidency cities of Calcutta, Bombay and Madras, and only 317 in the provinces–275 in that of Bengal and the rest scattered over the other two presidencies. *The Examiner*, 24 October 1857.

2. *The Nation*, 18 July, 8 August, 5 and 26 September and 10, 17, 24 and 31 October 1857. In fact, the paper went on producing analogies between the two parts of the British empire until the revolt was over.

3. In addition to publishing a large number of articles and poems which described the outbreak in India as a revolution, *The Nation* always gave the news from India under the title: 'The Indian Revolution'.

4. *The Nation*, 26 September 1857.

5. Hansard 3, CXLVI, 542.

6. *The Scotsman*, 29 June and 1 July 1857. In its issue of 29 June, the paper slighted the uprising and editorially observed:

   The proclamation of the King, though indicating an unusual concord and purpose among the insurgents, is really of no very great significance–anything like popular attachment to the Mogul dynasty, or indeed to any of the native dynasties, scarcely exists. The only probable result of this part of the affair will be putting an end to the mock court of the Moguls maintained at Delhi.

   Two days later the paper told its readers that no 'doubts were entertained of the rebellion being promptly and easily suppressed.'

7. 15 July 1857.

8. 4 July 1857.

9. 29 June and 4 and 16 July 1857. In its issue of 4 July, *The Times* editorially chided the French newspaper *Univers* for attributing the outbreak to a general dislike of the English. Ascribing this attitude to the malignant spirit of the French paper, *The Times* forcefully argued: 'This Indian Mutiny will be put down with a strong hand and in a few months will be forgotten, except as a guide for future policy.'

10. *The Times*, 29 June 1857, Cf., George D. Bearce, *British Attitudes towards India, 1784–1858* (London: Oxford University Press, 1961), p. 235.

11. Hansard 3, CXLVI, 1431–32; *Illustrated London News*, 18 July 1857.

12. Expression borrowed from Dr Ian W. Brown's unpublished twin dissertations, both entitled, *The Anglican Evangelicals in British Politics, 1780–1833* (M.A. thesis, McGill University, Montreal, Canada. Ph.D. Dissertation, Lehigh University, Bethlehem, Penns ylvania, USA), pp. 138 and 145 respectively. Six years of additional research did not change Dr Brown's thesis on the impact of British Evangelicals on their country's politics.

13. Hansard 3, CXLVIII, 1360, 1458 and 1718; CXLIX, 2097 and 2206 and CL, 1690.

14. Ibid., CXLVI, 1577–1654.

15. Ibid., CXLVIII, 1–131.

16. *Manchester Guardian,* 2 October 1857.

17. Hansard 3, CXLVII, 360 and CXLVIII, 71.

18. An Indian Missionary [Hargrave Jennings], *The Indian Religions: or, Results of Mysterious Buddhism* (London: Printed by Guildford, 1858), p. 139; 'The Coming Debate on the Indian Crisis', *Saturday Review,* 25 July, 1857; William Howard Russell, *My Diary in India* (7th Thousand; Two vols.; London: Routledge, Warne, and Co., 1860), vol. 1, p. 2; *Manchester Guardian,* 3 September 1857; 4 December 1857 (Letter from John Bright, MP, to Thomas Lloyd of Birmingham), and 3 February 1858; 'The Christianization of India,' *London Journal and Weekly Record of Literature, Science and Arts* (hereafter referred to as *London Journal*), XXVI, 1857, p. 109.

19. 'Has the Preservation of Caste Conduced to the Present Revolt in India–Affirmative Article 111,' *British Controversialist* (hereafter referred to as *BC.*) 1858, p. 119.

20. 17 and 21 October 1857.

21. 'English Assertions and Indian Facts,' *Saturday Review,* 7 November 1857.

22. Hansard 3, CXLVIII, 671–72.

23. *The Nation,* 3 October 1857.

24. William Forbes-Mitchell, *Reminiscences of the Great Mutiny, 1857–59, Including the Relief, Siege, and Capture of Lucknow, and the Campaigns in Rochilcund and Oude* (London: Macmillan and Co., 1894), pp. 153–9.

25. The Earl of Shaftesbury, *England's Apostasy in India and the Earl of Shaftesbury's Great Speech on Indian Cruelties, delivered at Wimborne* (London: Published by Patridge and Co., [1857], pp. 5–6; *The Times,* 2 November 1857. Cf. Puran Chandra Joshi (ed. by), *Rebellion 1857, a Symposium* (New Delhi: People's Publishing House, 1957), p. 295.

26. *Manchester Guardian,* 6 February 1858. Cf. Joshi, *loc. cit.*

27. Ibid., 3 November 1857.

28. 17 April 1858. Earlier on 26 September 1857, the paper had raised serious objection to the publication of anonymous 'horror letters' in the London newspapers. *The Nation* argued:
    > It will be seen that not one 'letter' in ten bears the name of the writer–or supposed writer. Why is this? Why any real witness of such scenes should have reluctance to attest the truth of these narratives by their names? Is it not rather far more likely that such persons would be anxious to give their names.

29. *Free Press,* 20 January 1858; Maj. W.S.R. Hodson, *Twelve Years of a Soldier's Life in India,* ed. The Rev. Geo. H. Hodson (2nd. ed.; London: John W. Parker, 1859), p. 218; *The Examiner,* 5 September 1857; *Manchester Guardian,* 2 January 1858.

30. Hansard 3, CXLVIII, 902–903.

31. Ibid., 929.

32. *The Examiner,* 21 November 1857. This petition was signed by 837 British inhabitants of Calcutta; of these 193 were merchants, forty-five barristers and solicitors, twenty-four planters, thirty-six brokers and ten doctors.

33. Henry Mead, *The Sepoy Revolt: Its Causes and Consequences* (London: John Murray, 1857), pp. 77–85.

34. Dr Edward Henry Nolan, *The Illustrated History of the British Empire in India and the East, from the Earliest Times to the Suppression of the Sepoy Mutiny in 1859* (Two vols.; London: publisher not given, n.d.), vol. II, p. 719.

35. Hansard 3, CXLVIII, 1485.
36. Ibid., 896–9.
37. See Chapter II, pp. 32–3.
38. For Smith's defence, see: Hansard 3, CXLVII, pp. 485–8.
39. 17 October, 1857.
40. Hansard 3, CXLVIII, 1132–4.
41. These were very widely held opinions.
42. In 1819, Mangal Pandy [sic], a Hindu sepoy at Meerut, had embraced Christianity. Apprehending wild reactions among the Hindu civil and military population of India, the government dismissed the new convert from his position in the army. The convert's testimony before the British officers that 'you will allow me to serve your King, but you will not allow me to serve your God' caused deep concern in Britain. (The Rev. Cadman, 'Fast-day Sermons. No. XI', *The Fast-day Sermons. The 'Indian Mutiny' Twelve Sermons*, pp. 134–5). The missionaries and the Church of England could never forget this incident. After the outbreak at Meerut, it once again came into the limelight and the government of the East India Company was put into a tight corner *de novo*. The fact that the mutiny had started at Meerut was offered as evidence that the outbreak was divine punishment which the Lord God in His great anger had sent down upon the people of Britain for this and various other neglects of the ill-fated Company and the British nation. The Bishop of Carlisle, 'Fast-day Sermons. No. V', *The Fast-day Sermons. The 'Indian Mutiny' Twelve Sermons delivered on Wednesday, 7 October 1857, being the Day appointed by Royal Proclamation as a Day of National Fasting, Humiliation, and Prayers* (Lond.: J.A. Berger, [1857]), p. 61; Cadman, *loc cit.;* 'Monthly Retrospect', *Christian Spectator* (hereafter referred to as *CS.*), VIII, 1858, p. 126; The Rev. James Charles, *The Lord's Voice to Britain from the Far East* (Edinburgh: Paton and Ritche. Glasgow: T. Murray and Son, 1857), pp. 14–15. In fact, it was a very widely shared opinion.
43. Bearce, *op. cit.,* p. 236.
44. For figures on the European and Native armies, see: Hansard 3, CLII, 359.

Chapter 2: Causes of the Military Mutiny

1. *The Press*, 12 September 1857.
2. 'India's Idolatry and England's Connexion With It', *Church of England Magazine* (hereafter referred to as *CEM.*), XLIII, 1857, p. 408; The Rev. Baptist Wriothesley Noel, *England and India–An Essay on the Duty of Englishmen towards the Hindoos* (London: James Nisbet and Co., 1859), p. V.
3. 'The Bengal Mutiny', *Blackwood's Edinburgh Magazine* (hereafter referred to as *Blackwood's*), LXXXII, 1857, p. 374. For a similar opinion, see also: *Manchester Guardian*, 25 September 1857. The paper reacted with extreme annoyance when Jones, a proprietor of the East India Company, attributed the Delhi mutiny and Kanpur massacre to the system of annexations lately followed by the government. It asserted that to accept the annexations of the Punjab, Sind and Awadh as the inciting cause of mutiny was tantamount to regarding the inhabitants of India as a single nation, 'one in blood, in language, in religion', animated by patriotism as warm as that of Italians in 1848, or of the Irish at the

beginning of the nineteenth century. It concluded with the remark: 'Such a theory does not deserve the labour of refutation. It is enough to state it and leave it to work its condemnation and that of its author in the minds of all who read it.'

The paper, however, accepted that the annexation of Awadh might have alienated the feelings of the Muslims, who regarded the English as usurpers and that this might account for Muslim conspiracies but not at all for the sepoy revolt.

4. *Saturday Review,* 3 October 1857. For similar opinions, see also: 'The Government of India and the Mutinies', *British Quarterly Review* (hereafter referred to as *BQR.*), XXVI, 1857, pp. 499–599; 'Hindooism and Mohammedanism in India', *CEM.*, XLIII, 1857, p. 191; *Manchester Guardian,* 17 August 1857.

5. *Manchester Guardian,* 17 August 1857.

6. Ibid.; 'The Bengal Mutiny', *Blackwood's,* LXXXII, 1857, p. 374.

7. 'The Bengal Mutiny', Ibid.

8. 'The English in India', *Westminster Review* (hereafter referred to as *WR.*), New . Series, XIII, 1858, p. 199.

9. 'The Bengal Mutiny', *Blackwood's,* LXXXII, 1857, p. 374.

10. Ibid. For a similar opinion, see also: *Manchester Guardian,* 25 September 1857.

11. 'The English in India', *WR.*, New Series, XIII, 1858, p. 199.

12. 1 July 1857.

13. *Manchester Guardian,* 7 and 16 September 1857; *Illustrated London News,* 1 August 1857; *The Scotsman,* 2 September 1857; Leopold Von Olrich, *Military Mutiny in India: Its Origin and its Results, with Observations by Maj.-Gen. Sir W.M.G. Colebrooke,* trans. Anonymously (London: T. and W. Brone, 1859), pp. 22–3; Wm. R. Aikman, *The Bengal Mutiny: Popular Opinions Concerning the Origin of the mutiny Refuted: The Real Cause Considered; with suggestions for the Future, in a Letter to Viscount Palmerston, 26 September 1857* (London: Richardson Bros.), p. 13; *Annual Register,* 1857, p. 239; Henry Beveridge, *A Comprehensive History of India, Civil, Military and Social, from the First Landing of the English, to the Suppression of the Sepoy Revolt, including an Outline of the Early History of Hindoostan,* (Three Vols.; London: Black and Son, 1862), III, pp. 553–4; Hansard 3, CXLVII, 284, 443 and CXLVI, 1333–4. Viscount Melville who had earlier served in the Indian army, was not even allowed to make public the deficiencies of the Bengal army. When he tried to do so on his return from India in 1850, he was asked to keep silent, lest 'foreign nations should be acquainted with the real state of affairs.'

14. This was almost a universal opinion.

15. *The Mutiny in the Bengal Army* (London: John Chapman, 1857), p. 5.

16. *Manchester Guardian,* 15 September 1857; Julius George Medley, *A Year's Campaigning in India, March 1857 to March 1858* (London: W. Thacker and Co., 1858), pp. 199–204; 'The Indian Mutiny', *Electic Review* (hereafter referred to as *ER.*), II, 1857, p. 535.

17. *Manchester Guardian,* 15 September 1857; Brig. General John Jacob, *Tracts on the Native Army of India, its Organization and Discipline* (London: Reprinted by Smith, Elder and Co., 1858), p. 27.

18. *Manchester Guardian,* 15 September 1857. For similar opinions, see also: Jacob, *op. cit.,* pp. 33–4; 'The Indian Mutiny', *ER.*, II, 1857, p. 538.

19. [W. Sinclair], *The Sepoy Mutinies: Their Origin and their Cure* (London: Wertheim and Macintosh, 1857), pp. 5–6; *Manchester Guardian*, 16 September 1857; 'The Sepoy Rebellion', *London Quarterly Review* (hereafter referred to as *LQR.*), IX, 1857–8, p. 236. Criticizing the composition of the sepoy regiments, which included 400 'hereditary priests', 200 Rajputs—with every one of them considering himself as 'the son of a King'—200 Muslims and 200 other low caste soldiers, the author of 'The Sepoy Rebellion' bitterly questioned: 'What should we think of a British statesman who would attempt to govern Ireland by regiments of Maynooth priests'.

20. Jacob died in service on 5 December 1858. Although his military writings were extensively quoted by the holders of the mutiny point of view, Jacob himself, strangely enough, never seems to have commented on the nature of the outbreak.

21. A learned Muslim; a Muslim priest; a Muslim theologian.

22. Poor, needy, indigent, destitute; a beggar; a religious mendicant; an ascetic; a devotee.

23. Jacob, *loc. cit.*; *Manchester Guardian*, 15 September 1857. Also quoted and reported by: 'The Indian Mutiny', *ER.* II, 1857, p. 538; [G.B. Malleson], *The Mutiny of the Bengal Army* (also called Red Pamphlet), (Two Parts; London: Bosworth and Harrison, 1858), pt. 1, p. 7.

24. Jacob, op. cit., p. 34; *Manchester Guardian*, 15 September 1857. For a similar opinion, see also: 'The Indian Mutiny', *ER.*, II, 1857, p. 538.

25. Jacob, *op. cit.*, p. 34. For similar opinions, see also: Martin Richard Gubbins, *An Account of the Mutinies in Oudh, and of the Siege of the Lucknow Residency with some Observations on the Condition of the Province of Oudh, and on the Causes of the Mutiny of the Bengal Army* (London: Richard Bentley, 1858), pp. 89–90; 'Has the Preservation of Caste Conduced to the Present Revolt in India– Affirmative Reply', *BC.*, 1858, p. 226; *Manchester Guardian*, 15 September 1857.

26. Henry Mead, *The Sepoy Revolt: Its Causes and its Consequences*, p. 22.

27. [Malleson], *op. cit.*, pt. I, p. 7.

28. The Rev. J. Smith, 'Resumption of the Mission in Delhi', *Missionary Herald* (hereafter referred to as *MH.*), LI, 1859, p. 389. For a similar opinion, see also: 'Has the Preservation...'Affirmative Article-I', *BC.*, 1858, p. 29.

29. Jacob, *op. cit.*, p. 35; *Manchester Guardian*, 15 September 1857.

30. Ghanta means bell, and Pande is a sub-caste among the Brahmans. Ghanta Pande apparently was the designation in the army of one employed for striking the bell.

31. Jacob, *op. cit.*, pp. 35–36; *Manchester Guardian*, 15 September 1857.

32. 16 September 1857.

33. See also: Jacob, *op. cit.*, p. 35.

34. *Manchester Guardian*, 16 September 1857.

35. Sinclair had earlier seen military service in India as a commissioned officer in the Madras cavalry. (*DNB.*, LII, pp. 310–11). Though he attributed the outbreak to a large number of governmental mistakes–civil, military and political—his main emphasis was on the role of the Muslims in the uprising. He emphatically called the followers of Islam the watchful and exasperated enemies of the British.

36. [Sinclair], op. cit., pp. 5–6.

37. Hansard 3, CXLVI, 524–5 and 1335. For a similar opinion also see col. 1590.
38. 14 October 1857. For similar opinions, see also *Manchester Guardian,* 31 October 1857; Kenneth Macqueen, *Who is to Blame for the Indian Mutinies* (Edinburgh: Thomas Constable and Co. London: Hamilton Adams and Co., 1857), p. 25; The Rev. James Wallace, *The Revolt in India: Its Causes and its Lessons, A Lecture delivered in Belfast, on 2 February 1859* (Belfast: C. Aitchison, 1859), p. 21; 'Has the Preservation of Caste…Affirmative Article II', *BC.*, 1858, pp. 32–4; 'The Outbreak in India', *CEM., XLIII*, 1857, p. 266.
39. *Investigation into Some of the Causes Which have Produced the Rebellion in India* (Printed for Private Circulation, 1857), p. 39. For similar opinions, see also: Henry Montgomery Lawrence, *Essays: Military and Political* (London: Wm. H. Allen, 1858), p. 29; 'The Native Troops in India', Letter to *The Spectator*, 1857, p. 675.
40. *Investigation into Some…*, p. 39; 'The Native Troops in India', Letter to *The Spectator*, 1857, p. 675. Calling the native Indian army 'a self-chosen corporation', this columnist of *The Spectator* had this to say:

   The district from which they [sepoys] are recruited is too limited: recruiting parties are sent down who recruit mostly amongst their relatives and connexions…the men are thus too much linked together; too many Brahamins are enlisted, and they being more intellectuals than the rest take the lead; an organization is thus introduced which would enable the soldiery, should they succeed to overthrow the English, to become the ruling elite in the state by a sort of military republic as was the case in the Punjab upon the death of Ranjit Singh.

   To avoid these pitfalls in the future, the author of *The Mutiny in the Bengal Army* suggested the formation of a multiracial army composed of Gorkhas, Marhatahs, Afghans, Rajputs, Jats, Gujars, the Balochis, the Punjabis, Negros from Africa, Arracanese, Mugs, Puguese, Burmese and Malays. p. 22. Cf. 'The Bengal Mutiny', *Blackwood's, LXXXII*, 1857, pp. 390–2; *Manchester Guardian,* 6 July, 11 August and 4 November 1857.
41. Almost universally emphasized by the advocates of the present school of thought as well as some adherents of other schools. Disraeli and his followers, however, refused to admit this as a cause of the outbreak. They drew their support by pointing to Meerut where there was no deficiency of European troops. Hansard 3, CXLVII, 495.

   According to the *Manchester Guardian* of 30 June 1857, the strength of European troops at Meerut was 2200 men of all arms, with a full complement of officers.
42. 'Indian Heroes', *WR.*, New Series, XIV, 1858, p. 353; *Investigation into Some…*, p. 15.
43. Hansard 3, CXLVIII, 1133.
44. *Investigation into Some…*, p. 15.
45. Scrutator [Sir Benjamin Colin Brodie]. *English Tenure of India. Practical Remarks Suggested by the Bengal Mutiny* (London: Smith, Elder and Co., 1857), pp. 4–5. For similar opinions, see also: Beveridge, *op. cit.*, p. 555; 'The Revolt of the Bengal Army', *Dublin University Magazine* (hereafter referred to as *DUM.*), L, 1857, p. 389.
46. Wallace, *op. cit.*, pp. 17–8; 'Indian Heroes', *loc. cit.*
47. One who holds a Ta'alluqah, a landholder, possessor of an estate, lord of a manor. Under the Mughals an officially appointed feudal lord, who had the

obligation to perform revenue, fiscal, civil and administrative duties in his
Ta'alluqah or estate.

48. Gubbins, *op. cit.*, p. 99. Gubbins had joined the service of the East India
    Company in 1830 as a writer. Twenty-six years later he was sent to Awadh as a
    member of the British Commission at the annexation of the state. Subsequently
    he made an extensive tour of Awadh as a financial commissioner in order to
    test the summary settlement of land revenue which had just been completed.
    Though averse to the idea of a popular uprising in the North-Western Provinces,
    Gubbins admitted the general character of the revolt in the state of Awadh.

49. *Manchester Guardian,* 14 October and 3 November 1857; 'Indian Military
    Mistakes', *Saturday Review,* 25 July 1857; Robert J. Roy Campbell, *The Indian
    Mutiny, its Causes and its Remedies. A Letter to Rt. Hon. Lord Viscount
    Palmerston* (London: Charles Evans, 1858), p. 5; *India, the Revolt and the Home
    Government* (London: Robert Hardwicke, 1857), p. 23; Oliver J. Jones,
    Recollections of a Winter Campaign in India in 1857–58 (London: Naundore and
    Otley, 1859), pp. X-XI.

50. *Manchester Guardian,* 26 August 1857; Joachim H. Stocqueler, *India: Its History,
    Climate, Products, with a full Account of the Origin, Progress and Development
    of the Bengal Mutiny and Suggestions as to the Future Government of India*
    (Lond.: George Routledge and Co., 1857), pp. 17–18; Jones, *op. cit.,* pp. X-XI;
    'Past Errors of Military Management in India, to be avoided in the Future', letter
    to *The Spectator,* 22 August 1857; Campbell, *op. cit.,* p. 5; 'The English in India',
    WR., New Series, XIII, 1858, p. 196; Sydney Cotton, *Nine Years on the North-
    West Frontier of India* (Lond.: Richard Bentley, 1868), p. 154.

51. Gubbins, *op. cit.,* p. 90.

52. 28 August 1857.

53. Stocqueler, *loc. cit.*

54. *Manchester Guardian,* 26 August 1857.

55. Campbell, *op. cit.,* p. 6.

56. 'Past Errors of Military…', *loc. cit.*

57. *Crisis in India, its Causes and Proposed Remedies* (Lond.: Richard Bentley, 1857),
    p. 15.

58. Ibid., pp. 15–6.

59. 'Our Indian Empire', *Quarterly Review* (hereafter referred to as QR.), CIII, 1858,
    p. 262.

60. Ibid.

61. Jones, *op. cit.,* pp. X-XI.

62. The Earl of Shaftesbury, *England's Apostasy in India and the Earl of Shaftesbury's
    Great Speech on Indian Cruelties, delivered at Wimborne,* p. 6. For similar
    reactions, see also: *Manchester Guardian,* 26 August 1857.

63. *India, the Revolt…,* p. 23.

64. *Manchester Guardian,* 7 September 1857.

65. Ibid., 29 September 1857.

66. Ibid., 7 September 1857.

67. Ibid.

68. Ibid.

69. Ibid.

70. Gubbins, *op. cit.,* pp. 90–1.

71. George B. Norton, *The Rebellion in India: How to Prevent Another* (London: Richardson Bros., 1857), p. 39. For a similar opinion, see also: Campbell, *op. cit.*, p. 5.

72. Campbell, *loc. cit.*

73. Mead, *op. cit.*, pp. 27–8. To support his contention the author gave the instance of Shaik Phutto, a sepoy of the 34th Native Infantry, who gallantly defended an English officer against the attack of Mangal Pande, while the rest of the regiment acted as silent spectators. Maj.-Gen. Hearsy, the commander of the division, promoted the sepoy to the rank of hawaldar. For this the major-general was reprimanded by Lord Canning, the Governor-General of India. The reprimand read:

    It is not in the power of the Major-General commanding the division to make this promotion, which can proceed only from the Government of India, and therefore should not have appeared in a Divisional Order without the sanction of the Government.

    Lord Derby, though not an exponent of the military mutiny thesis, also referred to the same instance and complained about this lack of power with the commanding officers. Hansard 3, CXLVII, 41.

    For other similar reactions, see also: *Manchester Guardian,* 26 August 1857; 'The Indian Mutiny', *ER.,* II, 1857, p. 535; Gubbins, *op. cit.*, pp. 90–1; [Malleson], op. cit., pt. I, p. 8; [Sinclair], *op. cit.*, p. 7; *Investigations into Some...*, p. 43; 'The Sepoy Rebellion', *LQR.,* IX, 1857–58, p. 234.

74. Jacob, *op. cit.*, pp. 30–1. Also quoted by the *Manchester Guardian* of 15 September 1857, and several other newspapers, periodicals and pamphlets.

75. Norton, *op. cit.*, p. 40.

76. Ibid., p. 39.

77. 'The English in India', *WR.,* New Series, XIII, 1858, p. 196; Medley, *op. cit.*, pp. 200–201; 'Our Indian Empire', *QR.,* CIII, 1858, p. 262.

78. Medley, *op. cit.*, pp. 199–204.

79. Norton, *op. cit.*, p. 43. For a similar opinion, see also: Miles, Letter to *The Times,* 7 July 1857.

80. Norton, *op. cit.*, pp. 43–5.

81. Miles, Letter to *The Times,* 7 July 1857.

82. 'India, the Revolt and the Native Troops', *Missionary Magazine and Chronicle* (hereafter referred to as *MMC.*), XXI, 1857, p. 182; *Manchester Guardian,* 29 September 1857; 'The English in India', *WR.,* New Series, XIII, 1858, p. 196.

83. Maj. Tucker, 'The Indian Army', Letter to *The Times,* 24 June 1857; Hansard 3, CXLVI, 1591 and CXLVIII, 426; 'The English in India', *loc. cit.*; Olrich, *op. cit.*, p. 8; Gubbins, *op. cit.*, p. 97; *The Spectator,* 25 July 1857; 'The Indian Mutiny', *ER.,* II, 1857, p. 535; Norton, *op. cit.*, p. 24; Medley, *op. cit.*, pp. 200–01; *The Mutiny in the Bengal Army,* p. 18; 'The Sepoy Rebellion', *LQR.,* IX, 1857–8, p. 233; Scrutator [Sir Benjamin Colin Brodie], *The Indian Mutiny* (London: W. Kent and Co., 1857), pp. 25–6; Mead, *op. cit.*, p. 29; J.L. Archer, *Indian Mutinies Accounted For: Being an Essay on the Subject* (London: Ward and Co., 1857), pp. 4–6; *Manchester Guardian,* 29 September 1857.

84. *The Examiner,* 3 October 1857. The figure also includes 416 officers who were either on sick or private leave.

85. Hansard 3, CXLVIII, 426. The Marquis of Clanricarde, attributing the mutiny to mismanagement in the army, reported to the House of Lords, how a son of

a friend of his had never gone near his regiment for twelve years before the outbreak and had remained away from it even after the mutiny had started.

86. *The Spectator*, 25 July, 1857; [Sinclair], *op. cit.*, pp. 7–8.
87. Archer, *op. cit.*, pp. 4–6; *Manchester Guardian*, 1 August and 29 September 1857.
88. 'The English in India', *WR.*, New Series, XIII, 1858, p. 196; Mead, *op. cit.*, p. 29.
89. *Manchester Guardian*, 1 August 1857.
90. Campbell, *op. cit.*, p. 6; [Sinclair], *loc. cit.;'* *Manchester Guardian*, 29 September 1857.
91. Gubbins, *op. cit.*, p. 95; Hansard 3, CXLVI, 1591.
92. Campbell, *op. cit.*, p. 6.
93. Archer, *op. cit.*, p. 6. Having attributed the outbreak to religious, political and military causes, Archer argued that it was a religious war which was quickly turned to political account.
94. Campbell, *loc. cit.*
95. 'India, the Revolt of the Native Troops', *MMC.*, XXI, 1857, p. 182; *Investigation into Some...*, p. 44.
96. Archer, *op. cit.*, p. 4.
97. Jacob, *op. cit.*, pp. 27–31. Also quoted by the *Manchester Guardian*, 15 September 1857.
98. *The Examiner*, 1 August 1857; *The Mutiny in the Bengal Army*, p. 18; T.C. Robertson, *The Political Prospects of British India* (London: Thomas Hatchard, 1858), p. 8.
99. Robertson, *loc. cit.; The Mutiny in the Bengal Army*, p. 18.
100. Hansard 3, CXLVII, 496–7.
101. Robertson, *loc. cit.*
102. 'The Indian Mutiny', *DUM.*, L, pp. 237–8.
103. May be translated as Haram.
104. 'The Indian Mutiny', *DUM.*, L, 1857, p. 238.
105. Robertson, *op. cit.*, p. 8.
106. Stocqueler, *op. cit.*, p. 16; *Manchester Guardian*, 25 August 1857.
107. 25 August 1857; Stocqueler, *loc. cit.*
108. Stocqueler, *loc. cit.*
109. *Manchester Guardian*, 25 August 1857.
110. *Investigation into Some...*, p. 48.
111. Jacob, *op. cit.*, pp. 31–2. Also quoted by the *Manchester Guardian*, 15 September 1857.
112. 'The Indian Army', *Fraser's Magazine* (hereafter referred to as *Fraser's*), LVI, 1857, p. 17; 'The English in India', *WR.*, New Series, XIII, 1858, p. 196; Hansard 3, CXLVI, 1333–34; Lawrence, *op. cit.*, p. 54; Manchester Guardian, 15 September, 1857 'The Indian Mutiny', *ER.*, II, 1857, p. 535.

If the *Eclectic Review* called the system of promotions 'mischievous', the *Manchester Guardian* of 15 September 1857, described it as a 'very bad and fatally injurious' one. However, there were conflicting opinions on the subject. Sir H. Wheeler, Sir Patrick Grant and W.H. Sleeman were all quoted by the *Edinburgh Review* as bestowing praises upon the system. The last named had called it the 'sheet anchor' of the Bengal army. The periodical itself, commenting on the system, held that the mutiny had started in spite of it and wondered how much sooner it might have broken out had that system been replaced. 'India', *Edinburgh Review* (hereafter referred to as *Edin. Rev.*), CVI, 1857, pp. 558–61.

113. *Manchester Guardian*, 15 September 1857.

114. Jacob, *op. cit.,* pp. 37–9; *Manchester Guardian*, 15 September 1857.

115. *Manchester Guardian*, 15 September 1857.

116. Ibid.; Jacob, *op. cit.,* pp. 30 and 39. For a similar opinion, see also: Medley, *op. cit.,* pp. 194–204. Referring to over-centralization, promotion by seniority and the withdrawal of European officers for civil employment, Medley argued that these three laid the groundwork for anybody to exploit the army for his own personal gains.

Here it should also be mentioned that the system of promotion for European officers too was not free from fault. In this case it was neither efficiency nor seniority that counted for promotion but the officer's buying and bidding capacity. For attaining the next step he could not but buy it because of the purchase system. The *Manchester Guardian* of 17 September 1857 was bitterly critical of it, when the paper pointed out the instance of Havelock who, in spite of his advanced age of sixty-two, in spite of the great capacity which he had shown in independent command, was still a colonel. Explaining that Havelock could not buy his promotion because of his poverty, the paper pointed out that his was one among several such instances.

117. A kind of litter or sedan, a palankeen or palanquin, generally used by a grandee or noble. Formerly the privilege of keeping a *palki* was granted by a king or viceroy.

118. Transliterated as *pankha*, meaning fan.

119. *Tattie* is a screen of fragrant grass hung on a doorway or a window during the hot months of summer, kept constantly wet for cooling and scenting the air in the room.

120. A serving-man, a servant, a table-servant.

121. Transliterated as Sardar.

122. *Manchester Guardian*, 15 September 1857; 'The English in India', WR., New Series, XIII, 1858, p. 196; Jacob, *op. cit.,* p. 28. Jacob discounted the climatic conditions as a reason or as an excuse for such behaviour. He held out the example of the Bombay Presidency where, in spite of a similar climate, European society was ten times more English than that of the Bengal Presidency.

123. *Manchester Guardian*, 16 September 1857.

124. Jacob, *op. cit.,* p. 30. Also quoted by the *Manchester Guardian* of 15 September 1857.

125. Hansard 3, CXLVII, pp. 496–7.

126. 'The Indian Mutiny', DUM., L, 1857, p. 237.

127. *Investigation into Some...,* pp. 46–7; *Manchester Guardian*, 1 August 1857; Hansard 3, CXLVII, pp. 496–7; Edward Smith Mercer, *A Letter to the Rt. Hon. the Earl of Ellenborough, on the Military, Religious and European Settlement Questions in the East Indies* (London: Edward T. Whitehead, 1861), p. 6.

128. *Investigation into Some...,* pp. 46–7; *Manchester Guardian*, 10 September 1857. It was perhaps because of the reasons described in the preceding pages that T.C. Robertson emphasized the character and capacity rather than the number of English officers stationed with sepoy battalions as the factor upon which the efficiency and loyalty of the native army depended. Robertson, *op. cit.,* p. 7.

129. *Manchester Guardian,* 1 and 17 August 1857; *The Mutiny in the Bengal Army,* p. 17; Review of *The Mutiny in the Bengal Army, The Athenaeum,* 1857, p. 1028.
130. *Manchester Guardian,* 1 August 1857.
131. 'The Camp and the Mission', *Saturday Review,* 22 August 1857.
132. Referring to the mission of Colonel Wheler, Sir George Trevelyan reported the Colonel himself having said:

> I beg to state that it has been my invariable plan to act on the broad line which scripture enforces, that is, to speak without reserve to every person. When I therefore address natives on the subject of religion, whether individually or collectively, it has been no question with me whether the person or persons I addressed belonged to this or that regiment, or otherwise, but I speak to all alike, as sinners in the sight of God; and I have no doubt that I have often in this way (indeed, am quite certain) addressed sepoys of my own regiment, as also of other regiments at this and other stations where I have been quartered. *Cawnpore* (3rd. ed.; London and Cambridge: Macmillan and Co., 1866), p. 29.

133. For other similar references, see: *The Scotsman,* 15 August 1857; *Manchester Guardian,* 30 June 1857 and 10 August 1858; *Free Press,* 19 August 1857; *Illustrated London News,* 4 July 1857.
134. An Indian missionary [Hargrave Jennings], *The Indian Religions; or, Results of Mysterious Buddhism,* p. 144. *The Tablet,* writing on Colonel Wheler, entitled its article: 'A Missionary Colonel–A Strong light on the Indian Mutinies'. 22 August 1857.
135. *Manchester Guardian,* 30 June 1857.
136. 'Indian Military Mistakes', *Saturday Review,* 25 July 1857; *Manchester Guardian,* 14 August 1857; 'The Bengal Mutiny', *Blackwood's,* LXXXII, 1857, p. 380; *Illustrated London News,* 4 July 1857; Scrutator [Brodie], *The Indian Mutiny,* pp. 15–16.
137. An Indian Missionary [Jennings], *loc. cit.*
138. Ibid.
139. 'The Bengal Mutiny', *Blackwood's,* LXXXII, 1857, p. 380. Another advocate of this school observed that earlier when officers were not so religious, the sepoys used to play with their children, and even carry the officer to his grave. But the situation, he went on, was changed now. *Mutiny in the Bengal Army,* p. 19.
140. There were two Sir Benjamin Colin Brodies, father and son, surgeon and chemist respectively. Apart from papers in their own fields, one of them seems to have been writing on religion and politics under the assumed name of 'Scrutator'. While the *DNB,* fails to list the latter publications, the important fact, from the point of view of the present research, remains that neither of them had ever been to India. *British Museum General Catalogue of Printed Books,* CCXVII, 859–63; *DNB.,* VI, pp. 378–80.
141. Scrutator [Brodie], *The Indian Mutiny,* pp. 15–6.
142. 'The Camp and the Mission', *Saturday Review,* 22 August 1857. For a similar opinion, see also: 'Indian Military Mistakes', 25 July 1857.
143. An Indian Missionary [Jennings], *op. cit.,* p. 144.
144. p. 18.
145. 'The Mutiny in India', *Illustrated London News,* 4 July 1857.
146. 15 August 1857.
147. Scrutator [Brodie], *The Indian Mutiny,* pp. 15–6.

148. Mercer, *op. cit.*, p. 5.
149. 'Errors of Indian Policy', *Illustrated London News*, 22 August 1857. For a similar opinion, see also: *The Scotsman*, 15 August 1857.
150. 30 June and 14 August 1857. See also: *The Scotsman*, 15 August 1857.
151. *Manchester Guardian*, 30 June 1857.
152. *Crisis in India, its Causes and Proposed Remedies*, (London: Richard Bentley, 1857), pp. 13–4.
153. Gubbins, *op. cit.*, pp. 94–5.
154. *Crisis in India, its Causes and Proposed Remedies*, pp. 13–4.
155. Gubbins, *op. cit.*, p. 97; Lawrence, *op. cit.*, pp. 27–8 and 390.
156. *Mutiny in the Bengal Army*, pp. 13–15. In an effort to bring the desperate condition of the sepoys home to his readers, the author also provided some figures pertaining to the salaries and expenses of the sepoys. He wrote:

> A sepoy's pay is fourteen shillings a month in cantonments and seventeen shillings a month in the field in India. After sixteen years' of service he obtains an increase of pay (one rupee of approximately two shillings) and again after twenty years' service (again one rupee). Out of this moderate sum he pays for the hire of cattle while marching; he builds and repairs his hut, towards which, however, Government contributes a small sum; he pays for his great coat; for his knapsack; his cup; his shoes; his white cotton uniform which he wears half the year; his undress off duty in native style, in which he is expected to be as clean—as on parade. p. 13.

All these expenses were in addition to the cost of his food.
157. Gubbins, *op. cit.*, pp. 97–8.
158. p. 15.
159. Gubbins, *loc. cit.*
160. Ibid.
161. *Manchester Guardian*, 26 October 1857; Medley, *op. cit.*, pp. 199–204; George Crawshay, *Proselytism Destructive of Christianity and Incompatible with Political Dominion. Speech of Mr Crawshay at the India House on the Vote of an Annuity to Sir John Lawrence, 25 August 1858, with Notes and an Appendix* (Lond.: E. Wilson, 1858), p. 29.
162. *Manchester Guardian*, 29 October 1857.
163. Gubbins, *op. cit.*, pp. 91–3.
164. *Manchester Guardian*, 29 October 1857.
165. William Wotherspoon Ireland, *History of the Siege of Delhi* (Edinburgh: Adams and Charles Black, 1861), p. 11.
166. 'An Anglo-Indian's View of the Indian Crisis', pt. 1 *Fraser's*, LVII, 1858, p. 271.
167. Norton, then a public prosecutor at Madras, did not, however, believe in the military character of the outbreak. As a Madras officer he severely criticized the government at Calcutta and held it responsible for the uprising. Emphasizing the political misdeeds of Dalhousie, he thought that the rebellion was caused by a large variety of political, religious and military causes.
168. Norton, *op. cit.*, pp. 21–2. For further information about the sepoy sensitivity regarding their religious and caste prejudices, also read: *The Mutiny in the Bengal Army*.
169. *Manchester Guardian*, 2 October 1857.
170. *Manchester Guardian*, 2 October and 19 November 1857. A writer in the *Illustrated London News*, however, provided an answer to the question raised by the *Manchester Guardian*, when he stated that all those Hindu and Muslim

sepoys who came from Awadh always transmitted their savings to their relatives in that country. It was a remarkable fact, he pointed out, and one that fully refuted Dalhousie's assertion about the misgovernment of Awadh, that 'not a single instance has been known of a sepoy settling down after the completion of his service in our provinces; he has invariably proceeded to Oude to invest his little fortune in the land'. 'History of the British Empire in India', *Illustrated London News*, 28 November 1857. For a similar opinion, see also: 'Our Relations to the Princes of India', *WR.*, New Series, XIII, 1858, pp. 457–8.

171. *Manchester Guardian*, 19 November 1857.

172. Ibid., 25 September 1857.

173. See Chapter I, pp. 5–6.

174. Hansard 3, CXLVII, 490. For a similar opinion, see also: 'An Anglo-Indian's View of the Indian Crisis', pt. 1, *Fraser's*, LVII, 1858, p. 272.

175. Hansard 3, CXLVII, 422–25 and CXLVI, 1613; 'The Revolt of the Bengal Army', *DUM.*, L, 1857, p. 390.

176. Hansard 3, CXLVII, 422–5.

177. Archer, *op. cit.*, pp. 6–7.

178. 'India in Mourning', *Fraser's*, LVI, 1857, p. 737.

179. Olrich, *op. cit.*, p. 6; *Saturday Review*, 7 November 1857; 'The Revolt of the Bengal Army', *DUM.*, L, 1857, p. 388; Charles Raikes, *Notes on the Revolt in the North-Western Provinces of India* (London: Longman, Brown, Green, Longmans, and Roberts, 1858), p. 151; *Free Press*, 17 February 1857.

180. 'The Revolt of the Bengal Army', *DUM.*, L, 1857, p. 388.

181. Ibid.: *Saturday Review*, 7 November 1857; Scrutator [Brodie], *English Tenure of...*, pp. 4–5; Hansard 3, CXLVIII, 1134; Wallace, *op. cit.*, pp. 17–8.

182. *Saturday Review*, 7 November 1857.

183. 'The Revolt of the Bengal Army', *DUM.*, L, 1857, p. 389.

184. Hansard 3, CXLVIII, 18.

185. Raikes, *op. cit.*, p. 151. Raikes firmly believed that the great disturbance in India was the outcome of a mutiny. Though the mutiny, he admitted, had grown into a rebellion, it was certainly not caused by any national discontent. While emphasizing that the vast majority of the people were with the government, he considered the Muslim community of India an exception to this generalization.

186. Stocqueler, *op. cit.*, pp. 17–8.

187. Norton, *op. cit.*, pp. 176–7; Ireland, *op. cit.*, p. 11.

188. The period during which the entire Muslim community in general, and the shi'ah sect in particular, mourn the martyrdom of Imam Hussain, the grandson of the Prophet Muhammad (PBUH).

189. Olrich, *op. cit.*, pp. 22–3. Olrich, however, felt sure that the revolt was caused by a wide combination of social, religious, political and military causes provided by the civil administration of the country. It was not just a military uprising caused by the neglect of army officers. Those who called the outbreak an army mutiny were, Olrich believed, attempting to shirk responsibility.

190. Major H.C. Tucker, former Adjutant General to the Military Secretary to the Government of India, wrote to inform the people that as early as 1853, he, with the authority of the Commander-in-Chief, had written to the Military Secretary that 'in greasing composition nothing should be used which could possibly offend the caste or religious prejudices of the natives'. For the present neglect,

therefore, he blamed the Military Secretary or the Ordinance Officer residing at Calcutta. *The Times,* 24 June 1857; *Free Press,* 19 August 1857.

However, the government was almost universally criticized for its folly in this regard. 'A Resident in the North-Western Provinces of India' went so far as to say that even a griff in India knew the consequences of introducing the greased cartridges. *Investigation into Some...,* p. 52.

191. Colonel Sykes, speaking in the Commons, quoted from a memorandum showing the reaction of the native troops towards the introduction of the greased cartridge and the new rifle. He narrated how a part of the 36th Regiment, then forming an escort to the Commander-in-Chief was detached and sent to Ambala. Later on when the Commander-in-Chief finished his inspection and returned to Ambala, the 36th refused to receive its detached part, saying 'Hookah Panee bund', that is, completely ostracized them, because they had used the polluted cartridge. Hansard 3, CLII, 197.

192. *Manchester Guardian,* 6 August and 1 September 1857.

193. Ibid., 2 July 1857.

194. Dr Edward Henry Nolan, *The Illustrated History of the British Empire in India and the East, from the Earliest Times to the Suppression of the Sepoy Mutiny in 1859,* II, p. 711.

195. Beveridge, *op. cit.,* p. 562.

196. 3 August 1857.

197. George Crawshay, *The Mutiny of the Bengal Army from Official Documents. A Lecture delivered in the Hall of Mechanics Institute, Gateshead, Wednesday, 4 November 1857* (Gateshead: Printed at the Observer Steam Press, 1857), p. 7. For a similar opinion, see also: 'The Bengal Mutiny', *Blackwood's,* LXXXII, 1857, p. 379.

198. *Manchester Guardian,* 17, 19 August and 2 November 1857.

199. Ibid., 3 August 1857.

200. Crawshay, *Proselytism Destructive of...,* p. 18.

201. 'Suppression of Important Passages in the Official Report of the Debate at the India House', *Free Press,* 17 February 1857.

Chapter 3: Variations on the Mutiny Theme

1. *The Times,* 6 August 1857.

2. *Saturday Review,* 18 July 1857. For a similar opinion, see also: The Rev. J.D. Massingham 'The Rebellion of the Sepoys traced to its True Source', (a sermon preached in St. Paul's Church, Derby, on 7 October 1857) *The Pulpit,* LXXII, 1858, p. 397.

3. See Chapters V, p. 166 and VII, pp. 248 and 257–8.

4. 'The Bengal Mutiny', *Blackwood's,* LXXXII, 1857, p. 389; *Crisis in India, its Causes and Proposed Remedies,* pp. 22–3. In fact, this was a very widely held opinion.

5. 6 August 1857. For similar opinion, see also: *The Scotsman,* 22 August 1857.

6. *The Examiner,* 1 August 1857.

7. Ibid., 8 August 1857.

8. 'Suppression of Important Passages in the Official Report of the Debate at the India House', *Free Press,* 17 February 1858. Comparing the sepoy with a pet

animal and the government with its master, Colonel Sykes absolved the former of all responsibility to revolt. According to the *Free Press*, the Colonel had observed before the Court of Directors at the India House, 'Suppose he pinched his dog's nose, although in play, and the dog bit his finger, he would leave the court to determine whether he was to blame or the dog was to blame in the matter.'

9. J.L. Archer, *Indian Mutinies Accounted For: Being an Essay on the Subject*, p. 11.

10. 'Extent of Missions in British India', *MMC.*, XXII, 1858, p. 44. For similar opinions, see also: George Crawshay, *The Mutiny of the Bengal Army from Official Documents. A Lecture delivered in the Hall of Mechanics' Institute, Gateshead, Wednesday, 4 November 1857*, pp. 7–10; *The Spectator*, 8 August 1857. How strong was the religious fear can be ascertained from the following extract of a letter from India, reproduced by *The Spectator*. Referring to the ten mutineers who were brought to be blown from guns at Ferozpur, the extract read:

> Some cried out, 'Do not sacrifice the innocent for the guilty!' Two others, 'Hold your snivelling! die men and not cowards–you defended your religion, why then do you crave for your lives?' 'Sahibs'! 'They are not Sahibs, they are dogs!'

While it clearly indicates that the mutinous sepoys were convinced that their religion was actually in danger and that they were dying in its defence, the last part of the conversation reveals the extent of hatred of the natives for the British. Unlike the west, even today a dog in India is regarded as an obnoxious and hated animal.

To realise what little regard the rulers and the ruled had for each other, compare this conversation with Colonel Sykes' statement before the Court of Directors. See n. 8.

11. [The Rev.] C.B. Lewis, Ext. from a letter of...quoted in the *MH.*, in an article 'India', XLIX, 1857, p. 513.

12. The Rev. James Smith, 'Resumption of the Mission in Delhi', *MH.*, LI, 1859, p. 389.

13. *The Examiner*, 4 July 1857. For similar opinions, see also: *The Times*, 30 July 1857; *India's Mutiny and England's Mourning; or Thoughts for the Fast Day* (London: Hatchard and Wertheim and Macintosh, 1857), p. 13.

14. *The Mutiny in the Bengal Army*, p. 16; *India's Mutiny and England's...*, p. 3; 'Suppression of Important Passages...', *Free Press*, 17 February 1858.

15. *The Mutiny in the Bengal Army*, p. 16.

16. Ibid.

17. Ibid.; Scrutater [Sir Benjamin Colin Brodie], *English Tenure of India: Practical Remarks Suggested by the Bengal Mutiny*, pp. 4–5.

18. Scrutater [Brodie], *loc. cit.*

19. *Manchester Guardian*, 6 July 1857.

20. *Saturday Review*, 8 August 1857. For similar opinions, see also: 'The Bengal Mutiny', *Blackwood's*, LXXXII, 1857, p. 389. *The Times*, however, commented that there was only one idea occupying the minds of the mutineers and that was to 'run off to Delhi...the traditional seat of the Indian Empire. From the most remote and opposite points there is still a flight to Delhi.... It is at least just what we should desire.... Yet, if Delhi is such a trap, we may possibly pay for it. We have made it ourselves a sort of Indian Sebastopol, strengthened it and

filled it with cannon and ammunition. Why we ever did this with a place of high Mahommedan fame, and then assigned it to the keeping of an exclusively native force...', 1 August 1857.

21. 'The Military Revolt in India', *National Review* (hereafter referred to as *NR.*), V, 1857, p. 455.

22. Hansard 3, CXLVII, 1437.

23. Scrutator [Brodie], *English Tenure of India, Practical...*, pp. 4–5.

24. 'Military Revolt in India', *NR.*, V, 1857, p. 452.

25. *Saturday Review*, 8 August 1857. For similar opinions, see also: 'The Bengal Mutiny', *Blackwood's*, LXXXII, 1857, p. 389; *Manchester Guardian*, 2 July 1857.

26. 'The Military Revolt in India', *loc. cit.*, p. 454.

27. *Manchester Guardian*, 3 August 1857. For similar opinions, also refer to the *Guardian* of 6 and 17 August and 2 November 1857.

28. *The Examiner*, 4 July 1857. For similar opinions, see also: 'The Military Revolt in India', *NR.*, V, 1857, p. 452; 'Calcutta and the Indian Question', *London Journal*, XXXVLL, 1858, p. 119; 'Operations of General Havelock', *Saturday Review*, 21 November 1857; Smith, 'Resumption of the Mission in Delhi', *MH.*, LI, 1859, p. 389; *The Indian Mutiny–Thoughts and Facts* (London: Seely, Jackson and Halliday, 1857), p. 5; *The Mutiny in the Bengal Army*, p. 3; 'The Bengal Mutiny', *Blackwood's*, LXXXII, 1857, p. 383; *The Times*, 6 August 1857; *Manchester Guardian*, 6 July and 7 August 1857; Hansard 3, CXXLVII, 1435.

29. 'Within Delhi'. *Saturday Review*, 26 September 1857. For similar opinions, see also: *Manchester Guardian*, 17 August 1857 and 18 January 1859; Scrutator [Brodie], *English Tenure of India, Practical...*, pp. 4–5; W.B. Adams, 'The Right to Govern and to Punish', Letter to *The Spectator*, 19 September 1857.

30. 'The Operations of General Havelock', *Saturday Review*, 21 November 1857; Adams, *loc. cit.*

31. 7 August 1857.

32. 30 July 1857.

33. *India's Mutiny and England's...*, p. 3.

34. 'Principles of Indian Government', *NR.*, VI, 1858, p. 3. For similar opinions, see also: 'The Military Revolt in India', *NR.*, V, 1857, p. 452; *The Examiner*, 19 September 1857; Hansard 3, CXLVII, 1435; *Manchester Guardian*, 6 July 1857; 'India and the Mutiny', *Wesleyan-Methedist Magazine* (hereafter referred to as *WMM.*), 5th Series, III, 1857, pp. 1032–3 and 1037. By maintaining that the uprising was 'purely a military rebellion' and that the 'masses had never risen against our authority anywhere', the writer in the *Wesleyan-Methedist Magazine* was, in fact, contradicting his earlier statement made in the same article that the 'true cause of the mutiny was a long-planned and well-laid Mahommedan conspiracy for their restoration to power. He further maintained, 'this was the chronic disease; the cartridge excitement only an inflammatory one'.

35. 'Principles of Indian Government', *NR.*, VI, 1858, p. 3. For similar opinions, see also: Hansard 3, CXLVII, 526; *Manchester Guardian*, 15 July 1857; *The Indian Mutiny–Thoughts and Facts*, p. 5.

36. 'Principles of Indian Government', *loc. cit.*

37. Ibid.; 'The Military Revolt in India', *NR.*, V, 1857, p. 452.

38. 15 July 1857.

39. 'The Military Revolt in India', *loc. cit.*

40. *The Examiner,* 8 August 1857.
41. Adams, 'The Right to Govern and to Punish', *The Spectator,* 19 September 1857.
42. Martin Richard Gubbins, *An Account of the Mutinies in Oudh, and of the Siege of the Lucknow Residency; with some Observations on the Condition of the Province of Oudh, and on the Causes of the Mutiny of the Bengal Army,* p. 53.
43. Hansard 3, CXLVI, 1331.
44. Ibid., 1589.
45. Ibid., CXLVII, 526.
46. Ibid., 482 and 526 and also CXLVIII, 98. A writer in *Blackwood's Edinburgh Magazine,* a firm supporter of the Mutiny theory, however, doubted the fidelity of the ruler of Gwalior. 'The Bengal Mutiny', LXXXII, 1857, p. 584.
47. Hansard 3, CXLVII, 526; *Manchester Guardian,* 6 July 1857.
48. Hansard 3, CXLVII, 526.
49. *Manchester Guardian,* 7 August 1857.
50. Earl of Shaftesbury, *England's Apostasy in India and the Earl of Shaftesbury's Great Speech on Indian Cruelties, delivered at Wimborns,* p. 6.
51. *Manchester Guardian,* 3 November 1857.
52. Ibid., 21 December 1857.
53. Ibid. A clear understatement of the enemy strength, for, if accepted, it would hardly do justice to the British civil and military administration in India. The government ended up deploying more than 90,000 European and 250,000 native soldiers to suppress the rebellion. Still it took more than two years to put down completely.
54. *Illustrated London News,* 26 December 1857.
55. Ibid.
56. 'Extent of the Indian Mutinies', *Fraser's,* LVII, 1858, p. 360.
57. p. 23.
58. See explanation n. 34. For similar opinions, see also: *The Indian Mutiny and Missions* (Dublin: Madden and Macintosh. London: Wertheim and Macintosh, 1857), p. 13; 'Has the Preservation of Caste Conduced to the Present Revolt in India–Affirmative Article 1', *BC.,* 1858, pp. 25–7.
59. 'Has the Preservation of…Affirmative Article 1', *BC.,* 1858, pp. 25–7.
60. See n. 34.
61. Richard Kidd, 'Causes of the Indian Mutiny', (A sermon preached on 7 October 1857), *The Pulpit,* LXXII, 1858, 393–4.
62. James Wallace, *The Revolt in India: Its Causes and its Lessons, A lecture delivered in Belfast on 2 February 1859,* 17–18.
63. The Rev. J.D. Massingham, 'The Rebellion of the Sepoys traced to its True Source', (A sermon preached on 7 October 1857), *The Pulpit,* LXXII, pp. 393–4.
64. Capt. Mowbray Thompson, *The Story of Cawnpore* (London: Richard Bentley, 1859), pp. 43–4.
65. 'The Military Revolt in India', *NR.,* V, 1857, p. 455.
66. Ibid., 453 and 455.
67. Ibid., 453.
68. Charles Raikes, *Notes on the Revolt in the North-Western Provinces of India,* pp. 159–60.
69. Ibid.
70. *Manchester Guardian,* 7 August 1857.

71. Ibid., 3 September 1857.

72. 'Extent of the Indian Mutinies', *Fraser's*, LVII, 1857, pp. 359–60.

73. Ibid.

74. Massingham, *op. cit.,* p. 395.

75. Crawshay, *the Mutiny of the Bengal Army...,* p. 10.

76. 'An Anglo-Indian's View of the Indian Crisis', *Fraser's*, LVII, 1858, p. 274.

77. Julius George Medley, *A Year's Campaigning in India, March 1857 to March 1858*, pp. 194–5. Medley was a Captain of the Bengal Engineers and Garrison Engineer, Lucknow.

78. Raikes, *op. cit.,* p. 156.

79. I have retained the old spelling of Hyderabad which, though wrong, is still current. A trend, however, has now started to spell it as Haiderabad.

80. *Manchester Guardian,* 9 September 1857.

81. 'Lucknow, Calcutta and London', *Saturday Review,* 12 December 1857.

82. 21 December 1857.

83. *The Examiner,* 3 October 1857.

84. Illustrated London News, 16 January 1858.

85. *Manchester Guardian,* 24 August 1857.

86. *The Examiner,* 3 October 1857.

87. 'India', *Illustrated London News,* 16 January 1858.

88. Medley, *op. cit.,* p. 198.

89. 'The English in India', *NR.,* New Series, XIII, 1858, pp. 194–5.

90. 'The Military Revolt in India', *NR., V,* 1857, pp. 454–5.

91. The writer regarded General Hearsey as an able officer, who was thoroughly acquainted with the natives.

92. 'The Military Revolt in India', *loc. cit.* Similarly the author of the article, 'The English in India', published in the *Westminster Review,* also held that the mutiny was not a sudden movement. He agreed with General Hearsey who maintained that the British were for a long time sitting on a mine ready to explode. Pointing to the warnings issued by the 'great men of India', i.e., Napier, Munro, Charles Metcalfe, Colonel Jacob, the writer argued that if at all the outbreak was a surprise, it was a 'surprise only to the Calcutta Government–poor Brigadier Hewitt and the rest, whom either imbecility or insolence of office had made obstinate'. *WR.,* New Series, XIII, 1858, pp. 194–5.

93. 'The Bengal Mutiny', *Blackwood's,* LXXXII, pp. 378 and 389.

94. Ibid., 390.

95. Gubbins, *op. cit.,* pp. 85–8.

96. Henry Mead, *The Sepoy Revolt: Its Causes and its Consequences,* p. 102.

97. 2 October 1857.

98. 14 September 1857.

99. 'The Bengal Mutiny', *Blackwood's,* LXXXII, 1857, p. 389.

100. 'The Military Revolt in India', *NR., V,* 1857, p. 453.

101. 'The Bengal Mutiny', *Blackwood's,* LXXXII, 1857, p. 389.

102. Ibid.

103. Having joined the Indian army in 1780, Munro served the government of India in various capacities, both in the civil and military administration. His career reached its climax in 1819, when he was appointed to the office of the Governor of Madras. He died in office on 6 July 1827.

104. Edward King, *A Bird's-eye View of India: Showing Our Present Position–its Dangers, and Remedy* (London: Patridge and Co., 1857), p. 45.
105. *India, the Revolt and the Home Government*, pp. 7–8.
106. 6 September 1857.
107. 20 August 1857.
108. 12 September 1857.

Chapter 4: Causes of the Revolution

1. The Rev. Alexander Duff, *The Indian Rebellion; its Causes and Results in a Series of Letters from...* (London: James Nisbet, 1858), p. 193; 'Indian Mutinies', *Fraser's*, LVI, 1857, p. 628.
2. Gen. Sir Robert William Gardiner, *Military Analysis of the Remote and Proximate Causes of the Indian Rebellion, drawn from the Official Papers of the Government of India: Respectfully Addressed to the Honourable the Members of the House of Commons* (2nd. ed.; London: Byfield, Hansworth and Co., 1858), p. 34. Earlier in the book Gardiner had made a still more unequivocal observation when he described the army outbreak as an 'attendant military mutiny' upon a 'social rebellion'. p. 18.
3. William Howard Russell, *My Diary in India*, (Two Vols.; 7th Thousand; London: Routledge, Warne and Co. 1860) I, p. 164. In continuation of the above thought and in the same breath, Russell went on to call the outbreak a war of religion, race and revenge as well.
4. *People's Paper*, 11 July 1857.
5. *Morning Herald*, cited in the *People's Paper*, 26 September 1857.
6. A seasoned general and an author of several pamphlets (16) on military matters, Gardiner had seen active military service in Gibralter, Hanover, Sicily, Portugal, Spain, France and Belgium, with generals like General Fox, Sir John More and Sir Arthur Wellesley. In 1848 he was appointed Governor-General and Commander-in-Chief of Gibralter, which offices he held until 1855. Though Gardiner never seems to have visited India, two lengthy papers by him on the Indian crisis were inspired by his desire to make a professional inquiry into the state of affairs in India based upon official papers. This Gardiner did on his own for the benefit of the House of Commons. Earlier too, he had done the same thing in the case of the Crimean and Peninsular wars. As was the case with his previous papers, his papers on the Indian crisis were also addressed to the House of Commons. *DNB.*, XX, pp. 417–8; *BMGG.*, LXXXII, cols, 66–7.
7. A graduate of St. Andrews University and a recipient of honorary degrees of DD and LLD from the universities of Aberdeen and New York respectively, Duff was ordained as a missionary to India in August 1829. As a devoted Christian missionary and educationist he founded a college at Calcutta, in which English was used for the first time as a medium of instruction in India. To acquaint himself with the country and its people, Duff virtually travelled all over the Indo-Pakistan subcontinent. During the revolt in India he addressed twenty-five letters to Dr Tweedie, Convener of the Free Church of Scotland's Foreign Missions Committee. The letters were first published in *The Witness* newspaper, and were afterwards collected in a volume which went through several editions. *DNB.*, XVI, pp. 125–8.

8. Throughout the outbreak this newspaper published scores of articles and poems on India, all of which sympathized with the rebels and wholeheartedly applauded their efforts at overthrowing the foreign yoke. In addition to this, the paper always gave a prominent place to the events in India and invariably published them under the title of 'Indian Revolution'.

9. Born in Germany of Welsh parents, Jones was a precocious boy. Before the age of ten he had written some poems which were published by Nesler of Hamburg. At eleven he ran away to join the Polish insurgents, but was overtaken and brought back home. At the age of twenty-three Jones was presented to the Queen by the Duke of Beaufort in 1841. In 1846 he joined the Chartist movement and soon became one of its most ardent members. A 'most persuasive orator' of his time, in 1847 Jones was connected with O'Connor's monthly magazine, *The Labourer,* and later became the editor of *The Northern Star.*

   In 1848 Jones parted company with O'Connor for their failure to advocate force. In the same year he was arrested at Manchester for making seditious speeches and sentenced to two years' imprisonment. It was during this period that he wrote his long and famous poem, *The Revolt in Hindostan,* with his own blood on loose leaves of a prayer book. In 1852 he became the editor of the Chartist newspaper, *The People's Paper.*

   During the Indian uprising Jones vigorously used *The People's Paper* to convince the people of Britain that the Indians were fighting for a noble cause. This writer has noticed that he was the only public speaker for whose speeches there was an admission charge, and which were publicized much in advance through the agency of his paper. Like Gardiner, Jones too never seems to have visited India. *People's Paper,* 1 August 1857; *DNB.,* XXX, pp. 99–100.

10. See n. 8 and Chapter 1, n. 2.

11. First published privately in 1850 under the title *The Revolt of Hindostan,* the poem was republished in 1857 under the name, *The Revolt of Hindostan; or, the New World by Effigham Wilson of London.*

12. Even the much criticized Subsidiary System of Lord Wellesley was designed to advance military rather than political frontiers. When towards the latter part of his Governor-Generalship, Welselley tried to pursue a more vigorous foreign policy, he was recalled, and Lord Cornwallis was sent back to India with the 'purpose of undoing the mischief' which his predecessor was 'supposed to have done'. The idea was henceforth to follow a policy of non-intervention; to end the hostilities with Holker and to pacify Sindhiya by the restoration to him of Gwalior and Ghoud. (R.R. Sethi and V.D. Mahajan, *British Rule in India and After, 1707–1956,* p. 88). To take another example, that of Henry Hardinge, whose Governor-Generalship preceded the uprising by less than a decade, one finds that he was faced with exactly the same situation *vis-a-vis* Awadh and the Punjab as Lord Dalhousie. Indeed, the situation in the Punjab was more serious and called for vigorous action. While Hardinge limited himself to remonstrances and friendly warnings in the case of Awadh and a far milder action in the case of the Punjab, Dalhousie acted decisively in both cases.

13. 'The Indian Nemesis', *The Nation,* 19 September 1857; 'Miscellaneous', *CEM.,* XLIV, 1858, p. 232.

14. Ernest Jones, *The Revolt of Hindostan: or, the New World* (Calcutta: Eastern Trading Co., 1957. Originally published in London by Effingham Wilson, 1857), pp. 6 and 11. Also see its review in *The Athenaeum,* 24 October 1857.

15. *The Athenaeum,* 29 August 1857.

16. Hansard 3, CXLVI, 1709–10.

17. Ibid., 538–40.

18. Ellenborough was the Governor-General of India from 1842 to 1844. In addition to this he had also served several times, both before and during the Indian uprising, as President of the Board of Control for India.

19. Hansard 3, CXLVIII, 66.

20. Ibid., 67. Later on the Conservatives took the government to task for not paying any heed to the warnings of Ellenborough, 42–3 and 570.

21. Ibid., CXLVI, 514 and 1324–5.

22. Ibid., CXLVII, 475.

23. Ibid., 440.

24. It was this firm belief which led Disraeli to suggest to the government the employment of civil remedies along with the application of military measures. He also advised that the reinforcement of twenty to twenty-five thousand soldiers would not be sufficient to quell the rebellion and pleaded that the militia be called up. (Hansard 3, CXLVII, 475–79). Although these suggestions were mostly unheeded, and the one relating to the militia turned down more than once, the government was ultimately compelled to adopt most of them, especially the one concerning the militia. It is no wonder that this later on led the Conservatives to taunt the government for its stubborn behaviour. Hansard 3, CXLVIII, 42–3.

25. Duff, *op. cit.,* p. 268. Sir Henry's own essays, written and contributed to various periodicals and magazines long before the outbreak, were also republished by Wm. N. Allen of London in 1859, under the title: *Essays: Military and Political.*

26. Duff, *loc. cit.*; Hansard 3, CXLVI, 525; *Free Press,* 11 November 1857; John Bruce Norton, *The Rebellion in India. How to Prevent Another,* pp. 85–6.

27. Hansard 3, CXLVI, 525; 'Prospects of the Indian Empire', *Edin Rev,* CVII, 1858, p. 3; Gardiner, *op. cit.,* pp. 24–5.

28. 'Prospects of the Indian Empire', *loc. cit.,* p. 4; *The Press,* 25 July 1857; Gardiner, *op. cit.,* pp. 45–63, 66–72, 74–5 and 82–3; Norton, *loc. cit.,* pp. 29–35 and 60; The Rev. William Brock, *A Biographical Sketch of Sir Henry Havelock* (London: James Nisbet and Co., 1858), p. 129.

29. 'Prospects of the Indian Empire', *loc. cit.,* p. 40; Hansard 3, CXLVIII, 42–3; *Free Press,* 3 March 1858; Gardiner, *op. cit.,* p. 26; Norton, *loc. cit.,* pp. 87–8, 136 and 216.

30. Hansard 3, CXLVI, 525.

31. *The Press,* 25 July 1857; 'Christianity in India', *Blackwood's,* LXXXV, 1859, p. 477; Norton, *loc. cit.,* p. 7.

32. *The Athenaeum,* 15 and 29 August and 10 October 1857; *Free Press,* 11 November 1857; Norton, *loc. cit.,* pp. 7 and 83–4.

33. *The Press,* 25 July 1857; Gardiner, *op. cit.,* pp. 19 and 34–8.

34. John Malcolm Ludlow, *Thoughts on the Policy of the Crown towards India* (London: James Ridgeway, 1859), pp. 16–7; Gardiner, *op. cit.,* pp. 25–6; Norton, *loc. cit.,* p. 87.

35. Edward Henry Nolan, *The Illustrated History of the British Empire in India and the East, from the Earliest Times to the Suppression of the Sepoy Mutiny in 1850,* 11, pp. 712–3.

36. 'The Indian Mutiny', *ER.,* New Series, IV, 1858, p. 338.

37. Gardiner, *op. cit.,* pp. 64–5.

38. Umara itself is a plural of Amir and, therefore, cannot be used as a double plural. Amir means: a governor, prince, noble, chief; a person of rank or distinction.

39. 'Our Indian Empire', *Blackwood's,* LXXXII, 1857, p. 644. Cf. Russell, *op. cit.,* II, p. 54.

40. 'Crisis of the Sepoy Rebellion', *LQR.,* IX, 1857–8, p. 567. For a similar opinion, see also: [George Dodd], *The History of the Indian Revolt and of the Expeditions to Persia, China and Japan, 1856-7-8* (London: W. and R. Chambers, 1859), p. 561.

41. Expression suggested by the title of Beckles Wilson's book, *Ledger and Sword or The Honourable Company of Merchants of England Trading to the East Indies (1599-1874)* (London: Longman's, Green and Co., 1903).

42. 'Our Indian Empire', *Blackwood's,* LXXXII, 1857, p. 644.

43. Gardiner, *op. cit.,* p. 65.

44. *Investigation into Some of the Causes Which have Produced the Rebellion in India,* pp. 53–4.

45. The Rev. Charles Stovel, *India: Its Crimes and Claims* (A lecture delivered on the Fast Day, 7 October 1857, and re-delivered on Wednesday, 14 October 1857, in the Commercial Street Chapel and published at the earnest request of those who heard for its circulation), (London: Jackson and Walford, 1857), p. 27.

46. Hansard 3, CL, 1652. For a similar opinion, see also: [G.B. Malleson], *The Mutiny of the Bengal Army,* pt. I, p. 29.

47. *Investigation into Some...,* pp. 53–4.

48. Hansard 3, CL, 1652.

49. Russell, *op. cit.,* I, p. VII.

50. [Malleson], *op. cit.,* pt. I, p. 29.

51. 'British India', *QR.,* CIV, 1858, pp. 229–30. It may be mentioned here that some of the Muslim rulers tried to set themselves up as rulers of the whole of India. Akbar the Great was a striking example of this phenomenon. He, much to the chagrin of orthodox Muslims, went to the extent of evolving something like a new religion, or what may more properly be called a religious code, purely Indian, that was a composite of native religions, Christianity and Islam. His successor Jahangir was the son of Akbar's famous Hindu wife Rani Jodha Ba'i.

52. *Investigation into Some...,* p. 24.

53. 'British India', *QR.,* CIV, 1858, pp. 229–30.

54. 'British India', *QR.,* CIV, 1858, p. 233. For a similar opinion, see also: Scrutator [Sir Benjamin Colin Brodie], *English Tenure of India. Practical Remarks Suggested by the Bengal Mutiny,* p. 7.

55. J.B. Norton, Review of the *Rebellion in India: How to Prevent Another,* Second Notice, *The Athenaeum,* 10 October 1857.

56. Russell, *op. cit.,* I, p. 180.

57. Scrutator [Brodie], *English Tenure of...,* pp. 6–7.

58. Review of *A Glance at the East, The Athenaeum,* 15 August 1857; 'British India', *QR.,* CIV, 1858, p. 235.

59. Scrutator [Brodie], *loc. cit.,* p. 6.

60. Henry Beveridge, *A Comprehensive History of India, Civil, Military and Social, from the First Landing of the English, to the Suppression of the Sepoy Revolt, including an Outline of the Early History of Hindoostan,* III, pp. 555–6; 'British

India', QR., CIV, 1858, p. 228; Norton, Review of *The Rebellion in...*, Second Notice, *The Athenaeum*, 10 October 1857; *Brief Observations Addressed to the General Reader on the Basis of the Reorganization of Our Power in India* (London: R.C. Lepage and Co., 1858), pp. 6–7.

61. Scrutator [Brodie], *English Tenure of...*, p. 7.
62. Norton, *The Rebellion in...*, p. 32. For a similar opinion, see also: Gardiner, *op. cit.*, pp. 46–7.
63. Gardiner, *op. cit.*, pp. 45–7.
64. Norton, *The Rebellion in...*, p. 32.
65. Hansard 3, CL, 1621.
66. Metcalfe quoted by Norton, *The Rebellion in...*, p. 30. For the same quotation, see also: Gardiner, *op. cit.*, pp. 46–7.
67. Martin R. Montgomery, *The Indian Empire—with a full account of the Mutiny of the Bengal Army; of the Insurrection in Western India; and an Exposition of the Alleged Causes* (Vol. II; London: The London printing and Publishing Co., n.d.) p. 2.
68. Beveridge, *op. cit.*, p. 555.
69. The Rev. Henry S. Polehampton, *A Memoir, Letters and Diary of...*, ed. The Revs. Edward Polehampton and Thomas Stedman Polehampton (2nd. ed.; London: Richard Bentley, 1858, pp. 235–6. For a similar opinion, see also: Beveridge, *op. cit.*, p. 556.
70. Hansard 3, CXLVII, 447. For similar opinions, see also: Beveridge, *loc. cit.*; Polehampton, *loc. cit.*
71. 4 November 1857.
72. Beveridge, *op. cit.*, p. 555.
73. 'Our Indian Sepoys', *Leisure Hour* (hereafter referred to as *LH.*), 1857, p. 630.
74. *Investigation into Some...*, p. 11.
75. 'British India', *QR.*, CIV, 1858, p. 232. The article quoted figures of native employment taken from the returns laid before the Parliament. The returns showed that in 1857 there were 856 native employees who received less than £120 a year; 1377 who received between £120 and £240 a year; only six who received between £840 and £960 a year, and just five with salaries more than £960 a year, while the average salary of an Englishman was £1750 a year. p. 237 n.
76. 'Our Relations to the Princes of India', *WR.*, New Series, XIII, 1858, p. 456.
77. Scrutator [Brodie], *English Tenure of...*, pp. 7–8.
78. Norton, Review of *The Rebellion in...*, Second Notice, *The Athenaeum*, 10 October 1857.
79. Ibid.
80. *Free Press*, 2 September 1857.
81. Malcolm Lewin, quoted by the *Free Press*, 17 March 1858.
82. 'Our Relations to the Princes of India', *WR.*, New Series, XIII, 1858, p. 456.
83. Hansard 3, CXLVII, 438; J.W. Kaye, *Christianity in India. An Historical Narrative* (London: Smith, Elder and Co., 1859), pp. 455–62. For a detailed information on the influence exercised by the Anglican Evengelicals in the shaping of the government policies, read: Ian W. Brown, *The Anglican Evangelicals in British Politics, 1780–1833*.
84. 'Christianity in India', *Blackwood's*, LXXXV, 1859, p. 477.
85. Review of the *Indian Infanticide: Its Origin, Progress and Suppression*, *The Athenaeum*, 1 August 1857. Commending the suppression of female infanticide

and other social evils, the reviewer argued that the step might have brought applause to the pioneers in Europe, but in their zeal they failed to take note of the gathering clouds in India. He firmly believed that the enmity of the people in the districts of Mainpuri, Etawah and other districts of the Agra division and the collectorate of Benaras was due to the suppression of the crime of female infanticide.

For similar opinions, see also: 'The Indian Mutiny and its Causes', *London journal*, XXV, 1857, pp. 405–6; Ludlow, *op. cit.*, pp. 210–11.

86. 'Religious Teaching in India', Letter to *The Scotsman*, 12 September 1857; 'A Suttee', *London journal*, XXV, 1857, p. 404; *Annual Register*, 1857, pp. 239–40; Ludlow, *op. cit.*, p. 209.

87. Norton, Review of *The Rebellion in India: How to Prevent Another*, First Notice, *The Athenaeum*, 3 October 1857; *Annual Register*, 1857, pp. 239–40; An Indian Missionary [Hargrave Jennings], Review of *The Indian Religions; or, Results of Mysterious Buddhism*, *The Athenaeum*, 26 June 1858; *The Press*, 11 and 18 July, 1857; 'Religious Teaching in India', *loc. cit.*; David Urquhart, 'The Legality of Acts Abolishing Native Customs and their Consequences', *Free Press*, 12 August 1857; Hansard 3, CXLVII, 465; 'Has the Preservation of Caste Conduced to the Present Revolt in India–Negative Article III', *BC.*, 1858, p. 128; T.C. Robertson, *The Political Prospects of British India*, p. 5. Commending the benevolent designs behind these reforms, Robertson bitterly complained about the manner in which they were carried out. He called them 'inflicted blessings' calculated more often to estrange than to conciliate the natives.

In fact, 58,000 people petitioned the government against and 55,000 for the Bill allowing widow remarriage. This was done at the time of the passage of the Bill through the Indian Legislative Council. *Manchester Guardian*, 16 August 1856.

88. 'Has the Preservation of...Negative Article III', *loc. cit.*; Norton, Review of *The Rebellion in...*, First Notice, *The Athenaeum*, 3 October 1857; An Indian Missionary [Jennings], Review of *The Indian Religions; or...*, *The Athenaeum*, 26 June 1858; T. Frost (ed.), *The Complete Narrative of the Mutiny in India, from its Commencement to the Present Time compiled from the most authentic sources; including many very Interesting Letters from Officers and Others on the Spot*, (London: Pub. by Read and Co., [1858]), p. 4.

In fact, female infanticide, and *sati*, allowing of widow remarriage and interference in the Hindu system of adoption were almost universally accepted as the causes of the outbreak. Female infanticide, *sati* and widowhood were practised in certain regions of India among some of the higher castes. Because of the rigours of the caste system as practised among the Hindus, it had become difficult to find a suitable husband for a daughter within the same caste or income group. While a high-caste man of the higher socio-economic status would not like his daughter to be wed to a man of lower status even in his own caste, with the poorer high-caste families the question of dowry posed an even more formidable problem. The natural result was that the birth of a female came to be dreaded among the higher castes. To save the family dignity and honour, many of the high-caste parents resorted to the cruel practice of female infanticide.

Just as female infanticide was based in the main on most selfish feelings of supposed social necessities, ostentation at wedding feasts, punctilious about inter-marriages and the relative position of either father-in-law or son-in-law, similarly *sati* and widowhood also had a kindred background. The pride of the high-caste husband would not permit that his wife should, after his death, cohabit with any other person. Once married, the union was regarded irrevocable both in life and death in so far as the wife was concerned.

89. Ludlow, *op. cit.,* p. 209. Ludlow supported his argument by further quoting an instance of a Lodhi cultivator's wife from Sir Wm. Sleeman's book *Rambles and Recollections.* In this case the widow, when denied the right of *sati,* herself 'stole a handful of ashes from his [deceased husband] pyre', and persuaded her people to burn her the next day.

90. 'The Indian Mutiny and its Causes', *London Journal,* XXV, 1857, pp. 405–6.

91. *Annual Register,* 1857, pp. 239–40.

92. Norton, Review of *The Rebellion in…,* First Notice, *The Athenaeum,* 3 October 1857; *The Press,* 11 July 1857; An Indian Missionary [Jennings], Review of *The Indian Religions; or…, The Athenaeum,* 26 June 1858; 'Religious Teaching in India', Letter to *The Scotsman,* 12 September 1857; 'The Sepoy Rebellion', *LQR.,* IX, 1857–58, p. 227; Urquhart, 'The Legality of Acts Abolishing Native Customs and their Consequences', *Free Press,* 12 August 1857; Kaye, *op. cit.,* pp. 455–62; Hansard 3, CXLVII, 820 and 822–3.

93. Kaye, *op. cit.,* p. 462. For a similar opinion, see also: Hansard 3, CXLVII, 518–19, 820–1 and 1414. J. Whiteside, an MP, calling the petition one of the 'most masterly papers he had ever read', deplored the indifference shown to it by the Company and the Parliament. Since the petition had 'emanated from some of the first men in Calcutta—not from armed sepoys…but from men of station, wealth and intelligence', Whiteside thought that it should have been given immediate attention.

94. Kaye, *loc. cit.*

95. A 'voluminous writer, and a constant contributor to periodical literature', Sir John was a graduate of Eton and Royal Military College, Addiscombe. He joined the Bengal artillery in 1832, but resigned his position in the army in 1841 and devoted himself to literature. Fifteen years later he joined the home civil service of the Company and at the abolition of this corporation in 1858, he succeeded John Stuart Mill as secretary of the political and secret department of the India office. His important works included, among others, *History of the War in Afghanistan* (3 Vols.); *Administration of the East India Company; The Life and Correspondence of Charles, Lord Metcalfe* (2 Vols.); *The Life and Correspondence of Henry St. Tucker; Life and Correspondence of Sir John Malcolm* (2 Vols.); *The History of the Sepoy War in India, 1857–58* (3 Vols.) and *Christianity in India. DNB.,* XXX, pp. 253–4.

96. In this case, however, it seems that the government was really forced into taking this step under the pressure of the missionaries and the Anglican Church in India. Kaye reports that as far back as 1832, the missionaries prominently brought this matter to the notice of the Court of Directors. The result was a partial remedy. A regulation was enforced in Bengal whereby in suits involving parties of different persuasions the matter was not to be decided in accordance with the laws of Hindu and Muslim religions. As the new rule was applicable to the Bengal Presidency only, in 1845 the Bishop of Bombay called the government's attention to this matter. In the same year a draft act was published which annulled the application of those sections of the Hindu and Muslim laws

which inflicted forfeiture of rights to property upon those who accepted another religion. The Hindus, thereupon, at once memorialized the government against the threatened innovation. The government was sufficiently alarmed not only to remove the relevant clauses from the Act, but even to go to the extent of expressing regrets upon the whole matter. The Bishop of Bombay, however, did not lose patience. Later on, he made another highly successful attempt to help new converts to Christianity. Consequently, a law enabling native converts to Christianity from Hinduism and Islam to retain their inheritance rights was enacted in April 1850. This happened in spite of the earnest petitions of the Hindus of Bengal, Bihar and Orrisa. Kaye, *op. cit.,* pp. 455–62.

97. *Free Press,* 2 September 1857.

98. An epithet of the goddess Durga, wife of Shiv, the Hectae of the Hindus, to whom human sacrifices were offered. John T. Platts, *A Dictionary of Urdu, Classical Hindi and English* (London: Oxford University Press, 1965), p. 804.

99. 'That inaccessible goddess', name of the daughter of Himavat and wife of Shiv. Also called Uma, Bhavani, Paravati, etc. In her character of Durga, she is a goddess of a terrific form and irascible temper, particularly worshipped by the Bengali Hindus at the Durga Puja festival. Platts, *loc. cit.,* p. 513.

100. A ceremony observed by the lower orders of Hindus on the day when the sun enters Aries, for the expiation of their sins. Platts, *loc. cit.,* pp. 429–30.

101. Norton, Review of *The Rebellion in...,* First Notice, *The Athenaeum,* 3 October 1857; *Free Press,* 11 July 1857.

102. Malcolm Lewin, *The Way to lose India* (London: J. Ridgeway, 1857), p. 18. For similar opinions and further information, see also: Scrutator [Brodie], *English Tenure of...,* p. 8; *Free Press,* 3 March 1858; Hansard 3, CXLVIII, 1155–6; The Rev. Baptist Wriothesley Noel, *England and India. An essay on the Duty of Englishmen towards the Hindoos,* p. 16. Noel had no hesitation in admitting the 'earnest and constant' help given by the officers in facilitating the task of the missionaries. Polehampton, the missionary at Delhi, happily wrote in August 1856, to inform his mother about the efforts of Dr Nai Smith of the 17th Native Infantry in converting his servants. (Polehampton, *op.cit.,* pp. 118–19). *The Press* in its issue of 11 July 1857 also lashed out against the entire administration of India. It complained that the Cannings had made their missionary zeal quite conspicuous, the members of the Indian Legislative Council presided at missionary meetings, and their daughters preached in the bazars 'in defiance of oriental propriety'.

103. Kaye, *op. cit.,* p. 448.

104. Hansard 3, CXLVII, 487.

105. Lewin, *op. cit.,* p. 16. For a similar opinion, see also: *Free Press,* 2 September 1857.

106. *Free Press,* 2 September 1857. Cf. Lewin, *loc. cit.*

107. Malcolm Lewin, *The Way to Regain India* (London: James Ridgeway, 1858), pp. 28–9.

108. Kaye, *op. cit.,* p. 449n.

109. Hansard 3, CXLVII, 487.

110. Ibid., 518–19 and 823 and also CXLVIII, 63.

111. Henry Care Tucker, *A Letter to the Rt. Hon. Lord Stanley, M.P., Secretary of State for India* (London: W.H. Dalton, 1857), pp. 5–6. The new policy reached its fulmination by Wood's Dispatch on Education in India in 1853. In this case as

well, outside influence, especially missionary, was brought to bear upon the Indian minister. Kaye, *op. cit.*, pp. 471–3.

112. Norton, *The Rebellion in...*, p. 199.

113. 'The Indian Army', *Fraser's*, LVI, 1857, p. 166. For similar opinions, see also: Hansard 3, CXLVII, 823; Lewin, *The Way to Lose India*, p. 16.

114. 'The Proselytising Danger in India', Letter to *The Scotsman*, 1 August 1857. The correspondent critically observed:

> It is not the unsupported efforts of the poor missionary, or even the private acts of a zealous commanding officer or civilian, that will ever stir up rebellion against the Government among the natives. It is that they see bishops and chaplains quartered upon the revenue of the country, just as soldiers and civilians are, and they rightly infer that supremacy will sooner or later be claimed for the faith of their rulers, and Christianity established by law.

In another letter to *The Scotsman* of 12 September 1857, the same correspondent attacked some of the contradictory policies pursued by the government *vis-a-vis* its avowal of religious neutrality. Pointing out the philosophical system of instruction at Banaras College; list of class books in the curriculum of the Calcutta University; government appointment and the high salary of the Lord Bishop of Calcutta, whose advent in any station through which he passed was announced with the thunder of the cannon, and his episcopal Lordship's ecclesiastical position as head of the missionary establishment of the Church of England, the writer sharply struck at the government efforts to convince the natives of its policy of religious impartiality as falsehood, political blunder and double error. While he applauded the Christian efforts of the government, he denounced the inconsistency in its attitude and regarded the native distrust as a natural corollary of such a policy.

115. Lieut.-Col. Sir H.B. Edwardes, *Christianity in India. The Speech of...delivered at an Extraordinary Meeting held at the Town Hall, Cambridge, on the 18th of June 1860* (Cambridge: T. Dixon. London: Wertheim and Co., 1860), pp. 9–10.

116. 'British India', *QR.*, CIV, 1858, p. 238.

117. 'Prospects of the Indian Empire', *Edin. Rev.*, CVII, 1858, p. 40. Ellenborough had deposed before a committee of the Commons in 1852, that in answer to his personal query from a native, Dawarkanath Taigor, 'You know if these gentlemen were to succeed in educating the natives of India to the utmost extent of their desire, we should not remain in the country for three months', the latter rejoined, 'Not three weeks'.

For similar opinions, see also: *Manchester Guardian*, 4 December 1857; 'The Indian Outbreak and its Connection with Climate', *The Spectator*, 8 August 1857; Leopold Von Olrich, *Military Mutiny in India: Its Origin and its Results*, p. 5.

118. 'Indian Mutinies and Indian Missions', *Church of England Quarterly Review* (hereafter referred to as *CEQR.*), XLII, 1857, p. 430.

119. Scrutator [Sir Benjamin Brodie], *The Indian Mutiny*, p. 17.

120. An Indian missionary [Jennings], Review of *The Indian Religions; or...*, *The Athenaeum*, 26 June 1858; 'The Indian Monopoly', *London Journal*, XXVI, 1857, p. 53.

121. 'The Indian Monopoly', *loc. cit.*

122. Ibid.

123. A Parliamentary Commission was set up in the 1840s to investigate into the complaints of torture as practised in India. The Commission conducted its

inquiry in the Presidency of Madras only, and the report was to be regarded as a fair representation of the situation in other parts of British India. It was submitted to the Governor of Madras after around seven years of investigation on 16 April 1855. The check-up unmasked 1690 cases of confession by torture in the Madras Presidency alone, out of which 890 were later acquitted. For figures and detail, see: Hansard 3, CXLV, 714–17; Review of the *Report of the Commissioners for the Investigation of alleged cases of Torture, in the Madras Presidency, The Athenaeum,* 20 October 1855.

124. *The Nation,* 19 September and 10 October 1857; Henry Mead, *The Sepoy Revolt: Its Causes and Consequences,* pp. 207–208; Hansard 3, CXLV, 714–17. The kinds of torture practised included: 'Keeping a man in the sun; preventing his going to meals or other calls of nature...the use of kittee [Kittee was an instrument consisting of two sticks tied together at one end, between which the fingers were placed 'as in a lemon-squeezer'. See: Review of the Report of...], *anundal* [Anundal was one of the most characteristic forms of torture. It consisted in 'tying a man down in a bent position, either with his own cloth or by a rope passed over his head and under his toes, with the ingenious addition of a heavy stone laid on his back, varied occasionally by the peons sitting astride upon him!' See: Review of the *Report of...*]; squeezing the crossed fingers with hands; pinches on the thighs; slaps, blows with fists or whip; running up and down; twisting the ears...striking two defaulters' heads against each other; tying them together with their back hair; tying the hair of the head to a donkey or buffalo's tail...sometimes arms and thighs are smeared with a hot iron, sometimes a coir rope is twisted tightly about the arm or leg, and then wetted with cold water, so as to contract to a degree utterly beyond endurance!

Regarding the absence of complaints, the report read, 'In most of these cases we find the painful confession: "We do not complain. What is the use of a poor man like me complaining to the gentlemen? Who will hear us? It is not useful to complain in such cases, for who will hear us?" Review of the *Report of...*, *loc. cit.*

125. Mead, *op. cit.,* pp. 208–209.

126. *The Press,* 22 August 1857; *The Tablet,* 22 August 1857.

127. *The Tablet,* 22 August 1857.

128. *The Press,* 22 August 1857.

129. Norton, Review of *The Rebellion in...,* Second Notice, *The Athenaeum,* 10 October 1857. Also read the book itself, p. 119n.

130. Author of the *Investigation into Some....* He called the administration of justice 'anomalous and idiosyncratic' in character. p. 31 For the criticism in the Commons, see below: p. 150.

131. 'The Indian Monopoly', *London journal,* XXVI, 1857, p. 53.

132. *Investigation into Some...,* p. 29.

133. Ibid., p. 32; The Rev. James Bradbury, (Notes of Bradbury's tour through the districts of Murshidabad and Rajshahi), *MMC.,* XXII, 1858, pp. 263–4. The 'Resident in the North-Western Provinces of India' observed:

The European head of a court is a mere puppet in the hands of the *vakeels* [Wakils, meaning advocates or lawyers] and *amlahs* ['Amlah is a plural, meaning staff]. He cannot be approached except through them. If one man has been injured by another, or an *asami* [Asami, meaning tenant or cultivator] has been oppressed by a *zamindar,* he cannot at once come into court and complain his grievance. He must present a petition to the *huzoor* [Huzur: honourable. Here it means judge], but in order to do so he must first bribe half a dozen persons. And after all this he may find himself so snubbed by the head official, who perhaps has received a valuable consideration from the opposite party, that he is afraid to have the petition presented.

Then, again, when a petition, or evidence of a witness, is taken down in writing, the writer being bribed distorts what is said in the most gross and audacious manner. Let it not be asserted that this is an unusual thing. It is practised everyday, of every year, in every court throughout the empire.

134. 'The Indian Monopoly', *London Journal*, XXVI, 1857, p. 53. For a similar opinion on the administration of justice, see also: Sir Eriskine Perry, Review of *A Bird's-eye View of India*, *The Athenaeum*, 12 January 1856.

135. 'The Indian Monopoly', *loc. cit.*

136. 'Our Indian Empire', *Blackwood's*, LXXXII, 1857, p. 658.

137. 'Our Relations to the Princes of India', *WR.*, New Series, XIII, 1858, p. 475n.

138. *Investigation into Some...*, p. 32. For a critical analysis of the judicial system in India, see also: Hansard 3, CL, 1652; Bradbury, (Notes of his tour through the districts of Murshidabad and Rajshahi), *MMC.*, XXII, 1858, pp. 263–4. Admitting that the British Indian Government was the best in its 'intentions towards the people than any preceding dynasty', the Rev. James Bradbury, an itinerant missionary in Lower Bengal, felt so disgusted with the judicial administration that he could not help calling the civil and criminal courts 'sinks of iniquity', where justice was 'bought and sold like any other marketable commodity'. A poor man, he asserted, preferred to suffer in silence than go and seek a remedy at these courts.

139. The Lala was compelled into signing a document of false charges against him on pain of confinement and denial of food. Hansard 3, CXLV, 250–7.

140. Ibid.

141. Ibid., CL, 1971–72. Bruce claimed that there was, in fact, no dearth of such 'cases of atrocious injustice committed on the natives', and that he personally knew many of them.

142. Hansard 3, CXLVII, 458. For similar opinions, see also: *Free Press*, 3 March 1858; Frost, *op. cit.*, p. 4; Disraeli regarded this 'disturbance of the settlement of property' as one among the three major causes of the outbreak, the other two being 'forcible destruction of native authority', and interference in the religion of the natives. Hansard 3, CXLVII, 448.

143. 'Indian Mutiny and the Land Settlement', *Blackwood's*, LXXXIV, 1858, p. 704. For a better appreciation of this grievance of the natives read the article itself and William Edwards' book, *Personal Adventures During the Indian Rebellion in Rochilcund, Futtehghur and Oude* (London: Smith, Elder and Co., 1859).

144. Hansard 3, CXLVII, 459.

145. 'Indian Mutiny and the Land Settlement', *Blackwood's*, LXXXIV, 1858, p. 707.

146. Ibid., p. 704.

147. Ibid., p. 707.

148. Dearer than life. Edwards, *op. cit.*, p. 17. For the same quote, see also: 'The Indian Mutiny and the Land Settlement', *loc. cit.*, p. 707.

149. 'Indian Mutiny and the Land Settlement', *loc. cit.*, p. 704.

150. Edwards, *op. cit.*, p. 14; 'Indian Mutiny and the Land Settlement', *loc. cit.*, p. 707. The author of the 'Indian Mutiny and the Land Settlement' further reported that H.S. Boulderson, a member of the Board of Revenue in the Upper

Provinces, had also been, along with William Edwards, criticizing and warning the government on its land settlement policies. The writer admonished the administration for not paying any heed to their public representations, p. 703.

151. Hansard 3, CXLVII, 458.

152. Meadows Taylor, *Letters from Meadows Esq., Deputy Commissioner of the Ceded Districts in the Deccan, written during the Indian Rebellion* (London: Printed by John Edward Taylor, 1857), pp. 17–18; Edwards, *op. cit.*, p. 12.

153. *A Short Review of the Present Crisis in India* (Dublin: McGlashan and Gill, 1857), p. 14.

154. *Investigation into Some...*, pp. 53–4.

155. L.E. Ruutz Rees, Review of a *Personal Narrative of the Siege of Lucknow, from its Commencement to its Relief by Sir Colin Campbell, The Athenaeum,* 6 March 1858.

156. Malcolm Lewin, *The Government of the East India Company and its Monopolies; or, the Young Indian Party and Free Trade* (2nd. ed.; London: J. Ridgeway, 1857), pp. 23–4.

157. 'The Indian Mutiny', *DUM.*, L, 1857, p. 239; *The Examiner,* 19 September 1857; Richard Congreve, India (London: Printed by A. Boner, 1907. First published in 1857 by Chapman. *The Athenaeum* reviewed it in its issue of 2 January 1858), p. 23; [W. Sinclair], *The Sepoy Mutinies: Their Origin and their Cure,* p. 9; Olrich, *op. cit.*, p. 21; Edwardes, *op. cit.*, p. 11; Hansard 3, CXLVII, 483.

158. 'The Indian Mutiny', *loc. cit.*

159. [Sinclair], *op. cit.*, p. 9.

160. The Examiner, 19 September 1857.

161. Olrich, *op. cit.*, p. 21.

162. Edwardes, *op. cit.*, p. 11.

163. 'The Indian Mutiny', *DUM.*, L, 1857, p. 239.

164. Lewin, *The Way to Lose India,* p. 10.

165. *The Press,* 11 July 1857. For a similar opinion, see also: Norton, Review of *The Rebellion in...*, Second Notice, *The Athenaeum,* 10 October 1857.

166. *Investigations into Some...*, pp. 23–5.

167. Congreve, *op. cit.*, p. 10. Having described the behaviour of his countrymen in India, Congreve observed:

> So mild a term as regret would not express my judgment on our bearing in India previous to the revolt. The bearing has been singularly concentrated by an Indian statesman in the bold expression: 'We have stalked as conquerors'. I see no reason to doubt the justice of this concentration. As little reason do I see to doubt that the horrors of the outbreak, as distinct from the outbreak itself, are attributable to the long sense of humiliation consequent on that stalking as conquerors.

168. Hansard 3, CL, 1650. Billingsgate is a London fish market, which is known for its coarse, vulgar, and abusive language. Random House Dictionary of the English Language.

169. An Indian missionary [Jennings], Review of *The Indian Religions; or...*, *The Athenaeum,* 26 June 1858. The following extract, though not representative of the British thought and treatment of the Indians, may still be regarded as a fair portrayal of the attitudes of a class of Britons in India. The extract is part of a letter signed 'Anglo-Indian'. It originally appeared in *The Times* and was later reproduced and censured in the Commons. It read:

I am happy to hear that evidence is being obtained both as to the Emperor of Delhi and the King of Oude. It will be pleasant to save £250,000 or £300,000 a year in their forfeited pensions.

I have some hope that the Nawab of Moorshidabad may be implicated too. That would save £120,000 a year more.

Once again, do allow me to plead earnestly that, instead of now yielding to caste, and pondering about the 'prejudices' of the natives, our future policy should be an unbending, stern, and avowed discouragement of everything opposed to civilisation, social morals, and British supremacy. If we now issue a proclamation declaring that, whereas caste has been used as a plea for sedition, and whereas it is based on falsehood, and the British Government regards all men as born equal, therefore, henceforth, it shall not be recognized in any form, the whole Hindoo population will bow, admit the justice of our indignation, and this monstrous anti-social absurdity will soon perish.

I am not for letting the State turn missionary; but, if our soldiers knock down every filthy idol they see, and lay every masjid [mosque] level with the ground; and if they pollute every shrine, and plunder everyone which is worth plundering, I shall not be sorry. For, as to these 'religions', what are they, in fact, but lust, lies, treachery, murder and social degradation? I should like to see our Government cause it to be known, that its past forbearance has been abused, and that now Mahomedans and Hindoos must look to it for no sort of countenance. Hansard 3, CXLVII, 1412–1413.

The present writer is of the opinion that such fanatics, of whom there certainly existed a large number in India, must surely have further spoiled the name of the British and immeasurably added to the great mass of discontent and dissatisfaction that already existed in the colony.

170. Hansard 3, CLI, 348–9. John Bright reported to the Commons an instance in which one of the officers whipped two of his servants to near murder or death. For a similar observation, see also: 'British India', QR., CIV, 1858, p. 235. In this article the author maintained that the 'very kindness which it is alleged is shown to the servants and those employed by the Government too generally partakes rather of that shown in England to a domestic animal, or of pitying condescension displayed by a superior to an inferior race'.

171. Congreve, op. cit., p. 10. For a similar observation, see also: An Indian Missionary [Jennings], The Indian Religions; or, Results of the Mysterious Buddhism, pp. 141–3 and 156–60.

172. 'British India', QR., CIV, 1858, p. 235.

173. Investigation into Some..., pp. 23–5.

174. Hansard 3, CLI, 340.

175. Investigation into Some..., p. 25.

176. Hansard 3, CL, 1650.

177. Norton, The Rebellion in..., pp. 224–6. For a similar opinion, see also: An Indian Missionary [Jennings], The Indian Religions: or..., pp. 141–3 and 156–60.

178. Hansard 3, CL, 1651–52. For similar opinions, see also: Norton, The Rebellion in..., pp. 6–7; 'Has the Preservation of...Negative Article III', BC., 1858, p. 126.

179. Norton, The Rebellion in..., p. 7.

180. Free Press, 16 December 1857; Hansard 3, CXLVI, 525 and CXLVIII, 1482; 'Prospects of the Indian Empire', Edin. Rev., CVII, 1858, p. 3; Investigations into some..., p. 11. Between 1846 and 1857, 207,637 square miles of territory with an annual revenue of 4,330,000 pounds and a population of eleven million people was added to the British Indian empire. (Hansard 3, CXLVI, 951–2). In

spite of this vast territorial expansion, the strength of European force stationed in India in 1857 was less than in 1835. The strength of native troops during this period, however, had increased by 100,000 men. (See Chapter II, pp. 42–3). On the civilian service side the situation was no better. In 1846 there were 431 covenanted civil servants in India and in 1857 this strength had risen to only 432. (Hansard 3, CXLVI, 952). The government, however, started to make up this deficiency by drawing upon the military service. The natural result was that while the civilian service could not be fully reinforced, the army was denuded of its experienced officers. (For figures see Chapter II, pp. 55 and 55a). According to the Earl of Malmesbury as many as 25 per cent of army officers were taken away from their regiments to fill civil vacancies. Hansard 3, CXLVI, 953.

181. Ludlow, *op. cit.*, p. 16.

182. Ibid.; Hansard 3, CXLVIII, 1482.

183. Scrutator [Brodie], *English Tenure of...*, p. 20. Ironically enough this fear turned out to be too true in the case of Sind itself. Even 'Ali Murad, the Amir of Khairpur, who had deserted his fellow Amirs in the Sind Wars in 1842–3, and had helped the British into power in that province, was not given a fair treatment. Retained in power by Charles Napier, the hero of Sind, and Lord Ellenborough, then Governor-General of India, for his loyal services, a 'charge of forgery was trumped up' against 'Ali Murad after the departure of Napier from India. As a result 'Ali Murad was deposed. Having given all the relevant facts of the case, the *Free Press* in its issue of 17 March 1858, was extremely critical of the government proceedings in this matter.

184. W.H. Sleeman, Review of *Journey Through the Kingdom of Oudh, The Athenaeum,* 13 March 1858; *The Press,* 25 July 1857; Hansard 3, CXLVII, 448–61 and CLI, 339–40. It is no wonder that a large section of the British public regarded the outbreak as a Dalhousie aftermath—a result of the different measures carried out by the Dalhousie administration, the most important being the extension of the territories.

185. Hansard 3, CXLVI, 525; Lawrence, *op. cit.*, pp. VIII–IX; 'Prospects of the Indian Empire', *Edin. Rev.,* CVII, 1858, p. 3.

186. Norton, *The Rebellion in...*, pp. 92–3. Norton regretfully observed:

> If we put on one side of the account what the natives have gained by the few offices that have lately been opened to them, with what they have lost by the extermination of these states, we shall find the net loss to be immense; and what the native loses, the Englishman gains. Upon the extermination of a native state, an Englishman takes the place of the sovereign, under the name of the commissioner; three or four of his associates displace as many dozens of the native official aristocracy, while some hundred of our troops take the place of many thousands that every native chief supports. The little court disappears–trade languishes–the capital decays–the people are impoverished–the Englishman flourishes and acts like a sponge, drawing up riches from the banks of the Ganges, and squeezing them down upon the banks of the Thames. Nor is this all. Native princes and their courts not only encourage native trade and native arts, but under them, and because of their very weakness, public spirit and opinion flourishes; all that constitutes the life of a people is strengthened; and though the Government may occasionally be oppressive, heavier far is the yoke of our institutions.

187. Robertson, *op. cit.*, pp. 13–14. For similar opinions, see also: An Indian Missionary [Jennings], *The Indian Religions: or...*, pp. 157–68; Hansard 3,

CXLVIII, 1482; Lewin, *The Way to Lose India*, p. 5. Himself firmly believing that the changes in the social, religious and political policies had occurred in the context of increasingly strong position of the British in India, Malcolm Lewin reproduced the feelings of a native intellectual conveyed to him long before the outbreak. The native of India had observed:

> The word of the English was formerly as if it were engraved upon granite; now it is written in water; as long it was politic to keep faith with the native, who could be more observant of your faith than you English; now that you have the country at your feet, you have fairly thrown off the mask; you may not believe me...we hate you and you deserve it.

188. 'Our Relations to the Princes of India', *WR.*, New Series, XIII, 1858, pp. 464–5. For a similar opinion, see also: Norton, *The Rebellion in...*, p. 137.

189. Robertson, *op. cit.*, pp. 11–14.

190. A very widely held opinion.

191. Norton, *The Rebellion in...*, p. 97; Ludlow, *op. cit.*, pp. 28–9.

192. 'Has the Preservation of Caste...Negative Article III', *BC.*, 1858, p. 126; *Free Press*, 5 August 1857; *Morning Herald*, quoted by the *People's Paper*, 26 September 1857; *Investigation into Some...*, pp. 2–4. Cf. 'The Sepoy Rebellion', *LQR.*, IX, 1857–8, p. 255; Beveridge, *op. cit.*, p. 556; Hansard 3, CXLVII, 444.

193. *People's Paper*, 1 August 1857.

194. Nana Sahib's agent in London. 'Azim was sent to London by the Nana, there to plead his master's case before the Queen and the Commons.

195. In fact, 'Azim's visit was prompted by the Allied defeat at Yalta. Having heard the news of the defeat, 'Azim got so excited that he specially went to Constantinople, and from there successfully endeavoured to get a passage to Balaklava. At Crimea through the courtesy of Doyne, the superintendent of the army works corps, and W.H. Russell, *The Times'* war correspondent in Crimea, 'Azim even visited the trenches, then under heavy bombardment of the Russians. According to Russell, who was later *The Times'* special correspondent in India to cover the Indian uprising, 'Azim felt quite happy at the slim chances of an Allied victory and he made no secret of his feelings. Russell, *op. cit.*, I, pp. 165–8.

196. A Persian equivalent of Hercules.

197. Russell, *op. cit.*, I, pp. 165–6.

198. Hansard 3, CXLVII, 474.

Chapter 5: The Conspiracy Theory: A Recurring Theme

1. Disraeli tried to put across his point of view in the Commons in these words:

> If the old principle–the principle upon which our empire was created and established and which prevailed until very recent times–was a respect for nationality, the principle of the new system seems to be the reverse, and may be described as one which would destroy nationality. Everything in India has been changed. Laws and manners, customs and usages, political organizations, the tenure of property, the religion of the people–everything in India has either been changed, or attempted to be changed, or there is a suspicion among the population that a desire for change exists on the part of our Government.

It was this consciousness, Disraeli stressed, which led to 'combination and the combination, in turn, led to conspiracy'. Hansard 3, CXLVII, 448.

2. *People's Paper,* 1 August 1857. Also read Chapter IV, pp. 160–2.

3. Alexander Duff, *The Indian Rebellion; its Causes and its Results in a Series of Letters,* pp. 219–20. Duff argued 'that it is a rebellion, and a rebellion of no mushroom growth, every fresh revelation tends more and more to confirm. And a rebellion long and deliberately concocted…'.

   N.A. Chick (ed.) *Annals of the Indian Rebellion, containing Narratives of the Outbreak and Eventful Occurrences, and Stories of Personal Adventures, during the Mutiny of 1857–58, with an Appendix Comprising Miscellaneous Facts, Anecdotes etc.* (Calcutta: Printed and Published by Sanders, Cones and Co., 1859), p. 1. In an attempt to prove that the uprising was a deep-laid conspiracy, Chick reproduced the argument put forward by the Deputy Judge Advocate General of the Army at the trial of the King of Delhi. The argument read:

   > The machinery that has set in motion, such an amount of mutiny and murder, that has made its vibrations felt almost at one and the same moment from one end of India to the other, must have been prepared, if not with forseeing wisdom, yet with awful craft, and most successful and commanding subtelity. We must recollect, too, in considering this subject, that in many of the places where the native troops have risen against their European officers, there was no pretence even in reference to cartridges at all.

   People's Paper, 1 August 1857. This newspaper editorially called it a 'long plan, matured with wonderful skill. Its ramifications were maintained with astonishing secrecy.… The time chosen was, while a Chinese war was afloat, and before the British force had returned from its Persian campaign,' The Rev. R. Meek, *The Martyr of Allahabad* (London: James Nisbet, 1858), p. 17. Meek called the outbreak 'the result of a deep-laid, well ordered and wide spread conspiracy for the overthrow of British dominion…'.

   For similar opinions, see also: *The Press,* 25 July 1857; CS., VII, 1857, p. 644; Meadows Taylor, *Letters from Meadows Esqr., Deputy Commissioner of the Ceded Districts in the Deccan, written during the Indian Rebellion,* pp. 4–5; Review of *Dacoitee in Excelsis; or, the Spoliation of Oude, by the East India Company, faithfully recounted, The Athenaeum,* 29 August 1857; The Rev. J.C. Miller, 'The fast-day Sermons. No. VI', *The Fast-day Sermons. The 'Indian-Mutiny' Twelve Sermons,* p. 81; *Morning Herald,* quoted by the *People's Paper,* 26 September 1857; The Rev. J.E.W. Rotton, *The Chaplain's Narrative of the Siege of Delhi, from the Outbreak at Meerut to the Capture of Delhi* (London: Smith, Elder and Co., 1858), pp. 4–5; The Rev. W.J. Newman, 'Our Mercies in the Past, and our Prospects for the Future', *The Pulpit,* LXXV, 1859, p. 441; Hansard 3, CXLVII, 469–71 and 1439–40; Review of *The Mutiny in the Bengal Army, A Glance at the East* and [David Urquhart's] *The Sraddha, The Athenaeum,* 15 August 1857; William Taylor, quoted by Duff, *The Indian Rebellion…,* pp. 299–300; The Rev. James Charles, *The Lord's Voice to Britain from the Far East,* p. 8; A.H. Layard, Speech of…editorially quoted in *The Scotsman* and the *Manchester Guardian,* 2 and 11 September 1857 respectively; [The Rev.] Robinson (letter from), *MH.,* XLIX, 1857, p. 569; 'An Anglo-Indian's View of the Indian Mutiny', *Fraser's,* LVII, 1858, p. 271 and also 'Indian Mutinies', *Fraser's,* LVII, 1858, p. 271 and also 'Indian Mutinies', LVI, 1857, p. 271; 'The Crisis in India', *CEM.,* XLIII, 1857, p. 193; 'Indian Mutinies of the Native Troops and Massacre of Europeans', *Illustrated London News,* 4 July 1857; *England's Troubles in India* (Taunton: Printed by T. Hiscock, 1857), p. 31; *The Spectator,* 26 September 1857; *The Times* (from the Agra Correspondent), 15 July 1857; *A Short Review of the Present Crisis in India*, pp. 10 and 14; 'Crisis of the Sepoy Rebellion', *LQR.*, IX, 1857–58, pp. 532–3; Henry Beveridge, *A Comprehensive History of India, Civil, Military and Political, from the First Landing of the English, to the Suppression of the Sepoy Revolt, including an Outline of the Early History of Hindoostan*, III, p. 570; *Crisis in India, its Causes and Proposed Remedies*, p. 45; William Taylor, *The Patna Crisis* (3rd. ed.; London: W.H. Allen and Co., 1857), pp. 65–9.

4. Edward Henry Nolan, *The Illustrated History of the British Empire in India and the East, from the earliest Times to the Suppression of the Sepoy Mutiny in 1859*, II, p. 722. Nolan quoted from the report of Major Abbot, a senior serving officer of the garrison in Delhi. The report which was submitted to the government clearly pointed out that the 'insurrection was organized and matured in the palace of the King of Delhi with his full knowledge and sanction, in the mad attempt to establish himself in the sovereignty' of India. To achieve this end the King also tampered with the loyalty of the 38th. Regiment, then stationed at Delhi. The 38th in turn corrupted the other two regiments in the city.

    For a similar opinion, see also: 'Our Relations to the Princes of India', *WR.*, New Series, XIII, 1858, pp. 468–9.

5. Nolan, *op. cit.*, p. 740; 'The Poorbeah Mutiny', *Blackwood's*, LXXXIII, 1858, p. 94; 'The Indian Mutinies', *Fraser's*, LVI, 1857, p. 628.

6. 'The Indian Mutinies', *loc. cit.* A conspiracy to murder every European in Calcutta was discovered by chance; its blueprint being found in a carriage by a company of sailors, after they had ejected its native occupants in order to be able to put the vehicle to their own use. The King of Awadh was found implicated in the plot and he was at once put under house arrest. Rev. W. Brock, *A Biographical Sketch of Sir Henry Havelock*, pp. 131–2.

7. [George Bruce Malleson], *The Mutiny of the Bengal Army*, pt. 11, p. 107.

8. William Howard Russel, *My Diary in India*, I, p. 168.

9. [Malleson], *op. cit.*, p. 131.

10. Nolan, *op. cit.*, p. 726. For a similar opinion, see also: Duff, *op. cit.*, p. 53.

11. 'Our Indian Sepoys', *LH.*, 1857, p. 630.

12. 'Our Indian Empire', *QR.*, CIII, 1858, p. 255. The author of this article observed:

    > There is no doubt, in fact, that these cartridges were the cause of the revolt, in the same sense that Gesseler's hat was the cause of the freedom of the Swiss Cantons, and the duty on tea the cause of the revolt of the American colonies. They were the spark that fired the train, but the combustible materials had been heaped together long before, and sooner or later an explosion was inevitable in Hindostan as in Switzerland or America.

    Gen. Sir Robert William Gardiner, *Military Analysis of the Remote and Proximate Causes of the Indian Rebellion, drawn from the Official Papers of the Government of India*, p. 35. Gardiner described the cartridge cause as a myth, laughed at by even the promoters of the revolt.

    [The Rev.] Sale (letter from), *MH.*, XIIX, 1857, p. 721. Sale, a Baptist missionary at Jessore, in his letter home described the cartridge as an invented cause—'invented to catch the more ignorant and credulous of the sepoys who would not appreciate, or could not be trusted with the conspiracy to turn out the Europeans and to restore the kings of Delhi and Oude.'

Lieut.-Gen. Sir S. Cotton, *Nine Years' on the North-West Frontier of India*, pp. 157–8. Cotton called the greased cartridges a 'fuse, by which the great mine of rebellion was ignited.'

For other similar opinions, see also: Rotton, *op. cit.*, p. 1; Hansard 3, CXLVII, 474.

13. Beveridge, *op. cit.*, p. 557.

14. Frederick H. Cooper, *The Crisis in the Punjab from the 10th of May until the Fall of Delhi* (London: Smith, Elder and Co., 1858), pp. 23–24 and 117–8; Nolan, *op. cit.*, pp. 714 and 740; Thomas Frost, (ed.), *Complete Narrative of the Mutiny in India, from its Commencement to the Present Time, Compiled from most Authentic Sources; including many very Interesting Letters from Officers and Others on the Spot*, p. 4.

15. *The Press*, 11 July 1857. There was a widespread rumour that Lord and Lady Canning had, before their departure for India, given a solemn pledge to the Queen to convert the natives of India to Christianity.

Capt. Mowbray Thomson, *The Story of Cawnpore*, p. 192. It was given out that the Nana had sent a Sawar on a camel to Russia in order to bring assistance from there. Thomson complained that the credulous sepoys (he came into contact with the soldiers of the 56th and 53rd Native Infantry regiments) had come to believe that the 'Russians were all Mahomedans and that the armies of the Czar are to liberate the faithful and their land from the yoke of the Feringhees.' For such other rumours also see the Nana's Proclamation given on pages 144–5 of Thomson's book. In fact dozens of such rumours can be counted here.

16. *Annual Register*, 1857, pp. 245–6.

17. Ibid.

18. Hansard 3, CXLVIII, 41; [Malleson], *op. cit.*, pt. 1, p. 33.

19. [Malleson], *loc. cit.*

20. *A Short Review of the Present Crisis in India*, p. 14.

21. Russell, *op. cit.*, I, pp. 167–8.

22. Maj.-Gen. Sir G. Le Grand Jacob, *Western India before and during the Mutinies* (henceforward referred to as G. Jacob), (London: Henry S. King, 1871), p. 204.

23. Hansard 3, CXLVII, 471. Thomson, *op. cit.*, p. 24. Thomson called the circulation of cakes and lotus flowers as 'occult harbingers of the mutiny'. Since the latter, he argued, was an 'emblem of war', it was distributed among the soldiers.

In an attempt to explain the mystery of lotus flowers, the author of *England's Troubles in India* pointed out that since lotus was a 'symbol of the throne' and since Hindu deities were 'represented as seated on lotus thrones', without any doubt all those regiments which accepted the flower belonged to the rebel group. Henceforth they were to unite in an attempt aimed at annihilating the British from India and reinstating the king of Delhi on his throne, p. 30.

Apparently the government or at least the regimental officers knew about the inexplicable circulation of the lotus flower, but they laughed at it 'as a practical joke, or an act of unmeaning absurdity'. ('History of the British Empire in India', *Illustrated London News*, 28 November 1857). Ironically enough the circulation of the flowers did become a practical joke.

For other similar opinions, see also: The Rev. A.C. Ainslie, *A Few Words about India and the Indian Mutinies* (3rd. ed.; Tuaton: Frederick May, 1857) pp.

12–13; 'Lotus Leaves and Pancakes. The Indian Mystery', *LH.*, 14 January 1858.

24. 'Sepoy Symbols of Mutiny', *Household Words* (hereafter referred to as *HW.*), XVI, 1857, p. 231.

25. The Rev. Henry S. Polehampton, *A Memoir, Letters, and Diary of...*, pp. 246–7; Nolan, *op. cit.*, p. 712; Mathew A. Sherring, *The Indian Church during the Great Rebellion: An Authentic Narrative of Disasters that Befell it: its Sufferings; and Faithfulness unto Death of many of its European and Native Members* (London: James Nisbet, 1859), p. 105; John Bruce Norton, *The Rebellion in India: How to Prevent Another*, p. 6.

26. John Malcolm Ludlow, *Thoughts on the Policy of the Crown towards India*, p. 25n.

27. Hansard 3, CXLVII, 821. It was so because of Hearsey's marriage with a Hindu lady and his knowledge of many Indian languages and customs which had made him popular with his men.

28. Hansard 3, CXLVII, 819. Cf. Beveridge, *op. cit.*, p. 558.

29. Hansard 3, CXLVII, 819; 'The Government of India and the Mutinies', *QR.*, XXVI, 1857, p. 488.

30. Hansard 3, CXLVIII, 39.

31. Ibid.; For similar opinions, see also: *The Spectator*, 8 August 1857; Beveridge, *op. cit.*, p. 558; Hansard 3, CXLVII, 1417.

32. 'Crisis of the Sepoy Rebellion', *LQR.*, IX, 1857–58, pp. 534–5.

33. 'The Poorbeah Mutiny: The Punjab, No. V', *Blackwood's*, LXXXIV, 1858, p. 31.

34. *A Lady's Diary of the Siege of Lucknow, Written for the Perusal of Friends at Home* (London: John Murray, 1858. New York: Henry Lyons and Co., 1858), p. 31.

35. *Illustrated London News*, 12 December 1857. Under the title 'Court Martial at Calcutta', this weekly informed its readers that a Mawlawi or Hafiz was tried by a general court martial 'for attempting to seduce the sepoys of the 70th Native Infantry in Calcutta from their allegiance by holding out to them promises of arms, ammunition and aid from 18,000 of the native population and that a similar scene might be enacted by them as that performed by their countrymen at Cawnpore.' It further informed its readers that many of 'the prisoners taken are priests among their people; if Mahometans, they are moulvis [Mawlawis] or hafiz [Hafiz], and, if Hindoos, they are Brahmins.'

36. Sherring, *op. cit.*, pp. 105 and 205; Norton, *The Rebellion in...*, p. 6.

37. Indophilus [Sir Charles Edward Trevelyan], *Letters of Indophilus on the Mutiny of Vallors,–its Parallelisms and its Lessons* (Calcutta, 1857), p. 7.

38. [W. Sinclair], *The Sepoy Mutinies: Their Origin and their Cure*, pp. 9–11.

39. Nolan, *op. cit.*, p. 712; Ainslie, *op. cit.*, pp. 12–13; 'The Poorbeah Mutiny', *Blackwood's*, LXXXIII, 1858, p. 96; *Annual Register*, 1857, p. 245; *Illustrated London News*, 28 November 1857; Hansard 3, CXLVII, 467–71; *Manchester Guardian*, 15 April 1857. Two and a half months before the arrival of the news of the outbreak in London, the Calcutta correspondent of the *Manchester Guardian*, a paper which insisted on the mutinous aspect of the revolt, put the King of Awadh at the bottom of the cake movement as well as the army commotions preceding the outbreak.

40. 'The Poorbeah Mutiny', *loc. cit.*, p. 94. For a similar opinion, see also: 'Pancakes', *Notes and Queries* (hereafter referred to as *NQ.*), Second Series, IV, 1857, p.161.

41. Nolan, *loc. cit.*
42. 'India', *Edin. Rev.,* CVI, 1857, p. 564n.
43. The time, size and the number of *chapatis* or cakes were variously reported: Nolan thought that the circulation of pancakes started soon after the annexation of Awadh; he put the number at six. Nolan, *loc. cit.*

    The *Notes and Queries,* on the other hand, put the date of their circulation one year before the outbreak had started. 'Pancakes', *loc. cit.*

    The *Annual Register* gave March 1857 as the starting date. 1857, p. 245. Meadows Taylor consigned the *chapati* distribution to the year 1856, *op. cit.,* pp. 4–5.

    Thomas Frost gave Awadh as the land of the origin of the cake movement and informed his readers that one cake was to be made by each one of the recipients for further distribution. Frost, *op. cit.,* p. 4.

    The *Manchester Guardian* first reported the news in its issue of 15 April 1857, and put the number of cakes at ten.

    However, the generally accepted time, number and place were: early 1857, six and the state of Awadh respectively.
44. 'India', *Edin. Rev.,* CVI, 1857, 564n; 'Sepoy Symbols of Mutiny', *Household Words* (hereafter referred to as HW.) XVI, 1857, p. 231; *Illustrated London News,* 28 November 1857; M. Taylor, *op. cit.,* pp. 4–5; Thomson, *op. cit.,* p. 24; Frost, *op. cit.,* p. 4; *The Spectator,* 26 September 1857; *Annual Register,* 1857, p. 245; Capt. G. Hutchinson, *Narrative of the Mutinies in Oudh* (London: Smith, Elder and Co., 1859), pp. 37–8; Nolan, *op. cit.,* p. 712; Ainslie, *op. cit.,* pp. 12–13; Norton, *The Rebellion in...,* p. 141. Even the *Manchester Guardian,* a paper which had earlier taken an opposing line to its Calcutta correspondent (see f.n. 39) and had in its issue of 16 April 1857, discounted the idea of any conspiracy behind this 'Newest Asian Mystery', was, four months later, compelled to admit the extreme probability of some connection between the cake circulation and the mutiny. 31 August 1857.
45. From two to six inches in diameter.
46. Nolan, *loc. cit.* The use of enigmatical signs does not appear to have been entirely unknown to the government. We have it on the authority of *The Spectator* that even before the outbreak the agents of the native chiefs, princes, Rajas and *zamindars,* stationed at the headquarters, used to keep their masters posted with the day to day developments, and that, at times, this correspondence was in ciphers to be deciphered only by the initiated.
47. Nolan, *loc. cit.* For similar opinions, see also: 'The Indian Mutinies', *Fraser's,* LVI, 1857, p. 238; 'Sepoy Symbols of Mutiny', *loc. cit.* Cf. William Edwards, *Personal Adventures during the Indian Rebellion in Rochilcund, Futtehghur and Oude,* pp. 15–16. Edwards observed:

    The leaders and promoters of this great rebellion, whoever they may have been, knew well the inflamable condition...of the rural society in the North-Western Provinces, and they, therefore, sent among them the chupatties, as a kind of fiery cross, to call them to action.... I truly believe that the rural population of all classes, among whom these cakes spread, were as ignorant as I was myself of their real object, but it was clear that they were a secret sign to be on the alert and the minds of the people were through them kept watchful and excited. As soon as the disturbances broke out at Meerut and Delhi, the cakes explained themselves, and the people at once perceived what was expected of them.

The author of *England's Troubles in India,* however, came up with another naive explanation. She thought that since the English ate *chapati* for breakfast, its distribution indicated that the natives no longer wanted the British to eat the 'bread of their industry', pp. 30–1.

48. Hansard 3, CXLVII, 470. Disraeli's reference to Russia was at once taken up by others, thus showing the influence he enjoyed in moulding certain sections of British public opinion. Dr Edward Henry Nolan was one of them. See Nolan, *loc. cit.*

49. 'Pancakes', *NQ.,* Second Series, IV, 1857, p. 161.

50. 'The Poorbeah Mutiny', *Blackwood's,* LXXXIII, 1858, p. 94.

51. Norton, *The Rebellion in...,* p. 141.

52. Hutchinson, *op. cit.,* pp. 37–8.

53. Brock, *op. cit.,* p. 130.

54. Thomson, *op. cit.,* p. 124; Rotton, *op. cit.,* pp. 4–5; Charles, *op. cit.,* p. 8. Cf. Col. George Bourchier, *Eight Month's Campaign against the Bengal Sepoys during the Mutiny* (London: Smith, Elder and Co., 1858), pp. 1–2.

55. Miller, *op. cit.,* p. 81; Charles, *loc. cit.*; Rotton, *loc. cit.*

56. Newman, *op. cit.,* p. 441; *The Indian Mutiny–Thoughts and Facts,* pp. 5–6; Rotton, *loc. cit.*; Bourchier, *loc. cit.*; Charles, *loc. cit.*; Miller, *loc. cit.* The Meerut outbreak, however, should not have come as a surprise to the military authorities at the station. We have it on the authority of Beveridge that on the 9 May, 'ominous warnings were given by placards which called upon the natives to rise and slaughter the hated Feringhees'. Beveridge naturally criticized that nothing but 'an actual rising seemed capable of arousing the authorities to a sense of their danger and as the 9th had passed away without disturbance, it was hoped that the 10th, a Sunday, would also prove fruitful'. Beveridge, *op. cit.,* pp. 564–5.

57. 1 August 1857. The Paper argued that the city of Delhi was chosen because it was the ancient seat of the Indian Empire, a sacred city and had a store of 100,000 muskets, masses of cannon and enough ammunition to meet the requirements of a large army for one year.

58. Beveridge, *op. cit.,* p. 570.

59. *Annual Register,* 1857, p. 305n.

60. 'The Poorbeah Mutiny, No. 111', LXXXIII, 1858, pp. 600–2. Letters were addressed even to the most loyal rulers of Rajputana.

For proclamations addressed to the army, see: Duff, *op. cit.,* p. 47.

61. Nolan, *op. cit.,* p. 740.

62. At Lucknow Birjis Qadar, a minor prince of eight or nine years of age, was raised as viceroy of Awadh under the King of Delhi. Nolan, *op. cit.,* p. 757; *Saturday Review,* 7 November 1857; L.G. Rutts Rees, *A Personal Narrative of the Siege of Lucknow, from its Commencement to its Relief by Sir Colin Campbell,* pp. 261–2.

Also see Nana's Proclamations given by Thomson, pp. 143–7.

63. Quoted by the *Manchester Guardian,* 31 October 1857. The concern of the sepoys for the cause of Delhi can be well imagined from the treatment of an English officer by a native subahdar. Treating his officer very kindly, while the subahdar allowed him to remove his private effects, he instructed him not to touch the public property as it belonged to the ruler of Delhi. Review of the *Crisis in India: Its Causes and Proposed Remedies, The Athenaeum,* 29 August 1857.

Another example of these feelings in an exaggerated form can be found in the repeated shouts of a soldier at the Rev. Heinig, the Baptist missionary at Banaras, 'Our God is in Delhi'. *Sixty-sixth Annual Report of the Baptist Missionary Society, ending March 1858,* (London: Printed by J. Haddan Brothers and Co.), p. 43.

64. See above, p. 173.
65. 3 October 1857.
66. Nolan, *op. cit.,* p. 740.
67. Thomson, *op. cit.,* pp. 144–7; *Annual Register,* 1857, p. 287.
68. *Morning Herald,* quoted in the *People's Paper,* 26 September 1857. For other similar opinions, see also: Rotton, *op. cit.,* pp. 100–2; *England's Troubles in India,* p. 31; 'Glance at Public Occurrences', *WMM.,* Fifth Series, III, 1857, p. 929; Brock, *op. cit.,* p. 129.
69. 'The Sepoy Rebellion', *LQR.,* IX, 1857–8, p. 255.
70. A religious mendicant, a beggar, poor.
71. Nolan, *op. cit.,* p. 740.
72. *The Press,* 8 August 1857.
73. *The Examiner,* 19 September 1857.

Chapter 6: Unity of the Revolution Theme

1. 18 July 1857.
2. 'British India', *QR.,* CIV, 1858, p. 227. For a similar opinion, see also: 'Fidelity of the Native Christians at Chhota Nagpur—An Abridgement of Sherring's 'The Indian Church during the Great Rebellion', *WMM.,* Fifth Series, V, 1859, p. 176.
3. *The Press,* 25 July 1857.
4. Capt. R.P. Anderson, *A Personal Journal of the Siege of Lucknow,* ed. by T. Carnegy Anderson (London: W. Thackers and Co., 1858), p. 1.
5. *Exeter Hall Versus British India* (London: Thomas Richard, n.d.), p. 7. For other similar opinions, see also: The Rev. Alexander Duff, *The Indian Rebellion; its Causes and its Results in a Series of Letters,* p. 33 and pp. 101–3; 'British India', *QR.,* CIV, 1858, p. 228; L.E. Ruutz Rees, *A Personal Narrative of the Siege of Lucknow from its Commencement to its Relief by Sir Colin Campbell,* p. 6; *The Press,* 8 August 1857: *A Lady's Diary of The Siege of Lucknow, written for the Perusal of Friends at Home,* p. 16; [The Rev.] W.H. Carey (ed.), *The Mahomedan Rebellion; its Premonitory Symptoms, the Outbreak and Suppression; with an Appendix* (Roorkee: Printed at the Directory Press, 1857), pp. 183–4; William Edwards, *Personal Adventures during the Indian Rebellion in Rochilcund, Futtehghur and Oude,* pp. 92 and 125.
6. William Howard Russell, *My Diary in India,* I, p. 161.
7. John Bruce Norton, *The Rebellion in India: How to Prevent Another,* p. 14.
8. Volunteer [Maj.-Gen. W.O. Swanston], *My Journal: or What I Did and Saw between the 9 June and 25 November, 1857, with an Account of General Havelock's march from Allahabad to Lucknow* (Calcutta: Printed by C.W. Lewis, Baptist Mission Press, 1858), p. 10; Martin Richard Gubbins, *An Account of the Mutinies in Oudh, and of the Siege of the Lucknow Residency: with Some Observations of the Condition of the Province of Oudh, and on the Causes of the Mutiny of the Bengal Army,* pp. 56–7.

9. Norton, *loc. cit.*

10. Extremely popular opinions.

11. Plain Speaker [John Henry Temple], *Justice for India. A Letter to Lord Palmerston* (London: Printed and Published for the author by Robert Hardwick, 1858), p. 18. For similar opinions, see also: John Bruce Norton, *Review of the Rebellion in India: How to Prevent Another*, First Notice, *The Athenaeum*, 3 October 1857; Henry Beveridge, *A Comprehensive History of India, Civil, Military and Social, from the First Landing of the English, to the Suppression of the Sepoy Revolt, including an Outline of the Early History of Hindoostan*, 111, p. 571; The Rev. T.C. Smyth, Letter to *The Scotsman*, 10 July 1857; Review of the *Mutiny in the Bengal Army, A Glance at the East*, A Kinnaird, *Bengal, its Landed Tenure and Police System*, and [David Urquhart's] *The Sraddha, the Keystone of the Brahminical, Buddhistic and Arian Religions, The Athenaeum*, 15 August, 1857; The Rev. Baptist Wriothesley Noel, *England and India—An Essay on the Duty of Englishmen towards the Hindoos*, p. 78.

   The result of this participation of the people of Delhi in the revolt was that cries for the total destruction of the city were frequently heard. Even Lord Ellenborough was reported to have lost his temper and demanded that every man in Delhi should be castrated after its fall and the city be named 'Euncuchabad'. (Richard Collier, *The Sound of Fury*, p. 152). Commenting upon these demands, *The Spectator* chided the advocates of such a policy. This magazine argued that Delhi with its past history already claimed immortality, and emphasized that any attempt on the part of the British to raze the city to the ground would make it still more immortal. 22 August 1857.

12. Very widely held opinion.

13. The Rev. W. Brock, *A Biographical Sketch of Sir Henry Havelock*, p. 155 and pp. 170–1. For similar opinions, see also: (George Bruce Malleson], *The Mutiny of the Bengal Army*, pt. II, pp. 93–96; *Morning Herald*, quoted by the *People's paper*, 266 September 1857; *Annual Register*, 1857, p. 257.

14. [Malleson], *loc. cit.*, p. 88.

15. The Rev. Henry S. Polehampton, *A Memoir, Letters and Diary of...*, pp. 303–4.

16. William Taylor, *The Patna Crisis*, p. 35.

17. Capt. Mowbray Thomson, *The Story of Gawnpore*, p. 246.

18. Sir Joseph Kingsmill, *British Rule and British Christianity in India* (London: Longman, Green, Longman and Roberts, 1859), pp. 62 and 64.

19. *The Times*, 29 June 1857.

20. Taylor, *The Patna Crisis*, pp. 54–5.

21. *Ibid.*, pp. 86–90.

22. Brock, *op. cit.*, p. 182; Plain Speaker [Temple], *op. cit.*, p. 18.

23. Dr. Edward Henry Nolan, *The Illustrated History of the British Empire in India and the East, from the Earliest Times to the Suppression of the Sepoy Mutiny in 1859*, II, p. 751.

24. Plain Speaker [Temple], *op. cit.*, p. 18.

25. *A Short Review of the Present Crisis in India*, p. 12.

26. 19 June 1858.

27. *Illustrated London News*, 17 September 1857; Maj. W.S.R. Hodson *Twelve Years of a Soldiers Life in India*, p. 259; *The Nation*, 21 August 1858; *People's paper* 19 June 1858.

28. 'Crisis of the Sepoy Rebellion, *LQR.*, IX, 1857–58, p. 534. The 'prayer' read:

Close up the mouths of tale-bearers, Having chewed the tale-bearers, eat them, Grind to pieces the enemies, Kill the enemies: Having killed the English, scatter them, O Mat Chundu, (O Mother Devee,) let none escape. Kill the enemy and their families Protect Sunkur Mahades and preserve your disciples, Listen to the calling of the poor, make haste, O Mat Hacbuka, (Devee,) Eat the unclean race, Do not delay, and devour them quickly, O Ghar mat Kalika (O terrible mother Devee).

Cf. Mathew A. Sherring, *The Indian Church during the Great Rebellion: An Authentic Narrative of Disasters that Befell it; its Sufferings; and Faithfulness unto Death of many of its European and native Members*, p. 316.

29. Hundreds of such instances were produced, reproduced and quoted by many advocates of the revolutionary theory.

30. Carey, *op. cit.*, pp. 130–3; Hansard 3, CXLVlII, 1155–6. In fact, all this was widely reported.

31. Carey, *op. cit.*, pp. 205–6; *People's Paper*, 3 October 1857; Frederick Henry Cooper, *the crisis in the Punjab from 10 May until the Fall of Delhi*, pp. 16–7; R.H.W. Dunlop, *Service and Adventure with the Khakee Ressallah; or, Meerut Volunteer Horse, during the Mutinies of 1857-58* (London: Richard Bentley, 1858), pp. 68–9 and 90; Oliver J. Jones, *Recollections of a Winter Campaign in India in 1857-58*, pp. 44–6; *The Spectator*, 24 October, 1857; *The Press*, 8 August and 26 September, 1857; *Annual Register*, 1857, pp. 257–8. Russell, *op. cit.*, 11, p. 425.

32. Duff, *op. cit.*, p. 99.

33. *Ibid.*, pp. 111–14, For a similar opinion, see also: *Crisis in India, its Causes and Proposed Remedies*, pp. 24–7. Here again the author, a military officer, contended with *The Times* over the same issue as Duff did.

34. Edwards, *op. cit.*, p. 142.

35. Malcolm Lewin, *The Way to Regain India*, pp. 9–10.

36. Maj.-Gen. [Sir James] Outram, *Outram's Campaign in India, 1857-58, comprising General Orders and Despatches relating to the Defence and Relief of Lucknow Garrison and Capture of the City by the British Forces*, ed. Anon. (London: Printed for Private Circulation by Smith, Elder and Co., 1860), pp. 40–1; [Mrs K.H. Bartrum], *A Widow's Reminiscences of the Siege of Lucknow* (London: James Nisbet and Co., 1858), p. 22; 'The Defence of Lucknow–Martial Incidents in Oude', *DUM.*, LI, 1858, pp. 488–9.

37. Sherring, *op. cit.*, p. 80.

38. Garey, *op. cit.*, pp. 130–31; [Bartrum], *loc. cit.*

39. Hodson, *op. cit.*, p. 196.

40. Outram, *loc. cit.*; [Bartrum], *loc. cit.*; 'The Defence of Lucknow–Martial Incidents in Oude', *loc. cit.*

41. *The Defence of Lucknow* (2nd. ed.; London: Smith, Elder and Co., 1858), p. 39.

42. O.J. Jones, *op. cit.*, pp. 45–6.

43. Outram, *op. cit.*, p. 34; 'British India', *QR.*, CIV, 1858, p. 226; Sir Sydney Cotton, *Nine Years on the North-West Frontier of India*, p. 186; Capt. G. Hutchinson, *Narrative of the Mutinies in Oudh*, p. 164.

44. Outram, *loc. cit.*; *The Defence of Lucknow*, p. 187; Brock, *op. cit.*, p. 162.

45. Duff, *op. cit.*, p. 287.

46. 'British India', *loc. cit.*

47. Rees, *A Personal Narrative of...*, p. 210.

48. Russell, *op. cit.*, I, pp. 401–2; British India', *loc. cit.*

49. Hodson, *op. cit.*, pp. 183 and 250; *The Defence of Lucknow*, p. 107; Outram, *op. cit.*, p. 109; 'The Defence of Lucknow–Martial Incidents in oude', *DUM.*, LI, 1858, p. 485; *The Times* (A Letter from Meerut), 5 October 1857.

50. *The Defence of Lucknow*, p. 107. For other similar complaints, see also: Outram, *op. cit.*, pp. 259, 311, 326, 341 and 349.

51. Hodson, *op. cit.*, pp. 183, 250 and 277; 'The Defence of Lucknow–Martial Incidents in Oude', *loc. cit.*; Edwards, *op. cit.*, p. 140.

52. Outram, *op. cit.*, p. 109.

53. Hodson, *op. cit.*, p. 261. Hodson was prepared to offer a bribe of 6000 rupees to anyone who would blow up the vital bridge linking Delhi with its outskirts.

54. *People's Paper*, 19 June 1858.

55. *Manchester Guardian* (An Historical Review of Events in India by an Umbala Officer), 31 October 1857. For a similar opinion, see also: Russel, *op. cit.*, I, p. 114.

56. *The Nation*, 15, 29 August and 19 September 1857; *The Spectator*, 14 November 1857.

57. *People's Paper*, 29 August 1857.

58. *Sixty-sixth Annual Report of the Baptist Missionary Society ending March 1858*, p. 46; *The Spectator*, 19 September 1857.

59. Sir G. Le G. Jacob, *Western India Before and During the Mutinies*, pp. 152–3.

60. Ibid.; *Sixty-sixth Annual Report of the Baptist...*, p. 46.

61. G. Jacob, *loc. cit.*, pp. 158–9. The result was that Satara princes were deported. Rangu himself had fled but his son along with other conspirators was hanged.

62. Ibid., pp. 214–5.

63. Ibid., pp. 154, 157–8, 161, 163, 171, 194–6, 201–5 and 207.

64. Ibid., pp. 222–7. He was attacked, defeated and killed during the first two days of June by Colonel Malcolm.

65. Ibid., pp. 217–8. Troops having been sent against him by the Resident at Hyderabad and from Belgaum in February 1858, the ruler surrendered, was taken prisoner and sentenced to transportation for life. The Raja, however, made short work of the sentence by committing suicide while on his way to the coast for transportation. His confession before death, according to Malcolm, unmasked the conspiracy, the details of which he fails to provide.

66. Ibid., pp. 204–5. The sword was found 'silver handled, the blade of wavering or serrated edge, covered with Sheeah [Shi'ah] inscriptions in gold,' p. 204n.

67. Ibid., pp. 205–6. Chimah Sahib's own minister preferred death to divulging the secret. In answer to government interrogation he said, 'Were I to open my mouth I should kindle a flame to burn up the land. I choose rather to meet my fate in silence,' and so he did.

68. Ibid., pp. 216–7.

69. Ibid., p. 217.

70. *The Spectator*, 16 January 1858. *The Spectator* gave the name of the village as Hulguttee.

71. G. Jacob, *op. cit.*, pp. 232–6. Jacob himself was sent to the Portuguese Governor-General, the Visconde de Novas Torres, at Goa to invoke the help of his Government.

72. 'British India', *QR.*, CIV, 1858, p. 225.

73. Ibid.; 'Our Indian Empire', *QR.*, CIII, 1858, p. 258; Norton, *The Rebellion in...*, p. 17; Nolan, *op. cit.*, p. 769.

74. Norton, *The Rebellion in...*, p. 17; Nolan, *op. cit.*, p. 769. For further information on the feelings of the people in the Madras Presidency, see also: *The Spectator*, 3 October and 14 November 1857.

75. 'India Under Dalhousie', *Blackwood's*, LXXXI, 1856, p. 239; George Grawshay, *Proselytism Destructive of Christianity and Incompatible with Political Dominion, Speech of Mr. Crawshay at the India House on the Vote of an Annuity to Sir John Lawrence, 25 August 1858, with Notes and an Appendix*, p. 20. In addition to the district listed above and below, several other districts to the south-east of Lahore were also awash in rebellion. The situation in Sahiwal, Chichawatni Mianchanu, Khanewal, and Gogira was very critical. Here, village after village was razed to the ground and the entire cattle wealth of the rebels was confiscated. For a broader comprehension of the situation in the Punjab, read: Salahuddin Malik, 'The Panjab and the Indian 'Mutiny': A Reassessment,' Islamic Studies, XV, 1976, pp. 81–110 and '1857 Gogira Rebellion in Southeastern Panjab: A Forgotten Chapter of Muslim Response to British rule in India,' Islamic Studies, XVI, 1977, pp. 65–95 Both papers are mostly based on the official Punjab Mutiny reports prepared by the government of the Punjab. As they were not part of the public debate in Britain, they are not included in this research.

76. Cooper, *op. cit.*, p. 41.

77. Ibid., p. 140.

78. 'The Poorbeah Mutiny: The Punjab–No. V', *Blackwood's*, LXXXIV, 1858, p. 78 and 78n.

79. 'The Poorbeah Mutiny: The Punjab–No. IV', *Blackwood's*, LXXXIII, 1858, p. 653; Cooper, *op. cit.*, pp. 16–17; Nolan, *op. cit.*, p. 769; [Malleson], *op. cit.*, pt. 11, p. 197. Referring to Hansi, Hissar and Sirsa, Malleson pointed out that every 'village in that part of the country is a castle on a small scale: the inhabitants, sympathizing with the mutineers, rose almost simultaneously with them and declared for the cause of the king of Delhi.'

80. Duff, *op. cit.*, p. 259.

81. 'The First Bengal European Fusiliers in the Delhi Campaign', *Blackwood's*, LXXXIII, 1858, p. 122.

82. 'The Poorbeah Mutiny: The Punjab–No. II', *Blackwood's*, LXXXIII, 1858, p. 239.

83. 'Missionary Records–Punjab–Its Loyalty', *CEM.*, XLIV, 1858, p. 33; Hodson, *op. cit.*, p. 224; Senior, 'The Man for India', Letter to *The Spectator*, 5 December 1857; The Rev. J.E.W. Rotton, *The Chaplin's Narrative of the Siege of Delhi, from the Outbreak at Meerut to the Capture of Delhi*, p. 222.

84. Cooper, *op. cit.*, pp. 24–5. No wonder George Crawshay who regarded the outbreak as a mutiny refused to commend the comparative calm in the Punjab. Speaking at the India House on the vote of an annuity to Sir John Lawrence, he referred to Sir John's success in the Punjab and observed:
   > But you will say he succeeded; so did Robespierre succeed. History is full of the names of men who have succeeded, but whose memory is not spared anymore than will be the memory of Sir John Lawrence. Crawshay, *Proselytism Destructive...*, p. 20.

85. *People's Paper*, 2 January 1858; *The Examiner*, 17 October 1857. The *Baptist Magazine*, however, offered a different theory on Sikh loyalty. Doubting the sincerity of Sikh intentions, it wrote:

> We hope that we do our present allies, but recent foes, injustice when we suspect them of playing their own game. That they are so eager to exterminate the sepoy regiments can hardly be ascribed to their love of us. May it not arise from the desire to crush the right arm of our strength in India, to be followed by an attempt to throw off the yoke which we, by the aid of the sepoy, so recently imposed upon them. XLIX, 1857, p. 639.

Sikh loyalty, however, was confined to the Punjab and the adjacent Sikh states. In Patna the Sikh high priest refused even to admit Rattray's Sikhs (name of a Sikh regiment) into the shrine, the reason being their help to the British. (Taylor, *The Patna Crisis*, pp. 33–4.) The British had also to pay the price of Sikh help. At times the British officers were taunted by their Sikh soldiers and at others they had to suffer insolent behaviour at the hands of the Sikhs. The British were always reminded of the value of Sikh help in the capture of Delhi and the consequent preservation of India for them. As a result the Sikh soldiers tended to become unruly and disobedient. The author of *The Future of India* reported on the basis of his conversation with some of the Sikh soldiers that the Sikhs did not revolt because they did not have a capable leader to guide them to victory, and that they were conscious of it. *The Future of India* (London: L. Booth, 1859), pp. 7–8.

86. *The Examiner,* 17 October 1857. Not only had the Sikhs acted out of vengeful feelings towards the Muslims, their spirit of vengeance was also exploited by the British. A prophecy was already current among the Sikhs that they were destined to reconquer Delhi with the help of the white man and so avenge themselves of the death of Guru Tegh Bahadur. It was to please his Sikh soldiers that Hodson 'deliberately shot' the two Mughal princes at Delhi and ordered their bodies to be thrown on the Chabutra in front of the Kotwali. After this event the Sikhs 'looked on Captain Hodson as the 'avenger of their martyred Gooroo [Guru]', and were even more ready than before to follow him anywhere'. Hodson, *op. cit.,* p. 302 and 302n.

87. *People's Paper,* 12 September, 24 October 21 and 28 November 1857; *Annual Register,* 1857, pp. 268–70; Nolan, *op. cit.,* p. 772; 'Lord Clyde's Campaign in India', *Blackwood's,* LXXXIV, 1858, p. 486; Charles Raikes, *Notes on the Revolt in the North-Western Provinces of India,* p. 43; Sir George Lawrence, *Forty Years' Service in India,* ed. by W. Edwardes (London: John Murray, 1875), pp. 295–6; *The Spectator,* 23 October 1858; O.J. Jones, *op. cit.,* p. 34; Plain Speaker [Temple], *op. cit.,* p. 19; Duff, *op. cit.,* p. 288; *The Press,* 8 August 1857.

88. Jas. Travers, *The Evacuation of Indore by Lieut.-Gen. Jas versus History of the Sepoy Revolt by Sir John Kaye* (London: Henry S. King and Co., 1876), pp. 5–6.

89. Plain Speaker [Temple], *op. cit.,* p. 19.

90. *Manchester Guardian,* 9 September 1857.

91. *The Press,* 8 August 1857. For similar opinions, see also: Duff, *op. cit.,* p. 288; *Saturday Review,* 19 December 1857; Leopold Von Olrich, *Military Mutiny in India: Its Origin and its Results, with Observation by Maj.-Gen. Sir W.M.G. Colebrooks,* pp. 26–7.

92. *The Press,* 8 August 1857.

93. O.J. Jones, *op. cit.,* p. 34.

94. 'The First Bengal European Fusiliers after the Fall of Delhi', *Blackwood's,* LXXXIII, 1858, p. 730.

95. Carey, *op. cit.,* p. 191.

96. See above, pp. 181 and 181a, n. 28.

97. Russell, *op. cit.*, I, p. 133.

98. *The Press*, 8 August 1857.

99. Gubbins, *op. cit.*, pp. 56–7. Both of these rulers paid the penalty of their 'treason' by being sentenced to death after the fall of Delhi.

100. 'The Poorbeah Mutiny: The Punjab–No. V', *Blackwood's*, LXXXIV, 1858, pp. 40–1. In this case as well Partap Singh, the ruler, and his accomplices were arrested and hanged.

101. *The Press*, 15 August 1857. After having risen in revolt, the ruler of Bhitoor [sic] was responsible for the murder of 132 Europeans.

102. *The Times* (from the Bombay Correspondent), 14 July 1857. The Rao was tried by a drumhead courtmartial and hanged.

103. *The Press*, 8 August 1857; Olrich, *op. cit.*, p. 21.

104. *The Press*, 8 August 1857.

105. Hodson, *op. cit.*, p. 342.

106. *What Shall We Do to the Mussulmans* (Calcutta: Sanders, Cones and Co., 1858), pp. 3–4.

107. M. Taylor, *op. cit.*, p. 20.

108. 'The Defence of Lucknow–Martial Incidents in Oude', *DUM.*, LI, 1858, p. 484.

109. Plain Speaker [Temple], *op. cit.*, pp. 19–20; Hansard 3, CXLVII, 508. Speaking in the Commons, Sir E. Perry attributed the loyalty of the Rajas of Gwalior and Patiala to their fear of the British power rather than to any liking for the foreign ruler.

110. Volunteer [Swanston], *op. cit.*, p. 12; Hodson, *op. cit.*, pp. 31–2; Travers, *op. cit.*, pp. 5–6; *Crisis in India, its Causes and Proposed Remedies*, pp. 24–7. The author of the *Crisis in India*, a military officer of thirty-two years' standing in India, reported from his personal knowledge how a Hindu Raja in the vicinity of Delhi played a three-fold game. Not only did he save some European lives, he also kept some of them as hostages and at the same time 'secretly attended the installation of the Delhi usurper. He was, however, so anxious to evade detection, in case of our [British] ultimate triumph, that in hurrying back to his own little territory he rode his best horse to death.'

111. Hodson, *op. cit.*, p. 181.

112. Ibid., p. 245.

113. Brock, *op. cit.*, pp. 190–1.

114. *The Press*, 22 August 1857.

115. Scrutator [Sir Benjamin Colin Brodie], *English Tenure of India. Practical Remarks Suggested by the Bengal Mutiny*, p. 21; *Manchester Guardian*, 20 August 1857; Nolan, *op. cit.*, p. 714; [Malleson], *op. cit.*, pt. II, p. 101; J.H. Stocqueler, *India: Its History, Climate, Products, with a full Account of the Origin, Progress and Development of the Bengal Mutiny and Suggestions as to the Future Government of India*, p. 20.

116. Malcolm Lewin, *The Way to Lose India*, p. 4.

117. Hansard 3, CXLVII, 1415. Thomas Frost (ed.), *Complete Narrative of the Mutiny in India, from its Commencement to the Present Time, compiled from most authentic sources; including many very Interesting Letters from Officers and Others on the Spot*, p. 3. Frost admitted the presence of a smouldering discontent among the civil and military populations of India, but he emphasized that the people were not mindful of its existence until recently when the native press started calling attention to it.

118. Hansard 3, CXLVII, 1415.

119. Ibid., 1429.

120. *Illustrated London News,* 4 July 1857.

121. 16 September 1857.

122. Ibid., 20 August and 10 November 1857. For a similar opinion, see also: Olrich, *op. cit.,* p. 20.

123. *Manchester Guardian,* 10 November 1857.

124. *Crisis in India, its Causes and Proposed Remedies,* p. 22. For a similar opinion, see also: Hansard 3, CXLVIII, 244.

125. Gen. Sir R. Gardiner, *Military Analysis of the Remote and Proximate Causes of the Indian Rebellion, drawn from the Official Papers of the Government of India: Respectfully Addressed to the Honourable Members of the House of Commons,* pp. 73–4.

126. *Manchester Guardian,* 16 September 1857.

127. Duff, *op. cit.,* p. 302.

128. [Malleson], *op. cit.,* pt. II, pp. 53 and 101–4.

129. Duff, *loc. cit.,* p. 199.

130. Lewin, *The Way to Regain India,* p. 4.

131. Chick, *op. cit.,* p. 6.

132. 1 August 1857.

133. Gen. Sir R. Gardiner, *Cursory View of the Present Crisis in India: together with the Military Power of England, respectfully addressed to the Members of the House of Commons* (London: Messers. Byfield, Hawksworth and Co., 1857), p. 18.

134. Ibid., pp. 15–17; Gardiner, *Military Analysis of...,* p. 33. For similar opinions, see also: [Malleson], *op. cit.,* pt. II, pp. 102–3; 'The Commons, the Ministers and the Forces', *The Spectator,* 17 October 1857; An Indian Missionary [Hargrave Jennings], *The Religions of India; or, Results of Mysterious Buddhism,* pp. 165–6.

135. Gardiner, *Military Analysis of...,* p. 34.

136. 8 August 1857.

137. *The Press,* 26 September 1857.

138. Richard Congreve, *India,* p. 35n.

139. Duff, *op. cit.,* p. 219.

140. 29 August 1857.

141. Duff, *op. cit.,* p. 223.

142. 5 September 1857.

143. 'British India', QR., CIV, 1858, p. 226. For similar opinions, see also: *People's Paper,* 2 and 16 January, 10 April and 19 June 1858; Hansard 3, CLI, 2041.

144. 12 June 1858.

145. Duff, *op. cit.,* p. 199.

146. Gardiner, *Military Analysis of...,* p. 41. In fact, no concern or doubt was ever entertained by the men in authority on the loyalty of the native army. Lord Dalhousie in his minutes written in 1856, had expressed complete satisfaction with its condition. He was so sure of the loyalty and affection of the Indian soldier that he did not even care to say much about him. In his forty-five page long minute his only reference to the native army was:

> The position of the native soldier in India has long been such as to leave hardly any circumstance of his condition in need of improvement. Hansard 3, CXLVII, 445.

Similarly General Anson, the Commander-in-Chief and the Military Member of the Governor-General's Council in 1857, had never sent a word of complaint either to the government, the Court of Directors, or the Board of Control, concerning the existence of any bad feelings in the native army. Hansard 3, CXLVI, 1461–62.

147. G. Hutchinson, *op. cit.,* pp. 40–1.

148. Cotton, *op. cit.,* p. 156.

149. Gardiner, *Military Analysis of...,* p. 45. It appears from Gardiner's pamphlet as if Metcalfe had constantly warned the government about the disaffection in India, against which, he further stressed there could be no practical remedy.

150. *India and its Future: an Address to the People of Great Britain and their Representatives* (London: L. Booth, 1858), pp. 47–8; Sir Henry Montgomery Lawrence, *Essays: Military and Political,* (London: Wm. H. Allen and Co., 1859), pp. 12–13; Russell, *op. cit.,* II, p. 248.

151. Russell, *op. cit.,* 11, p. 267.

152. Ibid., I, p. 161. For a similar opinion, see also: *Sixty-sixth Annual Report of the Baptist Missionary Society ending March 1858,* p. 46.

153. Norton, *The Rebellion in...,* pp. 96–7. For the harangue itself, see Chapter IV, p. 160.

154. Lewin, *The Way to Lose India,* p. 3.

155. Congreve, *op. cit.,* p. 30n.

156. Sir John Malcolm, famous for his travels to Persia, was the fourth son of George Malcolm of Burnfoot. Born in 1769, at the age of thirteen (in 1782) he joined the military service of the East India Company—which corporation he served in various capacities. In 1792, he was appointed Persian interpreter to the Nizam's troops. During his military, civil and diplomatic career in India, Malcolm exercised great influence upon the governors and governors-general of India, this being specially true insofar as Wellesley was concerned. In his case Malcolm was spoken of as 'Lord Wellesley's factotum and the greatest man in Calcutta'. Malcolm earned his great reputation by undertaking several visits to the Persian court as an emissary of the British government in India. This was specially important because the government of Britain had at that time transferred the control of Britain's diplomatic relations with Persia to the British Indian administration. In 1827, Malcolm reached the zenith of his Indian career when he was appointed Governor of Bombay. 'Simple, manly, generous and accessible, he made himself beloved by the natives of India and to his unvarying good faith and honesty much of his diplomatic success was due.'

During the few years which he spent in England after his retirement in December 1830, he joined politics as a Tory and represented the Borough of Launceston (in Cornwall) in the Commons. He also took great interest in the home politics of the East India Company. He died in 1833. *DNB.,* XXXV, pp. 404–12.

157. Duff, *op. cit.,* pp. 268–9.

158. Malcolm Lewin, *The Government of the East India Company and its Monopolies; or, the Young India Party and Free Trade,* pp. 6–9.

159. Lewin, *The Way to Lose India,* p. 3.

160. R.S. Fullerton, 'Last Days of the Futtehghur Missionaries', *Calcutta Christian Observer,* cited in *WMM.,* Fifth Series, IV, 1858, pp. 1133–4; 'The Sepoy Rebellion', *LQR.,* IX, 1857–58, p. 227; *England's Troubles in India,* p. 31.

161. *The Athenaeum,* 29 August 1857. I have not been able to identify this nephew of Canning.

The Church of England Magazine quoted Byron from his 'Curse of Minerva', in which Byron had similarly predicted the approach of a revolt in India. For reference, see Chapter IV, n. 13.

162. Lewin, *The Way to Lose India,* pp. 6–7.

163. 'Has the Preservation of Caste Conduced to the Present Revolt in India, Negative Article–No. 111', *BC.,* 1858, p. 126; Lewin, *The Way to Lose India,* p. 7.

It was because of this nature of the army that the 8th Cavalry when ordered for service in Bengal from Banglore halted at a distance of twenty-six miles from Madras. The regiment refused to proceed further on the pretext that their claims for increased pay, prize money and pensions were lying in abeyance since 1837. The Government, however, was quick to meet this subterfuge by immediately granting all these demands. Left with no excuse, the 8th Cavalry did march but for thirteen miles only and came to a halt again. This time the soldiers came out in their true colours and refused to go ahead on any terms whatsoever. Their firm stand was that they were not prepared to make war on their countrymen; the regiment was, thereupon, disarmed. *The Spectator,* 3 October 1857.

164. Hansard 3, CXLVIII, 930.

165. Lewin, *The Way to Lose India,* p. 7. For a similar opinion, see also: Norton, *The Rebellion in...,* pp. 90–1.

166. 'British India', *QR.,* CIV, 1858, p. 228. For similar opinions, see also: Cotton, *op. cit.,* p. 286; Hansard 3, CXLVII, 506 and CXLVIII, 930.

167. 'British India', *QR.,* CIV, 1858, pp. 227–8; Hansard 3, CXLVII, 444 and 506.

168. 'Our Indian Empire', *QR.,* C111, 1858, p. 256.

169. Capt. [Thomas] Evans Bell, *The English in India: Letters from Nagpore, written in 1857–58* (London: John Chapman, 1859), pp. 60–1.

170. Letter to *The Times,* 6 July 1857. Cf. *The Nation,* 29 August 1857.

171. *The Press,* 8 August 1857; Hansard 3, CXLVII, 444.

172. *The Tablet,* 5 September 1857.

173. *The Nation,* 18 July and 8 August 1857. For further clarification of this point, read: 'The Legal Position of the Sepoys', *Free Press,* 11 November 1857; 'The phrase–'Our Indian Empire'', *Free Press,* 16 December 1857; Russell, *op. cit.,* II, pp. 67–9.

174. Hansard 3, CLI, 2042.

175. *The Nation,* 8 August 1857.

176. *The Press,* 15 August and 5 September 1857. For similar opinions, see also: *People's Paper,* 22 August 1857; *Crisis in India, its Causes and Proposed Remedies,* pp. 12 and 17; *The Nation,* 29 August 1857.

177. *The Press,* 25 July 1857. The Paper argued that had the people not been involved in the outbreak, the cakes could not have passed through the villages, and the sepoys would not have dared to take such a desperate step.

178. *The Press,* 11 and 25 July and 1 August 1857; *People's Paper,* 28 November 1857; Duff, *op. cit.,* p. 139.

179. 18 July 1857.

180. 10 October 1858.

181. 17 August 1857.

182. Hansard 3, CL, 1616–17.

183. Ibid., CLI, 350 and 2041–2.

184. Ernest Jones, *The Revolt of Hindustan*, p. 52; *People's Paper*, 8 August and 5 September 1857 and 9 January 1858. For a similar opinion, see also: *Reynald's Newspaper*, 5 July 1857.
185. *The Nation*, 5 and 26 September and 3 October 1857.
186. Hansard 3, CXLVII, 520 and 544–6.
187. John Malcolm Ludlow, *Thoughts on the Policy of the Crown towards India*, p. 22.

Chapter 7: Muslim Conspiracy

1. The Rev. A.F. Lacroix (Letter from), *MM.*, XXI, 1857, p. 203; 'Foreign Intelligence–India', *MH.*, XLIX, 1857, p. 717; The Rev. Mathew A. Sherring, *The Indian Church during the Great Rebellion: An authentic Narrative of the Disasters that Befell it; its Sufferings; and Faithfulness unto Death of Many of its European and Native Members*, p. 208; Caritus, 'The Sane and the Insane', Letter to the *Free Press*, 21 October 1857.
2. W.H. Carey, *The Good Old Days of the Honorable John Company; being Curious Reminiscences Illustrating Manners and Customs of the British in India during the Rule of the East India Company, from 1600 to 1858* (Simla: Printed at the Argus Press, 1882–87). See the title of the sub-chapter on the Indian mutiny in chapter eight of Vol. III.
3. The Rev. A.C. Ainslie, *A Few Words about India and the Indian Mutinies*, p. 15; The Rev. Alexander Duff, *The Rebellion in India; its Causes and Results, in a Series of Letters from...*, p. 93; The Rev. Robinson (letter from), *MH.*, XLIX, 1857, p. 658 and also 'Foreign Intelligence–India', L, 1858, p. 50; The Rev. James Wallace, *The Revolt in India: Its Causes and its Lessons. A Lecture delivered in Belfast, on 2 February 1859*, pp. 8, 9 and 13; The Rev. Dr Daniel Wilson, *Prayer the Refuge of a Distressed Church* (Calcutta: T.J. M'Arthur, Bishop's College Press, 1857), pp. 6–7; Sherring, *op. cit.*, p. 208; 'The Mutiny in India', *United Presbyterian Mazagine* (hereafter referred to as *UPM.*), New Series, 1, 1857, p. 431 and also 'The Capture of Delhi', p. 569; 'India in 1807 and 1857', *CEM.*, XLIV, 1858, p. 151; *Illustrated London News*, 12 September and 28 November 1857; R.H.W. Dunlop, *Service and Adventure with the Khakee Ressalah; or, Meerut Volunteer Horse during the Mutinies of 1857–58*, pp. 152–5; Review of Mrs Colin Mackenzie's book *Delhi, the City of the Great Mogul, Literary Gazette*, (hereafter referr to as LG.), 1857, pp. 804–5; Dr A. Christian, Letter to *The Scotsman*, 2 September 1857; *Indian Mutiny to the Fall of Delhi* (London: G. Routledge, 1857), p. 7; William Howard Russell, *My Diary in India*, 11, pp. 77–8; 'The Christianization of India', *London journal*, XXVI, 1857, p. 109; *Investigation into Some of the Causes which have Produced the Rebellion in India*, p. 7; 'The Revolt of the Bengal Army', *DUM.*, L, 1857, p. 386; *The Times*, 1 September 1857; *Manchester Guardian*, 3 September 1857; *People's Paper*, 12 September 1857; *Crisis in India, its Causes and Proposed Remedies*, p. 54; *A Short Review of the Present Crisis in India*, p. 9.
4. 'India in 1807 and 1857', *CEM.*, XLIV, 1858, p. 151; *What Shall We Do to the Mussulmans*, p. 3; Christian, *loc. cit.*; 'The Crisis in India', (comments on Macleod Wylie's Pamphlet, *Commerce, Resources and Prospects of India*), *The Scotsman*, 9 September 1857; Caritas, 'The Sane and the Insane', Letter to the *Free Press*, 21 October 1857; *The Examiner*, 8 August 1857; 'The Revolt of the Bengal Army', *DUM.*, L, 1857, pp. 385–6.

5. Almost a universally held opinion.

6. 'India Under Dalhousie', *Blackwood's*, LXXX, 1856, pp. 254–5. For similar opinions, see also: *Investigation into Some...*, p. 7; 'India in 1807 and 1857', *CEM.*, XLIV, 1858, p. 151; Wallace, *op. cit.*, p. 9.

   The author of 'India Under Dalhousie', was so conscious and sure of Muslim antagonism towards the British rule that while vividly describing the moving scene of Dalhousie's departure from India he reports the friendly feelings of the Hindus and the Europeans as witnessed by him at the Calcutta harbour but fails to make any mention of the former ruling community of India.

7. Read: The Rev. William Beynon (letter from), *MM.*, XXI, 1857, p. 245; 'The Capture of Delhi', *UPM.*, New Series, 1, 1857, p. 569; 'The Revolt of the Bengal Army', *DUM.*, L, 1857, pp. 485–6; Dr A. Christian, Letter to *The Scotsman*, 2 September 1857; 'The Crisis in India', (comments on Macleod Wylie's pamphlet), *The Scotsmen*, 9 September 1857.

8. *Religious Neutrality in India–Delusive and Impracticable* (Occasional Paper No. IV on India, published by the Church Missionary Society in 1858), p. 16. For a similar opinion, see also: 'India in 1807 and 1857', *loc. cit.*

9. 'Our Indian Empire', *QR.*, CIII, 1858, p. 257.

10. The Rev. William Beynon (letter from), *MM.*, XXI, 1857, p. 245; Scrutator [Sir Benjamin Colin Brodie], *The Indian Mutiny*, p. 19; Russell, *op. cit.*, II, pp. 77–8; 'The Christianization of India', *London Journal*, XXVI, 1857, p. 109; 'India in 1807 and 1857', *CEM.*, XLIV, 1858, p. 151; *Walayat Ali of Delhi. A Martyr's Narrative of the Great Indian Mutiny of 1857* (London: Pub. by T. Pewtress and Co. for the Baptist Missionary Society, 1858), p. 8; Duff, *op. cit.*, pp. 176–7; *What Shall We...*, p. I; R.C. Mather, *Christian Missions in India, On the Present State and Prospects of Christian Missions in India; and the Duty of the Churches at the Present Crisis of Our Indian Affairs* (London: John Snow, 1858), p. 6.

11. Beynon, *loc. cit.*

12. Duff, *loc. cit.*, pp. 176–7.

13. Read: Dunlop, *op. cit.*, pp. 152–5; Russell, *loc. cit.*; Scrutator [Brodie], *The Indian Mutiny*, p. 19; Wallace, *op. cit.*, pp. 8–9; 'India in 1807 and 1857', *loc. cit.*; Duff, *loc. cit.*; *Investigation into Some...*, p. 14.

14. *Investigation into Some...*, p. 14. For similar opinions, see also: *Crisis in India...*, p. 29; J.L. Archer, *Indian Mutinies Accounted For. Being an Essay on the Subject*, pp. 7–8; Russell, *loc. cit.*; 'India in 1807 and 1857', *loc. cit.*

15. *Indian Mutiny to the Fall of Delhi*, p. 7. For similar opinions, see also: Scrutator [Brodie], *The Indian Mutiny*, p. 19; 'India in 1807 and 1857', *CEM.*, XLIV, 1858, p. 151.

16. 7 August 1857.

17. 'The Revolt of the Bengal Army', *DUM.*, L, 1857, pp. 385–6. For a review of and comments on this article, see also: *The Nation*, 10 October 1857.

18. *Indian Mutiny to the Fall of Delhi*, p. 7. For a similar opinion, see also: 'India', *Edin. Rev.*, CVI, 1857, pp. 567–8.

19. 'India', *loc. cit.*, p. 567. For a similar opinion, see also, *Indian Mutiny to the Fall of Delhi*, p. 7.

20. 'India', *Edin. Rev.*, CVI, 1857, p. 568.

21. Wallace, *op. cit.*, p. 9.

22. 'The Revolt of the Bengal Army', *DUM.*, L, 1857, p. 385. For similar opinions, see also: *Manchester Guardian*, 23 July 1858; *Indian Mutiny to the Fall of Delhi*, p. 7.

23. 23 July, 1857.

24. 'The Crisis in India', (comments on Macleod Wylie's pamphlet), *The Scotsman*, 9 September 1857.

25. *Indian Mutiny to the Fall of Delhi*, p. 7; *What Shall We...*, p. 1.

26. The Rev. Edward Storrow, *India and Christian Missions* (London: 1859), p. 15.

27. Ibid., p. 16.

28. Ibid., p. 15.

29. Henry Moad, *The Sepoy Revolt: Its Causes and Consequences*, p. 24.

30. Storrow, *op. cit.*, p. 16.

31. The author of *What Shall We Do to the Mussulmans*, a person who styled himself as a 'Friend to Mussulmans but not Mohammedanism', held the government responsible for disaffection among the Muslims. He complained that the introduction of English education was calculated to keep the Muslims out of service. Referring to a recommendation which called for excluding Muslims from all important posts unless they were proficient in English pronunciation, he reproachfully observed:

> They do not yet appreciate useful knowledge sufficiently, though given in their own language, and yet they are expected to acquire through a foreign medium. Protestants cried out against the Romish church, because she could give her religious knowledge through the medium of Latin chiefly. Do you not act much similarly in forcing the English language on the Mussulmans? Let us by all means give them English knowledge, but in a form adapted to them.
>
> The Mussulmans have more independence of character than the Hindoos; they have a strong and proper attachment to their literature which has won the admiration of the ablest European scholars. Why should we require them, as some propose, to renounce this, and compel them to get all education through an English medium, pp. 6–7.

Next referring to the spread of Western knowledge among the Muslims in the Presidency of Agra when communicated through the Urdu language, this friend of the Muslims further scolded his own nation for her failure to learn any lesson from the Irish experience. He observed:

> In Ireland the policy of the Government had been for centuries to give religious or secular knowledge to the Irish through the English language. The simple result was, the Irish would not take it, and were left entirely to the superstitious guidance and instruction of their own priests. In 1559, it was enacted by a Statute of Queen Elizabeth that as the Irish did not understand the common prayers in church in English language, the prayers were to be said in Latin, but not in Irish. The Irish looked at everything English as a badge of conquest, and hence the English Bible was regarded with detestation as the Saxon's symbol. Two centuries after the Reformation, when Bishop Bedell, an Englishman, at the age of sixty, encouraged by Usher and the great Boyle, undertook the translation of the Bible into Irish, he was opposed by his brethren, who thought the language ought to be extirpated; for two centuries the book remained unpublished, the masses revelled in rebellion and hostility to England; not until 1821 was Bedell's Bible first published. Alas, the policy of Bedell's countrymen is the policy now of many educationists, both missionary and government, with regard to the Mussulmans, pp. 7–8.

This may properly be regarded as the failure of history to teach by example.

32. *Investigation into Some...*, p. 7; Storrow, *op. cit.*, pp. 15–6; Beynon (letter from), *MM.*, XXI, 1857, p. 246; Duff, *op. cit.*, pp. 39–40. In his letter of 24 June 1857,

to Dr Tweedie, the Rev. Alexander Duff wrote to inform him that between 200 to 300 Muslims had attacked the government and missionary schools at Agarpara near Calcutta. Shouting that the rule of the East India Company had come to an end, they ordered the teachers not only to stop teaching English but also to destroy the English books, and to teach the Qur'an only.

33. Sherring, *op. cit.*, p. 175. For other similar information, see also: Beynon, *loc. cit.*

34. *Minute of the Marquis of Tweedale, Late Governor of Madras, on the Introduction of the Bible as a Class-book into Government Schools in India* (Occasional Papers on India, No. VII), (London: Church Missionary House, 1859), p. 14.

35. Sale (letter from), *MH.*, L, 1858, pp. 182–3. Sale, who was a Baptist Missionary at Jessore, wrote this to inform the people at his headquarters in London:

> Only last evening, a Mussulman schoolmaster, whom I have occasionally aided with books and in other ways, came to me saying that several Mussulmans had united and brought a new schoolmaster into the village where he taught his school, and were giving out a report that the reign of the English was fast drawing to a close, and that those who wished to save themselves from future punishment must leave the school where the Sahib's books were read, and come to the new school, for the ruler who would succeed the English would deal very severely with those who continued to go to such schools. This is going on within eight miles of our sudder [Sadar, meaning central] station; and after the fall of Delhi has been proclaimed, and with stringent laws for the punishment of treasonable practices lately passed and published. I think, therefore, that we may only judge what would have been our fate had the wretched mutineers been more successful.

Muslim animosity towards receiving Western education becomes easily understandable when one reads the observation made by the Reverend John MacKay, the missionary martyr of Delhi. Writing home on 25 January 1857, MacKay reported that in the case of Muslims 'it was not only the religious, but the national prejudices of the people against which we [the teachers, lay and missionary] have to contend.' James Culross, *The Missionary Martyr of Delhi. A Memoir of the Rev. John MacKay, Baptist Missionary, who was killed at Delhi, May 1857* (London: J. Heaton and Son, 1860), p. 121.

36. 'Young Bengal', *Chambers's Journal of Popular Literature, Science and Arts* (hereafter referred to as *Chambers's Journal*), XXIX, 1858, p. 199.

37. [The Rev.] John MacKay (letter from), *MH.*, XLIX, 1857, p. 583; *What Shall We...*, p. 6.

38. *Investigation into Some...*, p. 7.

39. Russell, *op. cit.*, II, p. 78; Mackay, *loc. cit.*; Culross, *op. cit.*, p. 121; Sherring, *op. cit.*, p. 266; Beynon (letter from), *MM.*, XXI, 1857, p. 246; Mather, *op. cit.*, p. 6.

40. Culross, *op. cit.*, pp. 104, 112 and 123.

41. Mather, *op. cit.*, p. 6

42. Culross, *op. cit.*, p. 123.

43. Ibid., pp. 123–4.

44. Sherring, *op. cit.*, p. 186. Sherring quoted Gopinath Nandi who, having explained how the Muslims tried to impede, one way or the other, all such missionary activity which could possibly lead to conversion, observed:

> Another time, when the baptism of six individuals took place, the Mohammedans, like the Jews of the old, said amongst themselves, 'What are we doing? At this rate, the whole of Futtehpore will soon become Christians'. They contrived a plan, which they felt quite sure would end in breaking up the mission; but He whose work we

were doing protected it. They gave out that my catechists, with my permission, took cartfuls of pigs' and cows' bones, and threw them into all the wells of the town. This was noised abroad, not only in the town, but also in the villages around.

45. 'Foreign Intelligence–India', *MH.*, XLIX, 1857, p. 717.

46. Storrow, *op. cit.*, p. 16.

47. Russell, *op. cit.*, 11, p. 78.

48. 'Foreign Intelligence–India', *loc. cit.*; [The Rev. John] Mackay (letter from), *MH.*, XLIX, 1857, p. 583; Russell, *loc. cit.*; Culross, *op. cit.*, pp. 104–24.

49. [The Rev.] Anderson (extracts of his journal), *MH.*, L, 1858, p. 255.

50. Storrow, *op. cit.*, p. 15.

51. 'The Christianization of India', *London Journal*, XXVI, 1857, p. 109.

52. *India, the Revolt and the Home Government*, pp. 80–1; Dunlop, *op. cit.*, p. 152.

53. Dunlop, *loc. cit.* For similar opinions, see also: *India and its Future; an Address to the People of Great Britain and Their Representatives*, p. 47; *The Indian Mutiny-Thoughts and Facts*, p. 20; Mackenzie, Review of *Delhi, the City of the Great Mogul*, *LG.*, 1857, pp. 804–5; Frederick Cooper, *The Crisis in the Punjab from 10th of May until the Fall of Delhi*, pp. 133–4; [The Rev.] J. Trafferd (letter from), *MH.*, XLIX, 1857, p. 514 and also 'Foreign Intelligence–India', pp. 649 and 717; The Rev. Dr Boaz (letter from), *MM.*, XXI, 1857, p. 222; *Investigation into Some...*, pp. 7–8; *India, the Revolt and the Home Government*, pp. 80–1.

54. 'The Sepoy Rebellion', *LQR.*, IX, 1857–58, p. 215. For similar opinions, see also: Mackay (letter from) *MH.*, XLIX, 1857, p. 583 and also 'Foreign Intelligence–India', L, 1858, p. 50; Wallace, *op. cit.*, pp. 8–9; Archer, *op. cit.*, pp. 8–10; 'India in 1807 and 1857', *CEM.*, p. 151; *Investigation into Some...*, pp. 7–8.

55. 'The Capture of Delhi', *UPM.*, New Series, I, 1857, p. 569; Caritas, 'The Sane and the Insane', Letter to the *Free Press*, 21 October 1857; Sherring, *op. cit.*, p. 208; Archer, *op. cit.*, pp. 11–2; The Rev. A.F. Lacroix (letter from), *MM.*, XXI, 1857, p. 203; Wallace, *op. cit.*, p. 13; Mackay, *loc. cit.*; 'Foreign Intelligence–India', *MH.*, XLIX, 1857, p. 717.

56. See above and below.

57. See above and below.

58. 'The Sepoy Rebellion', *loc. cit.* For other similar opinions, see also: *Investigation into Some...*, pp. 7–8; 'The Revolt of the Bengal Army', *DUM.*, L, 1857, p. 386; *Indian Mutiny to the Fall of Delhi*, p. 7; 'Foreign Intelligence–India', *MH.*, XLIX, 1857, p. 717; Lacroix, *loc. cit.*; Dunlop, *op. cit.*, pp. 152–5; *What Shall We...*, pp. 9–10; Archer, *op. cit.*, p. 7.

59. 'The Sepoy Rebellion', *loc. cit.*; Archer, *op. cit.*, p. 7; *Indian Mutiny to the Fall of Delhi*, p. 7.

60. 'The Sepoy Rebellion', *loc. cit.*

61. Mackenzie, Review of *Delhi, the City of the Great Mogul*, *LG.*, 1857, pp. 804–5; Indophilus [Sir Charles Edward Trevelyan] *The Letters of Indophilus on the Mutiny of Vellore,–its Parallelisms and its Lessons*, pp. 4–7; 'India in 1807 and 1857', *Cem.*, XLIX, 1858, p. 150.

62. William Taylor, *The Patna Crisis*, pp. 21–2.

63. Capt. G. Hutchinson, *Narrative of the Mutinies in Oudh*, pp. 35–6. For similar information, see also: *Manchester Guardian*, 15 April 1857; M. Wylie (ed.), *The English Captives in Oudh: An Episode in the History of the Mutinies of 1857–58* (London: W.H. Dalton. Calcutta: G.C. Hay, 1858), pp. 30–1.

64. 'The English in India', *WR.*, New Series, XIII, 1858, p. 196.

65. 'The Revolt of the Bengal Army', *DUM.*, L, 1857, p. 392.

66. *The Indian Mutiny–Thoughts and Facts*, p. 21. For a similar piece of information, see also: Sherring, *op. cit.*, p. 168.

67. 'The Wrongs of India and their Remedy', *CEM.*, XLIII, 1857, p. 341. For a similar opinion, see also: *India and its Future*, p. 47.

68. *Investigation into Some...*, pp. 4–5. For a similar opinion, see also: 'The Mutiny of the Bengal Army', *DUM.*, L, 1857, p. 385.

69. See below, pp. 239–42.

70. Scrutator [Brodie], *The Indian Mutiny*, p. 19. For a similar opinion, see also: [W. Sinclair], *The Sepoy Mutinies; Their Origin and their Cure*, p. 11.

71. *Investigation into Some...*, pp. 5–6; Archer, *op. cit.*, p. 7.

72. *Manchester Guardian*, 23 July 1858; Archer, *loc. cit.*; Wallace, *op. cit.*, pp. 7–9.

73. Wallace, *loc. cit.*; *Investigation into Some...*, pp. 5–6.

74. Archer, *op. cit.*, p. 8.

75. *Investigation into Some...*, pp. 5–6.

76. Archer, *op. cit.*, pp. 7–8.

77. *The Press*, 22 August 1857.

78. *Manchester Guardian*, 23 July 1858 and also 3 September 1857. For other similar opinions, see also: 'State Intervention in the Religions of India', *MM.*, XXI, 1858, p. 226; Duff, *op. cit.*, p. 177.

79. 'State Intervention in the Religions of India', *loc. cit.*

80. 'The Indian Mutiny', *ER.*, II, 1857, p. 542; 'A Few Words from the Khyber', *Blackwood's*, LXXXII, p. 613; *The Press*, 22 August 1857; *Indian Mutiny–Thoughts and Facts*, p. 20; N.A. Chick (ed.), *Annals of the Indian Rebellion, containing Narratives of the Outbreak and Eventful Occurrences, and Stories of Personal Adventures, during the Mutiny of 1857–58, with an Appendix Comprising Miscellaneous Facts, Anecdotes etc.*, (Calcutta: Printed and published by Sanders, Cones and Co., 1859), p. 4; 'India', *Edin. Rev.* CVI, 1857, p. 563. One of the prophecies attributed to some 'Saint, the revered Shah Niamut Ali Moulvy' was as follows:

> After the Fire-worshippers and Christians shall have held sway over the whole of Hindoostan for 100 years, and when injustice and oppression shall prevail in their Government, an Arab Prince will be born who will ride triumphantly to slay them. Chick, p. 4n.

The *Edinburgh Review,* however, reported that General Low had received some Persian couplets composed by one Ni'matullah 700 years ago. In them he had predicted the fall of the English in AH 1260., or AD 1864. And that these verses were circulated in the whole of North-Western India. 'India', *Edin. Rev., CVI,* 1857, p. 563n.

    The proximity between the names of the two soothsayers suggests that the reference is, perhaps, to the same prophecy.

81. 22 August 1857.

82. 22 August 1857.

83. 'The Revolt of the Bengal Army', *DUM.*, L, 1857, p. 389. Also see Chapter IV, pp. 138–44.

84. 'The Revolt of the Bengal Army', *DUM.*, L, 1857, p. 389; Archer, *op. cit.*, pp. 8–10. See also, Chapter IV, pp. 138–44.

85. 'The Revolt of the Bengal Army', *loc. cit.*

86. Almost universally accepted as such by the advocates of the present theme.

87. [G.B. Malleson], *Mutiny of the Bengal Army*, pt. I, p. 11. For a similar opinion, see also: [Sinclair], *op. cit.*, p. 8.

88. [Malleson], *loc. cit.; Investigation into Some...*, p. 8.

89. [Sinclair], *loc. cit.*

90. Maj. R.W. Bird, *The Spoliation of Oudh* (Lond.: Printed at Nassau Steam Press, 1857), p. 13.

91. *The Annexation of the Kingdom of Oude one of the Main Causes of Rebellion in India* (Manchester: Loony and Filling, [1857]), p. 1.

92. William Witherspoon Ireland, *History of the Siege of Delhi*, p. 8.

93. *Investigation into Some...*, p. 13. For similar opinions, see also: *India and its Future*, p. 47; Archer, *op. cit.*, p. 7; *The Mutiny in India–A Letter to the Honorary Clerical Secretary of the Church Missionary Society, dated Calcutta, 13 July 1857* (Lond.: T.C. Jones), p. 13; [Sinclair], *op. cit.*, p. 8.

94. *Investigation into Some...*, p. 8. For a similar opinion, see also: [Malleson], *op. cit.*, pt. I, p. 11.

95. [Malleson], *loc. cit.*; 'Has the Preservation of Caste Conduced to the Present Revolt in India–Negative Reply', *BC.*, 1858, p. 273.

96. 'British Ideas in India', *Illustrated London News*, 12 September 1857.

97. *Investigation into Some...*, p. 13.

98. Ireland, *op. cit.*, p. 8.

99. *Investigation into Some...*, p. 13.

100. 'The Revolt of the Bengal Army', *DUM.*, L, 1857, p. 389.

101. 3 June 1857.

102. *The Mutiny in India–A Letter to the Honorary Clerical...*, p. 13.

103. 'The Indian Mutiny', *ER.*, II, 1857, p. 542.

104. *Investigation into Some...*, p. 9.

105. Ibid.

106. Ibid. See also, Chapters II, pp. 79–81 and IV, pp. 160–2.

107. Leopold Von Olrich (tr. by A.R.), *Military Mutiny in India; Its Origin and its Results, with Observations by Maj.-Gen. Sir W.M.G. Colebrooke*, p. 6.

108. 'The Indian Mutiny', *ER.*, II, 1857, p. 542.

109. *Investigation into Some...*, p. 9; Ireland, *op. cit.*, p. 9; *Free Press*, 3 June 1857; Hansard 3, CXLVII, 468–69 and CXLVIII, 1158; Volunteer [Maj.-Gen. W.O. Swanston], *My Journal; or What I Did and Saw Between the 9th June and 25th November, 1857*, p. 54; *The Annexation of the Kingdom of Oude...*, p. 7.

110. *Investigation into Some...*, p. 9.

111. Ireland, *op. cit.*, p. 5; Olrich, *op. cit.*, p. 25.

112. Their title to the throne of Delhi had become purely nominal.

113. Ireland, *op. cit.*, p. 5.

114. Ibid., pp. 11–2. In his Indian diary W.H. Russell chided his countrymen for considering the King of Delhi ungrateful to his benefactors. He observed:

> The first knowledge the great mass of Englishmen had at home of the King of Delhi was that he was the nominal chief of a revolt which was shaking our Indian empire to its foundations. He was called ungrateful for rising against his benefactors. He was, no doubt, a weak and cruel old man; but to talk of ingratitude on the part of one who saw that all the dominions of his ancestors had gradually been taken from him, by force or otherwise, till he was left with an empty title, a more empty exchequer, and a palace full of penniless princesses and princes of his own blood, is perfectly preposterous. Was he to be grateful to the Company for the condition in which he

found himself? Was he to bless them forever because Polyphemus, in the shape of the British Government, snatched poor blind Shah Alum from the hands of Mahrattas and then devoured him peacemeal? We, it is true, have now the same right and the same charter for our dominions in India that the Mahomedan founders of the house of Delhi had for the sovereignty they claimed over Hindostan; but we did not come into India, as they did, at the head of great armies, with the avowed intention of subjugating the country. We crept in as humble barterers, whose existence depended on the bounty and the favour of the lieutenants of the kings of Delhi; and the 'generosity' which we showed to Shah Alum was but a small acknowledgment of the favours his ancestors had conferred on our race. Russell, *op. cit.*, II, pp. 53–4.

115. Chick, *op. cit.*, p. 4. For other similar information, see also: Duff, *op. cit.*, p. 301; Ireland, *op. cit.*, pp. 11–2.
116. Duff, *op. cit.*, p. 301.
117. Chick, *op. cit.*, p. 5.
118. Ibid.
119. Ibid.
120. Ibid., pp. 2–3 and 7–8.
121. Ibid., pp. 7–9.
122. Ibid., p. 8.
123. Ibid., pp. 8–9.
124. Daniel Wilson, *Prayer the Refuge of a Distressed Church,* pp. 6–7.
125. Daniel Wilson, *Humiliation in National Troubles* (Calcutta: T.J. M'Arthur, Bishop's College Press, 1857), p. 23.
126. Duff, *op. cit.*, p. 121; The Rev. A.F. Lacroix (letter from), *MM.,* XXI, 1857, p. 203; 'Has the Preservation of...', Negative Reply', *BC.,* 1858, p. 273; 'The Poorbeah Mutiny', *Blackwood's,* LXXXIII, 1858, p. 96.

It was reported as a 'significant fact' that the ruler of Awadh had protested as early as 29 January 1857, 'against the *surveillance* of a European officer, Major Herbert, who had been appointed to control his movements.' 'The Revolt of the Bengal Army', *DUM.,* L, 1857, p. 391.

127. Ireland, *op. cit.*, pp. 11–2.
128. *Free Press,* 3 June 1857; Hansard 3, CXLVII, 1485.
129. 'The Revolt of the Bengal Army', *DUM.,* L, 1857, pp. 388–9; 'The Government of India and the Mutinies', *BQR.,* XXVI, 1857, p. 487; 'Has the Preservation of...', Negative Reply,' *BC.,* 1858, p. 273.
130. 'The Revolt of the Bengal Army', *DUM.,* L, p. 390. It was rumoured that the pensions of the ruler of Delhi and the Nawab Nizam were to be cut down by 40 and 60 per cent respectively.
131. W.H. Carey, *The Mahomedan Rebellion; its Premonitory Symptoms, the Outbreak and its Suppression,* p. 5. For similar opinions, see also: *The Scotsman* (letter from a lady in Calcutta to a friend in Edinburgh), 19 August 1857; 'Has the Preservation of...', *loc. cit.*
132. *Indian mutiny to the Fall of Delhi,* p. 7.
133. See above, p. 241.
134. 'The Poorbeah Mutiny–The Punjab', *Blackwood's,* LXXXIII, 1858, pp. 94–5.
135. 'India', *Edin. Rev.,* CVI, 1857, p. 568.
136. See below and also Chapter V, pp. 164 and 173–4.
137. Russell, *op. cit.*, I, p. 130.
138. Chick, *op. cit.*, pp. 2–3; Dunlop, *op. cit.*, pp. 152–55; Cooper, *op. cit.*, pp. 13–4; L.E. Ruutz Rees, *A Personal Narrative of the Siege of Lucknow, from its*

Commencement to its Relief by Sir Colin Campbell, p. 37; Archer, *op. cit.*, pp. 8–10.

139. 'The Revolt of the Bengal Army', *DUM.*, L, 1857, p. 386.

140. R.P. Anderson, *A Personal Journal of the Siege of Lucknow*, pp. 9–10.

141. Rees, *A Personal Narrative...*, p. 37.

142. Daniel Wilson, *Humiliation in National Troubles*, p. 23.

143. 'Progress of the Indian Rebellion', *Illustrated London News*, 5 September 1857. For other similar opinions, see also: Mackenzie, Review of *Delhi, the City of the Great Mogul, LG.*, 1857, pp. 804–5; Archer, *op. cit.*, pp. 8–11; Ainslie, *op. cit.*, p. 15; *Observations on the Late Events in the Bengal Presidency* (Jersy: Joshua Coutanche, 1857), p. 7; Mead, *op. cit.*, pp. 94–5; *A Short Review of the...*, p. 9; Dr A. Christian, Letter to *The Scotsman*, 2 September 1857; 'A Few Words from the Khyber', *Blackwood's*, LXXXII, 1857, p. 613; *Manchester Guardian*, 3 September and 22 October 1857; [The Rev. Mathew A.] Sherring (letter from) *MM.*, XXI, 1857, p. 243 and also, The Rev. A.F. Lacroix (letter from), p. 203; [The Rev.] J. Trafford (letter from), *MH.*, XLIX, 1857, p. 514; Hansard 3, CXLVII, 1435; 'The English in India', *WR.*, New Series, XIII, 1858, p. 196; *Investigation into Some...*, pp. 4–5; 'The Revolt of the Bengal Army', *DUM.*, L, 1857, p. 386; *The Examiner*, 8 August 1857; 'The Government of India and the Mutinies', *BQR.*, XXVI, 1857, p. 487; Daniel Wilson, *Humiliation in...*, p. 23; Daniel Wilson, *Prayer the Refuge of...*, pp. 6–7; *The Times* (letter from a cavalry officer in India, 1 September 1857).

It was thought that the Muslims, in spite of inherent differences between Islam and Hinduism, had given, in order to entice and beguile the Hindus, a political colour to their religious war. This was viewed as a weak point in the unnatural alliance and a source of strength to the British cause in India. It not only prevented the outbreak from becoming universal, but it was regarded to be the only ray of hope amid dark clouds for the continuation of the British rule in India. The *Manchester Guardian* thus observed:

> The Hindoos have been all along mere tools in the hands of their former oppressors.... Sooner or later, the Hindoo part of the rebel force is sure to find this out. Report says that in Delhi they have already begun to discover it...and then the work of our army will be facilitated by an incurable disunion in the camp of the enemy.... The Hindoos will not fight to restore Mohammedan rule in India. 22 October 1857.

For other similar opinions, see also: Hansard 3, CXLVII, 1435; Archer, *op. cit.*, p. 12; *The Scotsman* (letter from India), 3 October 1857.

144. Ireland, *op. cit.*, pp. 11–12; 'The Government of India and the Mutinies', *BQR.*, XXVI, 1857, p. 487; 'The Indian Mutiny', *ER.*, New Series, IV, 1858, p. 542; 'Foreign Intelligence–India', *MH.*, XLIX, 1857, p. 658; 'Has the Preservation of Caste...–Negative Reply'. *BC.*, 1858, p. 274.

145. 'Has the Preservation of Caste...–Negative Reply', *loc. cit.*

146. *Investigation into Some...*, pp. 5–6. For a similar opinion, see also: 'The Government of India and the Mutinies', *loc. cit.*

147. *Investigation into Some...*, pp. 5–6. For a similar opinion, see also: 'A Few Words from the Khyber', *Blackwood's*, LXXXII, 1857, p. 613.

148. *Investigation into Some...*, pp. 5–6; 'The Poorbeah Mutiny', *Blackwood's*, LXXXIII, 1858, p. 95.

149. 'The Poorbeah Mutiny', *loc. cit.*

150. *Investigation into Some...*, pp. 5–6.

151. Carey, *The Mahomedan Rebellion...*, p. 179. For other similar opinions, see also: Daniel Wilson, *Prayer the Refuge...*, pp. 6–7; 'The Revolt of the Bengal Army', *DUM.*, L, 1857, pp. 388–9; 'The Government of India and the Mutinies', *BQR.*, XXVI, 1857, p. 489; Ireland, *op. cit.*, pp. 11–12.

152. Almost a universally held opinion.

153. *Investigation into Some...*, pp. 5–6. For a similar opinion, see also: 'The Government of India and the Mutinies', *BQR.*, XXVI, 1857, p. 487.

154. [Sinclair], *op. cit.*, p. 11.

155. Ibid.; Cooper, *op. cit.*, pp. 133–4; *The Indian Mutiny–Thoughts and Facts*, p. 20; 'The Government of India and the Mutinies', *BQR.*, XXVI, 1857, pp. 487–8; 'State Intervention in the Religions of India', *MM.*, XXI, 1858, p. 226; Sherring, *op. cit.*, p. 208; 'The Poorbeah Mutiny', *Blackwood's*, LXXXIII, 1858, p. 95; *Annual Register*, 1857, p. 240; Ireland, *op. cit.*, pp. 11–12; Duff, *op. cit.*, p. 121; [The Rev.] J. Trafford (letter from), *MH.*, XLIX, 1857, p. 514.

156. Duff, *op. cit.*, pp. 46, 63 and 121; Mackenzie, Review of *Delhi, the City of the Great Mogul, LG.*, 1857, pp. 804–5; Archer, *op. cit.*, pp. 10–11; Ainslie, *op. cit.*, p. 15; *Observations on the Events...*, p. 7; 'A Few Words from the Khyber', *loc. cit.*, p. 613; 'State Intervention in the Religions of India', *loc. cit.*; The Rev. A.F. Lacroix (letter from), *MM.*, XXI, 1857, p. 203; Sherring, *loc. cit.*; 'The Government of India and the Mutinies', *BQR.*, XXVI, 1857, p. 488; Dr A. Christian, Letter to *The Scotsman*, 2 September 1857; *Indian Mutiny–Thoughts and Facts*, p. 20; Cooper, *op. cit.*, p. 46; 'Foreign Intelligence–India', *MH.*, XLIX, 1857 and L, 1858, pp. 659 and 50 respectively; [Sinclair], *loc. cit.*

Believing that the Muslims had always longed to revolt, but had feared the Hindus, Archer asserted that the Muslims ultimately got their chance in various acts of the government affecting the Hindus—acts which finally climaxed in the greased cartridge. He was so sure of Muslim exploitation of the cartridge incident that he imaginatively cited a possible harangue addressed by a Muslim to Hindu soldiers for the latter's seduction. The chimerical sermon ran in these words:

> Brothers, we know you are men who would joyfully die in the cause of religion, but beware lest craft should accomplish that, the attempt to effect which by force you would resist by force, and gloriously defeat. Have you watched the conduct of your Christian rulers lately? If you have not, we have, and we will awaken you to a sense of imminent danger now impending over you; and what is more, we will assist you with our swords, for your cause is a common cause. First, then, did you mark the extension of civil right to Indian proselytes from your religion or our own? This was doubtless a cautious first step, by which the Christians wished to ascertain how far they could with safety venture on such ground. Their encroachment was unchecked, unresisted,–and what followed? The marriage of Hindoo widows and sisters was boldly declared legal; yes, your widows and sisters were tempted to disgrace themselves and you, and yet you murmured not; then, intoxicated by success, and forgetful that our arms maintained them in this country, unmindful too of the debt they owed to those who had freely bled for them on the plains of Aliwal and Sobraon [the two bloody battles, among several others, waged for the conquest of the Punjab], amidst the rugged mountain-passes of Afghanistan, in the pestilential swamps of Burmah, and on a hundred battlefields, they, by the advice of crafty men of their nation, deeply read in our religious books, formed a design for the suppression of our religion, towards which their first step has been to do what they now have done. Shall we, then, thousands in arms, permit a handful of treacherous foreigners to disgrace and ruin us for time and for eternity? Believe not that they have acted thus in ignorance, for

there is not a European in the land who does not know that the lowest of his Hindoo menials would lose his place a thousand time rather than touch this abomination. Nor because for a hundred years they have allowed us to enjoy our faith in safety, think that we wrongly suspect them now of such designs. Did you not mark their cautious and time-serving policy towards Oude? They waited, biding their time, and then with one fell swoop they robbed and ruined a royal family, when not another independent prince in India was left to avenge the injury. And now when Oude is theirs, and their sway extends from the Himalayas to the waters of the Indian Ocean, they think the time is come for christianizing us by guile and force. Hindoos, we will not insult you by pointing out to you your duty now in the cause of religion. Archer, *op. cit.,* pp. 8–10.

No wonder, Frederick Cooper, deputy commissioner of Amritsar, asserted that the true colours under which the sepoys were fighting 'have now long since been shown; they were simply armed tools of Mohammedan insurrection'. Cooper, *op. cit.,* p. 46.

157. 'The Poorbeah Mutiny', *Blackwood's,* LXXXIII, 1858, p. 95.
158. 'Monthly Retrospect', *CS.,* VII, 1857, p. 652.
159. 'The Government of India and the Mutinies', *BQR.,* XXVI, 1857, pp. 487–9.
160. Carey, *The Mahomedan Rebellion…,* p. 7; Cooper, *op. cit.,* pp. 117–8.
161. Cooper, *op. cit.,* pp. 33–4.
162. Rees, *A Personal Narrative of…,* p. 37.
163. Chick, *op. cit.,* pp. 5–7.
164. Carey, *The Mahomedan Rebellion…,* pp. 9–10.
165. Chick, *loc. cit.*
166. 'The Mutiny in India and the Government', *Free Press,* 16 December 1857. For a similar piece of information, see also: 'The Revelt of the Bengal Army', *DUM.,* L, 1857, p. 392.
167. [The Rev. Mathew A.] Sherring (letter from), *MM.,* XXI, 1857, p. 243. For a similar opinion, see also: 'Foreign Intelligence–India', *MH.,* XLIX, 1857, p. 658.
168. H.H. Greathed, *Letters written during the Siege of Delhi* (London: Longman, Brown, Green, Longmans, and Roberts, 1858), p. XIV.

Chapter 8: Muslim Rebellion

1. 'Foreign Intelligence–India', *MH.,* XLIX, 1857 and L, 1858, pp. 658 and 50 respectively; The Rev. James Wallace, *The Revolt in India, its Causes and its Lessons. A Lecture delivered in Belfast, on 2 February 1859,* pp. 8–9; R.P. Anderson, *A Personal journal of the Siege of Lucknow,* p. 11; [G.B. Malleson], *The Mutiny of the Bengal Army,* pt. 1, p. 43; The Rev. Mathew A. Sherring, *The Indian Church during the Great Rebellion: An Authentic Narrative of the Disasters that befell it; its Sufferings; and Faithfulness unto death of many of its European and Native Members,* p. 208; [The Rev. Mathew A.] Sherring (letter from), *MM.,* XXI, 1857, p. 243 and also, the Rev. William Beynon (letter from), p. 245; *The Press,* 25 July 1857; Volunteer [Maj.-Gen. W.O. Swanston], *My Journal; or What I Did and Saw between the 9th June and 25th November 1857, with an account of General Havelock's March from Allahabad to Lucknow,* p. 54.

2. 'The Progress of the Sepoy War', *Saturday Review* (hereafter referred to as SR.), 3 October 1857. For other similar opinions, see also: Volunteer [Swanston], *op. cit.*, p. 54; Henry Mead, *The Sepoy Revolt; Its Causes and Consequences*, pp. 94–95; [The Rev. Mathew A.] Sherring (letter from), *MM.*, XXI, 1857, p. 243; William Witherspoon Ireland, *History of the Siege of Delhi*, p. 5.

3. Mead, *loc. cit.*, p. 94. Commenting upon the reasons of Muslim enthusiasm for the Mughal ruler at Delhi, Mead went on to say:

> ...there is hardly a single monarch who has not at some time sworn fealty to the House of Tamerlane, and received investiture at its hands. The Mogul is the only person to whom the Mahomedans can look up as their natural head. The founders of the royal houses of the Deccan, Carnatic, and Oude, of Holkar and Scindiah, were the deputies and servants of his ancestors. His divine right to universal dominion still exists....

4. *Punch*, 12 September 1857.

5. Even in 1857 Delhi was the seat of the figurehead Muslim ruler.

6. 31 August 1857.

7. The *Manchester Guardian* emphasized this aspect of the revolt on several other occasions as well.

8. See Chapters V, p. 164 and VII, pp. 249–52.

9. See Chapter V, pp. 173–4.

10. Ibid.

11. Frederick Cooper, *The Crisis in the Punjab from the 10th of May until the Fall of Delhi*, pp. 32–3.

12. W.H. Carey (ed.), *The Mahomedan Rebellion; its Premonitory Symptoms, the Outbreak and Suppression; with an Appendix*, p. 179.

13. Cooper, *op. cit.*, pp. 117–18.

14. Ibid., p. 212.

15. 'Foreign Intelligence–India', *MH.*, XLIX, 1857, p. 722; The Rev. A.C. Ainslie, *A Few Words about India and the Indian Mutinies*, p. 15; *The Times* (letter from Bays Water), 25 July 1857; *Manchester Guardian*, 3 September 1857.

16. *The Times* (letter from Bays Water), 3 September 1857; *The Scotsman* (letter from India), 19 August 1857; *Manchester Guardian*, 3 September 1857; The Rev. Alexander Duff, *The Indian Rebellion; its Causes and Results in a Series of Letters from...*, p. 4.

17. 18 July 1857.

18. Henry Beveridge, *A Comprehensive History of India, Civil, Military and Social, from the First Landing of the English, to the Suppression of the Sepoy Revolt, including an Outline of the Early History of Hindoostan*, p. 555.

19. Cooper, *op. cit.*, pp. 196–7.

20. *The Examiner*, 1 and 8 August 1857. For similar opinions, see also: *The Press*, 25 July 1857; [Malleson], *op. cit.*, pt. I, p. 43.

21. Volunteer [Swanston], *op. cit.*, p. 54.

22. *Manchester Guardian*, 7 August 1857; Carey, *The Mahomedan Rebellion...*, pp. 187–8.

An interesting sidelight of this is that even European converts to Islam were reported to be participating in the fight against government forces. L.E. Ruutz Rees, one of the surviving defenders of the Lucknow Residency, bitterly complained by name of those European converts to Islam who could be, more or less, identified. They were: Capt. Savory, a retired officer of the East India Company–an Englishman who had for many years received the pension of a captain and who had embraced Islam; Capt. Rotton, a Lucknow-born Englishman, who had likewise accepted Islam and whose daughters were married to Muslims; Monsieur Lebland, a Frenchman, whom Rees had described as an 'apostate' to Islam and as great a 'villain' as 'ever breathed'; and a young man whose name Rees purposely held back 'on account of his family', and who 'most probably' was the person 'who commanded the enemy's cavalry at Chinhut'–a place where Henry Lawrence had suffered a heavy repulse. Calling them 'haters of their own race', Rees proposed the severest possible punishment for them. L.E. Ruutz Rees, *A Personal Narrative of the Siege of Lucknow, from its Commencement to its Relief by Sir Colin Campbell*, pp. 116–17 and 144.

23. H.H. Greathed, *Letters written during the Siege of Delhi*, p. 130; Maj. W.S.R. Hodson, *Twelve Years of a Soldier's Life in India*, p. 259.

24. *Manchester Guardian*, 23 July 1857.

25. *The Times* (letter from Meerut), 5 October 1857.

26. 'Young Bengal', *Chambers's Journal*, XXIX, 1858, p. 199. For similar opinions, see also: 'Foreign Intelligence–India', *MH.*, XLIX, 1857, p. 722; Cooper, *op. cit.*, p. 151; *Investigation into Some of the Causes which have Produced the Rebellion in India*, p. 14; *A Letter from a Layman on the Policy of the East India Company in Matters of Religion* (London: W.H. Dalton, 1858), p. 30; R.H.W. Dunlop, *Service and Adventure with the Khakee Ressalah; or, Meerut Volunteer Horse, during the Mutinies of 1857–58*, pp. 152–5.

To prove that the army mutiny and the Muslim rebellion were planned together and perhaps in conjunction with each other, Dunlop quoted an interesting piece of conversation between a Muslim civil servant 'Nawab Ahmud Oollah Khan of Nugeenah, nephew of the Nawab Mahmood Khan of Nujeebabad' (Nawab Ahmadullah Khan was a *tahsildar*, a high ranking revenue officer in the service of the East India Company) and Francis Sistan, a European inspector of police at Sitapur in Awadh, then on three month's leave in Meerut. Mistaking Sistan for a Muslim (Sistan was reportedly dressed in the Muslim style) and upon knowing his service, Nawab Ahmedullah instinctively inquired from him about the situation in Awadh. Dunlop reports the dialogue with his own comments as follows:

'What news from Oude?' said the *Tehsildar*; 'how does the work progress, brother?' 'If we have work in Oude, your Highness will know it well', replied Sistan, who had inherited a good deal of Hindoostanee suspicion, and made the Tehsildar thus think him not ignorant but cautious. The trifling mutinies at Barrackpore, as they were then thought, had commenced. 'Depend upon it, we will succeed this time', said the Tehsildar; 'the direction of the business is in able hands.'

Dunlop goes on to inform his readers that this *tahsildar* was later on the leader of the rebels at Bijnor. He complained that had Sistan reported the conversation to the authorities at that time, he would have been 'laughed at as an alarmist'.

27. 'Foreign Intelligence–India', *loc. cit.* Criticizing the recent appointment of a Muslim as asst. commissioner to Mr Samuells, the newly appointed commissioner of Patna Division, the Rev. Sale, Baptist Missionary at Jessore, observed:

The Mussulman is to receive 1,000 Rupees a month. I suppose the policy is to bribe him as a decoy duck to the disaffected Mussulmans. This is the true Company's policy.

The truth of the accusation of treachery against Mussulmans in Government employ is proved by the following instances:- The Commander-in-Chief of the rebel forces is a native commissioned officer. The Prime Minister of the King of Delhi is a Mussulman from the Company's civil service; as is also the man who is his Assistant Minister. So the man who led the wretches who murdered Mr Tucker, of Furruckabad, was high in the Company's service, and had been indebted greatly to Mr Tucker for his advancement. So the man who ordered the massacre at Bareilly, and headed the insurgents, and tried even to induce the ladies to come back by false promises of safety; this wretch and his father had both held judicial appointments, and was receiving, by a special act of favour, the double pension for himself and his father.

28. The Rev. William Beynon (letter from), *MM.*, XXI, 1857, pp. 245–6; Wallace, *op. cit.*, p. 10; 'The War in India', *Illustrated London News*, 19 September 1857; *Manchester Guardian*, 14 September 1857; Dr E.H. Nolan, *The Illustrated History of the British Empire in India and the East, from the Earliest Times to the Suppression of the Sepoy Mutiny in 1859*, II, p. 769.

29. 'Foreign Intelligence–India', *MH.*, XLIX, 1857, pp. 647–8 and 720, 'The Mutiny and the Missions', p. 578 and also, The Rev. Williamson (letter from), L, 1858, p. 562; *Sixty-sixth Annual Report of the Baptist Missionary Society, ending March 1858*, p. 35.

30. *Crisis in India, its Causes and Proposed Remedies*, p. 29; 'The Outbreak in India', *CEM.*, XLIII, 1857, p. 265.

31. *AGRA.* Charles Raikes, *Notes on the Revolt in the North-Western Provinces of India*, pp. 52–3; Sherring, *op. cit.*, p. 89; Dwarkanath Lahoree (letter from), *MH.*, L, 1858, pp. 253–4.

ALLAHABAD. The Rev. A.F. Lacroix (letter from), *MM.*, 1857, p. 203; Carey, *op. cit.*, pp. 187–8; Sherring, *op. cit.*, pp. 208–9.

AMRITSAR. Joseph Kingsmil, *British Rule and British Christianity in India*, p. 69; 'The Poorbeah Mutiny', *Blackwood's*, LXXXIII, 1858, p. 101.

BANARAS. Sherring, *op. cit.*, p. 260; The Rev. W. Buyers (letter from), *MM.*, XXI, 1857, p. 205.

BELGAUM. Manchester Guardian, 29 September 1857; The Rev. William Beynon (letter from), *MM.*, XXI, 1857, p. 245; Nolan, *op. cit.*, p. 769; Wallace, *op. cit.*, p. 10.

BAKARGANJ. 'The Mutiny and the Missions', *MH.*, XLIX, 1857, p. 578.

BHAGALPUR. 'Foreign Intelligence–India', *MH.*, XLIX, 1857, p. 649.

BOMBAY. See n. 28.

BUDAUN. 'Perils in India', *HW.*, XIX, 1859.

CALCUTTA. The Scotsman (letter from India), 19 August 1857; *Manchester Guardian*, 6 August 1857; 'Foreign Intelligence–India', *MH.*, XLIX, 1857, p. 655; The Rev. A.F. Lacroix (letter from), *MM.*, XXI, 1857, p. 203 and also, The Rev. Dr Boaz (letter from), pp. 222–3; 'The Revolt of the Bengal Army', *DUM.*, L, 1857, pp. 385–6.

CHITTAGONG. 'Foreign Intelligence–India', *MH.*, L, 1858, p. 120; *The Sixty-sixth Annual Report of the Baptist Missionary Society, ending March 1858*, p. 35.

DACCA. 'The Mutiny and the Missions', *MH.*, XLIX, 1857, p. 578; *The Sixty-seventh Annual Report of the Baptist Missionary Society, ending March 1859* (London: Printed by Yates and Alexander, 1859), p. 34.

FIROZPUR. Cooper, *op. cit.*, pp. 13–14.

FAIZABAD. Capt. G. Hutchinson, *Narrative of the Mutinies in Oudh,* p. 111.

FATEHGARH. Sherring, *op. cit.,* pp. 125–6.

FATEHPUR. Ibid., pp. 182 and 186–7.

GORAKHPUR. Ibid., pp. 279–80.

HYDERABAD. Carey, *The Mahomedan Rebellion...,* pp. 219–20; Nolan, *op. cit.,* p. 770; Capt. Hastings Frazer, *Our Faithful Ally, the Nizam. Being a Historical Sketch of Events Showing the Value of the Nizam's Alliance to the British Government in India and his Services during the Mutinies* (London: Smith, Elder and Co., 1865), pp. 285–6.

JESSORE. [The Rev.] J. Trafford *(letter from),* MH., XLIX, 1857, p. 514, and 'The Mutiny and the Missions', p. 578 and also 'Foreign Intelligence–India', L, 1858, pp. 182–3.

JAUNPUR. Sherring, *op. cit.,* p. 266.

LAHORE. Cooper, *op. cit.,* p. 20.

LUDHIANA. Sherring, *op. cit.,* pp. 319–20.

MONGHYR. Carey, *loc. cit.,* p. 216; 'Foreign Intelligence–India', MH., XLIX, 1857, pp. 648–9.

MORADABAD. Carey, *loc. cit.,* pp. 144–5.

MYMENSINGH. 'Foreign Intelligence–India', MH., XLIX, 1857, p. 647.

MADRAS. See n. 30.

NAGPUR. The Press, 8 August 1857.

PATNA. Carey, *loc. cit.,* p. 216; William Taylor, *The Patna Crisis,* pp. 44–50 and 71–72; Duff, *op. cit.,* p. 63; Kingsmill, *op. cit.,* p. 63; 'Foreign Intelligence–India', MH., XLIX, 1857, pp. 648–9.

PESHAWAR. Julius George Medley, *A Year's Campaigning in India, March 1857 to March 1858,* p. 26.

POONA. Wallace, *op. cit.,* p. 10; Nolan, *op. cit.,* p. 769; The Rev. William Beynon (letter from), MM., XXI, 1857, p. 245.

RAMPUR. Carey, *loc. cit.,* p. 144.

RATNAGIRI. Nolan, *op. cit.,* p. 769.

SAWANTWADI. Ibid.

Indeed, there is a long list of other cities and towns where Muslims were reported to be either in rebellion, or seething with discontent and waiting for a leader or an opportunity to revolt. This was especially true of south-eastern Punjab where the Sahu and Kharal tribes openly raised the standard of revolt and were crushed with a heavy hand.

32. Lieut.-Gen. Sir Sydney Cotton, *Nine Years on the North-West Frontier of India,* pp. 202–4. Cotton tells that a 'fanatical Mahommedan priest' Syyed Amir, had raised the Muslim standard in the Khyber Pass, beyond the reach of the British authorities—the region being in the tribal belt and not under British control. From there Syyed Amir attempted to undermine the loyalty of the British army stationed in the Peshawar region, 'raise a force of Hindostanee mutineers for a religious crusade', and launch an attack on the British frontier. The Syyed met sufficient success and was enabled to present himself twice at the frontier posts of 'Mitchnee' and 'Abazaie'. His attempts, however, were successfully foiled.

In the case of Khyber as well, I have retained the old spelling, which though incorrect is current. Now there is some tendency however, to spell the place as Khaiber.

33. *The Press,* 19 September 1857; *The Spectator,* 19 September 1857; 'The Poorbeah Mutiny–The Punjab, No. IV', LXXXIII, 1858, p. 652.

34. 'Foreign Intelligence–India', *MH.,* XLIX, 1857, pp. 648–9; Carey, *loc. cit.,* p. 216; Duff, *op. cit.,* p. 63.

35. 'Foreign Intelligence–India', *MH.,* XLIX, 1857, pp. 648–9; Carey, *loc. cit.,* p. 216.

36. Cooper, *op. cit.,* pp. 33–4.

37. Ibid., pp. 100–1. Another similar case was reported by L.E. Ruutz Rees. See: *A Personal Narrative...,* p. 269.

38. Cooper, *op. cit.,* p. 118.

39. Raikes, *op. cit.,* p. 64.

40. Sherring, *op. cit.,* pp. 84–5.

41. William Howard Russell, *My Diary in India,* II, p. 16.

42. Greathed, *op. cit.,* p. 130. For a similar piece of information, see also: Hodson, *op. cit.,* p. 259.

43. *People's Paper,* 22 August 1857; Carey, *The Mahomedan Rebellion...,* pp. 62–4. In fact, very largely reported.

44. *The Sixty-sixth Annual Report of the Baptist Missionary Society, ending March 1858,* p. 4; 'The Martyrs and Confessors of Delhi', *WMM.,* Fifth Series, IV, 1858, pp. 548–9; Kingsmill, *op. cit.,* pp. 70–84.

45. 'Foreign Intelligence–India', *MH.,* L, 1858, pp. 253–4.

46. The Rev. Robert Meek, *The Martyr of Allahabad, Memorials of Ensign Cheek of the 6th N.B.I., murdered by the Sepoys at Allahabad* (London: James Nisbet and Co., 1858), p. 30.

47. Sherring, *op. cit.,* pp. 278–81.

48. Ibid., p. 182.

49. Ibid., pp. 283–90.

50. Ibid., p. 151.

51. Ibid., pp. 303–4; 'India: Flight and Deliverance of Native Christians', *CEM.,* XLIV, 1858, pp. 319–20; Kingsmill, *op. cit.,* pp. 68–9.

52. All accounts which refer to such a dialogue between a Mawlawi and a native convert to Christianity at Allahabad furnish only one name and that is that of Gopinath Nandi. The name definitely indicates that he was a Hindu and, therefore, there could be no question of Nandi's being a 'slave of Mahomet' before his conversion to Christianity. For Nandi's story itself, read: 'India', *MM.,* XXIII, 1859, pp. 149–50; Kingsmill, *op. cit.,* pp. 64–8; 'The Courage of Faith: Gopinanth Nandy and Ensign Cheek', *CEM.,* XLIV, 1858, pp. 109–11; 'Converts in India under Trial'. Fifth Series, *WMM.,* III, 1857, p. 1045.

53. Meek, *op. cit.,* pp. 54–5. It should be noted here that Islam virtually forbids slavery. Islamic law is based upon the Qur'an and the sunnah—what Muhammad (PBUH), the Prophet of Islam did in his life. He not only freed slaves, he urged other Muslims to free slaves and secured the freedom of slaves who converted to Islam but were held in slavery by non-Muslims. Bilal Habshi, the most famous of all freed slaves was a very close friend of the Prophet. He was given the distinct honour of giving the call to prayers at the mosque of the Prophet. When Zaid bin Haris was gifted to Muhammad (PBUH) as a slave, he not only freed him but also adopted him as his son. Later on when Zaid's father came to claim his son, he preferred to stay with his foster father. Still later, Zaid's son, Usama, was appointed by the Prophet as commander of the army sent against

Najran. This army included a large number of Quraish, the leading tribe of Makkah. Subsequently, Muslims did practise slavery, but it was certainly not the Euro-American type in which slaves had no rights. Instead, it was a talent-based slavery, a 'system' which produced the two most powerful ruling dynasties in the world: the Mamelukes in Egypt and the Slave Dynasty of India. Muslim rule in India was established by slaves and they ruled the subcontinent for almost a hundred years during the thirteenth century. The Mamelukes, on the other hand, ruled the Egyptian empire for more than 200 years.

54. 'Reports of Mission Stations', *The Sixty-sixth Annual Report of the Baptist Missionary Society, ending March 1858.* Read the reports sent by the Baptist Missionaries stationed at Johnnugger, Dacca, Comilla, Chittagong and Mathura, pp. 17, 34, 35 and 45 respectively. Also see footnotes to Chapters VII and VIII.

55. Probably the reference is to Jaynagar in Bihar.

56. 'Reports of Missionary Stations', The Sixty-sixth Annual Report of the Baptist..., p. 17.

57. Ibid., pp. 17, 34 and 35.

58. *The Spectator,* 22 August 1857; 'India: Progress of Insurrection', *MM.,* XXI, 1857, p. 205. In fact, very largely reported.

59. 'India: Progress of Insurrection', *loc. cit.*

60. 'India', *MM., XXIII,* 1859, pp. 149–50.

61. Sherring, *op. cit.,* pp. 98–103.

62. The Rev. William Beynon (letter from), *MM.,* XXI, 1857, p. 245.

63. 'Foreign Intelligence–India', *MH.,* L, 1858, pp. 50 and 254; Sherring, *op. cit.,* pp. 29–30 and 134–5; *The Indian Crisis. A Special General Meeting of the Church Missionary Society at Exeter Hall, on Tuesday, 12 January 1858* (London: Church Missionary House, 1858), pp. 36–7.

64. Volunteer [Swanston], *op. cit.,* p. 56.

65. *The Times* (letter of an officer from Naini Tal), 5 October 1857.

66. 'The Christianization of India', *London Journal,* XXVI, 1857, p. 109. For a similar opinion, see also: Russell, *op. cit.,* II, p. 78.

67. J.L. Archer, *Indian Mutinies Accounted For. Being an Essay on the Subject,* pp. 7–8; 'State Intervention in the Religions of India', Letter to *The Times,* 1 September 1857.

68. The Rev. William Beynon (letter from), *MM.,* XXI, 1857, p. 246. For similar opinions, see also: Wallace, *op. cit.,* pp. 8–9; N.A. Chick (ed.), *Annals of the Indian Rebellion, containing Narratives of the Outbreak and Eventful Occurrences, and Stories of Personal Adventures, during the Mutiny of 1857-58, with an Appendix Comprising Miscellaneous Facts, Anecdotes etc., 1857-58,* p. 2.

69. *The Scotsman* (letter from India), 18 July 1857. For a similar opinion, see also: Wallace, *loc. cit.*

70. 'The Progress of the Indian Rebellion', *Illustrated London News,* 5 September 1857. For similar opinions, see also: Chick, *loc. cit.,* p. 6.; 'Foreign Intelligence–India', *MH.,* XLIX, 1857, p. 717.

71. Chick, *op. cit.,* p. 6. For a similar opinion, see also: *Investigation into Some...,* p. 7.

72. Dunlop, *op. cit.,* p. 152. For similar opinions, see also: *India, the Revolt and the Home Government,* pp. 80–1; Volunteer [Swanston], *op. cit.,* p. 54; Cooper, *op. cit.,* p. 134; *Investigation into Some...,* pp. 7–8.

73. [The Rev.] J. Trafford (letter from), *MH.*, XLIX, 1857, p. 514; Anderson, *op. cit.*, p. 13.
74. Chick, *op. cit.*, p. 6.
75. Archer, *op. cit.*, pp. 11–12.
76. 'Foreign Intelligence—India', *MH.*, L, 1858, p. 585.
77. Ibid., p. 652.
78. Ibid., p. 585.
79. Ibid., XLIX, 1857, p. 721.
80. Ibid., L, 1858, p. 585.
81. Maj.-Gen. [Sir James] Outram, *Outram's Campaign in India, 1857–58; comprising General Orders and Despatches relating to the Defence and Relief of Lucknow Garrison and Capture of the City by the British Forces* (London 1860), p. 285.
82. Raikes, *op. cit.*, p. 78 and 79 n.
83. *The Nation*, 24 October 1857. The paper, editorially reporting the suggestion, taunted: 'Such is the English humanity in the middle of the 19th century'.
    Since the press in India at that time was under government control, the paper held the British Government responsible for 'at least not disapproving' this tendency.
84. 'A Few Words from the Khyber', *Blackwood's*, LXXXII, 1857, p. 613.
85. 'Delhi As It Is', *Fraser's*, LVIII, 1858, p. 63.
86. The Rev. James Smith, 'Resumption of the Mission in Delhi', *MH.*, LI, 1859, p. 390.
87. 'Delhi As It Is', *Fraser's*, LVIII, 1858, p. 64.
88. Ibid., p. 63.
89. 'The Crisis in India', (Review of Macleod Wylie's book, *Commerce, Resources and Prospects of India*), *The Scotsman*, 9 September 1857.
90. 'A Few Words from the Khyber', *Blackwood's*, LXXXII, 1857, p. 614. Bahadur Shah Zafar, the octogenarian Mughal ruler of Delhi, was soon sent to Rangoon in perpetual exile and twenty-four Muslim princes were shot to death in a single day at Delhi. See: R.R. Sethi and V.D. Mahajan, *British Rule in India and After, 1707–1956*, p. 162.

Chapter 9: Worldwide Jihad or a Clash of Civilizations?

1. Edward Hoare, *England's Stewardship* (London, 1857), pp. 7–8; 'National Sins and National Responsibility', *The Pulpit*, LXXII, 1858, p. 349; 'The Religions of India', *CEQR*, XLIV, 1858, p. 63; Henry Allon, *Indian Rule And Responsibility* (London, 1857), p. 16; James Charles, *The Lord's Voice To Britain From The Far East* (Edinburgh and Glasgow: 1857), p. 23; John Hampdon Gurney, *The Moral Of A Sad Story. Four Sermons On The Indian Mutiny* (London: 1857), p. 69; Edward Whitehead, *I Wrought For My Name's Sake* (London & Jersey: 1857), p. 9; Joseph Mullens, *The Queen's Government And The Religions Of India* [Reprinted from The Eclectic] (London: 1859), p. 4.
2. Read Philip K. Hitti, *Islam And The West* (New York: 1962); John Victor Tolan (ed.), *Medieval Christian Perceptions Of Islam* (New York and London: Routledge, 1996).
3. Tolan, op. cit., pp. xii–xiii. As discussed above, both the Qur'an and the traditions of Muhammad (PBUH) give great importance to Jesus; by Islamic faith

he was born to a virgin, and therefore, was a miracle of God and a Prophet of Islam; he performed many miracles; he did not die but was lifted alive, and will return as Jesus/Isa before the end of time. Therefore, Muhammad (PBUH)could not have been the alleged mediaeval Antichrist.

4. 'Apollo Among Gods of the Saracens,' cited in Hitti, ibid. Reading No. 16, pp. 150-1.

5. Works of Francis Bacon, II (London, 1824), p. 279.

6. Hitti, op. cit., p. 56.

7. Henry Bergen (ed.) *Lydgate's Fall of Princes* (Washington: 1923), Pt. III, p. 921.

8. Peter Hardy, *The Muslims of British India* (Cambridge: Cambridge University Press, 1972), p. 62. Government support of the Anglican Church in India, in particular, and the British missionaries, in general, with Indian revenues and use of official position for conversions, treatment of subjugated natives by Muslim and by Christian rulers are very interesting topics for a comparative study.

9. George Sale, *The Koran*, with and Introduction by Robert D. Richardson, Jr. (New York and London: 1984), read the 'Dedication.'

10. Sale, op. cit. Read the 'Introduction' by Robert D. Richardson.

11. Sir James Stephen, Holt Mackenzie, Pringle, Thompson, and Henry Elliot were among the 'celebrated' scholars who received their initial training at Hailebury and who helped perpetuate the 'James Millian tradition 'in the historical accounts of India. Philips, pp. 221 and 226. Also read: Salahuddin Malik, 'Nineteenth Century Approaches to the Indian "Mutiny"', *Journal Of Asian History*, VII, no. 2, pp. 95-127.

12. The Rev. Harvey Brooks, '*God's Displeasure As Provoked By Indian Heathenism And Anglo-Saxon Policy* (London: 1857); C.F.S. Money, *The Indian Mutiny; Or India's Idolatry And England's Responsibility* (London: 1857) A condensed version of this was also published in the *Church Of England Magazine*, XLIII, 1857, pp. 406-8; Hansard, CXLVIII, 1857, pp. 20 and 94; [W.E. Gladstone] (Speech of...before the Friends of the Society for the Propagation of the Gospel) cited in the *Manchester Guardian*, 14 October 1857; Dean of Carlisle, *An Indian Retrospect; Or What Has Christian England Done For Heathen India* (London: 1859); *Minutes of The Church Missionary Society On Indian Mutiny In Its Connection With Christian Missions And The Future Government Of India Upon Christian Principles* (Calcutta: 1857); 'India, Its Government and Christianity,' MH, L, 1858, pp. 382-3; 'The Religions of India,' CEQR, 1858, p. 65; 'National Sins the Sources of National Calamities,' CMI, IX, 1858, pp. 241-5; Mullens, op. cit.; 'India, the Heaven of Satan,' CEM, 19 March 1859, pp. 177-8; W.. Eastwick, *Speech Of Captain W.J. Eastwick At A Special Court Of Proprietors Held At The East India House, On 20th Of January, 1858* (London: 1858), p. 15; 'God's Judgment on Idolatry,' MH, XLIX, 1857, pp. 782-3; R.B. Boswell, *Hope For India In England's God* (London: 1857), pp. 5-6; J.L. Porter, *National Christianity For India* (London: 1857); Rev. E.B. Squire, '*God's Prolonged Controversy With Britain* (Swansea: 1857); Charles Stovel, *India: Its Crimes And Claims* (London: 1857); Mullens, op. cit.; Baptist Wriothesley, *England And India: An Essay On The Duty Of Englishmen Toward The Hindoos* (London: 1859), pp. iv and 24-5; James Davis, 'India and Recent Events in Relation to Christianity,' and Alfred Jones, 'Lamentations and Woe Follow in the Steps of Unfaithfulness to God,' *The Pulpit*, LXXII, 1858, pp. 318-19 and 513-15 respectively; 'India, Its

Government and Christianity,' MH, L, 1858, pp. 382–3; 'Religions of India,'
CEQR, XLIV, 1858; 'How Shall Our Wrongs in India be Best Avenged,' CMI, IX,
1858, pp. 26–7; Edmund Kell, *What Patriotism, Justice And Christianity Demand
For India* (London: Hatchard and Wertheim, 1857); Rev. J.B. Heard, 'The
Analogy between the Decline of Paganism in the Roman Empire, and its Present
Decline in India,' DUM, LIII, 1859, pp. 129–46; Lt.-Col. Sir H. Edwardes, *The
Safety of a Christian Policy in India. A Speech Delivered at the Sixty-first
Anniversary Meeting of the Church Missionary Society*, 1 May 1860 (London:
1860), pp. 29–32; Rev. Edward Hoare, 'The Mutiny in India in Relation to
Mahometanism and its appointed Issues,' *The Pulpit*, LXXIII, pp. 241–7; Rev.
G.H. Curteis, *The Evangelization Of India* (Oxford, London: Lichfield, 1857);
Rev. James Smith, 'Resumption of the Mission in Delhi,' MH, LI, 1859, p. 389;
Sherring, op. cit., p. 175; Benyon (Letter from) MH, XXI, 1857, p. 246; Rev.
William Cadman, 'The Wide Proclamation of the Gospel among the Heathen,'
The Pulpit, LXXIII, 1858, pp. 221–8; Rev. Curteis, G.N., 'The Evangelization of
India,' (Oxford and London: J.H. and James Parker. Lichfield: Lomerx: 1857);
Dixon, Rev. James, 'The Sword of the Lord in the Indian Crisis,' (London: John
Mason, Manchester: Galt, Kerruish and Gent, nd); Davis, Rev. James, 'India and
Recent Events in their Relations to Christianity,' *The Pulpit*, LXXII, 1858, pp.
315–19; Fenn, Rev. Joseph, 'Britain's Burdens and Causes of Punishments,'
(London: W.H. Dalton, 1857); Jones, Rev. Alfred, 'Lamentations and Woe
Follow in the Steps Unfaithfulness to God,' *The Pulpit*, LXXII, pp. 511–16; Kell,
Rev. Edmund, 'Edmund Kell in Reply to a Reviewer of his Sermon entitled
"What Patriotism, Justice, and Christianity Demand for India",'(London: E.T.
Whitfield, 1858); Porter, Rev. J. Leech, 'National Christianity for India, or
National Acts and National Duties,' (London: Wertheim and Macintosh, 1857);
Puckle, Rev. John, 'Heathen Sin Through Fault,' (Dover: Printed by W. Batcheller,
nd).

13. Read: *The Policy Established By Law Of The Indian Government, Opposed To The
Neutral Policy In Respect Of Christianity*, Occasional Papers on India, No. IX,
(London: 1860), p. 19. The Church Missionary Society alone published a series
of nearly one dozen 'Occasional Papers' on India. Indeed, the British were
overwhelmed with articles, books, and pamphlets pertaining to the conversion
of Indians to Christianity. J.B. Heard, 'Prize Essay on Christianity in India,'
appeared in two instalments in *DUM*, LIII, 1859, pp. 513–39 and 641–63; J.E.W.
Rotton, *Chaplain's Narrative Of The Siege Of Delhi* (London: 1858); W.E.
Gladstone (Speech of...), *Manchester Guardian*, 14 October 1857; *Indian
Mutiny: Thoughts And Facts* (London: 1857), pp. 4 and 14–16, and 34; Rev.
Robert Meek, *The Martyr Of Allahabad: Memorials Of Ensign Cheek Of The 6th
N.B.I.* (London: 1858), p. 81; 'How We Talked about the Indian Mutiny, Part I,'
DUM, L, 1857, pp. 625–38; C.W. Martyn (address in answer to the Throne
Speech), Hansard 3, CXLVIII, p. 94; Rev. Redwar, 'The Uncertainty of Life,' *The
Pulpit*, LXXIII, 1858, pp. 44–5; *How To Keep India* (London: 1857), pp. 4–5; Lt.
Edward King, *A Bird's-Eye View Of India: Showing Our Present Position—Its
Danger And Remedy* (London: 1857), read the Introduction; Rt. Hon. Joseph
Napier, *The Bible In Government Schools In India. Speech Delivered At The
Annual Meeting Of The Church Missionary Society, Held At Xeter Hall*, 30 April
1861, pp. 9–11; the Dean of Carlisle, op. cit., pp. 35–6; Edwardes, op. cit., pp. 7,
15–19, and 48–51; Newman, op. cit., p. 443.

14. Very widely held view. To realize how anguished the British were at the tardiness of the East India Company to help spread Christianity in India, and the dire consequences thereof , read: Salahuddin Malik, 'God, England, and the Indian Mutiny: Victorian Religious Perceptions,' *The Muslim World*, LXXIII, 2, 1983, pp. 106–32.

15. *Manchester Guardian*, 14 October 1857; Hansard, CXLVIII, 94; *Indian Mutiny: Thoughts And Facts*, op. cit.; Stovel, op. cit.; Charles, op. cit.; 'How We Talked about the Indian Mutiny, Part I,' *DUM*, op. cit.

16. Hoare, op. cit., p. 6.

17. Cairns, op. cit., p. 4.

18. Gurney, op. cit., p. 12.

19. Mather, op. cit., p. 3.

20. Hoare, op. cit., pp. 7–8. Indeed, hundreds of similar statements can be cited here.

21. Both are unpublished dissertations. The Master's thesis was presented at McGill University, Montreal, Canada, in 1959, and the Ph.D. dissertation was submitted at Lehigh University, Bethlehem, Pennsylvania, USA, in 1965.

22. See Chapters 2, 3, and 7.

23. Read: Right Reverend Reginald Heber, Lord Bishop of Calcutta, *Narrative of a Journey through the Upper Provinces of India from Calcutta to Bombay, 1824– 1825 (with Notes upon Ceylon) an account of a Journey to Madras and the Southern Provinces*, 1826 (London: 3 vols., John Murray, 1928). Indeed, Bishop Heber travelled through all of the above provinces and places in pomp and glory at the expense of the native taxpayers. No such consideration was offered to Hindu, Muslim, or Sikh religious leaders.

24. See Chapter 7.

25. Ibid.

26. Vol. CXL, 1857, p. 127. How much did the contributor of this article in the *New Monthly Magazine* know about the history of India and its people is sufficiently evident from his spelling of various Indo-Pakistani names. A perusal of the article itself, which is full of errors, would further strengthen this impression. For similar views, see also: *Manchester Guardian*, 7 August and 3 September 1857.

27. *The Free Press*, 4 November 1857. The journal quoted a German newspaper, *Neue Preussische Zeitung*, which emphasized that the Muslim struggle against Christianity was not confined to India and Persia; indeed, it was global in nature and included Muslims of Asia Minor, Syria, and Egypt. It stressed that Muslims everywhere were buying arms and that even though the economies of Birmingham and Liege 'were reaping a golden harvest' from this 'massive' arms traffic, the paper cautioned that it was a matter of grave concern to the 'Franks and Christians.' For other similar views, see: *Manchester Guardian*, 13 July 1858; 'Great Mahometan Conspiracy against the Christians,' *The Tablet*, 24 October 1857; *The Economist*, 17 July 1858; *The Spectator*, 17 July 1858; 'The Jeddah Massacre,' *CEQR*, XLIV, 1858, pp. 218–9; *The New Monthly Magazine*, CXI, 1857, p. 127; 'Monthly Review of Public Events,' ER, New Series, IV, 1858, p. 191; 'Political Narrative,' TEM, XXV, 1858, p. 504; *Illustrated London News*, 17 July 1858; *The Times*, 27 July 1858. *The Spectator* called for another 'crusade' against the Muslims. Indeed, the diversity of British adventures into Muslim lands like North Africa, Turkey, Iran, Arabia, Afghanistan, and India backed up

by intense missionary zeal could easily lead to a countervailing theory 'hundred year old Christian crusade against the world of Islam.' The above events were unconnected and uncoordinated local resistance against high-handedness of European Christians. This topic is worth a penetrating scholarly study.

28. Rev. J.D. Massingham, 'The Rebellion of the Sepoys traced to its True Source,' (a sermon preached on 7 October 1857), *The Pulpit*, LXXII, 1857, pp. 393–4.
29. The name was also spelt as Muhammerah, Mohammerah, and Mohammareh.
30. 'Great Mahometan Conspiracy against the Christians,' *The Tablet*, 24 October 1857.
31. Dr E.H. Nolan, *The Illustrated History Of British Empire In India And The East, From The Earliest Times To The Suppression Of The Sepoy Mutiny In 1859*, II, p. 711; 'India,' *Edinburgh Review*, CVI, 1857, p. 567; *The Times*, 30 July 1858; *Illustrated London News*, 17 July 1858.
32. Tanzimat, or rather Tanzimat-i-Khairiye, meaning beneficent legislation, is the 'term used to denote the reforms introduced into the government and administration of the Ottoman empire from the beginning of the reign of Sultan 'Abdul Majid and inaugurated by the charter generally called the 'Khatt-i-Sharif of Gulkhane.' *Encyclopaedia Of Islam*, 1913 ed., IV: 2, p. 656.
33. Nolan, op. cit., p. 711. For a similar opinion, see also: 'India.' *Edinburgh Review*, CVI, 1857, p. 567.
34. 'The Great Mahometan Conspiracy' *The Tablet*, 24 October 1857.
35. 'India,' *Edinburgh Review*, CVI, 1857, p. 567.
36. 'The Great Mahometan Conspiracy', ibid.
37. 'India', *Edinburgh Review*, CVI, 1857, p. 567.
38. W.H. Carey (ed.), *The Mahomedan Rebellion: Its Premonitory Symptoms: The Outbreak and Suppression, With an Appendix*, p. 6. For similar opinions, see also: Frederick Cooper, *The Crisis in the Punjab from the 10th of May until the Fall of Delhi*, p. XIII; *Free Press*, 3 June 1857; *The Spectator*, 4 July 1858.
39. Carey, *The Mahomedan Rebellion*, p. 6.
40. Ibid., pp. 2–3.
41. Ibid., p. 3.
42. Ibid., pp. 3–4.
43. Ibid., p. 4.
44. Cooper, op. cit., p. XIII; *Free Press*, 3 June 1857.
45. Can be translated as, 'Edict', 'Order', 'Ordinance', or 'Decree'. Here, however, 'Edict' or 'Decree' seem to be better substitutes for Farman.
46. Rev. George Percy Badger, *Government in its Relation with Education and Christianity in India* (London: Smith, Elder and Co. Bombay: Smith, Taylor and Co., 1858), pp. 14–15.
47. Read Chapter 7, pp. 246–7 and 249.
48. *Annual Register*, 1857, p. 240.
49. Rev. Alexander Duff, *The Indian Rebellion; its Causes and Results in a Series of Letters*, p. 94.
50. *Manchester Guardian*, 15 April 1857.
51. N.A. Chick (ed.), *Annals of the Indian Rebellion, containing Narratives of the Outbreak and Eventful Occurrences, and Stories of Personal Adventures, during the Mutiny of 1857–58, with an Appendix Comprising Miscellaneous Facts, Anecdotes etc.*, p. 10.
52. 'The Fall of Delhi', *Saturday Review*, 31 October 1857.

53. *Free Press*, 4 November 1857. For an identical reference, see also: 'The Great Mahometan Conspiracy, *The Tablet*, 24 October 1857.

54. *Free Press*, 4 November 1857.

55. *The Times*, 16 July 1858. The paper editorially put the strength of the 'miscreants' at 5000. *The Tablet* also gave the same number, 17 July 1858.

56. *The Times*, 27 July 1858. An officer on board the steam frigate 'Cyclops', which was harbouring at Jeddah at the time of the bloody occurrence and was itself involved in the incident, writing to *The Times* of 27 July, reported the 'rabble' strength at 8000.

57. The total number of people slain in Jeddah was unanimously reported to be twenty-one. The first report of Turkish fatalities of the day came from the Earl of Malmesbury when he discussed the incident in the House of Lords. The media was so hyped up that it did not print the full story coming out of Jeddah. It did not analyse the reasons behind the Jeddah turbulence, mention the strenuous efforts of the Turkish government to contain the uprising, or even allude to Turkish fatalities of the day. A simultaneous mention of all these facts would have greatly pacified the public outrage.

58. Hansard 3, CLI, 1657–8.

59. Antoine D'Abbadie, Letter to *The Times*, 27 July 1858.

60. *The Spectator*, 1858, pp. 746 and 757; *The Times*, 15, 16, and 27 July 1858; *The Examiner*, 17 July 1858; *The Economist*, 17 July 1858.

61. *The Spectator*, 17 July 1858; *Manchester Guardian*, 13 July 1858; 'The Jeddah Massacre', CEQR, XLIV, 1858, pp. 218–9.

62. *The Nation*, 17 July 1858.

63. Antoine D'Abbadie, Letter to *The Times*, 27 July 1858. In today's terminology, D'Abbadie's assertive comment would be viewed as racial, ethnic, religious, or community profiling—certainly forbidden and frowned upon in North America.

64. D'Abbadie, letter to *The Times*, 19 July 1858. As proofs D'Abbadie mentioned that: a) In 1839 the English and the French Consuls were insulated at Jeddah in his own presence by 'the Jeddah rabble', b) in the same year a Christian doctor was assassinated because one of his patients had died; c) the things were still worse at Mocha [Mecca], where the Captain of a French warship having landed incautiously was detained along with other officers in the common jail; d) twice in 1839 and 1840 the British flag was trampled upon, in the second instance his own brother having been forced to tread upon the Union Jack before meeting the Sheriff of Mocha [Mecca]. These, he claimed, were some of the many instances which proved the permanent nature of Muslim hostility towards Christianity and the Christian powers.

65. *The Times*, 27 July 1858. For a similar opinion, see also: Hansard 3, CLI, 1656.

66. *The Times*, 27 July 1858.

67. Ibid.

68. 'The Jeddah Massacre', CEQR, XLIV, 1858, p. 219; *The Times*, 27 July 1858.

69. *The Spectator*, 17 July 1858.

70. Ibid.; *The Tablet*, 17 July 1858.

71. *The Spectator*, *The Nation*, 17 July 1858.

72. *The Nation*, 17 July 1858.

73. *The Spectator,* 17 July 1858; 'The Jeddah Massacre', *CEQR,* XLIV, 1858, pp. 218–9. *The Spectator* asserted that the Jeddah atrocity had received its 'first inspiration from Delhi'.

74. *Manchester Guardian,* 13 July 1858; 'The Jeddah Massacre', *loc. cit.*

75. *Illustrated London News,* 17 July 1858; *The Spectator,* 17 July 1858.

76. 'The Jeddah Massacre', *CEQR,* XLIV, 1858, pp. 218–9. Editorially commenting upon the Jeddah massacre, the *Manchester Guardian* similarly observed:

> The world of Islamism is in turmoil.... In India, a quasi-religious war, of which the most active and intelligent promoters are undoubtedly Mahometans, still rages against the English; having been provoked, as its authors assert by the discovery of a profound design to force the Christian faith upon native acceptance.... In the wild misrepresentations of current events put forth by Nana Sahib, and some other chiefs of the Indian mutiny, it is probable that we have seen fair illustrations of what is said and believed about England by Mahometan fanatics of every hue, from the banks of Ganges to the coast of Morocco and from the Danube to the Niger. 13 July 1858.

77. *The Spectator,* 17 July 1858.

78. 'The Jeddah Massacre', *CEQR,* XLIV, 1858, p. 219.

79. Rev. Edward Hoare, 'The Mutiny in Relation to Mahometanism and its Appointed Issues', (fourth of a course of twelve lectures on 'The Signs of Time'), *The Pulpit,* LXXXIII, 1858, pp. 241–7.

80. Ibid., p. 241.

81. Ibid.

82. According to Hoare the Euphrates or at least its canal system was actually drying up at that time, p. 242.

83. Hoare did not provide any instance in which the coffin of a Turk was carried from European Turkey across the Strait of Bosphorus. Historically, however, Hoare's contention appears to be quite untrue. The fact of the matter is that Abu Ayub Ansari, one of the companions of the Prophet Muhammad [PBUH], is buried in European Istanbul. Ever since its conquest Istanbul continued to be the capital of the Ottoman Empire until the time of the republic. Most of the Sultans since the conquest were buried in European Turkey. Also, European Turkey always received a greater amount of attention in the development of Muslim or rather Turkish art and architecture. The result is that some of the best specimens of art and architecture today are to be found on the western side of the Bosphorus. In Istanbul, for example, one can enumerate Cinili Kiosk, Sulaimaniyah mosque, the mosque of Sultan Ahmad, the mosque of Rustam Pasha, Fateh mosque, the mausoleum of Sulaiman, and above all, several palaces of the Sultans, the most important being Topkapi.

84. Hoare, op. cit., pp. 241–6.

85. Ibid., p. 247.

86. Ibid., pp. 246–7.

87. Ibid., p. 247.

88. *The Leader,* 17 July 1858.

89. *The Leader,* 24 July 1858. For more information, see also: *The Leader,* 7 and 14 August, 1858; *The Examiner,* 24 July 1858.

90. *Annual Register,* 1858, p. 268

Conclusion

1. For figures, see: *MM.,* New Series, 1860, I, p. 183. The amount collected was quite significant in view of the two other funds which were being raised simultaneously to aid the missionary programme in Africa and to relieve British sufferers in India.

Glossary

Afghan	An inhabitant of Afghanistan or the North-Western regions of Pakistan.
Banya	A Hindu merchant, trader, shopkeeper, vendor of provisions; niggard; petty-minded man; timid man.
Chabutra	A terrace; a raised and levelled piece of ground; a platform.
Chapati	A thin cake of unleavened bread.
Darbar	Royal court; hall of audience; royal audience; holding of court.
Devi	A female diety, a goddess, the wife of a deity.
Darwesh	Poor, indigent; a religious mendicant; a beggar.
Doab	The country between the Ganges and Jumna.
Farangi	A Frank; a European; an Englishman.
Fawj	An army.
Ghazi	A warrior, a conqueror, a hero; one who fights against infidels.
Guru	A Hindu or Sikh teacher or priest.
Hafiz	One who has the whole Qur'an by heart.
Haram	Woman's apartment.
Hawaldar	A native military officer of inferior rank, equivalent to a head constable.
Jama'dar	A native officer of the army.
Jami' Masjid	A Friday congregational mosque.
Jihadan	A Muslim female warrior.
Kachahri	A court of justice.
Kamarband	Sash.
Kotwali	The chief police station in a town.
Maharaja	Mighty or illustrious king.
Masjid	Mosque.
Masnad	A place in or upon which one leans or rests; a throne; a large cushion.
Mawalawi	A Muslim doctor of law, a professor, a learned man; a Muslim priest.
Mulla	A doctor, a learned man; a Muslim priest.
Munshi	An author, a composer; a writer, scribe, secretary; a tutor, a teacher of Persian or Urdu; a title of respect.
Na'ib	An assistant, lieutenant, deputy, viceroy.
Nawab	A governor, a viceroy; a lord; a prince.
Padshah (Persian) Badshah (Urdu)	King.
Puja	Worship, respect, reverence, veneration, adoration; idol-worship.
Purbiya	A native of the eastern parts of India (from Kanpur to Bihar).
Qasid	A messenger, a courier, letter carrier.
Quli	A coolie, labourer, porter.
Raja	King, sovereign, monarch, governor, lord.

Risalahdar/Risaldar	A native commander of a troop of horse.
Sadar court	High court.
Sahib	A word of respect like 'sir', 'Mr'.
Sanad	Order, royal ordinance, mandate or decree; any deed or grant etc. from one in authority.
Sa'is	A groom, a horse-keeper.
Sawar	A rider, horseman, cavalier, horse-soldier, trooper.
Shah	King, prince, monarch.
Subedar	A native military officer (non-commissioned) whose rank corresponded to that of a captain.
Sunni	An orthodox Muslim, one who receives the Sunnat or traditional portion of Islamic law.
Sultan	King, monarch, sovereign.
Tahsildar	An important officer of the revenue department.
'Ulama	Plural of 'Alim, meaning learned or doctor of religion.
Wazir	Minister.
Wahabi	Of or relating to Wahhab; a follower of the doctrines of Shaikh 'Abdul Wahhab.
Wakil	An attorney, a pleader, counsellor.
Zamindar	Landlord, landowner, landed proprietor; a farmer.

Bibliography

1. **Primary Sources:**
A) Hansard's *Parliamentary Debates*, Third Series, 1853-60, Vols. CXXIV-CLX.

B) **Parliamentary Papers. Readex Microprint Edition, Edited by Professor Edgar L. Erickson of the University of Illinois.**
Vol. XLVIII of 1854, Session, 31 January–12 August 1854.
Vol. XXIX of 1857, Session, 30 April–28 August 1857.
Vol. XXX of 1857, Session, 30 April–28 August 1857.
Vol. XLII of 1857-58, Session, 3 December 1857–2 August 1858.
Vol. XLIII of 1857-58, Session, 3 December 1857–2 August 1858.
Vol. XLIV, parts I to IV of 1857-58, Session, 3 December 1857–2 August 1858.
Vol. IV of 1859, Session, 3 February–19 April 1859.
Vol. VIII of 1859, Session 2, 31 May–13 August 1859.
Vol. XLII of 1861, Session, 5 February–6 August 1861.
Vol. XL of 1863, Session, 5 February–28 July 1863.

C) **Books and Pamphlets published contemporaneously:**
In this section are included books, pamphlets, speeches, diaries, journals, histories and annual reports which were published either during the mutiny or are eye-witness accounts published at the time (until 1862).
Much of this material was published anonymously, often by the civil and military servants of the East India Company (for fear of inviting retaliation from the government), or by those who like the East Indian interest wished to avoid public criticism. The latter section of writers was specially apologetic; they tried to advocate the continuation of the East India Company as disinterested parties. It was, however, not very difficult to determine the political, social, religious or service affiliations of the anonymous writers.

Adye, Lt.-Col. John, *The Defence of Cawnpore by the Troops under the Orders of Major-General Charles A. Windham, C.B., in November 1857* (London: Longman, Brown, Green, Longmans and Bros., 1858).

Aikman, Lieut. Wm. R., *The Bengal Mutiny: Popular Opinions Concerning the Origins of the Mutiny Refuted: The Real Cause Considered, with Suggestions for the Future, in a Letter to Viscount Palmerston* (London: Richardson Bros., 1857).

Ainslie, The Rev. A.C., *A Few Words about India and the Indian Mutinies* (3rd. ed.; Tauton: Frederick May, 1857).

Anderson, Capt. A.R., *A Personal Journal of the Siege of Lucknow*, ed. with a Preface and an Introduction by Anderson, T. Carnegy (London: W. Thackers and Co., 1858).

The Annexation of the Kingdom of Oude One of the Main Causes of the Rebellion in India (Manchester: Looney and Pilling, [1858]).

Appendix to 'The Oude Question Stated and Considered; with References to Published Official Documents' (London: Smith and Co., 1857).

Archer, J.L., *Indian Mutinies Accounted For: Being an Essay on the Subject* (London: Ward and Co., 1857).

Atkinson, George Franklin, *The Campaign in India, 1857-58 From Drawings made during the Eventful Period of the Great Mutiny by..., Illustrating the Military Operations before Delhi and its Neighbourhood* (London: Day and Son, 1859).

Badger, The Rev. Geo. Percy, *Government in its Relation with Education and Christianity in India* (London: Smith, Elder and Co. Bombay: Smith, Taylor and Co., 1858).

Bagot, Daniel, *Psalm XLVI–Suited to the Indian Crisis* (Dublin: Madden and Oldham, [1857]).

Ball, Charles, *The History of the Indian Mutiny: Giving a Detailed Account of the Sepoy Insurrection in India; and a Concise History of the Great Military Events which have tended to Consolidate British Empire in Hindostan* (Two Vols.; London and New York: The London Printing and Publishing Co., [1858-59]).

Baptist Missionary Society, Annual Reports:
1857-58 (London: Haddon Bros.)
1858-59 (London: Yates and Alexander).
1859-60 (London: Yates and Alexander).

[Bartrum, Mrs K.M.] *A Widow's Reminiscences of the Siege of Lucknow* (London: James Nisbet and Co., 1858).

Bell, Capt. [Thomas] Evans, *The English in India. Letters from Nagpore, written in 1857-58,* (London: John Chapman, 1859).

Beveridge, Henry, *A Comprehensive History of India, Civil, Military and Social, from the First Landing of the English, to the Suppression of the Sepoy Revolt, including an Outline of the Early History of Hindoostan* (Vol. III, London: Black and Son, 1862).

Bird, Maj. R.W., *The Spoliation of Oudh* (London: 'Nassau Steam Press', W.S. Johnson, 1857).

Bourchier, Col. George, *Eight Months' Campaign against the Bengal Sepoys During the Mutiny* (London: Smith, Elder and Co., 1858).

Brief Narrative of the Defence of the Arrah Garrison; with an Account of the Main Events in an Official Communication by H.C. Wake Esquire, Magistrate of Shahabad, to W. Taylor Esquire, Commissioner of the Patna Division (London: W. Thacker Spink and Co. Bombay: Thacker and Co. Allahabad: J. Hill and Co., 1858).

Brief Observations, Addressed to the General Reader, on the Basis of the Re-organization of Our Power in India (London: R.C. Lepage and Co., 1858).

British and Foreign Bible Society, Annual Reports: 1856-58 (London: F. W. Watkins). 1859-62 (London: Spottiswood and Co.).

Brock, The Rev. W., *A Biographical Sketch of Sir Henry Havelock* (London: James Nisbet, 1858).

Buchanan, [The Rev.] Claudius, *Christian Researches in India,* ed. by The Rev. W.H. Foy (London: G. Routledge and Co., 1858).

Campbell, Robert James Roy, *The Indian mutiny, its Causes and its Remedies. A Letter to the Right Honourable Lord Viscount Palmerston* (London: Charles Evans, 'United Service Gazette Office', [1858]).

Carey, The Rev. W.H. (ed.), *The Mahomedan Rebellion; its Premonitory Symptoms, the Outbreak and its Suppression; with an Appendix* (Roorkee: Printed at the Directory Press, 1857).

Case, Mrs Col., *Day by Day at Lucknow. A Journal of the Siege of Lucknow* (London: Richard Bentley, 1858).

Cator, P., *Christian Education in India. Why Should English be Excluded? A Letter to Honourable Arthur Kinnard, M.P.* (London: Seeley, Jackson and Halliday, 1858).

Cause and Effect: The Rebellion in India (London: John Farquhar Shaw, [1857]).

Cave-Brown, The Rev. J., *The Punjab and Delhi in 1857. Being a Narrative of the Measures by which Punjab was Saved and Delhi Recovered During the Indian Mutiny* (London and Edinburgh: William Blackwood and Sons, 1861).

Chick, N.A. (ed.), *Annals of the Indian Rebellion, Containing Narratives of the Outbreak and Eventful Occurrences and Stories of Personal Adventures during the Mutiny of 1857-58, with an Appendix comprising Miscellaneous Facts, Anecdotes etc.* (Calcutta: Printed and Published by Sanders, Cones and Co., 1859).

Christian Mission and Government Education in India. Review of a Letter Addressed to the Court of Directors of the East India Company by the Earl of Ellenborough, and of a Memorandum of Sir George Clerk (London: Church Missionary House, 1858).

Christianising India: What-How-And By Whom (London: Simpkon, Marshall and Co., 1859).

Christmas, The Rev. Henry, *The Hand of God in India A Series of Lectures Preached by...in the City of London* (London: Houlston and Wright, 1858).

Civicus [Russell, Sir Henry], *Thoughts on the Indian Crisis and its bearing on the Freedom of the Press* (London: Effingham Wilson, 1857).

Congreve, Richard, *India.* (London: A. Boner, 1907, First Published by John Chapman of London in 1857).

A Constitutional View of the Indian Question (London: William Penny, 1858).

Cooper, Frederick, H., *The Crisis in the Punjab from the 10th of May until the Fall of Delhi* (London: E. Wilson, 1858).

Crawshay, George, *The Mutiny of the Bengal Army from Official Documents. A Lecture delivered by the Mayor of Gateshead, in the Hall of Mechanics Institute. Wednesday, 4 November, 1857* Gateshead: Printed at the Observer Steem'Press, 1857).

Crawshay, George, *The Catastrophe of the East India Company* (London: 1858).

Crawshay, George, *Proselytism Destructive of Christianity and Incompatible with Political dominion. Speech of Mr Crawshay at the India House on the Vote of an Annuity to Sir John Lawrence, 25 August 1858, with Notes and an Appendix* (London: Effingham Wilson, 1858).

Crisis in India, its Causes and Proposed Remedies (London: Richard Bentley, 1857).

Culross, James, *The Missionary Martyr of Delhi: A Memoir of the Reverend John Mackay* (London: J. Heaton. Edinburgh: Paton and Ritchie, 1860).

The Defence of Lucknow (Diary of a Staff Officer) (2nd. ed.; London: Smith, Elder and Co., 1858).

Deputation to Lord Stanley (London: W.M. Watts, 1858).

Dodd, George, *The History of the Indian Revolt and of the Expeditions to Persia, China and Japan, 1856-7-8* (London: W. and R. Chambers, 1859).

Dodgson, Lieut.-Col. David, *General Views and Special Points of Interest of the City of Lucknow* (London: Day and Son, 1860).

Duberley, Mrs Frances Isabella, *Campaigning Experience in Rajpootana and Central India, during the Suppression of the Mutiny, 1857-58* (Smith, Elder and Co., 1859).

Duff, The Rev. Alexander, *The Indian Rebellion; its Causes and Results in a Series of Letters from...*, (London: James Nisbet, 1858).

Duff, The Rev. Alexander, Letter by the Reverend Dr Duff of Calcutta on the Present State of India, dated Calcutta, 7 November 1857.

Duff, The Rev. Alexander, What is Caste? How is a Christian Government to deal with it? (A paper prepared and read by the Reverend Alexander Duff at a meeting of the Calcutta Missionary Conference).

Dunlop, R.H.W., Service and Adventure with the Khakee Ressalah; or, Meerut Volunteer Horse, during the Mutinies of 1857-58 (London: R. Bentley, 1858).

Eastwick, Capt., Speech of...at a Special Court of Proprietors, held at the East India House, on the 20th of January 1858 (London: Smith, Elder and Co., 1858).

Edwardes, Lieut.-Col. Sir H., Christianity in India. The speech of...delivered at an extraordinary meeting held at the Town Hall, Cambridge, on the 18th of June 1860, together with addresses by the Reverend G. Phillips, D.D., President of Queen's College; and the Rev. C.K. Rohinson, Minister of St. Andrew's the Less (Cambridge: T. Dixon. London: Wertheim and Co. [1860]).

Edwardes, Lieut.-Col. Sir H., The Safety of a Christian Policy in India. A Speech delivered at the Sixty-first Anniversary Meeting of the Church Missionary Society, 1 May 1860 (London: Church Missionary House, 1860).

Edwardes, R., Extracts from Indian Journals [relating to the Indian Mutiny] (Cheltenham, n.d.).

Edwards, William, Personal Adventures During the Indian Rebellion in Rochilchund, Futtehghur and Oude (London: Smith, Elder and Co., 1859).

Lord Ellenborough's Blunder (Calcutta: Printed by J. Thomas, Baptist Mission Press, 1857).

England's Troubles in India (Tauton: Printed by T. Hiscock, 1857).

Exeter Hall Versus British India (London: Thomas Richard, n.d.).

A Few Remarks Earnestly Addressed to the Men of England, Political and Mercantile, upon the Present Crisis in Indian Affairs (2nd ed.; London: Darton and Co., 1857).

A Few Words on the Red Pamphlet [G.B. Malleson's The Mutiny of the Bengal Army] (3rd. ed.; London: James Ridgeway, 1858).

Firth, W.H.L., Correspondence etc. between the East India Company and W.H.L. Firth, relative to his Claims against the late Kingdom of Oude (London: Printed by Harrison and Co., 1858).

Five Letters to the Editor of the Daily News on Indian Re-Organization ([London]; 1858).

Freeman, John, A Reply to the Memorandum of the East India Company; or, An Insight into British India (London: Robert Hardwicke, 1858).

From London to Lucknow: With Memoranda of Mutinies, Marches, Flights, Fights and Conversations (2 Vols.; London: James Nisbet, 1860).

Frost, Thomas (ed.), Complete Narrative of the Mutiny in India, from its Commencement to the Present Time, Compiled from Most Authentic Sources; Including Many Very Interesting Letters from Officers and others on the Spot (London: Published by Read and Co., n.d.).

The Future of India (London: L. Booth, 1859).

Gardiner, Gen. Sir R., Cursory View of the Present Crisis in India: together with the Military Power of England, respectfully Addressed to the Members of the House of Commons (London: Messrs. Byfield, Hawksworth and Co., 1857).

Gardiner, General Sir R., Military Analysis of the Remote and Proximate Causes of the Indian Rebellion, drawn from the Official Papers of the Government of India.

Respectfully Addressed to the Honourable the Members of the House of Commons (2nd. ed.; London: Byfield, Hawksworth and Co., 1858).

[Gibney, Robert Dwarris], *My Escape from the Mutinies in Oudh* (London: Richard Bentley, 1858).

The Government of India and the Christian Movement in the 24th. Punjab Native Infantry, with a Memorandum by an Officer of the Indian Army (London: Church missionary house, 1861).

The Government of India, As It has Been, As It is, and As it Ought to Be (London: Robert Hardwicke, 1858).

Greathed, H.H., *Letters Written During the Siege of Delhi* ed. by Greathed, Mrs H.H. (London: Longman, Brown, Green, Longmans and Roberts, 1858).

The Great Indian Crisis in Five Minutes' Reading by a General Officer (London: Wm. H. Allen, 1858).

Gubbins, Martin Richard, *An Account of the Mutinies in Oudh, and of the Siege of the Lucknow Residency; with Some Observations on the Condition of the Province of Oudh, and on the Causes of the Mutiny of the Bengal Army* (London: Richard Bentley, 1858).

Hale, William P., *The Oude Question Stated and Considered; with References to Published Official Documents* (London: Smith and Co., 1857).

Hall, James John, *Two Months in Arrah in 1857* (London: Longman, Green, Longmans and Roberts, 1860).

Halliday, F.J., *Grants-in-aid to Mission Schools: minute by F.J. Halliday Esquire, Lieut.-Governor of Bengal, on the Earl of Ellenborough's Letter of 28 April 1858, with Sir George Clark's Memorandum* (London: Church Missionary House, 1859).

Halls, John James, *Two Months at Arrah in 1857* (2nd. ed.; London: Longman, Green, Longman and Roberts, 1860).

Herford, I.S.A., *Stirring Times Under Canvas* (London: Richard Bentley, 1862).

Hodson, Maj. W.S.R., *Twelve Years of a Soldier's Life in India*, ed. by Hodson, The Rev. Geo. H. (2nd. ed.; London: John W. Parker, 1859).

Home Government of India (London: Privately Printed, 1858).

On Home Views of Indian Affairs ([London, 1858]).

Hooper, Frederic E.E., *The Indian Revolt: A Poem in Two Parts* ([London]: Pub. by Robert Hardwick, 1858).

Hough, Lieut.-Col. William, *A Letter to the Court of Proprietors Regarding the Interests of India and Justice Due to the Court of Directors of the East India Company, Who have for More Than Hundred Years Promoted the Commercial Interests etc. of Great Britain* (London: B. Seeley and Co., 1858).

How to Keep India (London: Richardson Bros., 1857).

Hutchinson, Capt. G., *Narrative of the Mutinies in Oudh* (London: Smith, Elder and Co., 1859).

Hymn for the General Thanksgiving for the Suppression of the Indian Rebellion (London: John Henry and James Parker [1858]).

India and its Future; an Address to the People of Great Britain and Their Representatives (London: L. Booth, 1858).

India: Its Dangers Considered in 1856, by a Retired Officer, together with Some Suggestions for the Amelioration of the Condition of that Country and its Millions (Jersey: Joshua Coutanche, 1858).

India Its History, Religion and Government (London: 1858).

India, the Revolt and the Home Government (London: Robert Hardwicke, 1857).

The Indian Crisis–Special General meeting of the Church missionary Society at Exeter Hall, on Tuesday, 12 January 1858 (London; Church missionary House, 1858).

An Indian missionary [Hargrave Jennings], *The Indian Religions; or, Results of Mysterious Buddhism* (London: Printed by Guildford, 1858).

The Indian mutiny to the Evacuation of Lucknow, by a former editor of the *Delhi Gazette* (London: 1858).

The Indian mutiny to the Fall of Delhi, by a former editor of the *Delhi Gazette* (London: G. Routledge and Co., 1857).

The Indian mutiny–Thoughts and Facts (London: Seeley, Jackson and Halliday, 1857).

The Indian Retrospect; or, What has Christian England Done for Heathen India, by the Dean of Carlisle (London: T. Hatchard; Seeley, Jackson and Halliday, 1858).

India's Claim and Britain's Duty (3rd. ed.; Southampton: Printed by Forbes and Bennet, 1858).

Indophilus [Trevelyan, Sir Charles Edward], *The Letters of Indophilus on the Mutiny of Vellore,–its Parallelisms and its Lessons* (Calcutta: Sanders, Cones and Co., [1857])

Indophilus [Trevelyan, Sir Charles Edward], *The Letters of Indophilus to 'The Times' with Additional Notes* (London: Longman, Brown, Green, Longman and Roberts, n.d.).

Inglis, Lady [Sady], *Letter containing Extracts from a Journal kept by Lady Inglis during the Siege of Lucknow* (London: Printed for Private Circulation, 1858).

Investigation into Some of the Causes Which have Produced the Rebellion in India ([London], Printed for Private Circulation, 1857).

Ireland, William W., *History of the Siege of Delhi* (Edinburgh: Adam and Charles Black, 1861).

Jacob, Brig.-Gen. John, *Tracts on the Native Army of India, its Organization and Discipline* (London: Reprinted by Smith, Elder and Co., 1858).

Jeffreys, Julius, *The British Army in India: Its Preservation* (London: Longman, Brown, Green, Longmans and Bros., 1858).

Jones, Capt. Oliver, *Recollections of a Winter Campaign in India, in 1857-58* (London: Saunders and Otley, 1859).

Jones, Ernest, *The Revolt of Hindustan* (Calcutta: Eastern Trading Co., Books and Publications, 1957. Originally published in London by Effingham Wilson in 1857).

Be Just to India; Prevent Famine and Cherish Commerce (Manchester: B. Wheeler, 1861).

Kavanagh, Thomas Henry, *How I Won the Victoria Cross* (London: Ward and Lock, 1860).

Kaye, J[ohn] W[illiam], *Christianity in India. An Historical Narrative* (London: Smith, Elder and Co., 1859).

Kennedy, The Rev. James, *The Great Indian Mutiny of 1857, its Causes, Features and Results* (London: Ward and Co., [1857]).

Khan Bahadoor, Moulvee Mohummud Susseehoodeen, *Oude its Princes, and its Government Vindicated* (London: J. Davy and Sons, 1857).

King, Lieut. Edward, *A Bird's-eye View of India: Showing Our Present Position–its Danger and Remedy* (London: Patridge and Co., 1857).

Kingsmill, Sir Joseph, *British Rule and British Christianity in India* (London: Longman, Green, longmans and Roberts, 1859).

Kinloch, C.W., *The Mutinies in the Bengal* (London: Simpkin and Marshall, 1858).

A Lady's Diary of the Siege of Lucknow, written for the Perusal of Friends at Home (London: John Murray. New York: Henry Lyon and Co., 1858).

The Lament of an Indian Officer. A Poem.

Lang, John, Wanderings in India, and Other Sketches of Life in Hindostan (London: Routledge, Warne and Routhorpe, 1859).

Laverack, Alfred, A Methodist Soldier in the Indian Army. His Personal Adventures and Christian Experience (3rd. ed.; London: T. Woolner, n.d.).

Lawrence, Henry Montgomery, Essays: Military and Political (London: Wm. H. Allen and Co., 1859).

Lawrence, John, Despatches by Sir John Lawrence, G.C.B., Chief Commissioner of the Punjab, on Christianity in India (London: Church Missionary House, 1858).

Lawrence, J.B., Six Years in the North-West, from 1854 to 1860, being Extracts from a Private Diary, with a glimpse of the Rebellion of 1857-58 (Calcutta: G.C. Hay and Co. Allahabad: T. Andrews, n.d.).

Leckey, Edward, Fictions Connected with the Indian Outbreak of 1857 Exposed (Bombay; Chesson and Woodhall, 1859).

Lee, J., The Indian Mutiny: Events at Cawnpore, June 1857 (Lucknow: The London Printing Press).

A Letter from a Layman in India on the Policy of the East India Company in Matters of Religion (London: W.H. Dalton, 1858).

Letters from Futtehghur (Clifton: Shepherd, n.d.).

Lewin, Malcolm, The Way to Lose India (London: James Ridgeway, 1857).

Lewin, Malcolm, The Way to Regain India (London: James Ridgeway, 1858).

Lewin, Malcolm, The Government of the East India Company and its Monopolies; or, the Young Indian Party and Free Trade (2nd. ed.; London: James Ridgeway, 1857).

Lewin, Malcolm, Has Oude been Worse Governed by its Native Princes than Our Indian Territories by Leadenhall Street? (London: James Ridgeway, 1857).

Lewin, Malcolm (ed.), Causes of the Indian Revolt, by a Hindu of Bengal (London: Ed. Stanford, 1857).

Lowe, Thomas, Central India during the Rebellion of 1857-58 (London: Longman, Green, Longman and Roberts, 1860).

Ludlow, John Malcolm, Thoughts on the Policy of the Crown towards India (London: James Ridgeway, 1859).

Ludlow, John Malcolm, The War in Oude (Cambridge: Macmillan and Co., 1858).

Ludlow, John Malcolm, British India, its Races, and its History, Considered with reference to the Mutiny of 1857; A Series of Lectures Addressed to the Students of the Working Men's College (Two Vols.; Cambridge: Macmillan, 1858).

Majendie, Lieut. Vivan, Up among the Pandies: or, A Year's Service in India (London: Routledge, Warne and Routledge, 1859).

[Malleson, Col. G.B.], The Mutiny of the Bengal Army (Two Parts; London: Bosworth and Harrison, 1858).

Marlborough, The Duke of, Exclusion of the Bible from Government Schools (London: W.H. Dalton, 1860).

Martin, R. Montgomery, The Indian Empire—with a Full Account of the Mutiny of the Bengal Army; of the Insurrection in Western India; and an Exposition of Alleged Causes (Vol. II; London: The London Printing and Publishing Co., n.d.).

Mather, The Rev. R.C., Christian Missions in India. On the Present State and Prospects of Christian Missions in India; and the Duty of the Churches at the Present Crisis of our Indian Affairs (London: John Snow, 1858).

Mequeen, Kenneth, *Who is to Blame for the Indian Mutinies* (Edinburgh: Thomas Constable and Co. London: Hamilton Adams and Co., 1857).

Mead, Henry, *The Sepoy Revolt: its Causes and its Consequences* (London: John Murray 1857).

Mecham, Clifford Henry, *Sketches and Incidents of the Siege of Lucknow,* From drawings made during the Siege by Clifford Henry Mecham (London: Day and Son, 1858).

Medley, Julius George, *A Year's Campaigning in India, March 1857 to March 1858* (London: W. Thacker and Co. Calcutta: Thacker Spinner and Co. Allahabad: J. Hill and Co. 1858).

Meek, The Rev. R., *The Martyr of Allahabad, Memorials of Ensign Arthur Marcus Hill Cheek of the 6th. N.B.I., Murdered by the Sepoys at Allahabad* (London: James Nisbet, 1858).

A Memorial to the Queen from the Church Missionary Society on the Religious Policy of the Government of India, with an Explanatory Statement on the Past and Present Policy of the Indian Government in Respect to Religion, and the Education of Natives Occasional Papers on India, No. 1 (2nd. ed.; London: Church Missionary House, 1858).

Mercer, Edward Smith, *A Letter to the Rt. Hon, the Earl of Ellenborough, on the Military, Religious and European Settlement Questions in the East Indies* (London: Edward Whitehead, 1861).

The Moslem and Hindoo. A Poem on the Sepoy Revolt (London: Saunders and Otley, 1858).

The Moral of the Indian Debate (London: William Penny, 1858).

Mullen, The Rev. J., *The Queen's Government and the Religions of India* (London: Ward and Co., 1859).

The Mutiny in India.—A Well Known Intelligent Christian Gentleman's Letter, long resident in Calcutta, to the Honorary Clerical Secretary of the Church Missionary Society, dated at Calcutta, 13 July 1857 (London: T.C. Johns, n.d.).

The Mutiny in the Bengal Army (London: John Chapman, 1857).

My Escape from the Mutinies in Oudh (Two Vols.; London: Richard Bentley, 1858).

Napier, The Rt. Hon. Joseph, *The Bible in Government Schools in India, Speech delivered at the Annual Meeting of the Church Missionary Society, held at Exeter Hall, 30 April 1861* (London: W.H. Dalton, 1861).

Narrative of the Indian Revolt from its Outbreak to the Capture of Lucknow by Sir Colin Campbell (London: Geog. Vickers, 1858).

Noel, The Rev. Baptist Wriothesley, *England and India–An Essay on the Duty of Englishmen towards the Hindoos* (London: James Nisbet and Co., 1859).

Nolan, Dr. Edward Henry, *The Illustrated History of the British Empire in India and the East, from the Earliest Times to the Suppression of the Sepoy Mutiny in 1859* (2nd Vol; London: publisher not given, n.d.).

Norman, Maj. H.W., *Campaigning with the Delhi Army* (London: W.H. Dalton, 1858).

North, Maj. Charles Bruce, *Journal of an English Officer in India* (London: Hurst and Blackett, 1858).

Norton, George, *Proselytism in India; the Questions at Issue Examined in a Letter to Sir George Clark, K.C.B., etc., with an Appendix containing an Account of the Recent Tinnevelly Slaughter* (London: Richardson Bros. 1859).

Norton, John Bruce, *The Rebellion in India; How to Prevent Another* (London: Richardson Bros. 1857).

Observations on the Late Events in the Bengal Presidency (Jersey: Joshua Coutanche, 1857).

Observations on the Proposed Council of India (London: William Penny, 1858).

Olrich, Leopold Von, *Military mutiny in India; Its Origin and Its Results, with Observations by Maj.-Gen. Sir W.M. Colebrooke,* trans. Anonymously (London: T. and W. Brone, 1859).

O'Malley, P.F., *Religious Liberty and the Indian Proclamation* (London: W.R. Dalton, 1859).

The Oude Catchism or Answers to Questions Concerning Oude, its History and its Wrongs (London: J. Davy and Sons, 1857).

Outram, Maj.-Gen. [Sir James], *Outram's Campaign in India, 1857-58; comprising General Orders and Despatches Relating to the Defence and Relief of Lucknow Garrison, and Capture of the City by the British Forces,* ed. Anonymously (London: Smith, Elder and Co., 1860).

Owen, The Rev. Williams, *Memorials of Christian Martyrs and Other Officers for the Truth in India* (London: Simpkon, Marshall and Co., 1858).

Parker, Henry Meredith, *The Empire of the Middle Classes* (London: W. Thacker and Co. Calcutta: Thacker, Spink and Co. Bombay: Thacker and Co., 1858).

Peter the Pearker (pseud.) *Caste in India, Caste Everywhere. How to Keep or Lose an Empire* (London: J. Heaton, 1858).

Plain Speaker (John Henry Temple), *Justice for India. A Letter to Lord Palmerston* (London: Robert Hardwick, 1858).

Polehampton, The Rev. Henry S., *A Memoir, Letters and Diary of...,* ed. Polehampton, The Rev. Edward and Polehampton, The Rev. Thomas Stedman (London: Richard Bentley, 1858).

The Policy as Established by Law of the Indian Government, Opposed to the Neutral Policy in Respect of Christianity, Occasional Papers on India, No. IX (London: Church Missionary House, 1860).

Practical Observations on the First Two of the Proposed Resolutions on the Government of India (London: William Penny, 1858).

Pratt, Hodgson, *A Few Words on the Question of Teaching the Bible in Government Schools in India* (London: Chapman and Hall, 1859).

The Present Crisis in India, Reflections (London: John Chapman, 1857).

A President in Council the Best Government for India (London: William Penny, 1858).

Prichard, I., *The Mutinies in Rajputana* (London: J.W. Parker, 1860).

A Psalm of Lamentation and Supplication to Almighty God Concerning India (London: Simpsons and Co. Salisbury: Brown and Co. 1857).

Raikes, Chalres, *Notes on the Revolt in the North-Western Provinces of India* (London: Longman, Brown, Green, Longmans and Roberts, 1858).

The Real Difficulties in Bengal, and How to Settle Them? (London: Smith, Elder and Co., 1861).

Recent Policy of the Indian Government in respect of Christianity in India, Occasional Papers on India, No. VIII (London: Church Missionary House, 1860).

Rees, L.E. Ruutz, *A Personal Narrative of the Siege of Lucknow, from its Commencement to its Relief by Sir Colin Campbell* (London: Longman, Brown, Green, Longmans, and Roberts, 1858).

Rees, L.E. Ruutz, *Oude, its Past and its Future* (London: Longman, Brown, Green, Longmans and Roberts, 1859).

Religious Neutrality in India—Delusive and Impracticable, Occasional Papers on India, No. IV (London: Church Missionary House, 1858).

Richard, Henry, *The Present and Future of India under British Rule* (2nd. ed.; London: Ward and Co., 1858).

Robertson, H. Dundas, *District Duties during the Revolt in the North-West Provinces of India in 1857: with Remarks on the Subsequent Investigations during 1858-59* (London: Smith, Elder and Co., 1859).

Robertson, Thomas Campbell, *The Political Prospects of British India* (London: Thomas Hatchard, 1858).

Rotton, The Rev. J.E.W., *The Chaplain's Narrative of the Siege of Delhi. From the Outbreak at Meerut to the Capture of Delhi* (London: Smith, Elder and Co., 1858).

Russell, William Howard, *My Diary in India* (Two Vols.; 7th Thousand; London: Routledge, Warne and Co., 1860).

Scenes From the Late Indian Mutinies (in verse), (London: John and Charles Morley, 1858).

Scrutator [Sir Benjamin C. Brodie], *English Tenure of India. Practical Remarks Suggested by the Bengal Mutiny* (London: Smith, Elder and Co., 1857).

Scrutator [Sir Benjamin C. Brodie], *The Indian Mutiny* (London: W. Kent and Co., 1857).

Seaton, Maj.-Gen. Sir Thomas, *From Cadet to Colonel* (Two Vols.; London: Hurst and Blackett, 1858).

Shaftesbury, The Earl of, *England's Apostacy in India and the Earl of Shaftesbury's Great Speech on Indian Cruelties, delivered at Wimborne* (London: Published by Patridge and Co., [1857]).

Sherring, The Rev. M.A., *The Indian Church during the Great Rebellion: An Authentic Narrative of Disasters that Befell it; its Sufferings; and Faithfulness unto Death of many of its European and Native Members* (London: James Nisbet and Co., 1859).

A Short Review of the Present Crisis in India (Dublin: McGlashan and Gill, 1857).

[Sinclair, W.], *The Sepoy Mutinies: Their Origin and their Cure* (London: Wertheim and Macintosh, 1857).

Sleeman, W.H., *Journey Through the Kingdom of Oudh* (Two Vols.; London: Bentley, 1858).

State Intervention in the Religions of India (A letter dated at Calcutta, 20 July 1857).

Stocqueler, J.H., *India; its History, Climate, Products, with a Full Account of the Origin, Progress and Development of the Bengal Mutiny and Suggestions as to the Future Government of India* (London: George Routledge and Co., 1857).

The Storming of Delhi, 20 September 1857 (London: T. Goode n.d.).

Storrow, Edward, *India and Christian Missions* (London: 1859).

Stracham, J.M., *A Letter to Captain Eastwick, Occasioned by his Speech at a Special Court of Proprietors held at the East India House, on the 20th of January 1858* (London: Seeley, Jackson and Halliday, 1858).

Straith, Hector, *The Indian Missionaries* (London: Church missionary house, [1857-58]).

Sullivan, Edward, *Letters on India* (London: Saunders and Otley, 1858).

Sykes, Lieut.-Col. W.H., *The Speech of...on the India Bill–(No. 3) in the House of Commons, on Monday, 26 July 1858* (London: Printed and Published by Cornelius Buck, [1858]).

Sykes, Lieut.-Col. W.H., *Speech of...in the House of Commons on Thursday, 18 February 1858 on the Proposed India Bill, with Notes and Appendices* (London: Smith, Elder and Co., 1858).

Sylvester, John Henry, *Recollections of the Campaign in Malwa and Central India* (Bombay: Smith, Taylor and Co., 1860).

Taylor, Meadows, *Letters from Meadows Esqr., Deputy Commissioner of the ceded Districts in the Deccan, written during the Indian Rebellion, 1857* (London: Printed by John Edward Taylor, 1857).

Taylor, William, *The Patna Crisis* (3rd. ed.; W.H. Allen and Co., 1857).

Thomas, J.F., *Bible Education in India, Some Objections Considered* (London: W.H. Dalton, 1860).

Thomas, J.F., *The Bible in India* (London: T.C. John, 1857).

Thomas, J.F., *Christianity in India* (London: T.C. John, n.d.).

Thomson, Capt. Mowbray, *The Story of Cawnpore,* (London: Richard Bentley, 1859).

The Thoughts of a Native of Northern India on the Rebellion, its Causes and Remedies (London: W.H. Dalton, 1858).

The Timely Retreat, or, A Year in Bengal Before the Mutinies, (Two vols.; London: Richard Bentley, 1858).

Trevor, George, *India; its Natives and Missions* (London: The Religious Tract Society, [1859]).

Trevor, George, *India. An Historical Sketch* (London: The Religious Tract Society, [1858]).

The Truth About Oudh (Calcutta: Baptist Mission Press, [1858]).

Tucker, Henry Carre, *Letter to the Rt. Hon. Lord Stanley, M.P., Secretary of State for India* (London: W.H. Dalton, 1857).

Tucker, Henry Carre, *A Letter to an Officer Concerned in the Education of India* (W.H. Dalton, 1858).

Tucker, Henry Carre, *A Letter on Oudh and its Talookdars,* No Publisher, [1858]).

Tweedale, The Marquis of, *Minute of the Marquis of Tweedale on the Introduction of Bible as a Classbook into Government Schools in India,* Occasional Papers on India, No. VII (London: Church Mission House, 1859).

Unquhart, David, *The Rebellion of India* (London: D. Bryce, 1857).

Unquhart, David, *The Rebellion in India. The Wondrous Tale of the Greased Cartridges* (London: Bryce, [1857]).

Urquhart, David, *The Sraddha, the Keystone of the Brahminical, Budhistic, and Arian Religions, as Illustrative of the Dogma and Duty of Adoption among the Princes and the People of India* (Fourth ed.; London: Pub. by David Bryce, 1858).

Urquhart, David, [Speech of] *Mr Urquhart in Newcastle, 27 May 1858* (Newcastle-Upon-Tyne: Printed by Andrew Carr).

Venn, Henry, *A Plea for Open and Unfetterd Bible in the Government Schools of India* (London: W.M. Watts, 1859).

Verney, Edmund Hope, *The Shanon's Brigade in India: Being some Account of Sir William Peel's Naval Brigade in the Indian Campaign of 1857-58* (London: Saunders Otley and Co., 1862).

A Voice from India to the Men of Manchester (by a Manchester Man), (Manchester: Joseph Pratt, 1858).

Walayat Ali of Delhi: A Martyr's Narrative of the Great Indian Mutiny of 1857 (London: Pub. by T. Pewtress and Co. for the Baptist Church Missionary Society, 1858).

Wallace, The Rev. James, *The Revolt in India: Its Causes and its Lessons. A Lecture Delivered in Belfast, on 2 February 1859* (Belfast: C. Aitchison, 1859).

What Shall We do to the Mussulmans (Calcutta: Sanders, Cones and Co., 1858).

Watson, Edward Spencer, *A Naval Cadet with H.M.S. Shanon's Brigade in India* (Kettering: W.E. and J. Goss, n.d.).

Weitbrecht, Mrs, *Missionary sketches in Northern India with reference to recent events* (2nd. ed.; London; Nisbet and Co., 1859).

Wheeler, Edmund, *What Shall We Do at Delhi? An Englishman's Letter to The Humanitarians* (London: Daniel F. Okey, 1857).

Williamson, George, *Notes on the Wounded from the Mutiny in India* (London: John Churchil, 1859).

Wilson, John, D.D., *The Indian Military Revolt Viewed in its Religious Aspects* (London: Smith, Elder and Co. Bombay: Smith, Taylor and Co. Edinburgh: W. Whtye and Co., 1857).

Wylie, M., *The English Captives in Oudh: An Episode in the History of the Mutinies of 1857-58* (London: W.H. Dalton. Calcutta: G.C. Hay and Co., 1858).

Young, William Richard, *A Few Words on the Indian Question* (London: Smith, Elder and Co., 1858).

D) Sermons on the Indian Mutiny:

Sermons represented not only a distinct body of opinion on the revolt in India, but they also reveal the extent to which the pulpit influenced or attempted to influence the trend of public opinion. They were published either as pamphlets, or were contributed to church and missionary periodicals, or else in *The Pulpit*, which was a collection of sermons published every three or six months. In the case of sermons almost all of them carried the names of the preachers.

Only those sermons have been included here which were published as independent pamphlets, or which appeared in a collection of sermons, i.e., *The Pulpit*, *The Fast-day Sermons*. *The 'Indian Mutiny' Twelve Sermons*. All those sermons which appeared in periodicals, church or missionary, have been, like other periodical articles in section E, excluded from this list.

After Deliverance Trail (A sermon preached to a country congregation, on Sunday, 1 May 1859, being the Day of Thanksgiving for the restoration of peace in India), (London: Ravington, 1859).

Allon, The Rev. Henry, *Indian Rule and Responsibility* (A sermon delivered on 7 October 1857, being the Day of National Humiliation, Fasting and Prayer), (London: Aylott and Co., 1857).

Baillie, The Rev. John, *God's Avenger: or, England's Present Duty in India with a Glance at the Future* (preached on 7 October 1857), (London: Jackson and Halliday, 1857).

Beechey, The Rev. St. Vincent, *India, the Source of Wealth and Ruin to the Principal Nations of Antiquity,* (delivered on 7 October 1857), (Manchester: Hale and Roworwth. London: Rivington, 1857).

Blatch, The Rev. William, 'National Sins and Individual Responsibility', (preached on 13 September 1857), *The Pulpit*, LXXII, 1858, pp. 349-53.

Boswell, The Rev. R.B., *Hope for India in England's God,* (preached on 26 August 1857), (London: Seeley, Jackson and Halliday, 1857).

Brock, The Rev. William, 'A Christian Soldier', (a funeral sermon preached on 17 January 1858, occasioned by the death of the late Gen. Havelock), *The Pulpit*, XLIII, 1858, pp. 64-72.

Brooks, The Rev. Harvey, *God's Displeasure as provoked by Indian Heathenism and Anglo-Saxon Policy*, (preached on 7 October 1857), (London: Thomas Richard, 1857).

Cadman, The Rev. Carlisle, The Bishop of and others, *The Fast-day Sermons*. The '*Indian Mutiny*' *Twelve Sermons* (Each sermon was preached by a different preacher in different parts of the United Kingdom), (London: J.A. Berger, 1857).

Cadman, The Rev. William, 'The Wide Proclamation of the Gospel among the Heathen', (preached on 26 February 1858), *The Pulpit*, LXXIII, 1858, pp. 221-8.

Cairns, The Rev. John, *The Indian Crisis, Viewed as a Call to Prayer: A Discourse* (preached on Lord's Day), (Berwick: Melrose and Plenderleith. Edinburgh: William Oliphant. Glasgow: David Robertson. London: Houlston and Wright, 1857).

Cartie, The Rev. Jos. Mac., *Judgment Salutary or the Lesson Taught by the Present Crisis in India* (preached on 7 October 1857), (Manchester: John Gray Bell. London: James Rimell. Dublin: George Herbert, 1857).

Cator, The Rev. Charles, 'The Mutiny in India and its Causes', (preached on 7 October 1857), *The Pulpit*, LXXII, 1858, pp. 415-20.

Charles, The Rev. James, *The Lord's Voice to Britain from the Far East*, (preached on 7 October 1857), (Edinburgh and Glasgow: Paton and Ritche and T. Murray and Son respectively, 1857).

Charlesworth, The Rev. Samuel, 'National Righteousness a Nation's Safety', (preached on 13 September 1857), *The Pulpit*, LXXII, 1858, pp. 270-5.

Curteis, The Rev. G.N., *The Evangelization of India* (preached on 22 November 1857), (Oxford and London: J.H. and James Parker, Lichfield: Lomerx, 1857).

Dale, The Rev. Thomas, 'God's Judgment in the Earth', (preached on 7 October 1857), *The Pulpit*, LXXII, 1858, pp. 338–43. Also published by J. Berger in their collection of twelve sermons on the Indian mutiny.

Daniel, The Rev., Bishop of Calcutta and Metropolitan in India, *Humiliation in National Troubles* (preached on 24 July 1857), (Calcutta: T.J. M'Arthur, Bishop's College Press, 1857), Dr Daniel Wilson.

Daniel, The Rev. Bishop of Calcutta and Metropolitan in India, *Prayer the Refuge of a Distressed Church*, (preached on 28 June 1857), (Calcutta: T.J. M'Arthur, Bishop's College Press), 1857), Dr Daniel Wilson.

Davis, The Rev. James, 'India and Recent Events in their Relations to Christianity', (preached on 13 September 1857), *The Pulpit*, LXXII, 1858, pp. 315–9.

Dixon, The Rev. James, *The Sword of the Lord in the Indian Crisis*, (preached on 7 October 1857), (London: John Mason, Manchester: Galt, Kerruish and Gent, n.d.).

East, The Rev. Edward, *A Few Thoughts Suggested by the Present State of Affairs in India*, (preached on 7 October 1857), (Hounslow: J. Gotelee, n.d.).

Fenn, The Rev. Joseph, *Britain's Burdens and Causes of Punishment* (preached on 7 October 1857), (London: W.H. Dalton, 1857).

Garden, The Rev. Francis, *Vengeance Right and Holy*, (preached on 7 October 1857), (London: Rivington. Edinburgh: Grant and Son, 1857).

Glover, The Rev. Richard, 'Queen Esther an Example of Intercession: A Pastor's Plea for India', (preached on 30 August 1857), *The Pulpit*, LXXII, 1858, pp. 320–4.

Gurney, The Rev. John Hampdon, *The Moral of a Sad Story, Four Sermons on the Indian Mutiny* (London: Ravington, 1857).

Hardinge, The Rev. John, *Hopes for the Future* (A Lecture delivered in St. Mary's Church, Poona, on 26 August 1857), (Bombay; 1857).

Hingston, The Rev. George Cotter, 'Indian Crisis: Its Lessons for Home Use', (preached on 7 October 1857), *The Pulpit*, LXXII, 1858, pp. 420–8.

Hoare, The Rev. Edward, 'The Mutiny in India in Relation to Mahometanism and its Appointed Issues', (The fourth of a course of twelve lectures on 'The Signs of Time', delivered on 2 March 1858), *The Pulpit*, LXXIII, 1858, pp. 241–7.

Hoare, The Rev. Edward, *England's Stewardship*, (preached on 7 October 1857), (London: Thomas Hatchard, 1857).

An Indian Mutiny Sermon, (London: James Darling, 1857).

Indian Mutiny and England's Mourning, or Thoughts for the Fast Day, 7 October 1857. (London: Hatchard and Wertheim and Macintosh, 1857).

Jessopp, The Rev. John, 'Indian Rebellion', (preached on 7 October 1857), *The Pulpit*, LXXII, 1858, pp. 357-61.

Jones, The Rev. Alfred, 'Lamentation and Woe Follow in the Steps of Unfaithfulness to God', (preached on 7 October 1857), *The Pulpit*, LXXII, pp. 511–6.

Keane, The Rev. William, *The Present Crisis in India* (preached on 7 September 1857), (York: Printed by J.L. Foster, 1857).

Kell, The Rev. Edmund, *A Sermon Preached on 11 October 1857, at the Chapel, Canal Walk, Southampton* (5th Ed.; London: E.T. Whitfield. Southampton: Forbes and Benett, 1858).

Kell, The Rev. Edmund, *Rev. Edmund Kell in Reply to a Reviewer of his Sermon, entitled 'What Patriotism, Justice and Christianity Demand for India'* (London: E.T. Whitfield, 1858).

Kidd, The Rev. Richard B.R., 'The Occasion of Queen's Proclamation', (preached on 7 October 1857), *The Pulpit*, LXXII, 1858, pp. 412–4.

Kidd, The Rev. Richard B.R., 'Causes of the Indian Mutiny', (preached on 7 October 1857), *The Pulpit*, LXXII, 1858, pp. 449–52.

Laughlin, The Rev. John William, 'The Devout Soldier', (preached on 24 January 1858, in reference to the death of Gen. Havelock), *The Pulpit*, LXXIII, 1858, pp. 117–24.

Macgregor, The Rev. Sir C., *India* (preached on 7 October 1857), (London: Longman and Co. Caistor: George Parker, n.d.).

Magurie, The Rev. Robert, 'The Indian Mutiny', (preached on 16 August 1857), *The Pulpit*, LXXII, 1858, pp. 165–72.

Massingham, The Rev. J.D., 'The Propriety of Seeking God in the Time of National Trouble', (preached on 7 October 1857), *The Pulpit*, LXXII, 1858, pp. 388–92.

Massingham, The Rev. J.D., 'The Rebellion of the Sepoys Traced to its True Source', (preached on 7 October 1857), *The Pulpit*, LXXII, 1858, pp. 393–8.

Maurice, The Rev. F.D., *The Indian Crisis: Five Sermons*, (Cambridge: Macmillan and Co., 1857).

Melvill, The Rev. Henry, 'Thanksgiving', (preached on 1 May 1859, the Day of General Thanksgiving for the Success in India), *The Pulpit*, LXXV, 1859, pp. 421–6.

Moffat, The Very Rev. Hugh B., 'Victory and Thanksgiving', (preached on 1 May 1859, the Day of General Thanksgiving for the recent success in India), *The Pulpit*, LXXV, 1858, pp. 580–2.

Money, The Rev. C.F.S., *The Indian Mutiny; or, India's Idolatry and England's Responsibility* (preached on 7 October 1857), (London: Wertheim and Macintosh, 1857). Also published under the same title in the *Church of England Magazine*, XLIII, 1857, pp. 406–8.

Monk, The Rev. E.G., 'Our Duty to Ourselves and to Our Indian Brethren', (preached on 7 October 1857), *The Pulpit*, LXXII, 1858, pp. 504-10.

Mursell, The Rev. James, *Our Relations with India, and the Lessons to be Derived from the Events passing in that Country* (A Discourse delivered in the Baptist Chaper Kettering, on 11 October 1857), (London: J. Heaton and Son. Leister: J. Burton. Kettering: J. Toller, 1857).

Newman, The Rev. W.J., 'Our Mercies in the Past and Our Prospects for the Future', (preached on 1 May 1859, being the Day of General Thanksgiving for the success in India), *The Pulpit*, LXXV, 1859, pp. 441-5.

Nicholson, The Rev. Aldwell J., 'Peace in India', (preached on 1 May 1859, being the Day of General Thanksgiving for the success in India), *The Pulpit*, LXXV, 1859, pp. 446-9.

Nicholson, The Rev. Maxwell, *Britain's Guilt and Duty with Reference to Her Indian Empire* (Edinburgh: Paton and Ritchie. Glasgow: Thomas Murray and Son, 1857).

Porter, The Rev. J. Leech, *National Christianity for India, or National Acts and National Duties* (preached on 7 October 1857), (London: Wertheim and Macintosh, 1857).

Prayer for our Cause in India. A Sermon (London: 1857).

Puckle, The Rev. John, *Heathen Sin Through Fault* (preached on 7 October 1857), (Dover: Printed by W. Batcheller, n.d.).

Redwar, The Rev. T.R., 'The Uncertainty of Life', (preached on New Year's Day, 1 January 1858), *The Pulpit*, LXXIII, 1858, pp. 43-6.

Reeve, The Rev. John William, 'Our Duty to India', (preached on 1 May 1857), *The Pulpit*, LXXV, 1858, pp. 437-40.

Salmon, The Rev. George, *The Indian Mutiny and Missions* (A sermon preached on behalf of the Church missionary Society, on 5 September 1857), (Dublin: Madden and Macintosh. London: Wertheim and Macintosh, 1857).

A Sermon preached in the Catholic Apostolic Church, Gordon Square, on Wednesday, 7 October 1857, the day appointed for National Humiliation (London: Bosworth and Harrison, 1857).

A Sermon, preached on Sunday, 4 October 1857, preceding the Day of Humiliation, appointed for Wednesday, 7 October 1857 (Winchester: Hugh Barclay, 1857).

Sinclair, The Ven. John, *Carthaginian and British Mercenaries Compared,* (preached on 7 October 1857), (London: Ravington, 1857).

Squire, The Rev. E.B., *God's Prolonged Controversy with Britain,* (preached on 7 October 1857), (Swansea: Printed at Cambrian Office, 1857).

Statham, The Rev. Francis, 'The Indian Mutiny', (preached on 13 September 1857), *The Pulpit*, LXXII, 1858, pp. 276-80.

Stovel, The Rev. Charles, *India: Its Crimes and Claims* (A lecture delivered on the Fast-day, 7 October 1857, and by special request re-delivered on Wednesday, 14 October 1857, in the Commercial St. Chapel at the earnest request of those who heard of its circulation), (London: Jackson and Walford, 1857).

Thanksgiving Thoughts on the Indian Mutiny (London: James Darling, 1859).

Thompson, The Rev. Edward, 'The Signs of Time', (preached on 6 September 1857), *The Pulpit*, LXXII, pp. 244-52.

Venables, The Rev. George, 'Shall Our Troubles in India Return?' (preached on 8 May 1859), *The Pulpit*, LXXV, 1859, pp. 599-604.

Venables, The Rev. George, 'But What? Even Now', (preached on 7 October 1857), *The Pulpit*, LXXII, pp. 359-65.

Whitehead, The Rev. Edward, *I Wrought For My Name's Sake* (preached on 7 October 1857), (London: Thomas Hatchard. Jersey: S.C. Gossett, 1857).

[Wordsworth, The Rev.], *A Plea for India* (preached in the Westminster Abbey, on Sunday, 27 September 1857), ([London]: n.d.).

E)   **Periodical Literature:**

Periodicals, church, missionary and lay, provided a wealth of material in the shape of articles, sermons, diaries, journals, editorials, dialogues, poems, letters, extracts of letters and on the spot reports. The importance of these cannot be overemphasized.

Annual Register (London: printed for F. and J. Rivington; Longman and Co.; Hamilton and Co. etc.), 1857-62.

The Athanaeum, (London: Published and Printed respectively by J. Francis and James Holmes), 1855-60.

Baptist Magazine, (London: Pewtress and Co. and J. Heaton and Son), 1857-59, Vols. XLIX-LI.

Blackwood's Edinburgh Magazine, (Edinburgh: William Blackwood and Son), 1856-60, Vols. LXXIX-LXXXVIII.

British Controversialist (London: Houlston and Wright), 1857-58.

British Quarterly Review, (London: Jackson and Walford), 1857-60, Vols. XXV-XXXII.

The Builder, (London: Conducted by George Godwin) 1857-60, Vols. XV-XVIII.

Chambers's Journal of Popular Literature, Science and Arts, (London: William and Robert Chambers), 1857-60, Vols. XXVII-XXXIV.

Christian Spectator, (Monthly), (London: Houlston and Wright. Edinburgh: Adam and Charles Black), 1857-59, Vols. VII-IX.

Church Missionary Intelligencer (London: Seeley, Jackson, and Halliday), 1857-59, Vols. VIII-X.

Church Missionary Record (London: Seeley, Jackson, and Halliday), New Series, 1857-59, Vols. II-IV.

Church of England Magazine, (London: William Hughs) 1857-59, Vols. XLIII-XLVII.

Church of England Quarterly Review, (London: Patridge and Co.), 1857-58, Vols. XLII-XLIV.

Dublin University Magazine, (Dublin: Hedges, Smith, and Co.), 1857-59, Vols. IL-LIV.

Eclectic Review (London: Ward and Co.), New Series, 1857-60, Vols. I-VII. (In the endnotes I forgot to list the series in the case of Vol. II. The reader should not be confused by this omission).

Edinburgh Review (Edinburgh: Longman, Brown, Green, Longmans and Roberts), 1856-60, Vols. CIII-CXI.

Evangelical Magazine and Missionary Chronicle (London: Ward and Co.), New Series, 1857-59, Vols. XXXV-XXXVII.

The Family Friend (London: Ward and Lock), 1857-61.

Fraser's Magazine (London: John W. Parker and Son), 1856-60, Vols. LIII-LXII.

Gentleman's Magazine, New Series (London: John Henry and James Parker), 1857-62, Vols. III-XIII.

Household Words (London: Conducted by Charles Dickens), 1857-58, Vols. XVI-XVIII.

Illustrated London News (London: William Little), 1857-62.

Leisure Hour (London: Printed by William Stevens), 1857-60.

Literary Gazette and Journal of Archaology, Science and Arts (in the book referred to as *Literary Gazette*), (London: Printed and Published by Lovell Reeve), 1857-June 1858, Vol. numbers not given, New Series (London: Printed by Bradburg and Evans), July 1858-1859, Vols. I-III.

London Journal and Weekly Record of Literature, Science, and Arts (London: G. Vickers), 1857-58, Vols. XXIV-XXVIII.

London Quarterly Review, (Dublin: John Robertson London: Alexander Haylin), 1857-58, Vols. IX-X.

London University Magazine (London: Arthur Hall, Virtue And Co.), 1856-58, Vols. I-III.

Missionary Herald (London: Then printed by Pewtress and Co. and J. Heaton and Son for the Baptist Missionary Society as a section of the *Baptist Magazine*), 1857-59, Vols. XLIX-LI.

Missionary Magazine and Chronicle (London: Pub. by the Directors of the London Missionary Society), 1857-59, Vols. XXI-XXIII and New Series, 1860, Vol. I.

National Review (London: Chapman and Hall), 1857-58, Vols. IV-VII.

Notes and Queries (London: Bell and Daldy), Second Series, 1857-61, Vols. II-XII.

The Punch (London: Printed and Published by William Bradbury and Frederic Mullet Evans), 1857-62, Vols. XXXII-XLIII.

Quarterly Review (London: John Murray), 1857-62, Vols. CI-CXII.

The Spectator (London: Pub. by Joseph Clayton), 1857-62.

Saturday Review (London: J.W. Parker and Son), 1857-62.

United-Presbyterian Magazine (Edinburgh: William Oliphant and Co. London: Houlston and Wright), New Series, 1857-59, Vols. I-III.

Wesleyan-Methodist Magazine (London: Pub. by John Mason), Fifth Series, 1857-60, Vols. III-VI.

Westminster Review (London: John Chapman), New Series, 1857-60, Vols. XII-XVIII.

F)   Newspapers (Dailies, Biweeklies and Weeklies):

Daily Scotsman, Edinburgh, 1857-58.

Daily Telegraph, London, 1857-58.

The Examiner, London, 1857-60.

Free Press, London, 1857-58.

Manchester Guardian, Manchester, 1854-60.

The Nation, Dublin, 1857-60.

People's paper, London, 1857-58 (discont'd. on 4 September 1858).

The Press, London, 1857-61.

Reynolds' Newspaper (Reynolds' Weekly Newspaper), London, 1857-58.

The Scotsman, Edinburgh, 1857-60.

The Tablet, London, 1857-61.

The Times, London, 1857-61.

Weekly Dispatch, London, 1857-58.

G)   Materials published after 1862

These were published by those who were personally involved in the mutiny or in forming British public opinion when it was a subject of intense controversy. These works were published too late to influence public opinion during the years of controversy but throw light on attitudes of participants and controversialists:

Adye, Sir John, *Recollections of a Military Life* (London: Smith, Elder, 1895).

Alexander, Lieut.-Col. William Gorden, *Recollections of a Highland Subaltern, during the Campaigns in India, 1857-59* (London: Edward Arnold, 1898).

Anson, Octavius Henry St. George, *With H.M. 9th Lancers during the Indian Mutiny. The Letters of Brevet-Major...,* ed. H.S. Anson (London: W.H. Allen, 1896).

Bagley, F.R., '1857 A Small Boy in the Indian Mutiny', *Blackwood's,* 1930, CCXXVII, pp. 427-42.

Bennett, Mrs Amelie, 'Ten Months' Captivity After the Massacre at Cawnpore', *Nineteenth Century,* Part I, 1913, LXXIII, pp. 1212-34, Part II, 1913, LXXIV, pp. 78-91.

Bonham, John, *Oude in 1857: Some Memories of the Indian Mutiny* (London: William and Norgate, 1928).

Bright, John, *Speeches on Questions of Public Policy by...,* M.P., ed. Rogers, James E. Thorold, (2nd. ed.; Two Vols.; London: Macmillan and Co., 1869).

Bright, John, *The Public Letters of Rt. Hon....,* M.P., collected by M.J. Leech (London: Sampson Low, 1885).

Campbell, Sir George, *Memoirs of My Indian Career,* ed. Barnard, Sir Charles E., (Two vols.; London: Macmillan and Co., 1893).

Carey, W.H., ed., *The Good Old Days of the Hon. John Company; being Curious Reminiscences Illustrating Manners and Customs of the British in India during the Rule of the East India Company, from 1600 to 1858* (Three Vols.; Simla: Printed at the Argus Press, 1882).

Cavenagh, Sir Orfeur, *Reminiscences of an Indian Official* (London; W.H. Allen and Co., 1884).

Cotton, Gen. Sir Sydney, *Nine Years on the North-West Frontier of India* (London: Richard Bentley, 1868).

Cust, Robert Needham, *Pictures of Indian Life, sketched with the pen from 1852 to 1881* (London: Trubner and Co., 1881).

Edwardes, Maj.-Gen. Sir H.B., *Memorials of the Life and Letters of...,* ed. Edwardes, Emma Lady (London: Kegan Paul and Co., 1886).

Frazer, Capt. Hastings, *Our Faithful Ally, the Nizam: Being a Historical Sketch of Events Showing the Value of the Nizam's Alliance to the British Government in India and his Services during the Mutinies* (London: Smith, Elder and Co., 1865).

Grant, Sir J.H., *Incidence in the Sepoy War of 1857-58,* ed. Knollys, Maj. H., (Edinburgh and London: William Blackwood and Sons, 1873).

Groom, William Tate, *With Havelock from Allahabad to Lucknow,* ed. Mrs Groom (London: Sampson Low and Co., 1894).

Halls, John James, *Arrah in 1857: Being an Account of the Splendid Defence of Arrah house during the Indian Mutiny,* ed. Leather, Lieut. G.F.T. (Bever: Privately Printed, 1893).

Holloway, John, *Essays on the Indian Mutiny* (London: Dean and Son, [1865]).

Hunter, W.W., *The Indian Mussulmans: Are They Bound in Conscience to Rebel Against the Queen?* (London: Trubner and Co., 1871).

India before and after the Mutiny (2nd ed. enl.; Edinburgh: E. and S. Livingstone, 1886).

Inglis, Hon, Lady Sady, *The Siege of Lucknow, a Diary* (London: James R. Osgood, 1892).

Jacob, Sir G. Le G., *Western India before and during the Mutinies* (London: King and Co., 1871).

Johnson, William Thomas, *Twelve Years of a Soldier's Life, From the Letters of...*, ed. Mrs Johnson, (London: A.D. Innes, 1897).

Kaye, John William, *A History of the Sepoy War in India. 1857-58* (5th ed.; Two Vols.; London: W.H. Allen and Co., 1870).

Kennedy, James, *Life and Work in Benares and Kumaon, 1839-77* (London: T. Fisher Unwin, 1864).

Lawrence, Sir George, *Reminscences of Forty-three Years in India*, ed. Edwardes, W., (London: John Murray, 1874).

Malet, H.P., *Lost Links in the Indian Mutiny* (London: T. Cautley Newby, 1867).

Malleson, Col. G.B., *The Indian Mutiny of 1857* (Three Vols.; London: W.H. Allen, 1878-88).

Marshman, John Clark, *Memoirs of Maj.-Gen. Sir Henry Havelock* (3rd ed.; London: Longmans, Green, Reader and Dyer, 1867).

Maude, Francis Cornwallis, *Memories of the Mutiny* (Two Vols.; London and Sydney: Remington and Co., 1894).

Metcalfe, Charles Theophilus, trans., *Two Native Narratives of the Mutiny in Delhi* (Westminster: Archibald Constable and Co., 1898).

Mitchel, William Forbes, *Reminiscences of the Great Mutiny of 1857-59, including the Relief, Siege and Capture of Lucknow, and the Campaigns in Rohilcund and Oude* (London: Macmillen and Co., 1894).

Mullens, The Rev. J., *A Brief Review of Ten Years' Missionary Labour in India between 1852 and 1861. Prepared from Local Reports and Original Letters* (London: James Nisbet and Co., 1863).

Mullens, The Rev. J., *Statistical Tables of Missions in India, Ceylon, and Burmah at the Close of 1861. Compiled from Original Letters and Local Reports* (London: Messrs. James Wiscot and Co., 1863).

Muter, Mrs D.D., *Travels and Adventures of an Officer's Wife in India. China, and New Zealand* (Two Vols.; London: Hurst and Blackett, 1864).

Norman, Gen. Sir Henry Wylie and Mrs Keith Young, ed., *Delhi–1857. The Siege, Assault and Capture as given in the Diary and Correspondence of the Late Col. Keith Young, C.B., Judge-Advocate General, Bengal* (London and Edinburgh: W. and R. Chambers, 1902).

Parry, Sydney Henry Jones, *An Old Soldier's Memories* (London: Hurst and Blackett, 1897).

Pitt, F.W., ed., *Incidents in India and Memories of the Mutiny with some Records of Alexander's Horse and the 1st. Bengal Cavalry* (London: Kegan Paul, Trench, Trubner and Co., 1896).

Ramsay, Belcarres Dalrymple W., *Rough Recollections of Military Service and Society* (Two Vols.; Edinburgh: Blackwood and Sons, 1882).

Roberts, Fred (Later Field Marshal Earl Roberts), *Letters Written During the Indian Mutiny* (London: Macmillan and Co., 1924).

Roberts, Field-Marshal Lord, *Forty-One Years in India. From Subaltern to Commander-in-Chief,* (Two Vols.; London: Richard Bentley, 1897).

Shepherd, W.J., *A Personal Narrative of the Outbreak and Massacre at Cawnpore during the Sepoy Revolt of 1857* (Agra: Delhi Gazette Press, 1863).

Showers, Lieut.-Gen. Charles Lionel, *A Missing Chapter of the Indian Mutiny* (London: Longmans, Green and Co., 1888).

Stewart, Charles Edward, *Through Persia in Disguise, with Reminiscences of the Indian Mutiny*, ed. Stewart Basil (London: G. Routledge and Sons. New York: E.P. Dutton and Co., 1911).

Taylor, William, *Thirty-eight Years in India* (Two Vols.; London: W.H. Ellen and Co., 1882).

Taylor, W., *A Narrative of the Events Connected with My Removal from Patna Commissionership,* Three Parts (Calcutta: 1867-68).

Temple, Sir Richard, *Men and Events of My Time in India* (Second Thousand; London: John Murray, 1882).

Thackeray, Col. Sir Edward, 'Recollections of the Siege of Delhi', *Cornhill Magazine,* 1913, XXXV, Part I, pp. 314-29., Part II, pp. 456-69.

Thornhill, Mark, *The Personal Adventures and Experiences of a Magistrate during the Rise, Progress and Suppression of the Indian Mutiny* (London: John Murray, 1884).

Travers, Lieut.-Col. Jas., *The Evacuation of Indore in 1857 by Lieut.-Col...Versus History of the Sepoy Revolt by Sir John Kave* (London: Henry S. King, 1876).

Trevelyan, Sir George, *The Competition Wallah* (London: Macmillan and Co., 1907. First Published in 1864).

Trevelyan, Sir George, *Cawnpore* (3rd ed.; London and Cambridge: Macmillan and Co., 1866).

Vibart, Col. Edward, *The Sepoy Mutiny as seen by a Subaltern from Delhi to Lucknow* (London: Smith, Elder and Co., 1893).

Walker, Col. Thomas Nicholas, *Through the Mutiny: Reminiscences of Thirty Years' Active Service and Sport in India, 1854-83* (London: Gibbings and Co., 1907).

Wilberforce, R.C., *An Unrecorded Chapter of the Indian Mutiny, being the Personal Reminiscences of...* (3rd ed.; London: John Murray, 1895).

Wilson, Francesca H., *Rambles in Northern India, with Incidents and Descriptions of Many Scenes of the Mutiny* (London: 1876).

Yeoward, G. *An Episode of the Rebellion and Mutiny in Oudh of 1857 and 1858* (Lucknow: Printed at the American Methodist Mission Press, 1876).

2. Secondary Sources:

Ahmed, Akbar S., *Islam under Siege. Living Dangerously in a Post-Honour World* (Cambridge, UK: Polity Press, 2003).

Ahmad Khan, Sir Sayyid, *Asbab-i Baghawat-i Hind* (Karachi: Urdu Academy, 1957. First published in 1858).

Ahmad Khan, Sir Sayyid, *Hunter par Hunter* (Lahore: Iqbal Academy, 1949).

Albig, William, *Public Opinion* (New York and London: McGraw–Hill, 1939).

Atkins, John Black, *The Life of William Howard Russell* (Two Vols.; London: John Murray, 1911).

Atkinson, Geo. Franklin, *'Curry and Rice', on Forty Plates, or the Ingredients of Social Life at 'Our Station' in India* (London: John B. Day, 1856).

Aziz, K.K., *Britain and Muslim India* (London: Heinemann, 1963).

Bakshi, S.R., *Mutiny to Independence* (New Delhi: Deep and Deep Publications, 1988).

Baird, J.G.A., *Private Letters of Marquess of Dalhousie* (2nd Impression; Edinburgh and London: William Blackwood and Sons, 1911).

Bearce, George D., *British Attitudes Towards India, 1784-1856* (London: Oxford University Press, 1961).

Bergen, Henry (ed.), *Lydgates's Fall of Princes,* Part III (Washington: 1923)

Binns, L.E. Elliot-, *The Early Evangelicals: A Religious and Social Study* (Greenwich, Conn.: Seabury Press, 1953).

Binns, L.E. Elliot-, *Religion in the Victorian Era* (2nd ed.; London and Redhill: Latterworth Press, 1946).

Bodelson, C.A., *Studies in Mid-Victorian Imperialism* (New York: Alfred A. Knopf, 1925).

Briggs, Asa, *Chartist Studies* (London: MacMillan and Co., 1959).

Brinton, Crane, *English Political Thought in the 19th Century* (Harper Torchbook edition; New York: Harper and Bros., 1962).

Brown, Ian W., *The Anglican Evangelicals in British Politics, 1780-1833* (Unpublished M.A. thesis, McGill University, 1959).

Brown, Ian W., *The Anglican Evengelicals in British Politics, 1780-1833* (Unpublished Ph.D. thesis, Lehigh University Bethlehem, Pennsylvania, U.S.A. 1965).

Brown, Ford, K., *Fathers of Victorians; the Age of Wilberforce* (Camb.: Cambridge University Press, 1961).

Buckler, F.W., 'Political Theory of the Indian Mutiny', *Royal Historical Society, Transactions of the,* Fourth Series, V, 1922, pp. 71-100.

Cambridge History of India, Vols. V and VI, ed. by H.H. Dodwell (Cambridge University Press, 1929 and 1932 respectively).

Campbell, Col. Walter, *My Indian Journal* (Edinburgh: Edmonston and Douglas, 1854).

Carey, Eustace, *Memoir of William Carey, D.D.* (London: Jackson and Walford, 1836).

Chand, Tara, *History of the Freedom Movement in India,* Vol. I; Delhi: The Publications Division, Ministry of Information and Broadcasting, 1961).

Chattapahyaya, Haraprasad, *The Sepoy Mutiny, 1857. A Social Study and Analysis* (Calcutta: Bookland Private Ltd., 1957).

Collier, Richard, *The Sound of Fury. An Account of the Indian Mutiny* (London: Collins, 1963).

Cooper, Leonard, *Havelock* (London: The Bodley Head, 1957).

Cox, Homersham, *Whig and Tory Administrations during the Last Thirteen Years* (London: Longmans, Green and Co., 1868).

Creighton, Donald J., 'The Victorians and the Empire', *Canadian Historical Review,* 1938 (March), Vol. XIX, pp. 138-53.

Dawar, Douglas and Garrett, H.L., "Political Theory of the Indian Mutiny'-A Reply', *Royal Historical Society, Transactions of the,* Fourth Series, 1924, VII, pp. 131-65.

Dicy, Albert, *Lectures on the Relations between Law and Public Opinion in England during the 19th Century* (London: MacMillan and Co., 1905).

Edwardes, Michael, *Battles of the Indian Mutiny* (London: B.T. Batsford, 1963).

Embree, Ainslee T. ed., *1857 in India, Mutiny or War of Independence?* (Boston: D.C. Heath and Co., 1963).

Esposito, John L., *The Islamic Threat: Myth or Reality?* (New York: Oxford University Press, 1999)

Forbes, Archibald, *Havelock* (London: MacMillan and Co., 1890).

Forrest, G.W., *History of the Indian Mutiny* (Two Vols.; Edinburgh and London: William Blackwood and Sons, 1904).

Foster, Sir William, *John Company* (London: John Lane The Bodley Head Ltd., 1926).

Freedom Struggle in Uttar Pradesh, Source Material, Six Vols.:
Vol. I, 1857-59: *Nature and Origin,* ed. Rizvi, S.A.A. and Bhargava, M.L. (Publications Bureau, Information Dept., Uttar Pradesh, 1957).
Vol. II, *Awadh: 1857-59,* ed. Rizvi, S.A.A. and Bhargava, M.L., (Publications Bureau, Information Dept., Uttar Pradesh, 1958).
Vol. III, *Bundelkhand and Adjoining Territories: 1857-59,* ed. Rizvi, S.A.A. and Bhargava, M.L. (Publications Bureau, Information Dept., Uttar Pradesh, 1959).
Vol. IV, *Eastern and Adjoining Districts: 1857-59,* ed. Rizvi, S.A.A. (Information Dept., Uttar Pradesh, 1959).
Vol. V, *Western Districts and Rohilkhand: 1857-59* ed. Rizvi, S.A.A. (Information Dept., Uttar Pradesh, 1960).
Vol. VI, *Consolidated Index and Chronology,* ed. Rizvi, S.A.A. (Information Dept., Uttar Pradesh, 1961).

Goldsmid, Maj.-Gen. Sir F.J., *James Outram. A Biography* (Two Vols.; London: Smith, Elder and Co., 1880).
Guedalla, Philip, *Palmerston* (London: E. Benn Ltd., 1926).
Gupta, P.C., *Nana Sahib and the Rising at Cawnpore* (Oxford: Clarendon Press, 1963).
Hardy, Peter, *The Muslims of British India* (Cambridge: Cambridge University Press, 1972).
Haldane, Alex. *The Lives of Robert Haldane of Airthrey and of his Brother J.A. Haldane* (5th ed.; Edinburgh: W.P. Kennedy. London: Hamilton Adams and Co., 1855).
Harding, Ewing, *From Palmerston to Disraeli, 1856-1876* (London: Bell and Sons, 1913).
Heasman, Kathleen, *Evangelicals in Action. An Appraisal of their Social Work in the Victorian Era* (London: Geoffrey Bles, 1962).
Heber, Reginald, *Narrative of a Journey through the Upper Provinces of India from Calcutta to Bombay, 1824-25* (4th ed.; Three vols.; London: John Murray, 1829).
Heeley, Sibyl, 'Delhi, 1857. A Man Hunt', *Blackwood's,* 1930, CCXXVIII, pp. 682-705.
Henderson, P.A. Wright, 'The Story of Cawnpore', *Blackwood's,* 1904, CLXXV, pp. 628-45.
Hitti, Philip K, *Islam and the West* (New York: 1962).
Holmes, T. Rice, *A History of the Indian Mutiny* (5th ed. Rev. and Enl.; London: MacMillan and Co., 1898).
Hovell, Mark, *The Chartist Movement,* ed. Tout, T.F., (Manchester: At the University Press, 1925).
Hunt, The Rev. J., *Religious Thought in England in the Nineteenth Century* (London: Gibbings and Co. Ltd., 1896).
Husain, Mahdi, *Bahadur Shah II and the War of 1857 in Delhi with its Unforgettable Scences* (Delhi: Atma Ram and Sons, 1958).
Husayan, Sayyid 'Abid, *Hindustani Musalman A'inah-'i Ayyam Men* (Delhi: Maktabah Jamia, 1965).
Imlah, Albert Henry, *Lord Ellenborough* (Cambridge: Harvard University Press. London: Humphery Milford, Oxford University Press, 1939).
Innes, Lieut.-Gen., McLeod, *Lucknow and Oude in the Mutiny* (New and Revised Edition; London: Innes and Co., 1896).

Innes, Lieut.-Gen. McLeod, *The Sepoy Revolt. A Critical Narrative* (London: A.D. Innes and Co., 1897).

Ja'fari, Ra'is Ahmad, *Wajid, 'Ali Shah awr unka 'ahd* (Lahore: Kitab Manzil, 1958).

Jones, Wilbur D., *Lord Derby and the Victorian Conservatism* (Athens: The University of Georgia Press, 1956).

Joshi, P.C., ed., *Rebellion 1857. A Symposium* (New Delhi: People's Publishing House, 1957).

Keene, H.G., *Fifty-Seven. Some Accounts of the Indian Districts during the Revolt* (London: W.H. Allen, 1883).

Khan, Muin-ud-Din Ahmed, *Muslim Struggle for Freedom in Bengal, 1757-1947* (Dacca: Public Relations Department, Bureau of National Reconstruction, East Pakistan, 1960).

Knorr, Klaus, *British Colonial Theories, 1570-1850* (Reprinted in the USA: University of Toronto Press, 1964).

Lal, Kanahya, *Tarikh Baghawat-i Hind, 1857, Musamma bih Muharabah-'i 'Azim* (Lucknow: Nawalkishor, n.d. A contemporary account).

Levi, Albert William, *A Study in the Social Philosophy of John Stuart Mill* (Chicago University Ph.D. thesis, 1938. Private ed.; Chicago: Distributed by the University of Chicago Libraries, 1940).

Lippincott, B.E., *Victorian Critics of Democracy* (Minneapolis: The University of Minnesota Press, 1957).

Lowell, A.L., *Public Opinion in War and Peace* (Cambridge: Harvard University Press, 1923).

Lutfullah, Syed, *The Man Behind the War of Independence, 1857* (Karachi: Mohamedan Educational Society, 1957).

Maclagan, Michael, *'Clemency' Canning* (London and New York: MacMillan and Co., 1962).

MacMunn, Maj. G.F., 'Jan Compani Kee Jai', *Cornhill Magazine*, New Series, 1910, XXVIII, pp. 671–8.

MacMunn, Lieut.-Gen. Sir George, 'Some New Light on the Indian Mutiny', *Blackwood's*, 1928, CCXXIV, pp. 433-46.

MacMunn, Sir George, *The Indian Mutiny in Perspective* (London: G. Bell and Sons, 1931).

Majumdar, R.C., *The Sepoy Mutiny and the Revolt of 1857* (Calcutta: Pub. by Srimati S. Chaudhari, 1957).

Majumdar, R.C., *History of the Freedom Movement in India* (Vol. I; Calcutta: Pub. by Firma K.L. Mukhopadhyay, 1962).

Malik, Salahuddin, 'Nineteenth Centry Approaches to the Indian 'Mutiny', *Journal of Asian History*, Vol. VII, 2, 1973, pp. 95–127.

————, 'God, England, and the Indian 'Mutiny': Victorian Religious Perceptions', *The Muslim World*, LXXIII, 2, 1983, pp. 106–132.

————, 'British Russophobes and the Indian 'Mutiny', *The New Review*, Vol. X, 2, 1970, pp. 81–110.

————, 'The Punjab and the Indian 'Mutiny': A Reassessment', *Islamic Studies*, XV, 2, 1976, pp. 81–110.

————, '1857 Gogira Rebellion in South-eastern Panjab: A Forgotten Chapter of Muslim Response to British Rule in India', *Islamic Studies*, XVI, 2, 1977, pp. 65–95.

Mallick, A.R., *British Policy and the Muslims in Bengal* (Dacca: Asiatic Society of Pakistan, 1961).

Mehta, Asoka, *1857 The Great Rebellion* (Bombay: Hind Kitabs Ltd., 1946).

Metcalf, Thomas R., *The Aftermath of Revolt–India, 1857-70* (Princeton, New Jersey: Princeton University Press, 1964).

Mihr, Ghulam Rasul, *1857 ke Mujahid* (Lahore: Kitab Manzil, 1957).

Misra, B.B., *The Central Administration of the East India Company, 1773-1834* (Manchester: Manchester University Press, 1959).

Miyan, Muhammad Shafi, *1857: Pahli Jang-i Azadi* (Lahore: Muktabah Jadid, 1957).

Monneypenny, W.E. and Buckle G.E., *The Life of Benjamin Disraeli, Earl of Baconsfield* (New and Rev. ed.; Two Vols.; New York: Macmillan and Co., 1929).

Morley, John, *The Life of Richard Cobden* (Two Vols.; London: T. Fisher Unwin, 1905).

Muir, Sir William, *Records of the Intelligence Department of the Government of the North-Western Provinces of India during the Mutiny of 1857, including Correspondence with the Supreme Government, Delhi, Cawnpore, and other Places,* ed. Coldstream, William, (Two Vols.; Edinburgh: T. and T. Clark, 1902).

Mukherjee, Ramkrishna, *The Rise and Fall of the East India Company* (Berlin: Veb Deutscher Verlag Der Wissenschaften, 1958).

Mullen, The Rev. Joseph, *The Results of Missionary Labour in India* (3rd improved ed.; London: W.H. Dalton, 1856).

Napier, Sir Charles James, *Defects, Civil and Military of the Indian Government,* ed. Napier, Lieut.-Gen. Sir W.F.P., (3rd. ed.; London: Charles Westerton, 1854).

Nizami, Khwajah Hasan, *Bahadur Shah Ka Muqaddamah* (Delhi: n.d.).

Owen, The Rev. William, *The Martyrs of the Indian Rebellion* (London: Ward, Lock and Co., [1891]).

Philips, C.H., 'The East India Company 'Interest' and the English Government', *Royal Historical Society, Transactions of the,* Fourth Series, 1937, XX, pp. 83-101.

Philips, C.H., *The East India Company, 1784-1834* (Manchester: Manchester University Press, 1940).

Powell, Avril Ann, *Muslims and Missionaries in Pre-Mutiny India* (Richmond, U.K.: Curzon Press, 1993).

Pollock, T.C., *Way to Glory. The Life of Havelock of Lucknow* (London: John Murray, 1957).

Qureshi, Ishtiaq Husain, *The Muslim Community of the Indo-Pakistan Subcontinent (610-1947). A Brief Historical Analysis* (The Hague: Mouton and Co., 1962).

Reynolds, Reginald, *White Sahibs in India* (3rd ed.; London: The Socialist Book Centre Ltd., 1946).

Roberts, P.E., *History of British India* (3rd ed.; London: Oxford University Press, 1952).

Routledge, James, *English Rule and Native Opinion in India* (London: Trubner and Co., 1878).

Rowbotham, Commander W.B., ed., *The Naval Brigades in the Indian Mutiny, 1857-58* (London: Printed for the Navy Records Society, 1947).

Said, Edward W., *Covering Islam. How the Media and the Experts Determine How We See the Rest of the World* (New York: Vintage Books, 1997).

————, *Orientalism.* (New York and Toronto: Random House, 1978).

Sale, George with Introduction by Robert D. Richardson, Jr., *The Koran* (New York and London: Garland Publishing, 1984).

————, *The Koran* (London, 1734).

Savillo, John, *Ernest Jones: Chartist* (London: Lawrence and Wishart Ltd., 1952).

Sen, Surendre Nath, *Eighteen Fifty-seven* (Delhi: Publications Division, Ministry of Information and Broadcasting, Government of India, 1957).

Shackleton, Robert, 'A Soldier of Delhi', *Harper's Magazine*, 1909, CXIX, pp. 673-8.

Shadwell, Lieut.-Gen., *The Life of Colin Campbell, Lord Clyde* (Two Vols.; Edinburgh and London: William Blackwood and Sons, 1881).

Solano, E. John, 'The Siege of Arrah: An Incident of the Indian Mutiny', *Blackwood's*, 1904, CLXXV, pp. 228-42.

Spear, Percival, *India. A Modern History* (Ann Arbor: The University of Michigan Press, 1961).

Stokes, Eric, *The English Utilitarians and India* (Oxford: Clarendon Press, 1959).

Struggle for Freedom, 1857 (Karachi: Pakistan Publications, April 1957).

Sutherland, Lucy Stuart, *The East India Company and the Eighteenth Century Politics* (Oxford: Clarendon Press, 1952).

Temperley, H.T.V., *Foundation of British Foreign Policy from Pitt (1792) to Salisbury (1902)*, (Cambridge: Cambridge University Press, 1938).

Thorner, Daniel, *Investment in Empire, British Railway and Steam Shipping Enterprise in India, 1825-1849* (Philadelphia: University of Pennsylvania Press, 1950).

Thornton, Archibald Paton, *The Imperial Idea and its Enemies; a Study in British Power* (London: Macmillan and Co. Ltd., 1903).

Tolan, John Victor (ed.), *Medieval Christian Perceptions of Islam* (New York and London: Routledge, 1996).

Torrens, W.M., *Empire in Asia. How we came by it* (London: Trubner and Co., 1872).

Townsend, Meredith, *Asia and Europe* (Westminster: Archibald, Constable and Co., 1901).

Trevelyen, G.O., *The Life and Letters of Lord Macaulay* (London: Longmans, Green and Co., 1959).

Trotter, Capt. Lionel J., *The Life of Hodson of Hodson's Horse* (London: J.M. Dent and Sons. New York: E.P. Dutton and Co., 1912).

Trotter, Capt. Lionel J., *The Bayard of India. A Life of General Sir James Outram* (Edinburgh and London: William Blackwood, 1903).

Vaughan, The Rev. James, *The Trident, the Crescent, and the Cross: A View of the Religious History of India during the Hindu, Buddhist, Mohammedan, and Christian Periods* (London: Longmans, Green and Co., 1876).

Wilson, Beckles, *Ledger and Sword or the Honourable Company of Merchants of England Trading to the East Indies (1599-1879)* (Two Vols.; London: Longmans, Green, and Co., 1903).

Wilson, James, *Letter to John Bright Esqr., M.P., on the India Question* (London: Edward Stanford, 1854).

Winks, Robin, W., ed., *British Imperialism–Gold, God, Glory* (New York: Holt, Rinehart and Winston, 1965).

Wood, Evelyn, *The Revolt in Hindustan, 1857-59* (London: Methuen and Co., 1908).

Woodruf, Philip, *The Men Who Ruled India* (Two Vols.; London: Jonathen Cape, 1953-54).

Woodward, M.L., *The Age of Reform, 1815-1870* (Oxford: At the Clarenden Press, 1949).

Young, G.M., *Early Victorian England, 1830-65* (London: Oxford University Press, 1934).

Young, G.M., *Mr Gladstone* (Oxford: Clarendon Press, 1944).

Zahir Dihlawi, Sayyid Zahiru-d-Din, *Dastan-i Ghadar* (Lahore: Panjab Academy, 1955).

Dictionaries, Directories, Encyclopaedias, etc.

Catholic Directory, Ecclesiastical Register, and Almanac for 1858-59 (London: Burns and Lambart).

Census of India, 1963 Census (Delhi: Census Commissioner, 1962).

Dictionary of National Biography.

Encyclopaedia Britannica, 1957 ed.

Encyclopaedia of Islam (London: Luzac and Co. Leyden: E.J. Brill, 1913-38).

Encyclopaedia of Religion and Ethics, ed., Hastings, James, (New York: Charles Scribner's Sons, 1955).

Gazetteer of India and Pakistan (Two Vols.; Published under the direction of the Director of Military Survey, Army Headquarters, India, 1950).

Lippincott Gazetteer of the World, The Columbia, ed., M. Seltser (New York: Columbia University Press, 1961).

Newspaper Press Directory, 1857-58 (London: Published by Charles Mitchell).

Platts, John T., *A Dictionary of Urdu, Classical Hindi, and English* (London: Oxford University Press, 1965).

Index